Law as a Means to an End

The contemporary U.S. legal culture is marked by ubiquitous battles among various groups attempting to seize control of the law and wield it against others in pursuit of their particular agendas. This battle takes place in administrative, legislative, and judicial arenas at both the state and federal levels. This book identifies the underlying source of these battles in the spread of the instrumental view of law – the idea that law is purely a means to an end – in a context of sharp disagreement over the social good. It traces the rise of the instrumental view of law in the course of the past two centuries, then demonstrates the pervasiveness of this view of law and its implications within the contemporary legal culture, and ends by showing the various ways in which seeing law in purely instrumental terms threatens to corrode the rule of law.

Brian Z. Tamanaha is the Chief Judge Benjamin N. Cardozo Professor of Law at St. John's University School of Law. He delivered the inaugural Montesquieu Lecture (2004) at the University of Tilburg. He is the author of *On the Rule of Law* (Cambridge 2004), *Realistic Socio-Legal Theory* (1997), and *A General Jurisprudence of Law and Society* (2001), which won the Herbert Jacob Book Prize in 2001 and the inaugural Dennis Leslie Mahoney Prize in Legal Theory (2006) for the outstanding contemporary work in sociological jurisprudence. He has published many articles and is the Associate Editor of *Law and Society Review*.

The Law in Context Series

Editors: William Twining (University College London)
and Christopher McCrudden (Lincoln College, Oxford)

Since 1970, the Law in Context Series has been in the forefront of the movement to broaden the study of law. It has been a vehicle for the publication of innovative scholarly books that treat law and legal phenomena critically in their social, political, and economic contexts from a variety of perspectives to bear on new and existing areas of law taught in universities. A contextual approach involves treating legal subjects broadly, using material from other social sciences and from any other discipline that helps to explain the operation in practice of the subject under discussion. It is hoped that this orientation is at once more stimulating and more realistic than the bare exposition of legal rules. The series includes original books that have a different emphasis from traditional legal textbooks, while maintaining the same high standards of scholarship. They are written primarily for undergraduate and graduate students of law and of the disciplines, but most also appeal to wider readership. In the past, most books in the series have focused on English law, but recent publications include books on European law, globalization, transnational legal processes, and comparative law.

Books in the Series

Continued after the index

Law as a Means to an End

Threat to the Rule
of Law

Brian Z. Tamanaha

CAMBRIDGE
UNIVERSITY PRESS

CAMBRIDGE UNIVERSITY PRESS
Cambridge, New York, Melbourne, Madrid, Cape Town, Singapore, São Paulo

Cambridge University Press
32 Avenue of the Americas, New York, NY 10013-2473, USA

www.cambridge.org
Information on this title: www.cambridge.org/9780521869522

First published 2006

Printed in the United States of America

A catalog record for this publication is available from the British Library.

Library of Congress Cataloging in Publication Data

Tamanaha, Brian Z.
Law as a means to an end : threat to the rule of law / Brian Tamanaha.
    p. cm.
Includes bibliographical references and index.
ISBN-13: 978-0-521-86952-2 (hardback)
ISBN-10: 0-521-86952-8 (hardback)
ISBN-13: 978-0-521-68967-0 (pbk.)
ISBN-10: 0-521-68967-8 (pbk.)
1. Rule of law – United States – History.   2. Law – United States – Philosophy.
3. Legal positivism.   4. Instrumentalism (Philosophy).   I. Title
KF382.T36   2007
340′.11 – dc22   2006013845

ISBN-13   978-0-521-86952-2 hardback
ISBN-10   0-521-86952-8 hardback

ISBN-13   978-0-521-68967-0 paperback
ISBN-10   0-521-68967-8 paperback

For

Lawrence M. Friedman

Marc Galanter

Morty Horwitz

William Twining

Contents

Acknowledgments

An outline of this book was presented as the inaugural Montesquieu Lecture (2004) at the University of Tilburg. I thank the law faculty at the University of Tilburg for this honor, and for encouraging me to set out my views on the most significant contemporary developments in legal theory. I thank John Berger of Cambridge University Press for his enthusiastic support for this book from the very first day I suggested it to him, and I thank the two anonymous reviewers John procured for their helpful critical comments on the entire manuscript. I appreciate their patience in wading through the messy initial draft I submitted; their input fundamentally shaped the final product. I thank Susan Fortney, Rob Vischer, Peter Margulies, Gary Minda, John Barrett, and Marc Galanter for their helpful comments on particular chapters, and I thank Tim Zick, Nelson Tebbe, and William Twining for their comments on the entire manuscript. I thank Lawrence M. Friedman for responding to several detailed inquiries on various historical issues early in the writing of the book. I thank the Berkeley Center for the Study of Law and Society, the Stanford Law School faculty, and the University of Groningen legal theory faculty group, for inviting me to present aspects of this book, and for the feedback I received. I thank Mike Schindhelm for his excellent research support. I thank Astrid Emel and Jaenne Legrow and the rest of the library staff for responding with good humor and promptness to my many requests for books and articles from old or obscure sources. I thank Mary Cadette and Linda Smith for their superb assistance in the editorial process. My special thanks go to Honorata, Jolijt, and Kats for their understanding and unflagging support for this project and to Sava for inspiring me to get the book done.

This book is dedicated to Lawrence M. Friedman, Marc Galanter, Morty Horwitz, and William Twining. About a dozen years ago, each of them reached out to me under different circumstances and expressed an interest in my work and in me as a person. For an obscure academic just starting out, there can be no greater boost than the chance to interact with scholars who have accomplished so much. Over the years, I have enjoyed lunches, dinners, long walks, and even a few sleep-overs and many personal and intellectual conversations with each. I have learned from their work, as well as from their personal examples. I know each of them will object to various aspects of this book, but all will support my writing of it. They have each mentored many individuals, and I feel lucky to be included. This dedication is a token of my gratitude for their generosity and to show how much I cherish our relationships.

Introduction

An instrumental view of law – the idea that law is a means to an end – is taken for granted in the United States, almost a part of the air we breathe. This operates in various ways: as an account of the nature of law, as an attitude toward law that professors teach students, as a form of constitutional analysis, as a theoretical perspective on law, as an orientation of lawyers in their daily practice, as a strategic approach of organized groups that use litigation to further their agendas, as a view toward judges and judging, as a perception of legislators and administrators when enacting laws or regulations. In all of these contexts, people see law as an instrument of power to advance their personal interests or the interests or policies of the individuals or groups they support. Today, law is widely viewed as an empty vessel to be filled as desired, and to be manipulated, invoked, and utilized in the furtherance of ends.

A few centuries ago, in contrast, law was widely understood to possess a necessary content and integrity that was, in some sense, given or predetermined. Law was the right ordering of society binding on all. Law was not entirely subject to our individual or group whims or will. There were several versions of this. Law was thought to consist of rules or principles immanent within the customs or culture of the society, or of God-given principles disclosed by revelation or discoverable through the application of reason, or of principles dictated by human nature, or of the logically necessary requirements of objective legal concepts. These ideas about the nature and content of law, each of which had its day, have mostly fallen by the wayside in the past century. Their obsolescence opened the way for an instrumental view to seep through and permeate every legal context. Now this view thrives throughout law.

Although instrumental views of law have taken hold in many societies, the U.S. legal culture has moved the furthest in this direction. In a sense, we have embarked upon a vast social experiment with no prior examples to provide guidance or warn of pitfalls. There are manifold signs that this experiment may be ill-fated.

The root danger can be stated summarily: In situations of sharp disagreement over the social good, when law is perceived as a powerful instrument, individuals and groups within society will endeavor to seize or co-opt the law in every way possible; to fill in, interpret, manipulate, and utilize the law to serve their own ends. This will spawn a Hobbsean conflict of all against all carried on within and through the legal order. Rather than function to maintain social order and resolve disputes, as Hobbes suggested was the role of law, combatants will fight to control and use the implements of the law as weapons in social, political, religious, and economic disputes. Law will thus generate disputes as much as resolve them. Even when one side prevails, victory will mark only a momentary respite before the battle is resumed. These battles will take place in every state and federal arena – legislative, executive, judicial – from struggles over the content of laws to struggles over how those laws will be enforced, applied, and interpreted, and by whom. Even those groups that might prefer to abstain from these battles over law will nonetheless be forced to engage in the contest, if only defensively to keep their less restrained opponents from using the law as a hammer against them. Spiraling conflicts will ensue with no evident halting point or termination short of exhaustion of resources or total conquest by one side.

Such struggles over and through law are openly visible today, and worsening. Beneath the surface of these battles lies a more subtle and insidious threat: The spread of instrumental thinking about law harbors the potential to damage the rule of law. An instrumental view of law and the rule of law ideal are two fundamental pillars of the U.S. legal tradition. Anyone raised in this tradition would naturally think that they are complementary, as I did. Not until completing the research for my previous book, *On the Rule of Law: History, Politics, Theory*, did I realize that this joinder of ideas has a relatively recent provenance, and, furthermore, that in several distinct ways an instrumental view of law has a powerful tendency to corrode the rule of law ideal.

It is not my contention that instrumental views of law are unique to the modern period. Instrumental strains of thinking about law can be found in earlier periods in the United States and elsewhere. Nor is it my contention that *only* instrumental views of law circulate in the United States today. Non-instrumental understandings of law are still present. In one context after another, however, they have been (or are in the process of being) shunted to the margins as instrumental views take over. The shift I identify herein is one of emphasis and proportion. Instrumental and non-instrumental views of law have circulated together, and continue to do so, but across the full gamut of legal contexts a sea change is occurring in the direction of consummately instrumental views. The problems I identify in each arena of legal activity will be familiar to many; what is less familiar is that they are linked by the shared phenomenon of creeping instrumentalism.

I do not assert that the all-out Hobbsean war fought through and over law just laid out is our inevitable fate. Rather, my contention is that we have traveled far down this path, and that intellectual developments and the logic of the situation portend a worsening that, if not somehow contained, may well eventuate in this nightmarish scenario. Events have yet to play out in their fullness, and human ingenuity is irrepressible, so the denouement of these trends cannot be known with certainty. This book is an attempt to convey in broad strokes where we have come from, where we stand now, and where we are headed, in the conviction that we must become cognizant of the attendant risks.

This is not the first time a theorist has written about rampant instrumental uses of and battles over law. John Dewey, a founding figure of philosophical pragmatism, wrote a startlingly blunt essay on law in 1916, entitled "Force and Coercion," that raised a similar set of issues:

> [I]s not the essence of all law coercion?.... Are our effective legislative enactments anything more than registrations of results of *battles* previously fought out on the field of human endurance? In many social fields, reformers are now *struggling* for an extension of governmental activity by way of supervision and regulation. Does not such action always amount to an effort to extend the exercise of force on the part of some section of society, with a corresponding restriction of the forces employed by others?[1]

Dewey portrayed law in thoroughly instrumental terms: "since the attainment of ends requires the use of means, law is essentially a formulation of the use of force."[2]

Four decades before Dewey's essay, Rudolph von Jhering, a German legal theorist prominent in his day but now largely forgotten, published two books, *The Struggle for Law* and *Law as a Means to an End* (the latter of which provides the title for this book). Jhering elaborated the thesis that the driving force behind legal development is continuous struggles among individuals and groups within society to have their interests reflected in and backed up by legal coercion. "In the course of time," Jhering wrote, "the interests of thousands of individuals, and of whole classes, have become bound up with the existing principles of law in such a manner that these cannot be done away with, without doing the greatest injury to the former . . . Hence every such attempt, in natural obedience to the law of self-preservation, calls forth the most violent opposition of the imperiled interests, and with it a struggle in which, as in every struggle, the issue is decided not by the weight of reason, but by the relative strength of opposing forces . . . "[3] Jhering asserted that law is coercive state power that individuals and groups utilize instrumentally to achieve and advance their often selfish purposes (frequently in the name of right).

Both Jhering and Dewey were critical of prevailing non-instrumental views of law. Jhering scoffed at the notions popular among jurists of his day that law is an emanation of the culture or consciousness of the people, or a matter of natural principles. Putting a skeptical, purely instrumental cast on what were sacrosanct ideas at the time, Dewey wrote that "liberty" and "rights" are "finally a question of the most efficient use of means for ends."[4] Law can be whatever we want it to be, they asserted, for it is the product of our will. These were shocking views, expressed at a time when non-instrumental understandings of law still held sway among the legal elite. Jhering's work influenced Oliver Wendell Holmes, Roscoe Pound, and the Legal Realists, and Dewey was an early contributor to Legal Realism.

Collectively, these were the figures most responsible for promoting an instrumental view of law in the United States. A century later it is possible to take stock of

1 John Dewey, "Force and Coercion," 26 *International J. of Ethics* 359, 359 (1916)(emphasis added).
2 Id. 367.
3 Rudolph von Jhering, *The Struggle for Law* (Westport, Conn.: Hyperion Press 1979) 10–11.
4 Dewey, "Force and Coercion," supra 366.

what has been wrought by the understanding of law they promoted. This is not to say that these legal theorists and reformers are responsible for the situation today. The views of law they advocated, as we shall see, in key respects were merely catching up with the reality of instrumental legal activity. Their intention was to improve the functioning of the legal system, not to undermine it. In hindsight, their main failing was perhaps excessive optimism (Holmes aside) about the human capacity to strive for and achieve the greater good.

A difference of great moment exists between the circumstances today and the period when they wrote. Jhering envisioned a generally cohesive society with laws that matched, so he construed the incessant struggles surrounding law in positive terms, as an engine of healthy legal change. Dewey believed that the proper social ends to be served by law could be identified by sound judgment and with the assistance of social science. Pound and most Legal Realists were secure in the faith that beneficial balances among competing interests could be found or that socially optimal ends could be arrived at in law. The critical difference between then and now lies not in the existence of conflicts among groups, which was also present at a high level at the close of the nineteenth century. The critical difference is that in the intervening period, faith in the existence of common social purposes, or in our collective ability to agree upon them, has progressively disintegrated.

This is the key point. The notion that law is an instrument was urged by its early proponents in an integrated two-part proposition: Law is an instrument *to serve the social good*. The crucial twist is that in the course of the twentieth century, the first half of this proposition swept the legal culture while the second half became increasingly untenable. As the century wore on, the seemingly inexorable penetration of moral relativism, combined with the multiplication of groups aggressively pursuing their own agendas, convinced in the rightness of their claims, dealt a deep wound to the notion of a shared social good. This book traces out the myriad worrisome implications of this twist. Rather than represent a means to advance the public welfare, the law is becoming a means pure and simple, with the ends up for grabs.

Many readers of this Introduction may be skeptical that a real transition from a non-instrumental to an instrumental view of law has taken place or is in the process of taking place. So inured have we become to an instrumental view of law that it is difficult to give credence to non-instrumental views of law: Law has always been seen and treated instrumentally, has it not, regardless of claims to the contrary? Chapters 1 and 2 articulate several versions of non-instrumental views of law that circulated for centuries in the Anglo-American common law system, continuing into the early twentieth century in the United States. The presence, consistency, and longevity of these views are impressive and undeniable.

It is also undeniable, however, that there were large mythical components to these non-instrumental views; they invoked abstractions and offered accounts of law and judging that, in hindsight, appear patently implausible. Nonetheless, they were widely espoused and sincerely believed, especially by the legal elite – by judges, legal scholars, and prominent lawyers. The only way to understand these views, to grasp what they meant and what their consequences were, is to strive to get beyond our consummate instrumentalism to participate in a mindset that was less jaded about law.

Skeptics of a more radical ilk will insist that law has always served elite or particular interests, that lawyers have always manipulated the law to achieve ends, or that judges have always shaped and interpreted legal doctrine with class or personal biases, which non-instrumental accounts of law – whether sincerely held or offered as a subterfuge – served to conceal. According to this view, the core change entailed in modern legal instrumentalism is making explicit and known to everyone what covertly was happening all along. Former domination of law by specific interests *sub silentio* has been replaced by an open contest over the power of law in which all (or at least those with resources) can engage. This is a real change with real consequences, but it is not a change from a fundamentally non-instrumental law to an instrumental law. The law has been instrumental beneath the surface all along. Exposing this underlying reality is a positive change because engaging in an overt contest for law will produce better results, or at least exposes legal domination for what it is.

Without the accompanying radical politics, this was, in essence, the position of Jhering and Holmes. They argued that the non-instrumental view of law was descriptively incorrect, an erroneous depiction of the reality of legal development. Holmes began *The Common Law* with his famous declaration that "The life of the law has not been logic: it has been experience. The felt necessities of the time, the prevalent moral and political theories, intuitions of public policy, avowed or unconscious, even the prejudices which judges share with their fellow-men, have a good deal more to do than the syllogism in determining the rules by which men should be governed."[5] Holmes contended that "hitherto this process has been largely unconscious,"[6] and he thought the law could be made more socially optimal if this process was instead done consciously.

The retort of the skeptic contains a large measure of truth. Law has always been used instrumentally to advance particular interests. Even when it was characterized in non-instrumental terms, law regularly originated in and changed through instrumentally motivated contests. Chapter 3 shows that legislation and the actual practice of law in the nineteenth century were seen in largely instrumental terms, notwithstanding the many non-instrumental accounts of law repeated during this period.

But this is not the whole story. Non-instrumental accounts of law were widely expressed and believed, and these beliefs were acted upon accordingly. In important ways the law had achieved autonomy or semi-autonomy, with its own internal integrity, because lawyers and judges treated it that way, not always and not entirely,

---

5 Oliver Wendell Holmes, *The Common Law* (New Brunswick, N.J.: Transaction Publishers 2005 [1881]) 5.
6 Id. 32.

but often enough to matter. Many critically important consequences – some good, some bad – have followed from the removal of the old non-instrumental cloak that had been draped over law for more than a thousand years.

One of the themes of this study is that ideals have the potential to create a reality in their image only so long as they are believed in and acted pursuant to. This might sound fanciful, like suggesting that something can be conjured up by wishful thinking; or it might sound elitist, like the "noble lie," the idea that it is sometimes better for the masses to believe in myths because the truth is too much to handle. But it is neither. It is a routine application of the proposition widely accepted among social theorists and social scientists that much of social reality is the construction of our ideas and beliefs.

Another theme, which rubs against but is no less true than the one just discussed, is that unintentional consequences often follow from intentional actions. This book recounts a long string of good intentions by reformers – from the Enlightenment philosophers, to the Realists, to the Warren Court, to liberal cause litigators – leading to unanticipated results that were contrary to their hopes and expectations.

The thrust of these comments make it easy to misread my position. Although this book explores the implications of a pervasive instrumental view of law with a sense of urgent foreboding, this should not be interpreted as a wholesale rejection of the idea that law is an instrument. This view of law was promoted for sound reasons and offers many advantages. More to the point, this view of law is here to stay. Circumstances in the economy, in politics, and in culture have changed in ways that preclude a return to non-instrumental views of law. A broad society-wide movement toward instrumental rationality, Max Weber argued a century ago, is characteristic of capitalist economics and mass bureaucratic organizations. This is the modern condition. The solution to the problems identified herein lies not in repudiating the view that law is an instrument, but in setting limits and restraints on this view, in recognizing the situations in which it is inappropriate, and in recognizing that certain uses of this instrument are dangerous and must be guarded against.

An Instrumental Mindset Toward Law

The proposition that law is pervasively understood and utilized as a means to an end, when stated as such, is clear enough. What this means in concrete terms varies depending upon the context, however. An instrumental understanding of law thus appears in markedly different forms. Beneath this apparent variety they are united by a common underlying orientation. An instrumental view of law means that law – encompassing legal rules, legal institutions, and legal processes – is *consciously* viewed by people and groups as a *tool* or *means* with which to achieve *ends*. The supply of possible ends is open and limitless, ranging from personal (enrichment, harassment, or advancement), to ideological (furthering a cause), to social goals like maximizing social welfare or finding a balance of competing interests.

Several examples will make this point more concrete. Lawyers with a purely instrumental view of law will manipulate legal rules and processes to advance their clients' ends; lawyers with a non-instrumental view, in contrast, will accord greater respect for the binding quality of legal rules and will strive to maintain the integrity of the law. Cause lawyers incite litigation to bring about desired social change, an exclusively instrumental course of action for which there is no non-instrumental counterpart. An instrumental judge manipulates the applicable legal rules to arrive at a preferred end, whereas a non-instrumental judge is committed to following the applicable legal rules no matter what the outcome. Groups that take an instrumental view of judging strive to secure the election or appointment of judges they expect will interpret the legal rules to favor their ends; groups with a non-instrumental view of judging seek the appointment of judges who will diligently apply the law with no preconceived controlling end in mind. Legislators with an instrumental view will promote whatever law will help secure their re-election (personal end), or further their ideological position (political end), or advance the public good (social end); a legislator with a non-instrumental view, a view that had currency two centuries ago but has long been defunct, will seek to declare the immanent norms of the community or natural principles.

Running through the aforementioned examples, legal instrumentalism takes on two distinct but interacting forms. The first is the *conscious attitude toward law* held by legal actors and others in society – the attitude that law (including legal rules, judges, enforcement officials, etc.) is a tool to be utilized to achieve ends. The second is a *theory or account of the nature of law* held by legal actors and others in society – the theory that law is purely a means to an end, an empty vessel devoid of any inherent principle or binding content or integrity unto itself. These are independent propositions that can coexist in different combinations with non-instrumental views of law at various levels. In the late nineteenth century, for example, the prevailing theory of the nature of law among the legal elite was non-instrumental, while conscious attitudes toward law among legislators and lawyers often were instrumental in one of the ways mentioned earlier.

The story told herein involves tracing the consequences of the collapse of the non-instrumental theory of the nature of law, the second sense discussed, in unleashing a purely instrumental conscious attitude toward law, the first sense discussed. Our contemporary legal culture pairs a pervasively held instrumental theory of the nature of law with consummately instrumental attitudes toward law, a unique combination in which the attitude and theory are mutually reinforcing.

Plan of the Book

The references just given may be too abbreviated to be enlightening at this early juncture, but they are offered as general words of guidance that will become more meaningful as the text progresses. The book proceeds chronologically and thematically, divided into three Parts. The first Part begins with non-instrumental views of the nature of law and traces out the emergence and spread of instrumental views. This mostly historical exploration conveys non-instrumental views of the common law that circulated in the eighteenth and nineteenth centuries (Chapters 1 and 2). Legislation and the practice of law, already viewed in largely instrumental terms in the nineteenth century, are covered next (Chapter 3). This is followed by the early twentieth-century promotion of an instrumental view of law by Holmes, Pound, and the Legal Realists (Chapter 4). Finally, a series of watershed events and themes in connection with the twentieth-century Supreme Court that fueled the instrumental perception toward law and judges is taken up (Chapter 5).

The second Part surveys contemporary instrumental views of law in the following contexts: legal education (Chapter 6), legal theory (Chapter 7), the practice of law (Chapter 8), cause litigation (Chapter 9), judging and judicial appointments (Chapter 10), and legislation and administrative law (Chapter 11). The 1960s and 1970s, it turns out, was a pivotal period that combined the entrenchment of an instrumental view of law in the legal culture with irresolvable disputes over the social good. A harshly politicized tone set in at that time, with consequences that continue to reverberate in the legal culture.

The third Part unpacks the ways in which an instrumental view of law and the battles it generates are detrimental to the rule of law. Four separate developments are covered: The collapse of fundamental legal limitations that required the law to conform to right, and deterioration of belief in the public good (Chapter 12).The reduction in the binding quality of legal rules, and spreading doubts about judicial objectivity (Chapter 13). Legal theorists recognize these problems for the rule of law separately; this discussion shows they are connected by a common antipathy to, and pressure from, an instrumental view of law.

As this summary indicates, a great deal of ground is canvassed in this work. Depth of coverage has been sacrificed to maintain a focused narrative. Each chapter is limited to conveying an instrumental view of law and its implications in the particular context covered. Only in this way can the broad scope of the situation be presented in a single work. Liberally mixing intellectual history with rational reconstruction, supported by empirical studies whenever available – drawing from the fields of legal theory, legal history, constitutional theory, professional ethics, public interest law, political science, and legal sociology – this book lays out an extended argument that the view that law is purely a means to an end lies at the heart of many of our most intractable problems, and that matters are worsening. This book offers a diagnosis of our worrisome time.

Part 1

The spread of legal instrumentalism

1

Non-instrumental views of law

It is characteristic of non-instrumental views that the content of law is, in some sense, given; that law is immanent; that the process of law-making is not a matter of creation but one of discovery; that law is not the product of human will; that law has a kind of autonomy and internal integrity; that law is, in some sense, objectively determined.

In the Medieval period in Europe, two distinct but commingled types of law possessed these characteristics. The first type was natural law and divine law in the Catholic tradition – the Ten Commandments, for example. Divine and natural law were thought to be binding upon and to be infused in the positive law that governed society. They were pre-given by God and were the product of God's will, unalterable by man. They were objective in that they constituted absolute moral and legal truths that were binding on all, providing the content of and setting limits upon positive law. These laws and principles were disclosed through revelation (mainly scripture) and discerned through the application of reason implanted in man by God. As medieval scholar Walter Ullmann put it, "the law itself as the external regulator of society was based upon faith. Faith and law stood to each other in the relation of cause and effect effect."[1]

The second type was customary law. Everyday life during the Medieval period was governed by customary law, or, more accurately, by overlapping and sometimes conflicting regimes of customary law: feudal law, the law of the manor, Germanic customary law, residues of Roman law, trade customs, and local customs. Customary law was said to have existed from time immemorial. It was derived from and constituted the very way of life of the community, the byways and folkways of the people. Law was "'the law of one's fathers,' the preexisting, objective, legal situation..."[2] As such, the content of customary law was not the product of any particular individual's or any group's will, but was a collective emanation from below. Accordingly, the process of explicitly articulating and applying the law was a matter of discovering and declaring the unwritten law that was already manifested or immanent in the community life.

1 Walter Ullmann, *A History of Political Thought: The Middle Ages* (Middlesex: Penguin 1965) 103.
2 Fritz Kern, *Kingship and Law in the Middle Ages* (New York: Harper Torchbooks 1956) 70–1.

These intertwined understandings of law, which dominated for at least a millennium, were non-instrumental in the core respect that they represented a pre-given order that encompassed everyone. It was a law for all that was the product of no one. The law was not subject to the will of anyone and not in the specific interest of anyone. It was the law of the community. Certain groups were in more favorable positions than others, to be sure, as nobles were to serfs, but everyone had a place within an organic social order governed by law. Legislation in the modern sense of the enactment of positive legal norms (by emperors, kings, princes, and parliamentary bodies) took place, but was relatively sparse and understood to mainly involve making explicit the already existing immanent law. The power to declare law was bounded by and took place within a framework of natural, divine, and customary law.

Traditional understandings of the common law

Historical understandings of the common law in the United States provide two distinct examples of non-instrumental law. The first one, which held sway through the first half of the nineteenth century, is continuous with the aforementioned two Medieval understandings of law; the second one, which grew in the course of the nineteenth century and dominated into the early twentieth century, characterized law as a science.

Medieval scholar Father Figgis's characterization of the traditional understanding of the common law displays the interwoven inheritance of its medieval forebears:

> The Common law is pictured invested with a halo of dignity peculiar to the embodiment of the deepest principles and to the highest expression of human reason and of the law of nature implanted by God in the heart of man. As yet men are not clear that an Act of Parliament can do more than declare the Common Law.... The Common Law is the perfect ideal of law; for it is natural reason developed and expounded by a collective wisdom of many generations.... Based upon long usage and almost supernatural wisdom, its authority is above, rather than below that of Acts of Parliament or royal ordinances..."[3]

The "common law mind" dominated English political and legal thought from the late sixteenth century. Historian J.G.A. Pocock summarized this mentality:

> In the first place, it is asserted that 'the ancient constitution' was an 'immemorial' constitution, and that belief in it was built up in the following way. The relations of government and governed in England were assumed to be regulated by law; the law in force in England was assumed to be the common law; all common law was assumed to be custom, elaborated, summarized and enforced by statute; and all custom was assumed to be immemorial, in the sense that any declaration or even change of

---

3 Quoted in Edward Corwin, *The "Higher Law" Background of American Constitutional Law* (Ithaca, N.Y.: Cornell Univ. Press 1955) 34–5.

custom – uttered by a judge from his bench, recorded by a court in a precedent, or registered by king-in-parliament as a statute – presupposed a custom already ancient and not necessarily recorded at the time of the writing.[4]

Although the common law in the United States took its own path, it was heavily influenced by its English inheritance. In the seventeenth century, the law within each colony was a mixture of scripture and common law understandings brought by settlers and based on what they were familiar with at home. The colonists had a strong belief that they were governed by the ancient constitution and common law of England. There was a dearth of trained lawyers in the colonies, and most judges had no legal training. The separation between legislatures and courts was not sharp, with legislatures rendering court-like determinations. In the late eighteenth century and thereafter, Blackstone's *Commentaries on the Laws of England* had an inestimable impact on the development of American law. It was the basic training material for apprentices who wished to become lawyers and the leading text in early law schools.[5]

The common law in England and the United States integrated two basic under-pinnings with distinct forms of legitimation.[6] First, as described above, the common law was thought to be a product of the customs of the people from time immemorial, an "ancient collection of unwritten maxims and customs," wrote Blackstone.[7] The law was said to represent the lived ways of the community, their collective wisdom recognized and refined into law – "the expression or manifestation of commonly shared values and conceptions of reasonableness and the common good."[8] Its purported origin in custom gave the law a claim to being consensual. "This consent is deeper than agreeing to have other persons represent one in a legislative assembly. It comes from a recognition that the rules that govern one's life are *one's own*, they define that life, give it structure and meaning, are already practiced and so deeply engrained that they appear to one as purely natural."[9]

Second, the common law was also said to be the very embodiment of natural rights and principle. Universal custom and usage were thought to reflect and be evidence of natural principle, and, furthermore, judges refine the common law and its principles through reasoned analysis. When engaging in this activity, judges were declaring law, not creating law. "Coke . . . had presented law as customary and judge-made, the fruits of centuries of constant adaptation, and had argued that

---

4 J.G.A. Pocock, *The Ancient Constitution and the Feudal Law: A Study of English Historical Thought in the Seventeenth Century* (Cambridge: Cambridge Univ. Press 1987) 261.
5 See Dennis R. Nolan, "Sir William Blackstone and the New American Republic: A Study of Intellectual Impact," 51 *N.Y.U. L. Rev.* 731 (1976).
6 A superb discussion of Blackstone's Commentaries can be found in Daniel J. Boorstin, *The Mysterious Science of Law: An Essay on Blackstone's Commentaries* (Chicago: Univ. of Chicago Press 1996).
7 1 Commentaries 17, quoted in Gerald Postema, *Bentham and the Common Law Tradition* (Oxford: Clarendon Press 1986) 4.
8 Postema, Id. 6–7.
9 Id. 16–17.

each maxim or rule of law embodied reason and experience so great and ripe that no individual mind with its limited horizon could attain to the height of its wisdom."[10]

Jesse Root, in 1789, writing in the newly created United States, articulated all these elements of the non-instrumental understanding of the common law: "[Our] common law was derived from the law of nature and of revelation; those rules and maxims of immutable truth and justice, which arise from the eternal fitness of things, which need only to be understood, to be submitted to; as they are themselves the highest authority; together with certain customs and usages, which had been universally assented to and adopted in practice, as reasonable and beneficial."[11] According to Root, the common law: "is the perfection of reason"; "universal"; "embraces all cases and questions that can possibly arise"; "is in itself perfect, clear and certain"; "is superior to all other laws and regulations"; "all positive laws are to be construed by it, and wherein they are opposed to it they are void"; "It is immemorial."[12]

There is a remarkable continuity to these views of the common law within the Anglo-American legal tradition that extends back centuries. Compare Blackstone's and Root's descriptions of the common law with the following statement by Sir John Davies in his 1612 Irish Reports:

> For the *Common Law of England* is nothing else but the *Common Custome* of the Realm: and a Custome which hath obtained the force of a Law is always said to be *Jus non scriptum*: for it cannot be made either by Charter, or by Parliament, which are Acts reduced to writing, and are alwaies matter of Record; but being only matter of fact, and consisting in use and practice, it can be recorded and registered no-where but in the memory of the people.
>
> For a Custome taketh beginning and froweth to perfection in this manner: When a reasonable act once done is found to be good and beneficiall to the people, and agreeable to their nature and disposition, then do they use it and practice it again and again, and so by often iteration and multiplication of the act it becometh a *Custome*; and being continued without interruption time out of mind, it obtaineth the force of a Law.
>
> And this *Customary Law* is the most perfect and most excellent, and without comparison the best, to make and preserve a Commonwealth. For the *written Laws* which are made either by the Edicts of Princes, or by Councils of Estates, are imposed upon the Subject before any Triall or Probation made, whether the same be fit and agreeable to the nature and disposition of the people, or whether they will breed any inconvenience or no. But a Custome doth never become a Law to bind the people, until it hath been tried and approved time out of mind, during all which time there did thereby arise no

---

10 Pocock, *Ancient Constitution and the Feudal Law*, supra 170.
11 Jesse Root, "The Origin of Government and Laws in Connecticut," Preface to Volume 1, *Root's Reports* (1798), excerpted in Mark De Wolfe, *Readings in American Legal History* (Cambridge, Mass.: Harvard Univ. Press 1949) 17, 16–24.
12 Id. 19.

inconvenience: for if it had been found inconvenient at any time, it had been used no longer, but had been interrupted; and consequently it had lost the virtue and force of a Law.[13]

Scientific understandings of the common law

In the course of the nineteenth century in the United States, a marked shift took place in which science, which enjoyed unmatched prestige as the font of knowledge in the Enlightenment age, became the ascendant form of legitimation for law. Blackstone, whose *Commentaries* were based on a series of lectures he delivered at Oxford commencing in 1753, claimed that "law is to be considered not only as a matter of practice, but also as a rational science;"[14] as such, it was "an object of academic knowledge" that ought to be studied in the University.[15] The *Commentaries* were an exercise in organizing the common law scientifically.

Richard Rush, a leading U.S. lawyer, published an essay in 1815 on "American Jurisprudence," which declared: "The law itself in this country, is, moreover, a science of great extent. We have an entire substratum of common law as the broad foundation upon which every thing else is built."[16] An unattributed 1851 essay in a leading law journal elaborated on the sense in which law is a science: "Like other sciences, [law] is supposed to be pervaded by general rules, shaping its structure, solving its intricacies, explaining its apparent contradictions. Like other sciences, it is supposed to have first or fundamental principles, never modified, and the immovable basis on which the whole structure reposes; and also a series of dependent principles and rules, modified and subordinated by reason and circumstances, extending outward in unbroken connection to the remotest applications of law."[17] Among the legal elite this was a standard understanding. Nationally renowned law reformer David Dudley Field proclaimed in 1859 that there is no science "greater in magnitude or importance" than "the science of law."[18] Edward Ryan, a Justice of the Wisconsin Supreme Court, stated in a law school graduation address (1873): "The law is a science."[19]

13 John Davies, quoted in Pocock, *The Ancient Constitution and the Feudal Law*, supra 32–3.
14 II *Commentaries* 2, quoted in Boorstin, *The Mysterious Science of Law*, supra 20.
15 I *Commentaries* 26–7, quoted in David Lieberman, *The Province of Legislation Determined: Legal Theory in Eighteenth Century England* (Cambridge: Cambridge Univ. Press 1989) p. 32.
16 Richard Rush, *American Jurisprudence* (1815), reprinted in *Readings in American Legal History*, p. 217, 268–80.
17 "Nature and Method of Legal Studies," 3 *U.S. Monthly Law Mag.* 381–2 (1851)
18 David Dudley Field, "Magnitude and Importance of Legal Science" (1859), reprinted in Stephen B. Presser and Jamil S. Zainaldin, *Law and Jurisprudence in American History*, 5th ed. (St. Paul, Minn.: West Pub. 2000) p. 740, 740–5.
19 Edward G. Ryan, Address to the Graduating Law Students of the University of Wisconsin (1873), reprinted in Dennis R. Nolan, *Readings in the History of the American Legal Profession* (Charlottesville, Va.: Michie 1980) p. 153, 153–9.

Christopher Columbus Langdell, appointed in 1870 to be the first Dean of the Havard Law School, offered the articulation most often cited today:

> Law, considered as a science, consists of certain principles or doctrines.... Each of these doctrines has arrived at its present state by slow degrees; in other words, it is a growth, extending in many cases through centuries. This growth is to be traced in the main through a series of cases.... It seems to me, therefore, to be possible to take such a branch of the law as Contracts, for example, and, without exceeding comparatively moderate limits, to select, classify, and arrange all the cases which had contributed in any important degree to the growth, development, or establishment of any of its essential doctrines...[20]

Law, according to this account, is a science with inductive, analytical and deductive aspects.[21] Decided cases are the raw material of law (its empirical component). Decisions fall into patterns, from which the governing rules, concepts and principles can be derived through induction. These rules, concepts and principles can be logically organized and their necessary content and implications made evident, then applied deductively to determine the appropriate rules and outcomes in future cases. Lawyers, judges, and law professors engage in this process on an ongoing basis. The common law and rights together form a coherent and gapless whole that objectively determines the decision in every case. These ideas formed the basis of a school of thought known as the formalists, to be discussed later.

By the end of the nineteenth century, the non-instrumental portrayal of law as a science was well entrenched among the legal elite. Beneath the science overlay remain many of the old views of the common law, as is evident in the following characterizations of the common law by contributors to an 1892 *Yale Law Journal* symposium on the "Methods of Legal Education":

> The very first and indispensable requisite in legal education... is the acquisition of a clear and accurate perception, a complete knowledge, a strong, tenacious grasp of those unchangeable principles of the common law which underlie and permeate its whole structure, and which control all its details, its consequences, its application to human affairs.[22]

Here is a like-minded passage from another contributor:

> The adjudicated cases constitute nothing more than materials out of which the scientific jurist is to construct a science of jurisprudence. They are not law in themselves, they are but applications of the law to particular cases. Law is not *made* by the courts, at most promulgated by them.... [N]either the judge nor the legislator makes living law, but

---

20 Christopher Columbus Langdell, Preface, Selection of Cases on the Law of Contracts, reprinted in *Law and Jurisprudence in American Legal History*, p. 747, 746–8. A similar characterization of law as a science was written by the Dean of Columbia Law School, William A, Keener, "Methods of Legal Education," 1 *Yale L.J.* 143 (1892).

21 A superb study of Langdell's ideas is Thomas C. Grey, "Langdell's Orthodoxy," 45 *U. Pitt. L. Rev.* 1 (1983).

22 Edward J. Phelps, "Methods of Legal Education," 1 *Yale L.J.* 139, 140 (1892).

only declares that to be the law, which has been forced upon them, whether consciously or unconsciously, by the pressure of the popular sense of right, that popular sense of right being itself but the resultant of the social forces which are at play in every organized society.[23]

These essays emphasize the principled nature of the common law, its consistency with reason, and that it is the immanent product of society.

An illustrative account of the common law that combines all of these aspects can be found in the 1890 Annual Address to the American Bar Association delivered by James C. Carter, one of the most acclaimed lawyers of the day. His address is especially revealing because his specific target of criticism was the growing instrumental view that legislatures have the power to declare law at their will. After centuries in which the common law had been the dominant source of law-making, this period witnessed the rise of legislation. Legislation was being promoted by reformists as more democratic, more systematic, clearer and more certain, than the common law, which critics complained was the preserve of manipulative lawyers and elite judges.[24] Carter responded (emphasizing what he saw as the key words):

> That the judge can not *make* law is accepted from the start. That there is already a rule by which the case must be determined is not doubted. . . . It is agreed that the true rule must somehow be *found*. Judges and advocates – all together – engage in the *search*. Cases more or less nearly approaching the one in controversy are adduced. Analogies are referred to. The customs and habits of men are appealed to. Principles already settled as fundamental are invoked and run out to their consequences; and finally a rule is deduced which is declared to be the one which the existing law requires to be applied to the case. . . . [O]ur unwritten law – which is the main body of our law – is not a command, or a body of commands, but consists of rules springing from the social standard of justice, or from the habits and customs from which that standard has itself been derived.[25]

Carter repeatedly insisted that the common law reflects the ways of the people. The job of the judge and jurist is to observe and formulate, organize, and rationalize these customs and habits. As such, "the law reveals itself in its true character as an Inductive Science."[26] "The law is a department of sociology. It is the unconscious resolve of society that all its members shall act as the great majority act."[27]

Carter attacked the century-old views of Jeremy Bentham, champion of legislation and the most vociferous critic of the common law. Carter thought it obvious

---

23 Christopher G. Tiedeman, "Methods of Legal Education," 1 *Yale L.J.* 150,154 (1892).
24 A general discussion of the time can be found in Robert W. Gordon, "'The Ideal and Actual in the Law': Fantasies and Practices of New York City Lawyers, 1870–1910" in *The New High Priests: Lawyers in Post-Civil War America*, edited by Gerard W. Gawalt (Westport, Conn.: Greenwood Press 1986) 51–74.
25 James C. Carter, "The Ideal and the Actual in the Law," Annual Address, *American Bar Assoc. Reports* (1890) 224–5.
26 Id. 231.
27 Id. 236.

that "no legislature can make what laws it will."[28] Legislatively mandated reforms are partial, not representative of the ways of the people or their sense of justice, and therefore doomed to failure. With a rhetorical flourish, he dismissed Bentham as someone who "may be accurately described by the vulgar designation of *crank*..."[29]

The embrace of a scientific posture had its own consequences, reinforcing certain tendencies already manifested within legal thought. Science in the nineteenth century was oriented toward logical abstractions and the identification of laws of economic and social order.[30] John Burgess, who briefly studied law, was a leading developer of the nascent field of political science in the 1880s and 1890s, which he characterized in terms redolent of legal science: "The task of political science was first to arrange 'the facts of history in the forms and conclusions of science,' and then to discern in those facts 'political ideals not yet realized.' These ideals in turn 'become principles of political science, the articles of political creeds, and at last, laws and institutions.'"[31]

Non-instrumental views of law as a science survived into the first third of the twentieth century. Yale law professor Walter Wheeler Cook observed in the *American Bar Association Journal* in 1927:

> Prominent teachers of law still tell us that we must preserve what they call the logical symmetry of the law, that after all the law is logical; and talk about deducing the rule to be applied to a new situation by logic from some 'fundamental principle.' Back of all this, it is submitted, is nothing but the old logic; the assumption that in some way or other we can discover general 'laws,' 'general principles,' Aristotelian 'universals', which by means of logical, that is, syllogistic reasoning, we can deal with new cases as they arise as merely new samples of preexisting classes. The nineteenth century notion of science as the ascertainment of all-embracing laws of nature, holding for all occasions [is still prevalent].
>
> It would be safe to assert that essentially the same ideas underlie nearly all the teaching in our law schools.[32]

Cook wrote these words shortly before non-instrumental views of law as a science were to collapse.

Myths with consequences

As alluded to earlier, the notion of the common law as descending from time immemorial was largely a myth. Nonetheless, it was a set of unshakable assumptions

---

28 Id. 241.
29 Id. 244 (emphasis in original).
30 See Morton White, *Social Thought in America: the Revolt Against Formalism* (Boston: Beacon Press 1957).
31 Dorothy Ross, *The Origins of American Social Science* (Cambridge: Cambridge Univ. Press 1991) 71 (quoting Burgess).
32 Walter Wheeler Cook, "Scientific Method and the Law," 13 *A.B.A. Journal* 303, 306 (1927).

posited about the common law, as Pocock described:

> The common law was by definition immemorial custom. For hundreds of years before
> Coke and Davies it had been accepted, by an assumption common in medieval thought,
> that English law was *jus non scriptum* and that the function of the courts was to declare
> the ancient custom of the realm. Even statutes could be so interpreted, and Coke eagerly
> takes at least the earliest of them to be declaratory judgments. Innumerable decisions
> were consequently on record as declaring that everything which they contained, down
> to the most minute and complex technicality, had formed part of the custom of England
> from time out of mind; or at least so the common lawyers read them to mean, and this
> fact is at the root of their interpretation of history.[33]

That these views were not entirely true – many common law rules had their origins
in transplanted feudal notions, or were introduced by relatively recent legislation,
or were the customs of judges and the legal profession rather than of the people –
did not lessen their clutch. "This delusion . . . had been accepted and believed by a
great many Englishmen of the politically minded classes."[34] The fact of this belief
turned out to have greater significance than its falsity: It shaped understandings and
debates about the political-legal order in seventeenth, eighteenth, and nineteenth
century England.

The same can be said of common law understandings in the United States. It is
perhaps difficult from a contemporary perspective to understand how these claims
could have been uttered or taken seriously. And, as with all myths, not everyone
was under its spell. Consider this startlingly realistic 1836 characterization of the
common law by Robert Rantoul, an advocate of codification:

> The judge is human, and feels the bias which the coloring of the particular case gives.
> If he wishes to decide the next case differently, he has only to distinguish, and thereby
> make new law. . . .
>
> The Common Law is the perfection of human reason, – just as alcohol is the perfection
> of sugar. The subtle spirit of the Common Law is reason double distilled, till what
> was wholesome and nutritive becomes rank poison. Reason is sweet and pleasant to
> the unsophisticated intellect; but this sublimated perversion of reason bewilders, and
> perplexes, and plunges its victims into mazes of error.
>
> . . . Almost any case, where there is any difference of opinion, may be decided either
> way, and plausible analogies found in the great storehouse of precedent to justify the
> decision. The law, then, is the final will or whim of the judge, after counsel for both
> parties have done their utmost to sway it to the one side or the other.[35]

---

33 Pocock, *The Ancient Constitution and the Feudal Law*, supra 37.
34 Id. 233.
35 Robert Rantoul, "Oration at Scituate" (1836), reprinted in *American Legal History*, 2nd ed., edited
   by Kermit L. Hall, William M. Wiecek, and Paul Finkelman (New York: Oxford Univ. Press 1996)
   318.

Rantoul still held an idealized view of the common law as an abstract matter, but described it as twisted in the hands of judges.

Neither the statements of skeptics, however, nor awareness that reality does not match the ideal, provide convincing reasons to doubt sincerity of belief in these descriptions. The legal elite had described law in such terms, updated into the language of science, for centuries. Members of the general populace also expressed similarly idealized views of law. As myths cum ideals, later chapters will show, they extended beyond the realm of rhetoric to establish standards of accountability and norms that affected the behavior of legal officials. To dismiss them as insignificant because they are myths, therefore, is a mistake.

Enlightenment and its aftermath

The eighteenth-century Enlightenment was characterized by the subjection of tradition and custom to critical scrutiny and the rise in the prestige of science and reason as the most reliable sources of truth and knowledge. After the miraculous discoveries of Newton, who announced a handful of natural laws that governed all physical relations in the heavens and on earth, it was thought that all of the secrets of the natural order would be uncovered. Advancements in physics, biology, and chemistry added to the expanding quantum of knowledge, transforming technology in their wake. Enlightenment *philosophes* believed that, just as the natural order could be understood and beneficially exploited, so too could the social order be mastered. "With Newton's achievement at their back men turned confidently to the formulation of the inherently just and reasonable rules of social and political relationships."[36] "Ultimately the Enlightenment aimed at nothing less than discovering the hidden forces in the moral world that moved and help people come together, forces that could match the great eighteenth-century scientific discoveries of the hidden forces – gravity, magnetism, electricity, and energy – that operated in the physical world."[37] A science of man focusing on human nature and society would yield knowledge about the natural principles of law and morality, enabling mankind to use reason to shape society to achieve material and political progress. "Entire systems were elaborated which purported to deduce with Euclidean precision the whole duty of man, both moral and legal, from a few agreed premises."[38] "Premised upon the belief that the universe is a rational whole, in the sense that it can be rationally understood, and that 'every detailed occurrence can be correlated with its antecedents in a perfectly definite manner, exemplifying general principles,' nineteenth century science led men to believe that by empirical methods alone they could discover 'positive facts' and 'universal laws' about all phenomena, human as well as physical."[39]

---

36 Corwin, "*'Higher Law' Background of American Constitutional Law*," supra 59.
37 Gordon S. Wood, *The Radicalism of the American Revolution* (New York: Vintage 1991) 218.
38 Corwin, "*'Higher Law' Background of American Constitutional Law*," supra 59.
39 John H. Hallowell, "Politics and Ethics," 38 *Am. Pol. Sci. Rev.* 639, 643 (1944)(citations omitted).

Blackstone and his contemporaries, including the founding generation of the United States, saw themselves as participants in the Enlightenment. Blackstone's organized presentation of the common law, the unprecedented feat which earned him great renown, was a classic Enlightenment exercise in the science of man. As these views carried over into the nineteenth century, when the prestige of the natural sciences rose to even greater heights, they fed into the scientific versions of non-instrumental law in the manner mentioned earlier.

Although the scientific approach was overlaid on preexisting non-instrumental views of law, and in many respects they overlapped, within the scientific mindset was the germ for a crucial change of perspective on law. Science is oriented toward uncovering causal relations, effects, and functions, formulated in terms of principles or laws. Non-instrumental views portrayed law *as* an immanent ordering (of the universe or of the community). Under a scientific view, law would come instead to be seen as the *source of* social order – to produce social order is the function or purpose or end of law. In turn, this new perspective, over time, would open up questions about the efficiency and utility of law in carrying out its functions. The subtle but fundamental difference can be put thus: law *is* order, versus law *maintains* order. While the implication of this was not immediately evident – indeed, it was concealed because the scientific perspective built on and incorporated non-instrumental accounts of law – this change in orientation is a key step in moving away from seeing law as an end in itself to seeing law as a means to an end.[40]

The resort to science initially bolstered non-instrumental views of law, as indicated, but over the longer term the critical thrust of the Enlightenment undermined the Medieval underpinnings of the common law – natural and divine law, and long-standing custom. Many Enlightenment thinkers were deists or atheists hostile to institutionalized religion. Divine revelation and Catholic natural law thus became less acceptable as sources of law. Additionally, the Enlightenment emphasis on critical scrutiny of received tradition undermined the prestige that had always attached to custom in connection with law. "Everywhere in the Western world people were making tiny piecemeal assaults on the ignorance and barbarism of the past."[41] What was once seen as the wisdom of the ages came to be seen as blind fetters of the past holding back progress. Historical studies, another product of the Enlightenment, showed that historical times and longstanding custom and usage were, often as not, tyrannical and uncivilized, not worthy of emulation or continuing deference.[42] These views were by implication corrosive of the longstanding identification of the common law with immemorial custom and scripture.

Many contemporaries of the period, including Blackstone, simultaneously held onto pre-Enlightenment views and Enlightenment views, notwithstanding their

40 See Roger Berkowitz, *The Gift of Science: Leibniz and the Modern Legal Tradition* (Cambridge, Mass.: Harvard Univ. Press 2005).
41 Wood, *Radicalism of the American Revolution*, supra 192.
42 See, for example, John Milton Goodenow, *Historical Sketches of the Principles and Maxims of American Jurisprudence* (New York: Arno Press 1972).

tension. Historian Bernard Bailyn found this combination in the ideas circulating during the American Revolution:

> The common lawyers the colonists cited, for example, sought to establish right to appeal by precedent and to an unbroken tradition evolving from time immemorial, and they assumed, if they did not argue, that the accumulation of the ages, the burden of inherited custom, contained within it a greater wisdom than any man or group of men could devise by the power of reason. Nothing could have been more alien to the Enlightenment rationalists whom the colonists also quoted – and with equal enthusiasm. These theorists felt that it was precisely the heavy crust of custom that was weighing down the spirit of man; they sought to throw it off and to create by unfettered power a framework of institutions superior to the accidental inheritance of the past.[43]

A combination of ideas like this would continue through the end of the nineteenth century.[44]

Enlightenment arguments ultimately undercut not just the foundations of law but also those of morality, for they shared the same foundations. The *philosophes*, it must be emphasized, were not moral relativists or anarchists. To the contrary, their goals were to establish more rational and scientific footings for law and morality to bring about a better organized and more just society. At the outset they had no doubts that they would be successful in the search for rational moral and legal principles.

Today we know that they failed in the quest to formulate objective principles of law and society. The reasons for this are many, only three of which will be recited here. First, exploration of the world made it increasingly evident that there were a multitude of divergent moral, legal, and customary systems, suggesting that morality and law were largely conventional. Second, human nature at its most common level is base and could at most be used to come up with a set of minimum rules necessary to survive in society, but it could not provide the basis for any higher moral or legal principles. Third, the power and scope of reason became restricted. Reason was once thought capable of producing substantive principles of the right and good. But in the course of the Enlightenment and its aftermath, reason was emptied of substance and increasingly seen in purely instrumental terms. Reason enables people to efficiently achieve their ends, but it cannot identify the proper ends to be desired. Notions about the good and right came to be seen as the product of surrounding cultural views and individual tastes or passions. The Romantic reaction against the Enlightenment celebrated passion and cultural forms of life as the wellsprings of all that is worthy, denigrating the limited, mechanical operations of reason.

Utilitarianism formalizes the implications of this complex of ideas into a moral system which holds that the individual good is whatever one desires or derives pleasure from; achieving the social good involves maximizing the total aggregate of

---

43 Bernard Bailyn, *The Ideological Origins of the American Revolution*, enlarged edition (Cambridge, Mass.: Harvard Univ. Press 1992), 33–4.
44 Ross, *Origins of American Social Science*, supra Chap. 3.

pleasure over pain among the individuals in a society. This transforms moral questions into an empirical science which quantifies pleasure and pain, sums the cumulative results, and produces an objective answer. Although utilitarianism spread within liberal societies in the course of the nineteenth century,[45] it has never proven satisfactory. Among other problems, the quantification of pain and pleasure on a single common scale has proven elusive. Without such a scale, however, it is impossible to provide concrete answers to a moral calculus. More objectionably, utilitarianism is hedonistic in bent, unable distinguish among pleasures – the pleasure of a sadist counts the same as the pleasure of an altruist – which has never comported with prevailing intuitions about morality. Furthermore, the maximizing approach suggests that it is legitimate to impose burdens upon a minority within a community if the majority thereby derives greater benefits overall.

An enduring, bedeviling legacy of the Enlightenment is that it undercut former beliefs in divine and natural law and in the wisdom of custom and tradition, once thought to provide correct principles for morality, law, and life, without supplying any persuasive replacements. The Enlightenment confidence that humans can shape and improve the conditions of their existence encouraged the instrumental view of law, but the relativism that also followed from the Enlightenment left the uses of this powerful instrument a matter of irresolvable dispute.

---

45 According to Peter Gay, natural law theory dominated the first half of the Enlightenment, whereas utilitarianism dominated the second half. Peter Gay, *The Enlightenment: The Science of Freedom* (New York: W.W. Norton 1996) 459.

2

A changing society and common law in the nineteenth century

Legal historians and theorists are in nearly complete agreement that the non-instrumental views of the common law described in the preceding chapter held sway through the eighteenth century. They agree also that the instrumental view of law took hold in the course of the twentieth century. This generally accepted time frame, however, leaves large unanswered questions with respect to the nineteenth century.

Many legal historians appear to accept that legal instrumentalism flowered in the United States in the first quarter of the nineteenth century and lasted until the mid-nineteenth century, when it was supplanted by a lengthy non-instrumental period running from the Civil War until after the turn of the century. The leading source of this chronology of the emergence and subsequent eclipse of instrumental views of law is Morton Horwitz's *Transformation of American Law* (1977).[1] Horwitz begins his account positing the non-instrumental conception of law: "In eighteenth century America, common law rules were not regarded as instruments of social change; whatever legal change took place generally was brought about through legislation. During this period, the common law was conceived of as a body of essentially fixed doctrine to be applied in order to achieve a fair result between private litigants in individual cases."[2]

According to Horwitz, after the Revolution, "merchant and entrepreneurial groups" forged an "alliance with the legal profession to advance their own interests through a transformation of the legal system."[3] Judges adopted a consciously instrumental view of law to shape the common law in a manner friendly to economic development. "What dramatically distinguished nineteenth century law from its eighteenth century counterpart," Horwitz wrote, "was the extent to which

---

1 The chapter on legal instrumentalism in Horwitz's book was published separately earlier as an article. Karl Llewellyn set out a version of this swing in views in *The Common Law Tradition: Deciding Appeals* (Boston: Little Brown 1960). Roscoe Pound, in "Mechanical Jurisprudence," 8 *Columbia L. Rev.* 605 (1908) also talked about the earlier "classical" style of judging, which appears to be the main reference for Llewellyn's claim.

2 Morton Horwitz, *The Transformation of American Law, 1780–1860* (Cambridge, Mass.: Harvard Univ. Press 1977) 1.

3 Id. 253.

common law judges came to play a central role in directing the course of social change."[4]

"By the middle of the nineteenth century the legal system had been reshaped to the advantage of men of commerce and industry at the expense of farmers, workers, consumers, and other less powerful groups within society."[5] Once this transformation in favor of capital interests had been completed, according to Horwitz, the legal profession returned to a non-instrumental account of law as a means to lock in the advantages obtained:

> The rise of legal formalism can be fully correlated with the attainment of these sub-stantive legal changes. If a flexible, instrumental conception of law was necessary to promote the transformation of the post revolutionary American legal system, it was no longer needed once the major beneficiaries of that transformation had obtained the bulk of their objectives. Indeed, once successful, those groups could only benefit if both the recent origins and the foundations in policy and group self-interest of all newly established legal doctrines could be disguised.[6]

Horwitz used this two-part explanatory paradigm to trace out nineteenth-century developments in the common law.

There is an immediate difficulty for Horwitz's account. As the preceding chapter documents, the nineteenth century produced an unbroken string of characterizations of law in consummately non-instrumental terms. These characterizations increasingly emphasized law as science as the nineteenth century progressed, but the underlying non-instrumental characterization of the common law remained constant throughout. This continuity would seem to belie the assertion that legal instrumentalism flowered in the early nineteenth century before giving away to a resurrected non-instrumental understanding of law.

Consider Justice Joseph Story, the most influential jurist of the early nineteenth century. Horwitz presents Story as a prime example of an early-nineteenth-century legal instrumentalist because Story took into consideration the economic conse-quences of common law rules and was willing to modify the law to accommodate commercial development. Instrumentalist judges, according to Horwitz, "no longer conceived [of law] as an eternal set of principles expressed in custom and derived from natural law."[7] In *Terrett v. Taylor*, however, Justice Story invalidated a Virginia statute as a violation of "principles of natural justice" and "fundamental laws of every free government"[8]; he added that the immediate principle of the common law "is equally consonant with the common sense of mankind and the maxims of eternal justice."[9] "Story wrote from an eighteenth-century natural law perspective

4 Id.
5 Id.
6 Id. 254.
7 Horwitz, *Transformation of American Law*, supra 10.
8 *Terrett v. Taylor*, 13 US 43,52 (1815).
9 Id. 50.

in *United States v. Coolidge*," observed historian Stephen Presser, "which announced the inevitable existence of a federal common law of crimes."[10] In the famous case *Swift v. Tyson*, which declared that federal courts must apply general common law, Story wrote "it will hardly be contended, that the decisions of courts constitute laws. They are, at most, only evidence of what the laws are, and are not, of themselves, laws."[11] The "true interpretation and effect" of commercial laws are to be found "in the general principles and doctrines of commercial jurisprudence."[12] These are classic, unselfconscious articulations by Story of the non-instrumental view of the common law as a controlling body of immanent rules and principles that judges discovered and applied to cases before them. Story's views were typical of his generation.

"The common law adopts the principles of natural law"[13] – this statement can be found in many early nineteenth-century court decisions. A historical study by Harry Scheiber showed that although judges in the first half of the nineteenth century were interested in promoting economic growth, nonetheless they adhered to common law principles and "continued to honor formalistic precedents that had relied upon higher notions of inalienable property rights."[14] In judicial opinions, speeches, and writings, there is strong historical evidence that the founding generation and several successor generations continued to believe in natural law principles and held a traditional non-instrumental understanding of the common law.[15] Belief in natural law, although shifting in orientation over time, continued to hold among intellectuals and people generally for much of the nineteenth century.[16]

In addition to not matching the plentiful non-instrumental characterizations of the law that can be found in the early nineteenth century, Horwitz's chronology of the rise and demise of instrumentalism has an odd feature. By this account, prevailing understandings about law managed to swing from non-instrumental (eighteenth century) to instrumental (first half of nineteenth), back again to non-instrumental (second half of nineteenth), then once again to instrumental (first third of twentieth), in a relatively short span of about 150 years. Historian Edward Purcell covers the first three legs in a single sentence: "Although the eighteenth-century concept of natural law and rigid theories of common law precedent had

---

10 Stephen B. Presser, "Revising the Conservative Tradition: Towards A New American Legal History," in *Law in the American Revolution and the Revolution in the Law*, edited by Hendrik Hartog (New York: NYU Press 181) 131.

11 *Swift v. Tyson*, 41 US 1,18 (1842).

12 Id. 19.

13 *Surocco v. Geary*, 3 Cal. 69 (1853).

14 Harry N. Scheiber, "Instrumentalism and Property Rights: A Reconsideration of American 'Styles of Judicial Reasoning' in the 19th Century," 1975 *Wisconsin L. Rev.* 1,5,7 (1975).

15 See Bailyn, *Ideological Origins of the American Revolution*, Chaps. III, and V; Corwin, "The 'Higher Law' Background of American Constitutional Law," 42 *Harvard L. Rev.* 149 (1928–29); T. Grey, "Do We Have an Unwritten Constitution," 27 *Stanford L. Rev.* 703 (1975).

16 See Ross, *Origins of American Social Science*, supra Chaps. 2 & 3.

been eclipsed in the early decades of the nineteenth century, both had returned to a central position in American legal thinking by the 1880's."[17]

Major shifts in prevailing ideas occur in the course of history – indeed that is the subject of this book – but such rapid *back-and-forth* movements would appear to be rare. To revive and return to a surpassed ideology, which happened twice by this account, is no simple feat. Under Horwitz's account, historians are called upon to explain why a set of ideas that prevailed for centuries was superseded, then revived, then eclipsed again; *and* they must explain why its successor arose, was eclipsed, then arose again.

Historian Neil Duxbury criticized what he identified as the exaggerated "'pendulum swing' vision of American Jurisprudential history,"[18] which reflects the penchant of American theorists to emphasize contrasting schools of thought. A more nuanced position would soften the contrast: Non-instrumental and instrumental understandings of law coexist; statements that reflect each can be found at all times; what happens is an ebb and flow in the primacy accorded to one over the other. Horwitz acknowledges that a mixture of the two was present in the views of jurists like Story.[19] But this still leaves open the question of what view of law – non-instrumental or instrumental – was dominant in the first half of the nineteenth century.

It is beyond the scope of this book to conclusively resolve this question. The lack of historical work bearing on the issue is a major lacuna in the field. Fortunately, a definitive answer to it is not necessary to this exploration. Agreement is uniform among legal historians and theorists that instrumental views of law became entrenched in the course of the twentieth century, which subsequent chapters will fully trace.

Nevertheless, an indirect confrontation with Horwitz's account will advance this study. Depth must be added to the non-instrumental views of law recited in the preceding chapter, which consisted of idealized representations of the common law at a level removed from ongoing events. This chapter connects these idealized accounts more closely to circumstances on the ground, first by focusing on how the common law dealt with social change and, second, by conveying prevailing social ideas and beliefs in the nineteenth century. From a modern instrumental perspective, the non-instrumental mindset is hard to grasp or take seriously; this exploration will render it understandable from within their own complex of ideas. With these accounts in hand, Horwitz's chronology is re-engaged to clarify the distinguishing

---

17 Edward Purcell, *The Crisis of Democratic Theory: Scientific Naturalism and the Problem of Value* (Lexington, Ky.: Univ. Press Kentucky 1973) 74. Many legal historians appear to accept this basic chronology. Another prominent historian who accepts this is G. Edward White, *Patterns of American Legal Thought* (Charlottesville, Va.: Michie 1978).

18 Neil Duxbury, *Patterns of American Jurisprudence* (Oxford: Clarendon Press 1997) 2. Duxbury aimed his criticism at the sharp contrast drawn typically between formalists and Realists. See also Grant Gilmore, *The Ages of American Law* (New Haven: Yale Univ. Press 1977).

19 Horwitz, *Transformation of American Law*, supra 254–6.

characteristics of an instrumental view of law. The information conveyed in this chapter provides a more textured background for events to come.

A period of rapid change

The latter half of the eighteenth century in England was a time of dynamic change. The Enlightenment was in its heyday, science was entering a period of rapid advancement, and the industrial revolution was well under way. These changes in society resounded in the law. Reform of the common law and legislation were burning issues of the day.[20] Influenced by Beccaria, a leading Enlightenment figure, penal reform – emphasizing deterrence over retribution and certainty of enforcement over harshness – was a major public topic. The vitality of commerce demanded changes in the law, which Lord Mansfield attempted to bring about. Much of the focus in England was on the reform of legislation, a disorganized body of enacted rules which, to observers of the day, was proliferating at an alarming rate. Bentham extended this criticism to the common law. Blackstone, who was the target of some of Bentham's sharper criticisms, emphasized that the law must change if it was to be amenable to the novel requirements of commerce thrown up by the fast pace of industrial development.[21] As the need arose, judges circumvented rules that stood in the way by declaring them to be inconsistent with reason and therefore void, or sidestepping them through the use of legal fictions.[22] No one doubted that legislation and the common law must keep up with a quickly evolving society. This was, after all, the self-conscious dawning of a new age.

The American colonies in this period were even more dynamic than England, undergoing manifold social, political, economic, and legal changes. The dominant social force in the middle of the eighteenth century was "the growth and movement of people."[23] English, Scots, Irish Protestants, and Germans "poured into the New World by the tens of thousands."[24] The population of the colonies doubled every twenty years – from one million at mid-century, to two million by 1770, then to four million by 1790 – with successive waves of people pushing settlements farther inland and westward, away from the long-settled coastal areas. Yeoman farmers spread throughout the land. The prevailing method of cultivation involved successive plantings until the soil was exhausted, then moving on to plant elsewhere. Fueled by this movement, "speculative land fever seemed to infect all levels of the society."[25] New towns were formed at a rapid rate in Western parts of Virginia, Pennsylvania,

---

20 An excellent background source for this discussion is Lieberman, *The Province of Legislation Determined*, supra.
21 Boorstin, *The Mysterious Science of Law*, supra 73–84.
22 Id. Chap. 1.
23 Wood, *Radicalism of the American Revolution*, supra 125. This discussion is substantially indebted to Wood's superb history of this period, along with Daniel Boorstin's *The Americans: The Colonial Experience* (New York: Vintage Books 1958).
24 Wood, *Radicalism of the American Revolution*, supra 125.
25 Id. 128.

Connecticut, New York, and the Carolinas, and later in Ohio, Tennessee, Kentucky, and Mississippi. As new towns filled, people sold their land and left to start anew elsewhere, while others bypassed them to create new settlements farther on. Social bonds were tenuous in such transient communities. Town officials often were relative newcomers and turnover was high.

"Coupled with this demographic expansion – and nearly equal a force in unsettling the society – were the spectacular changes taking place in the American economy."[26] American farms in the mid and southern colonies produced large quantities tobacco, corn, and wheat for export to the West Indies and Europe. Consumer items were manufactured in the northern cities and sold throughout the colonies. Most households remained self-sufficient producers of their necessities, and many people made surplus goods at home for exchange or sale in the market. Commercial "traffick" by just about everyone was a way of life.

The unique circumstances in the colonies led to differences from the common law of England. In the early colonial period, there were few trained lawyers and judges, so early cases were not developed in the same rigid, encrusted English way, although a good deal of the law they produced was recognizably consistent with English common law.[27] Juries often made decisions about the law and the facts. Many people had some knowledge about basic legal matters, which they needed for their own purposes, especially relating to land transactions.

Novel issues and circumstances in America lacked ready parallels in the English common law, so innovation was forced upon judges by necessity.[28] An important social difference in the colonies was the absence of an hereditary aristocracy, which prevented the entrenchment of class distinctions in the law. Feudalistic aspects of the English common law that did not fit the more freewheeling land situation were rejected or modified. Real property rules such as primogeniture (upon death property goes to the eldest son) and entail (property reverts to grantor if grantee line lacks an heir), for example, which had the effect of restricting alienation and maintaining large family estates, were abolished by statute almost everywhere.[29]

The purchase of land and the establishment of farming and businesses required legal doctrines that encouraged the availability of credit. Debt previously was viewed in moral terms, a matter of assistance for the needy within a community, sought only when necessary and expected to be duly repaid. Increasingly, debt came to be seen and treated in the law as an aspect of productive entrepreneurial activity, to be encouraged, not shunned. Bankruptcy laws were enacted that freed future earnings from past creditors. The increase in transactions between people at a distance also prompted changes in contract law, which previously enforced pre-established

26 Id. 134.
27 See Boorstin, *The Americans*, supra.
28 See Ford W. Hall, "The Common Law: An Account of its Reception in the United States," 4 *Vanderbilt L. Rev.* 791, 805–7 (1950–51).
29 See Morris, "Primogeniture and Entailed Estates in America," 27 *Columbia L. Rev.* 24 (1927).

rights and duties determined by status-based relationships. "[I]n the commercialized eighteenth century contracts became much more voluntary, explicit, and consensual.... Contracts came to be thought of as positive bargains deliberately and freely entered into between two parties who were presumed to be equal and not entirely trustful of one another."[30] A growing number of transactions were legally formalized.

Another major change in the law that began during this period was prompted by the widespread distrust of common law crimes. Judges would convict people of common law crimes without the criminal offense having been set forth in advance in legislation or otherwise; many calls were issued for state and federal crimes to be specified legislatively. A remarkably learned work published in 1812 by John Goodenow, canvassing English legal history and citing Enlightenment figures, laid out a powerful attack on common law crimes as barbaric, obscure, indeterminate, and granting excessive leeway to unaccountable judges who were prone to abuse the power.[31] Within a few generations, crimes would be established legislatively almost everywhere.

Finally, though not last in significance, this was the period of the founding of the country. About half the people involved in the Declaration of Independence, the drafting and ratification of the Constitution, and elected to early Congresses were lawyers. The Constitution was a spectacular example of an instrumental application of law: written in whole cloth in a few sittings (assisted by the examples of existing state constitutions[32]) to create a workable government system acceptable to all. Its design and content carried the stamps of political and economic compromises among conflicting concerns and interests, to meet the goal of creating a new nation made up of disparate people that would survive politically and thrive economically.

New national pride, combined with a hatred for the English that many Americans felt following the Revolution, also had legal consequences. The Revolution was a rejection of English tutelage, especially throwing off "tyrannical" English legislation. Countering this attitude, however, was the practical reality that the common law was the law they were familiar with, along with the sense that the common law in the United States was not an exclusively English creature. *The* common law was the epitome of reason, principle, and community order.

To say that an unbroken string of non-instrumental views of the common law were expressed through the close of the nineteenth century, therefore, is not to say that there were no changes in the law during this period. Many changes occurred, not only in specific legal rules but also with respect to understandings about natural rights and natural principles. One important change was a subtle metamorphosis in the orientation of natural principles in the course of the eighteenth and nineteenth

30 Wood, *Radicalism of the American Revolution,* supra 162.
31 Goodenow, *Historical Sketches of the Principles and Maxims of American Jurisprudence,* supra.
32 See Herman Belz, "The Constitution in the Gilded Age: The Beginnings of Constitutional Realism in American Scholarship," 13 *Am. J. Legal Hist.* 110 (1969).

centuries, from moral and religious principles (good and right), to political principles (political liberty and justice), to economic principles (laissez faire).[33]

The dual nature of the common law

How could the legal elite continue to insist upon and project a centuries-old image
of the common law as principle and custom from time immemorial in the face
of so much dramatic change in the late eighteenth and early nineteenth centuries?
Several answers can be given to this perplexing question.

A threshold reminder and a separate clarification will help. The reminder is that
characterizations of law set out in the first chapter were meant by prominent jurists
to describe the *common law*, not legislation. Jurists regarded the common law as
the law – the unquestioned center of gravity of the legal world. During this period
much dynamic legal change took place through legislation, which by then had come
to be understood in mostly instrumental terms. Champions of the common law
pointed to the instrumental character of legislation as precisely the quality that
magnified its potential for mischief. The separate clarification is that the foregoing
non-instrumental characterizations of law were idealized statements of the nature
of the common law made by the legal elite. Although the populace shared in these
idealizations, people also knew well that the everyday reality of law was messier
than these idealized descriptions indicated. Both of these points are elaborated in
the next chapter.

What must also be borne in mind is the extraordinary hold of the centuries-
old beliefs about the immemorial and principled nature of the common law. To
our eyes, never having been under this spell, these beliefs appear untenable in the
face of so much rapid and radical change. However, as Pocock argued, inconsis-
tencies or contrary indications were suppressed because prevailing understandings
of the common law shaped how contemporary observers interpreted events. Evidence of this controlling mindset can be found in Goodenow's book, mentioned
earlier. Goodenow compartmentalized his critique, which included sophisticated
arguments about legal indeterminacy, to apply exclusively to common law crimes.
Although the import of his attack could easily have extended to the entirety of the
common law, Goodenow declined to take this step, observing that "private rights
and private wrongs are founded on and measured by the immutable principles of
natural law and abstract justice."[34]

Another essential point to remember is that rhetoric surrounding the Revolution
was suffused with legalistic claims that the English government was violating the
ancient constitution and liberties and rights of the colonists.

> As late as 1774, appeals to natural law were often combined with a hodgepodge of
> other claims to liberty, as in the 'ancient, constitutional, and chartered Rights' invoked

---

33 See Pound, *Formative Era of American Law*, supra 22–3.
34 Goodenow, *Historical Sketches of the Principles and Maxims of American Jurisprudence*, supra 36.

by Virginians. In the same year, the first Continental Congress [in 1774] defended its actions by appealing to the 'principles of the English constitution' and the 'liberties . . . of free and natural-born subjects, within the realm of England.'[35]

As the Revolution progressed, and in its aftermath, claims about ancient liberties were universalized away from the English connection to represent the rights of free men, but they remained the same claims. What we see today as a revolutionary act they saw as consistent with and, indeed, justified by, their common law rights. The political revolution was not, in this sense, a legal revolution.

Above all else, the central answer to how claims about continuity could be made in the face of major change has to do with a fundamental feature of the common law: its inherently dual character. The common law repeatedly was said to represent both immemorial custom and principle *and* to be up to date by virtue of its ongoing application and conformity to society. The common law was likened to a ship on a voyage in which each plank is replaced en route, thereby always remaining in good repair, continuously absorbing new material, while remaining fundamentally the same. "Behind this doctrine there clearly lies the notion that law is custom and custom perpetual adaptation."[36]

John Selden wrote in 1617:

> Then were natural laws limited for the conveniency of civil society here, and those limitations have been from thence, increased, altered, interpreted, and brought to what now they are; although, perhaps saving the meerly immutable part of nature, now, in regard of their first being, they are not otherwise than a ship, that by often mending had not piece of the first materials, or of the house that's so often repaired, . . . which yet, by the civil law, is to be accounted the same still.[37]

Drawing upon these ideas, the common law simultaneously claimed ancient prescription, correct principle and reason, ongoing adaptability, conformity to society, and general social consent.

Hence the common law was rational and principled and descended from time immemorial, and was, in that sense, unchanging, yet it also was up to date and accommodated ongoing developments. Pocock observed, "The idea of the common law was twofold – men might treat it primarily as that which was continually adapted, or as that which was constantly preserved. The former emphasis would lead . . . to the idea that law was the ever-changing product of a historical process; the latter to the idea that law was fixed, unchanging, immemorial."[38] Blackstone, who espoused traditional non-instrumental views, also believed that the common law throughout its history demonstrated a tendency toward progress apace with society.[39]

35 Eric Foner, *The Story of American Freedom* (New York: Norton 1998) 13.
36 Pocock, *The Ancient Constitution and the Feudal Law*, supra 170.
37 John Selden, *Opera* (1616), quoted in Richard Tuck, *Natural Rights Theories: Their Origin and Development* (Cambridge: Cambridge Univ. Press 1979) 84.
38 Pocock, *Ancient Constitution and the Feudal Law*, supra 173–4.
39 Boorstin, *The Mysterious Science of Law*, supra 73–84.

The same understanding prevailed in the United States. An 1860 testimonial in honor of Chief Justice Lemuel Shaw contains a representative statement of this sensibility:

> It was the task of those who went before you, to show that the principles of the common and the commercial law were available to the wants of communities which were far more recent than the origin of those systems. It was for you to adapt those systems to still newer and greater exigencies. . . . Thus it has been, that in your hands the law has met the demands of a period of unexampled activity and enterprise; while over all its varied and conflicting interests you have held the strong, conservative sway of a judge, who moulds the rule for the present and the future out of the principles and precedents of the past.[40]

Molding the law in this manner was the time-honored process of making evident under new social and economic circumstances the reason and principle underlying the common law. It was the common law craft of maintaining the continuity of the law while managing change.

Non-instrumental attention to consequences

This idea helps explain how Justice Story could flexibly shape legal doctrines to facilitate commercial development, while repeating classical non-instrumental views that court decisions do not make law but are only evidence of preexisting principles. A judge operating within an understanding of the dual nature of the common law would find no inconsistency here.

The significance of the point can be drawn out in connection with Horwitz's argument. Horwitz observed that "American judges before the nineteenth century rarely analyzed common law rules functionally or purposively, *and* they almost never self-consciously employed the common law as a creative instrument for directing men's energies toward social change."[41] This sentence contains two distinct senses of legal instrumentalism. The first indicates that the effects or consequences of the law are considered by instrumentalists but not by non-instrumentalists; the second indicates that law can be used instrumentally to bring about social change.

The dual perspective on the common law suggests that Horwitz's first assertion may be wrong in a crucial respect. A judge who holds a traditional non-instrumental view of law, to repeat, believes that the common law does and should accommodate ongoing social and economic change. This perspective is entirely consistent with viewing the law functionally (Horwitz's first sense of legal instrumentalism). In order to successfully accommodate ongoing social changes, particularly to keep up with commercial development, which everyone saw as important to society, a judge *must* consider the consequences of legal rules. That is precisely what Story was doing, and, contrary to Horwitz's suggestion, he did so in a manner consistent with

---

40 Reprinted in Charles Warren, *History of the American Bar* (Boston: Little Brown 1911) 448.
41 Horwitz, *Transformation of American Law*, supra 253 (emphasis added).

his generally non-instrumental views of law. Because the economy was undergoing rapid development that might be inhibited by the operation of older common law rules, Story and other judges were willing to modify the common law to match and further this economic development. That was the dynamic side of the dual nature of the common law. This is not using the law to "direct the course of social change" (Horwitz's second sense of legal instrumentalism).

To articulate this crucial point more fully, a judge who holds a non-instrumental view of law can view the law functionally so long as the judge does this with the aim of striving to accommodate changes in society consistent with the reason, principles, and customs within law. Even in seventeenth-century England, the judges viewed common law rules in connection with their social utility,[42] as indicated in the earlier quotes from Selden and Davies that describe the common law as changing for the "conveniency" of society. Judges who engaged in this task did not think of the law as being utilized "instrumentally." They were engaging in the time-honored common law task of maintaining law in sync with society. As the nineteenth century wore on, as scientific thought, with its own emphasis on function, penetrated law, and as law (especially legislation) came to be seen in more instrumental terms, an imperceptible shift in understanding took place which paved the way for judges to engage in functional analysis with an instrumental orientation. But it would be anachronistic to project the modern instrumentalist perspective on earlier generations whose functional perspective on law had an important place within their non-instrumental understanding.

Based upon the same analysis, Horwitz's second point about an instrumental view of law is sound. A judge with a non-instrumental view of the common law *cannot* adopt the social engineering view of law as an instrument of social change. That is anathema. That is not matching or reflecting changes in society, but generating or directing changes. Horwitz correctly identifies this as what "dramatically distinguishes" later instrumental views from earlier non-instrumental views of law. The core non-instrumental view of law within the common law was that the law at once matches society and comports with reason and principle. This is a truly conservative conception in which society was as it should be (evolving as it should evolve), law was as it should be, and their relationship was as it should be. Not until the close of the nineteenth century, when this tight conceptual package fell apart, could the idea take hold that law should be used to direct social change.

Skepticism about non-instrumentalism as a facade

Horwitz pressed the separate argument that the non-instrumental formalist approach to law espoused by judges in the post-bellum period was a guise taken on for instrumental reasons to lock in and conceal a bias in favor of capital interests within the legal doctrine. The common law was not truly seen in non-instrumental

42 See Tuck, *Natural Rights*, supra.

terms by the judges, if Horwitz is correct. Rather, the judges recognized that the common law contained an instrumentally oriented bent, and their touting of non-instrumental ideals was purely strategic.

This line of argumentation prompts the larger question of whether any version of non-instrumentalism is truly non-instrumental. Horwitz, it should be noted, does not extend his skepticism this far. His account characterizes eighteenth-century law as being truly non-instrumental. His book is about a real transition from being non-instrumental law to being instrumental, then reverting to a fraudulent form of non-instrumentalism. It is not obvious, however, why this earlier period should be insulated from the same skepticism. English common law judges were drawn from the landed gentry and shaped common law doctrines in a way that favored their own property holding classes.[43] Prior to that, and intermingled with it, the transplanted customary feudal law favored hereditary aristocracy in terms of property rights and the obligations of those who worked the land. More generally, natural law and natural rights thought has a long history of justifying slavery and protecting propertied classes.[44] Thus it can be said that in all of these circumstances the law was favoring certain groups within society at the expense of others – that it was an instrument of their domination. It must also be contemplated whether at bottom law is always instrumental, regardless of what is claimed, because law seemingly everywhere in one way or another favors some groups at the expense of others.

Another clarification can now be offered. Seeing legal instrumentalism in such broad terms, which makes sense for other purposes, is beyond the narrow focus of this exploration. The idea of taking an instrumental view of law gets its meaning from a specific historical contrast with a predecessor combination of ideas that took a non-instrumental view of law. To see law as an instrument entails perceiving and describing its nature in instrumental terms – law *is* a means to an end.

The common law was used instrumentally by individuals and groups in society, to be sure, but the common law as such – whether chracterized as natural law, principle and reason, or customs from time immemorial – was not perceived to be instrumental in nature in the centuries' long primacy of non-instrumental view of law that continued through the nineteenth century. Law was not seen as an empty vessel that could be filled in with whatever content might be desired by law makers to serve whatever end was desired. That is a quintessentially modern instrumental view of law.

Dominance of laissez faire and Social Darwinism

The question prompted by Horwitz remains: Did the judges in the late nineteenth century who espoused non-instrumental views of law do this for instrumental

---

43 See Norman Cantor, *Imagining the Law: Common Law and the Foundations of the American Legal System* (New York: Harper Perennial 1997).
44 See Tuck, *Natural Rights*, supra.

reasons? That is, did they have as their goal to serve capital interests, did they recognize that the common law doctrines in place achieved this, and did they secure this favorable bias by reviving and concealing it within non-instrumental accounts of law? If true, this was impressively Machiavellian maneuvering on the part of the judges. Horwitz charges the elite bar with entering a Faustian bargain with their corporate clients to do just that. Although he suggests that the entire legal profession was party to this bargain, his account of legal scholars and judges appears to operate in an indirect fashion. Jurists produced a "scientific, objective, professional, and apolitical conception of law," according to Horwitz, because it served the interests of "a status-hungry elite of legal thinkers" who would enjoy more power if the law had autonomy from political interference.[45] According to this account, the revival of non-instrumental views of law was calculated, but came about through a combination of different sets of motivations: a corporate bar serving the interests of corporate clients, and legal scholars and judges serving their own respective interests.

There is something to the idea that a confluence of interests among the legal elite led to mutual support for the non-instrumental common law, a similar version of which is discussed at the end of the next chapter. Yet it is inadequate to rest so heavily upon a late-nineteenth-century combination of self-interest and pro-fessional interest to explain ideas about the common law that had such longevity and power. The legal tradition into which they were indoctrinated had enshrined this understanding of law for centuries. Many judges and legal scholars sincerely believed in the non-instrumental accounts of law they espoused. They were not all corrupt or self-aggrandizing. They were not all dupes for corporate lawyers or their clients, and would not have molded their ideal of the law solely to enhance their status or further personal objectives.

A brief look at a seminal figure, Thomas Cooley, is illuminating on this point. By all accounts, Cooley had a major influence in shaping the jurisprudence of late-nineteenth-century "formalist" courts. One of fourteen children, his father was a farmer, an active Jacksonian democrat.[46] Cooley emerged from these modest circumstances to become a justice on the Supreme Court of Michigan and a professor at the University of Michigan, and later served as the first Chairman of the Interstate Commerce Commission. He worked briefly as a lawyer for the railroads, but the bulk of his career was spent as a judge, a legal academic, and a government official. Citing his main influences as Blackstone, Kent, and Story, in his publications and speeches Cooley expressed a typical non-instrumental view of the common law, including faith in the dual nature of the common law.[47]

45 Horwitz, *Transformation of American Law*, supra 266.
46 Alan Jones, "Thomas M. Cooley and 'Laissez-Faire Constitutionalism': A Reconsideration," 53 *Am. J. Legal Hist.* 751,753 (1967).
47 Jones, "Thomas M. Cooley and Laissez Faire Constitutionalism," supra 758.

The limits on government power were the focus of his celebrated *Constitutional Limitations* – credited as being "the most fecund source of laissez faire constitutional principles during the period."[48] His core ideas, which were not original, were that taxation and spending were limited to public purposes, that legislation favoring a particular class was strictly prohibited, and that constitutional rights and common law property rights were protected by the due process clause from legislative infringement.

Although judges routinely cited Cooley's text when they struck legislation favorable to employees, Cooley warned against the "merciless power of concentrated capital."[49] He expressed concern about "the great and wealthy corporations having greater influence in the country and upon the legislation of the country."[50] As a judge, he ruled against the railroads in a number of cases. When serving as the Chairman of the Interstate Commerce Commission, he defended rate setting, which was vehemently opposed by railroads as a violation of liberty and property rights. Judging from these words and actions, Cooley cannot be pegged as a rigid advocate of laissez faire. When opposing class legislation, aside from his genuine belief that this was wrong in principle, Cooley's main concern appears to have been the potential for abuse by capital interests; the fact that this principle would disallow legislation favoring employees was a matter of consistency of application. Reading his work lends strong support to the conclusion that he was truly committed to the non-instrumental views of law he espoused.

Corporate lawyers seized upon Cooley's ideas, and the similar work of influential legal writers like Christopher Tiedeman and John Dillon, to further the interests of their clients.[51] And there is no question that many judges were easily persuaded by legal entreaties from the corporate bar. But again it is distorting to see this in entirely self-interested terms. Cooley's ideas were persuasive because other judges and jurists thought much as he did. They shared a set of ideas held "in common with most people living at that time, especially those of a conservative cast of mind such as members of the bar."[52] Among broad swaths of the elite, the intelligentsia, and the middle class, the late nineteenth century in the United States and England was the apotheosis of laissez faire ideas,[53] reinforced in salient respects in the United States by the popularity of Social Darwinism.

The political culture of the United States throughout history has revolved around a cluster of liberal ideas about individual liberty, equality, democracy, capitalism,

---

48 Clyde E. Jacobs, *Law Writers and the Courts: The Influence of Thomas M. Cooley, Christopher G. Tiedeman, and John F. Dillon Upon American Constitutional Law* (Berkeley: Univ. Ca. Press 1954) 30.
49 Quoted in Jones, "Thomas M. Cooley and Laissez Faire Constitutionalism," supra 767.
50 Thomas Cooley, *Constitutional Limitations*, 6th ed. revised (Boston: Little Brown 1890) 335.
51 See Benjamin R. Twiss, *Lawyers and the Constitution: How Laissez Faire Came to the Supreme Court* (Princeton: Princeton Univ. Press 1942).
52 Id. 20.
53 See generally John Gray, *Liberalism*, 2nd ed. (Minneapolis: Univ. Minnesota Press 1995) Chap. 4.

and fear of government power. In his survey of American political thought, Richard Hofstadter identified a common core of agreed-upon beliefs:

> The sanctity of private property, the right of the individual to dispose of and invest it, the value of opportunity, and the natural evolution of self-interest and self-assertion, within broad legal limits, into a beneficent social order have been staple tenets of the central faith in American political ideologies. . . . The business of politics – so the creed runs – is to protect this competitive world, to foster it on occasion, to patch up its incidental abuses, but not to cripple it with a plan for common collective action. . . .

> Almost the entire span of American history under the present constitution has coincided with the rise and spread of modern industrial capitalism. In material power and productivity the United States has been a flourishing success. Societies that are in such good working order have a kind of mute organic consistency. They do not foster ideas that are hostile to their fundamental working arrangements.[54]

As integral participants in the established order, judges, and the legal elite generally, were raised in and committed to this creed, and saw the law in its terms. Judges who interpreted and formulated the common law to further economic development were not, in this understanding, favoring capital interests, but rather were furthering the collective good that depended upon economic development.

The laissez faire ideal that government should not interfere in the natural workings of the market found fertile soil in this native bed of American ideas. These ideas underwrote a seamless transition from the initial Revolutionary emphasis on political liberty to an emphasis on economic liberty as commerce took center stage in the American polity. Distrust of government oppression became distrust of regulation of the market and of economic activities. Liberty that focused on freedom from government tyranny became non-interference with one's property rights and the right to contract. The core of laissez faire thought was this: "The individual – especially the owner of property – is the basic unit of society and economics. It is his natural right to do what is most advantageous to him, since it is man's tendency to better his condition. He is the best judge of his own welfare, hence of where to invest his labor and property. . . . The government is but a necessary evil whose function is to preserve liberty and property."[55] According to laissez faire theory, the proper role of the state is to "suppress force and fraud, keep property safe, and aid men in enforcing contracts"[56] – nothing more.

Social Darwinism – the work of Herbert Spencer and William Graham Sumner building on the sensation created by Darwin's ideas of natural selection – was immensely influential in the final quarter of the nineteenth century. Spencer

---

54 Richard Hofstadter, *The American Political Tradition: And the Men Who Made It* (New York: Vintage 1989 [1948]) xxxvii.
55 Twiss, *Lawyers and the Constitution*, supra 8.
56 L. T. Hobhouse, *Liberalism* (Oxford: Oxford Univ. Press 1964 [1911]) 49.

presented his work as a naturalistic biology-based science of society. The natural social order involves a competitive struggle that leads to the "survival of the fittest" – a phrase now identified with Darwin but coined by Spencer. Government interference in this process inhibits the progress of society:

> [Spencer's] categorical repudiation of state interference with the 'natural,' unimpeded growth of society led him to oppose all state aid to the poor. They were unfit, he said, and should be eliminated. 'The whole effort of nature is to get rid of such, to clear the world of them, and make room for better.' Nature is as insistent upon fitness of mental character as she is upon physical character, 'and radical defects are as much causes of death in the one case as in the other'.... Under nature's laws all alike are put on trial. 'If they are sufficiently complete to live, they do live, and it is well they should live. If they are not sufficiently complete to live, they die, and it is best they should die.'[57]

Spencer opposed aid to the poor, public education, tariffs, and all regulation beyond what was required to maintain social order.

Laissez faire thought and Social Dawinism made a complementary match. They were different scientific programs, economic and biological, which emphasized the primacy of individual striving under competitive circumstances, the benevolent working of natural laws of society, and the futility and self-defeating consequences of government attempts at interference in this natural order. This pair of streams of thought, moreover, found a comfortable home in the American ideal of liberty, with its emphasis on individual freedom and on fear of government. These ideas matched one another and the culture of the time.

For the captains of capitalism in the Gilded Age at the end of the nineteenth century, the attraction of this combination of ideas is obvious. John D. Rockefeller stated in an address, "The growth of a large business is merely a survival of the fittest.... This is not an evil tendency in business. It is merely the working-out of a law of nature and a law of God."[58] Social Darwinism was interpreted by business leaders to endorse their tactics, no matter how mean, as justified by their success.

These ideas, which were consistent with the ethic of individual striving and distrust of government that have been constant features of American culture, also appealed to members of the middle class, who saw themselves as due winners in the struggle for survival, and who attributed their relative success to their worthy character, ability, and hard work. The poor were widely seen as deserving of their abysmal fate. Consistent with these ideas, in reaction to the labor disputes erupting at the time, the sympathies of many in the middle class aligned with employers, thinking that the actions and demands of the unions were harmful to society. This attitude is reflected in the condemnatory tenor of news reports taken from the 1870s:

---

57 Richard Hofstadter, *Social Darwinism in American Thought* (Boston: Beacon Press 1992) 41, citations omitted. This discussion is indebted to Hofstadter's account.
58 Quoted in Id. 45.

Labor unions violated certain immutable 'natural and moral laws' and deterred economic development and capital accumulation. The *Chicago Times* put it another way in its discussion of workers who challenged the status quo: 'The man who lays up not for the morrow, perishes on the morrow. It is the inexorable law of God, which neither legislatures nor communistic blatherskites can repeal. The fittest alone survive, and those are the fittest, as the result always proves, who provide for their own survival.'

Unions and all forms of labor protest, particularly strikes, were condemned. The *New York Times* described the strike as 'a combination against long-established laws,' especially the law of supply and demand. The *New York Tribune* wrote of 'the general viciousness of the trades-union system,' and the *Cleveland Leader* called 'the labor union kings...the most absolute tyrants of our day.' Strikes, insisted the *Chicago Tribune*, 'implant in many men habits of indolence that are fatal to their efficiency thereafter.'[59]

From a viewpoint infused by laissez faire Social Darwinism, labor unions were seen as engaged in anti-social attempts at circumventing the natural laws of the social and economic order, which would hasten the downfall of all. The middle class feared these actions as a threat to social order and to their own hard-earned position. That is not to say there were no dissenters, of course, but these ideas permeated the population until the turn of the century.

The reasoning and decisions of formalist judges and jurists cannot be understood without attention to these ideas. They formed a background prism through which the judges viewed the common law, natural rights, the Constitution, and their role as judges within the government system. This is on display in the following passage by James Carter, whose speech was quoted in Chapter 1 as an example of late-nineteenth-century non-instrumental views of law:

This is what I have so often insisted upon as the sole function both of law and legislation, namely, to secure to each individual the utmost liberty which he can enjoy consistently with the preservation of the like liberty to all others. Liberty, the first of blessings, the aspiration of every human soul, is the supreme object. Every abridgement of it demands an excuse and the only good excuse is the necessity of preserving it. Whatever tends to preserve this is right, all else is wrong. To leave each man to work out in freedom his own happiness or misery, to stand or fall by the consequences of his own conduct, is the true method of human discipline.[60]

This set of beliefs ran deep through the legal culture. Roscoe Pound labeled Carter's statement an "authoritative exposition of current juristic thought in America."[61] The next two chapters recount the transition away from this entrenched view.

59 Herbert G. Gutman, "The Workers Search for Power," in *The Gilded Age*, edited by H. Wayne Morgan (Syracuse, N.Y.: Syracuse Univ. Press 1969) 50.
60 James C. Carter, *Law, Its Origin, Growth and Function* (New York: Putnam 1907) 337.
61 Roscoe Pound, "Law in Books and Law in Action," 44 *American L. Rev.* 12, 28 (1910).

3

Nineteenth-century legislation and legal profession

Although non-instrumental views of law were widely repeated through the end the nineteenth century, as the foregoing two chapters establish, in two important arenas instrumental views of law had already take hold earlier. Legislation was seen in throughly instrumental terms throughout this period, and expanded in volume and significance with the passage of time; the practice of law, in crucial respects, was also described and perceived in instrumental terms. Both of these arenas of instrumental understandings of law – explored in this chapter – fed into and set up the more pervasive instrumentalism to come in the twentieth century.

Contest between legislation and common law

In eighteenth-century England, and for at least a century before that, legislation was an increasing source of law-making. Classical views of the common law allowed little place for the active creation of law by legislation, however. Within the common law tradition, the proper role of legislation was mainly to declare preexisting customary law (although it often did more than that). Jurists claimed that the common law was coherent, ordered, and comprehensive. Legislation posed a threat to the systematic and rational nature of the common law.[1] Jurists accorded supremacy in the hierarchy of law-making to the common law, for only common law judges were trained in rational science of law, not legislators, and only judges could be trusted to faithfully recognize the customs of the people. Judges were openly hostile to the increase in the frequency and scope of legislation, which they opposed at every turn.

The contest for supremacy between the common law and legislation, between judges (and the legal profession) and legislators, respectively, carried on for centuries in both England and the United States. It was a central dynamic during the post-Revolutionary period, as historian Gordon Wood explained:

> Protecting private property and minority rights from the interests of the enhanced public power of the new republican governments eventually became, as Madison had foreseen, the great problem of American democratic politics. As early as the 1780s

---

1 See Grey, Langdell's Orthodoxy, supra 10, 12.

many were already contending that only the judiciary in America was impartial and free enough of private interests to solve that problem and defend people's rights and property from the tyrannical wills of interested popular majorities. The state legislatures, it was argued, should not 'leave the great business of the state, and take up private business, or interfere in disputes between contending parties' as the colonial assemblies had habitually done. The evils of such legislative meddling were 'heightened when the society is divided among themselves; – one party praying the assembly for one thing and opposite party for another thing' . . . These efforts to carve out an exclusive sphere of activity for the judiciary, *a sphere where the adjudication of private rights was removed from politics and legislative power*, contributed to the remarkable process by which the judiciary in America suddenly emerged out of its colonial insignificance to become by 1800 the principal means by which popular legislatures were controlled and limited.[2]

The forces behind the expansion of law-making by legislatures were powerful. The democratic rhetoric that permeated the Revolution led to a broad grant of suffrage (women and slaves excluded) and gave a boost to legislation as a source of law. The populist wave of Jacksonian egalitarianism that came a generation after the founding delegitimized the idea that an aristocracy of judges should have the power to control the declaration of what law is. One manifestation of this sentiment was the wave of legislation that required state judges to stand for election, either initially or upon reappointment. Another manifestation of the weakening position of the common law vis-à-vis legislation was the movement to codify the common law, which briefly enjoyed momentum mid-century.

In a temporarily effective maneuver, judges emphasized that the common law, as custom and usage, embodied the consent of the people, which entitles it to a claim of democratic legitimacy. Legislation that is inconsistent with prevailing social usages, it was said, will remain a dead letter, resisted by the people. Defenders of the common law argued, moreover, that legislation suffers from unavoidable blindness. Legal rules are framed by legislators in general terms in advance, ignorant of future circumstances, in contrast to the more cautious, particularized case-by-case creation of the common law. Legislation, furthermore, was denigrated as the product of special interests and unreliable passion and will, to be distrusted and constrained, in contrast to reason and principle embodied in the common law. "Placing legal boundaries around issues such as property rights and contracts had the effect of isolating these issues from popular tampering, partisan debate, and the clashes of interest groups politics. Some things, including the power to define property and interpret constitutions, became matters not of political interest to be determined by legislatures but of the 'fixed principles' of law to be determined only by judges."[3]

Advocates of legislation as a source of law, most famously Bentham and his followers, pressed their case by pointing out the failings of the common law. Bentham

---

2 Wood, *Radicalism of the American Revolution*, supra 322–3 (emphasis added).
3 Id. 324–5.

made his reputation by launching a polemical attack on Blackstone's celebrated *Commentaries*, which he characterized as an exercise in rationalization that concealed the egregious mess of the common law.[4] Bentham asserted that the common law was purposely kept in an obscure state by lawyers and judges to artificially prop up their prestige and income. He argued that the common law does not actually exist. "In these words [common law] you have a name, pretended to be the name of a really existing object: look for any such existing object – look for it till doomsday – no such object you will find."[5] Echoing Bentham, reformers in the United States in the early nineteenth century urged that common law adjudication "be purged of its 'professional mystery.'"[6]

According to Bentham, law involves the coercive enforcement of rules by legal officials.[7] Laws should be designed and implemented to maximize the greatest happiness of the greatest number. Bentham promoted a utilitarian science of legislation that would produce a clear, comprehensive, and coherent code of laws that would enable each person to be his own lawyer.

Although Bentham is recognized as a leading progenitor of instrumental views of law, it is wrong to place too much emphasis on him in direct causal terms. While his views were known, he was considered too theoretical for the practical sensibilities of nineteenth-century lawyers and jurists in the United States.[8] Bentham's work nevertheless offers an important conceptual insight for this exploration through its linkage of legislation, legal instrumentalism, and legal positivism. Legal positivism is a theory which holds that "law" is whatever the recognized authority sets out as "law," known as the "will" or "command" theory of law; legal instrumentalism is the idea that law is an instrument or tool to achieve ends; and legislation is the most adaptable and efficient form that law takes. They combine in a mutually reinforcing fashion. If the law is to serve ends efficiently, it must be open with respect to content, which must vary according to the end identified and the anticipated circumstances of its achievement; legislation is the best ready mechanism for willfully shaping law instrumentally – for determining ends and filling in content.

By the end of the nineteenth century, the momentum had shifted markedly away from the common law in favor of legislation as a source of law-making, both in terms legitimating ideals and in actual practice. In 1908, Roscoe Pound, one of the leading jurists of the generation, observed (in a legal positivist vein) that "much of American legislation . . . is founded on an assumption that it is enough for the State to command . . ."[9]

---

4 See Jeremy Bentham, *A Fragment on Government* (Cambridge: Cambridge Univ. Press 1988).
5 Jeremy Bentham, "Bentham's Letter, Letter IV," in *Codification of the Common Law* (New York: John Polbemus Printer 1882) 3.
6 Wood, *Radicalism of the American Revolution*, supra 323.
7 See Jeremy Bentham, *Of Laws in General: Principles of Legislation*, edited by H.L.A. Hart (London: Athlone Press 1970).
8 C. W. Everett, "Bentham in the United States," in *Jeremy Bentham and the Law*, edited by George W. Keeton and Georg Schwarzenberger (Westport, Conn.: Greenwood Press 1970) 188, 185–232.
9 Roscoe Pound, "Mechanical Jurisprudence," supra 613.

The shift in momentum to legislation was not only a matter of its superior claim to democratic legitimacy. Traditional common law concepts, frozen in a mode of abstract analysis, were becoming obsolete, no longer functional, no longer able to adequately meet problems thrown up by rapidly changing circumstances. If not modified, the common law would "obstruct the way of social progress."[10] Legislation, according to Pound, was the solution:

> A period of legislative activity supervenes to supply, first new rule, then new premises, and finally a systematic body of principles as a fresh start for juristic development. . . . The further step, which is beginning to be taken in our present era of legal development through legislation, is in reality an awakening of juristic activity, as jurists perceive that they may effect results through the legislator as well as through the judge or the doctrinal writer.[11]

Marking the beginning of a new era, Pound gave a clear nod to legislation as the preferred mode of law-making for the present and future.

A major impetus for legislation in this period, which fueled an instrumental view of law, were economic battles fought out in legislatures and courts. In the final quarter of the nineteenth century, "American law was an essential instrument or weapon in economic struggle," wrote historian Lawrence Friedman. "This meant . . . that law could serve as a social instrument of great power."[12]

Conflict fought through law at the close of the century

The rise of legislation as an active source of law and mode of changing law was at the epicenter of intense social conflict. "Between the Civil War and the end of the nineteenth century," observed historian Eric Foner, "the United States underwent one of the most profound economic revolutions any country has ever experienced, and witnessed some of the most violent struggles between labor and employers in the history of capitalism."[13]

At the opening of the nineteenth century, society and the economy revolved mainly around small land owners, agriculture, and household production of goods for sale at local markets. At the close of the century, crowded urban areas with large-scale workplaces were dominant. The economy became fully industrialized, launched on its way by mechanization and by the development of railroads. People spread across the Great Plains to the Pacific coast. Land speculation was rampant. Commerce exploded, catching and overtaking the leading economies of Europe, with textile factories, coal mines, oil production, and steel production, generating internal and external trade. A greater proportion of employment was found in corporations and small businesses with separate workplaces, which enjoyed economies

10 Id. 616.
11 Id. 612.
12 Lawrence M. Friedman, *A History of American Law*, 2nd ed. (New York: Touchstone 1985) 340.
13 Foner, *The Story of American Freedom*, supra 116.

of scale, shunting the once-prevalent phenomenon of household production permanently to the margins of economic activity. Previously given existence by individual legislative grants, general laws of incorporation were enacted to make it easy to create corporations, limiting liability for investors and facilitating the raising of capital. Financing mechanisms to support large commercial enterprises became more sophisticated. Mass production and payment plans made consumer goods more affordable. Economic boom and bust occurred with regularity. Modern society was fitfully being born. All the while, technology was changing the conditions of daily life. Electricity illuminated the cities; telegraph and telephones allowed immediate communication across a distance. Mechanized trams and, later, automobiles, enabled cities to spread out further. The airplane was on the horizon.

A society was coming into being that was radically different from the economy upon which the common law was constructed. Prior to this time, tort law was a small part of the common law. In this period, railroads killed and maimed thousands of people a year, and industrial accidents added massively to the toll. Huge corporations ran the lives of employees, shaped consumers' tastes and purchases, and controlled the economic fates of towns and cities, rivaling and in some instances exceeding the power of government. The very notions of customs of the people were hopelessly antiquated in this context and natural principles spoke to little of this. Longstanding common law notions were becoming irrelevant or inadequate.[14]

Heightened by severe depressions in the 1870s and 1890s, conflict between organized groups with divergent economic interests became more focused, organized, and intense. Much of this combat took place in the legal arena.[15] Contests were fought out in legislatures and courts between debtors and creditors, between mortgagors and mortgagees, between capital and labor, between urban and rural interests, between industrial and agrarian sectors, between the major trusts or business combinations and the government. Hofstadter vividly conveyed the time:

> The very sharpness of the struggle, as the Populists experienced it, the alleged absence of compromise solutions and of intermediate groups in the body politic, the brutality and desperation that were imputed to the plutocracy – all these suggested that failure of the people to win the final contest peacefully could result only in a total victory for the plutocrats and total extinction of democratic institutions, possibly after a period of bloodshed and anarchy. "We are nearing a serious crisis," declared Weaver. "If the present strained relations between wealth owners and wealth producers continue much longer they will ripen into frightful disaster. This universal discontent must be quickly interpreted and its causes removed." "We meet," said the Populist platform of 1892, "in the midst of a nation brought to the verge of moral, political, and material ruin. Corruption dominates the ballot-box, the Legislatures, the Congress, and touches even the ermine of the bench. . . ."[16]

14 See William Wiecek, *The Lost World of Classical Legal Thought* (New York: Oxford 1998) 246–50.
15 See Friedman, *The History of American Law*, supra 237–370.
16 D. Hofstadter, *The Age of Reform* (New York: Vintage Books 1955) 66–7.

This was not the first time such battles had occurred. What was novel, however, is that courts had greater institutional autonomy in the late nineteenth century and were not reluctant to exercise it.

Late-nineteenth- and early-twentieth-century contests among economic interests "molded, dominated, shaped American law,"[17] observed Friedman. A loser in the legislature turned to the courts to re-fight the battle, and vice versa. The history of labor injunctions offers a prime example of this back-and-forth combat within and through law. To prevent or break strikes, employers implored judges to issue injunctions in labor disputes.[18] Judges were receptive to such requests, drawing upon the courts "inherent" equity power to order injunctions to avoid irreparable harm to property interests. According to one study, "roughly 105 labor injunctions were issued in the 1880s, 410 in the 1890s, 850 in the 1910s, and 2,130 in the 1920s."[19] Union leaders who failed to call off a strike (even when they lacked the power to control it) were cited for contempt by the judge and jailed.[20] At the behest of labor unions, state legislatures enacted anti-injunction statutes to halt judicial intervention, but courts invalidated twenty-five of these statutes, and those that survived were narrowly interpreted.[21] The federal Clayton Act was passed in 1914, which explicitly restricted labor injunctions to situations of utmost necessity; undaunted, courts continued to liberally issue labor injunctions.[22] These back-and-forth battles through courts and legislatures took place for decades.

The power of judicial review gave judges an advantageous position. Although in theory this power could be exercised only for violations of constitutional limits, state and federal courts acted more expansively.[23] Citing the liberty of contract and the right to property, citing the Due Process clause, the Commerce clause, the Equal Protection Clause, or using common law principles, and sometimes offering nothing more than vague references to reason and natural justice, state and federal courts began, in the 1880s and continuing for decades, to invalidate legislation, particularly legislation friendly to labor. One study found that sixty-seven pro-labor statutes were invalidated by courts in this period, while twenty-six were upheld.[24] Much of this was the work of state courts, but the U.S. Supreme Court was also active. "According to one count, in the period before 1898, the Supreme Court invalidated a total of twelve federal statutes and 125 state laws, while in the single generation after 1898, it trebled those figures (fifty federal and 400 state)."[25]

---

17 Friedman, *History of American Law*, supra 339.
18 See David Bicknell Truman, *The Government Process* (New York: Knopf 1951) 497.
19 William Forbath, *Law and the Shaping of the American Labor Movement* (Cambridge, Mass.: Harvard Univ. Press 1991) 193.
20 See Friedman, *History of American Law*, supra 556–7.
21 Forbath, *Law and the Shaping of the American Labor Movement*, supra 151–52.
22 See Lawrence M. Friedman, *American Law in the 20th Century* (New Haven: Yale Univ. Press 2002) 74–7.
23 See e.g. *Hepburn v. Griswold*, 75 US 603 (1870); see also William E. Nelson, "The Impact of the Antislavery Movement Upon Styles of Judicial Reasoning in Nineteenth Century America," 87 *Harvard L. Rev.* 513,530–1 (1974); Wiecek, *Lost World of Classical Legal Thought*, supra 100.
24 Wiecek, Id. 133 (citation omitted).
25 Id. 135 (citation omitted).

The problem was not just that these court actions frustrated legislative policy initiatives; it was that they lined up time and again on the side of protecting capital interests. These decisions reeked of obstructionist favoritism for the rich. Lending credence to this view is this outburst in a case from Supreme Court Justice Stephen J. Fields: "The present assault on capital is but the beginning. It will be but the stepping stone to others, larger and more sweeping, till our political contests will become a war of the poor against the rich, – a war constantly growing in intensity and bitterness."[26]

In his famous 1897 essay, "The Path of the Law," Justice Oliver Wendell Holmes described the ongoing class battle fought through legal institutions:

> When socialism first began to be talked about, the comfortable classes of the community were a good deal frightened. I suspect that this fear has influenced judicial action both here and in England, yet it is certain that it is not a conscious factor in the decisions to which I refer. I think that something similar has led people who no longer hope to control the legislatures to look to the courts as expounders of the Constitution, and that in some courts new principles have been discovered outside the bodies of these instruments . . . [27]

Why formalist judges struck legislation

A formalist view of law has been blamed as the culprit behind court decisions striking social welfare legislation. An early articulation of formalism can be found in Pound's 1908 "Mechanical Jurisprudence" article. Pound began by attacking the contemporary identification of law as an abstract, logical science. "Law is not scientific for the sake of science."[28] He chastised adherents of this approach, what he called a "jurisprudence of concepts,"[29] for emphasizing logical deduction from assumed dogmas of law with little attention to social consequences:

> . . . the jurisprudence of conceptions tends to decay. Conceptions are fixed. The premises are no longer examined. Everything is reduced to simple deduction from them. Principles cease to have importance. The law becomes a body of rules. This is the condition against which sociologists protest, and protest rightly.[30]

> That our case law at its maturity has acquired the sterility of a fully developed system, may be shown by abundant examples of its failure to respond to vital needs of present-day life.[31]

To serve as the exemplar of flawed formalist reasoning, Pound offered *Lochner v. New York*,[32] an infamous case in the annals of American jurisprudence. The

---

26 *Pollock v. Farmers' Loan and Trust Co.*, 157 US 429,607 (895) (Field, J., dissenting).
27 Oliver Wendell Holmes, "The Path of the Law," *Harvard L. Rev.* 457, 467–8 (1897).
28 Pound, "Mechanical Jurisprudence," supra 605.
29 Id. 611.
30 Id. 612.
31 Id. 614.
32 *Lochner v. New York*, 198 US 45 (1905).

New York legislature imposed limits on the working hours of bakers to no more than ten hours a day and sixty hours a week. The Court invalidated the statute as an: "unreasonable, unnecessary and arbitrary interference with the right of the individual to his personal liberty or to enter into those contracts in relation to labor which may seem to him appropriate or necessary for the support of himself and his family."[33] Basing the decision on the abstract liberty of contract, the Court ignored the reality that the bakers had no freedom to bargain – they took the conditions of employment imposed upon them by the employers, or didn't get the job. Justice Holmes issued a still-echoing dissent that lacerated the majority for reading their own laissez faire views into the Constitution.

Any generalizations about so-called formalists must be offered advisedly, with awareness of the tendentious nature of the label, appended by critics and slung at the judges as a pejorative. One study of the *Lochner* court revealed that judges labeled "formalists" did not all espouse the same collection of ideas or adhere to the same styles of legal reasoning.[34] Nevertheless, the "formalist" characterization stuck, and became an often-repeated foil for later arguments.

With these provisos in mind, formalist views of the law can be pared down to two core notions, conceptual formalism and rule formalism. *Conceptual formalism* was the idea that legal concepts and principles, like property ownership, liberty of contract, and duty in torts, had necessary content and logical interrelations with one another, which could be discerned through reason, constituting a coherent, internally consistent, comprehensive body of law. *Rule formalism* was the idea that that judges could reason "mechanistically" from this body of law to discover the right answer in every case.

Conceptual formalism, it is important to recognize, is continuous with non-instrumental accounts of law in that both describe the content of law as in some sense pre-given. Rule formalism, however, was distinct from non-instrumental law. Non-instrumental views of the common law were about the nature and content of legal principles and concepts, whereas rule formalism was an account of judicial decision-making.

In the late nineteenth century, for reasons indicated in the preceding chapter, the conviction of the legal elite was that "The only function of the state was to protect property and enforce contracts; otherwise, classical creed taught, the state must get out of the way lest it disturb the beneficial workings of the natural order."[35] To modern ears, the reasoning of *Lochner* and its ilk sounds absurd, raising suspicions about bad faith on the part of judges. Historians and theorists in the past two decades, however, have begun to emphasize that formalism (in both senses) constituted a sincerely held and coherent set of beliefs and understandings about law and legal principles.[36] A study of the legal consciousness of the time found a genuine

33 Id. at 56.
34 See Walter F. Pratt, "Rhetorical Styles on the Fuller Court," 24 *Am.J. Legal Hist.* 189 (1980).
35 Wiecek, *Lost World of Classical Legal Thought*, supra 260.
36 See Duncan Kennedy, "Toward an Historical Understanding of Legal Consciousness: the Case of Classical Legal Thought in America, 1850–1940," 3 *Research in Law and Soc.* 3 (1980); Robert

"experience that appears to have been common at the turn of the century: that of the compulsion by which an abstraction dictates, objectively, apolitically, in a non-discretionary fashion, a particular result."[37] Formalist thinking permeated many areas of thought in the final quarter of the nineteenth century, when the natural sciences were supreme in prestige and provided the model emulated by all other bodies of knowledge. Philosophy, ethics, economics, and the social sciences emphasized internal coherence, logic, abstraction, typology and categorization, unchanging laws or immanent patterns, and order, often to the neglect of close attention to reality.[38]

Moreover, for reasons stated earlier, the legitimacy of judge-made common law in a democracy became more precarious as the nineteenth century progressed. Both conceptual formalism and rule formalism, in different ways, reaffirmed that judges were not making law. John Dewey described the late-nineteenth-century formalistic style of judging as an attempt by judges to bolster the legitimacy of judge-made law:

> Just because the personal element cannot be wholly excluded, while at the same time the decision must assume as nearly as possible an impersonal, objective, rational form, the temptation is to surrender the vital logic which has actually yielded the conclusion and to substitute for it forms of speech which are rigorous in appearance and which give an illusion of certitude.[39]

Whereas the conventional wisdom today, and of Progressives at the time, is that formalist judges intentionally favored capital interests, a strong case can be made that in their own minds they were doing the opposite: They were vigilantly remaining true to republican ideals about the impropriety of special interest legislation.[40] "This older tradition insisted that, to be valid, legislation must promote the general welfare and not the interest of one or another interest group or class."[41] Jacksonian aversion to special privilege was a guiding principle. Cooley championed the notion that "class legislation" was constitutionally prohibited. A passage often quoted by judges from his *Constitutional Limitations* emphasized this point:

> The doubt might also arise whether a regulation made for any one class of citizens, entirely arbitrary in its character, and restricting their rights, privileges, or legal capacities in a manner before unknown to the law, could be sustained notwithstanding its

---

W. Gordon, "Legal Thought and Legal Practice in the Age of American Enterprise, 1870–1920," in *Professions and Professional Ideologies*, edited by Gerald L. Geisen (Chapel Hill: Univ. North Carolina Press 1983). See generally Gary D. Rowe, "*Lochner* Revisionism Revisited," 24 *Law & Soc. Inquiry* 221 (1999); Jack M. Balkin, " 'Wrong the Day it was Decided': Lochner and Constitutional Historicism," 85 *Boston U. L. Rev.* 677 (2005); Stephen A. Siegal, "The Revision Thickens," 20 *Law & Hist. Rev.* 631 (2002).

37 Kennedy, "Toward an Historical Understanding of Legal Consciousness," supra 3.

38 White, *Social Thought in America*, supra; Richard Hofstadter, *The Progressive Historians* (New York: Vintage 1970) 183.

39 John Dewey, "Logical Method and Law," 10 *Cornell L. Quarterly* 17,24 (1924).

40 A powerful historical study that makes this point is Howard Gillman, *The Constitution Besieged: The Rise and Demise of Lochner Era Police Powers Jurisprudence* (Durham, N.C.: Duke Univ. Press 1993).

41 Wiecek, *Lost World of Classical Legal Thought*, supra 267.

generality. Distinctions in these respects must rest upon some reason which renders them important, – like the want of capacity in infants, and insane persons; and if the legislature should undertake to provide that persons following some specified lawful trade or employment should not have capacity to make contracts, or to receive conveyances, or to build such houses as others were allowed to erect, ... it can scarcely be doubted that the act would transcend the due bounds of legislative power, even if it did not come into conflict with express constitutional provisions. The man or the class forbidden the acquisition or enjoyment of property in a manner permitted to the community at large would be deprived of *liberty* in particulars of primary importance to his or their "pursuit of happiness."[42]

This is the understanding that lay behind *Lochner*. Paternalistic legislation – intended to protect a purportedly vulnerable group – was permissible only in traditionally recognized situations of incapacity (infants and insane, sometimes women and children). To treat the employees of bakers in this fashion was demeaning to them and trampled their liberty. Such legislation, it was thought, treated employees in a manner akin to slaves by prohibiting them from selling their labor under whatever terms and conditions they saw fit.[43]

Formalist judges viewed all forms of class legislation as a threat to the law that had to be rebuffed.[44] Legislation that genuinely advances the public interest was fine. "Government regulation of economic affairs ... was invalid only where the state moved beyond the sphere of its inherently limited authority by using its powers to help some citizens at the expense of others, rather than to promote genuinely public purposes to benefit the citizenry as a whole."[45] "[N]ineteenth century courts were on guard against not all regulations of the economy, but only a particular kind of government interference in market relations ... 'class' or 'partial' legislation; that is, laws that (from their view) promoted only the narrow interests of particular groups or classes rather than the general welfare."[46]

The judges applied their principles across the board in a manner that did not always favor capital interests.[47] Judges invalidated attempts by municipalities to subsidize railroad construction, for example. It was impermissible under the "public purpose" doctrine, courts reasoned, to use the taxing and spending power in a manner that directly advances private interests, even when there might be an indirect public benefit (the towns wanted rail service and would only get it if they helped bear some of the initial cost). In a Michigan Supreme Court opinion striking such legislation, Cooley wrote:

> But when we examine the power of taxation with a view to ascertain the purpose for
> which burdens may be imposed upon the public, we perceive at once that necessity

42 Cooley, *Constitutional Limitations*, supra 434–5.
43 See Foner, *The Story of American Freedom*, supra Chap. 6.
44 See Friedman, *History of American Law*, supra 361–2.
45 Lawrence Tribe, *American Constitutional Law*, 2nd ed. (Mineola, N.Y.: Foundation Press 1988) 564.
46 Gillman, *The Constitution Besieged*, supra 7.
47 See Jacobs, *Law Writers and the Courts*, supra Chap. 4.

is not the governing consideration, and that in many cases it has little or nothing to do with the question presented . . . . [C]ertain things of absolute necessity to civilized society the State is precluded, either by express constitutional provisions, or by necessary implication, from providing for at all; and they are left wholly to the fostering care of private enterprise and private liberality . . . . Certain professions and occupations in life are also essential, but we have no authority to employ the public moneys to induce persons to enter them. The necessity may be pressing, and to supply it may be, in a certain sense, to accomplish a 'public purpose'; but it is not a purpose for which the power of taxation may be employed.[48]

In sum, the world view of these judges was composed of natural rights, laissez faire, a natural order of competitive struggle, and limited government powers exercisable only for the public welfare. Many judges, including Cooley, accepted the propriety of regulation of business for public purposes, and were not doctrinaire laissez faire adherents in that sense; legislation that promoted particular interests was their target. When the justices were persuaded of heath or safety benefits, social welfare legislation would survive challenge, as it did a great deal of the time.

Under this interpretation, formalist judges who invalidated legislation favoring employees were, at least in their own minds, operating with studied neutrality, not favoring capital but rather denying favoritism on behalf of labor. Yet there is no question that the judges were cognizant that capital interests in many cases benefited from their decisions. It is also true that many of them sought this result. This would not have struck them as objectionable from a legal standpoint, first, because they thought they were duly living up to what the law (constitutional and common law principles) required, and second, because within the complex of prevailing ideas, the general welfare was served by facilitating economic development, which was accomplished by freeing competitive capitalism.

Formalist judges saw themselves as heroically staving off the threat to the non-instrumental integrity of the law posed by special interest legislation. They were not especially disturbed by the anti-democratic tenor of their decisions. Chief Justice Fuller wrote in the opinion invalidating the federal income tax that the constitution was "manifestly designed . . . to prevent an attack upon accumulated property by mere force of numbers."[49] The judges were simply doing their constitutional duty. This sentiment permeates a 1905 speech by Judge John Philips, which inveighs against the contemporary explosion of legislation as "a growing evil," in which "the people are encouraged to believe that the remedy for every imaginary ill in state and society lies in legislation."[50] "Legislators strive to meet the unreasonable demands of these interests and classes . . . "[51] "Woe unto the judge who must pass upon their legality!"[52] This required great courage of the judge, "who must bow his devoted

48 20 Mich. 452,483–84 (1870), quoted in Jacobs, *Law Writers and the Courts*, supra 117–18.
49 *Pollock v. Farmers Loan and Trust Co.*, 157 U.S. 429,583 (1895).
50 John Philips, "The Law and Lawyers," 17 *Green Bag* 433,437 (1905).
51 Id.
52 Id.

head to the vials of wrath. . . . [T]o stand firm, and vindicate the supremacy of law."[53] Judges, according to Philips, were defending the integrity of the law pursuant to the framer's constitutional mandate. The judge "can only lift his beaming forehead to the heavens, and let the tempest expend its fury . . . [with] the consciousness of having done duty as an enlightened conscience gives him to see it."[54]

While courts remained entrenched in traditional ways of seeing the legal world, however, surrounding views shifted quickly at the turn of the century.[55] The frozen mode of analysis of conceptual formalism and rule formalism, which judges adverted to in part owing to their shaky basis for legitimation and in part owing to the rigidifying influence of law as science, became a tight straightjacket that handicapped their ability to engage in the age-old common law task of modifying the law to keep up with social and economic change. The conservative views of elite lawyers and judges, casting their allegiance with the protection of property, contributed to this failure to accommodate the law to the new social-economic reality. Judges continued to espouse the philosophy of self-standing individualism and property rights at a time when the dominant social and economic features were the rise of large institutions and collective action.

The severe depression of the 1890s, strikes and riots violently responded to by police and private security forces, Tammany Hall–type corruption of politics by money, and flamboyant robber barons flouting the law, all brought to light by turn-of-the-century muckraking journalism, made the middle class more sympathetic to labor. In mass, urbanized society in which everyone is a cog in a large corporation or bureaucracy, or works in an insignificant small business struggling to make it in an economy indifferent to hard work, individuals are buffeted about by forces and institutions beyond their control. The individualist laissez faire common law views seemed absurd when measured against the lives of most people. The manifest contrast between surrounding reality and the judges' words and decisions left them exposed and ripe for criticism.

Instrumental views of the nineteenth-century legal profession

Criticism of the avarice of lawyers goes way back, as reflected in this observation made in 1583 England: "The lawyers . . . handle poor men's matters coldly, they execute justice partially, & they receive bribes greedily, so that justice is perverted, the poor beggared, and many a good man in[j]ured thereby. They respect the persons and not the causes; money, not the poor; rewards and not conscience."[56] For centuries it has been said that lawyers instrumentally manipulate the law for

---

53 Id.
54 Id.
55 See Pound, "Law in Books and Law in Action," supra.
56 Quoted in Marc Galanter, *Lowering the Bar: Lawyer Jokes and Legal Culture* (Madison, Wisc.: Wisconsin Univ. Press 2005) 3. The quote was taken from E.W. Ives, "The Reputation of the Common Lawyers in English Society, 1450–1550," 7 *Univ. of Birmingham Historical J.* 130 (1960).

the benefit of their clients and themselves. How does this square with the idealized non-instrumental accounts of the law set forth in Chapter 1?

A part of the agenda of the legal elite in their glorified renderings of the common law was to persuade the public of the sanctity, objectivity, social value, and justice of law. They had a closer audience in mind as well. Many of these accounts were made in addresses to the bar or to graduating law students: They were exhortations to lawyers and judges to engage in honorable conduct in defense of the law (and their collective livelihoods). Carter's 1890 speech to the bar espousing a non-instrumental view of law, quoted earlier, explicitly acknowledged expressions of public outrage about rapacious lawyers and corrupt judges.

Complaints about lawyers have been a constant companion of the profession in the United States. "On the eve of the Revolution, Virginians debated in the newspapers as to whether or not lawyers practiced a 'grovelling, mercenary trade,' and engaged in 'petit Larceny.'"[57] A particular low point for the esteem of the legal profession, according to historian Charles Warren,[58] was the Revolution and its aftermath (despite the prominent role played by lawyers therein). Among others heaping scorn upon the profession, in 1786 "Honestus" published popular tracts about greedy, fee-chasing lawyers manipulating the legal process for their own gain.[59] He proposed that the legal profession be abolished. The town of Braintree outside of Boston, in 1786, requested of the legislature "that there may be such laws compiled as may crush or at least put a proper check or restraint on that order of Gentlemen denominated Lawyers . . . "[60] Another exasperated town voiced "the almost universally prevailing complaints against the practice of the order of lawyers."[61] Marc Galanter summarized prevailing views of lawyers at the time:

> "There existed a violent universal prejudice against the legal profession as a class" and its members "'were denounced as banditti, as blood-suckers, as pickpockets, as wind-bags, as smooth-tongued rogues . . . . In March 1789, two months before the Constitutional Convention convened in Philadelphia, future president John Quincy Adams, then a Harvard senior, addressed a college "conference:" "The profession of the Law labours under the heavy weight of popular indignation; . . . it is upbraided as the original cause of all the evils with which the Commonwealth is distressed."[62]

Several explanations have been offered for this period of heightened unhappiness with lawyers: post-revolutionary animus against English common law and against

---

57 Wood, *The Radicalism of the American Revolution*, supra 107.
58 Charles Warren, *History of the American Bar* (Boston: Little Brown 1911).
59 Honestus [Benjamin Austin], "Observations on the Pernicious Practice of the Law (1786), reprinted in Dennis R. Nolan, *Readings in the History of the American Legal Profession* (Charlottesville, Va.: Michie 1980) 93–5.
60 Warren, *History of the American Bar*, supra 215; also Gerard W. Gawalt, "Sources of Anti-Lawyer Sentiment in Massachusetts, 1740–1840," 13 *Am. J. Legal Hist.* 283 (1970).
61 Warren, *History of the American Bar*, supra 215.
62 Galanter, *Lowering the Bar*, supra 4–5 (citations omitted).

lawyers with Tory sympathies (many of whom left);[63] the primary business of lawyers in this period involved debt collections and the recovery of property,[64] generating widespread anger;[65] resentment about a legal aristocracy that erected barriers to entry to practice while expanding opportunities for income by taking over activities that did not previously require lawyers; and concern that lawyers held an inordinate number of public positions.[66] Adding to these particular resentments, Jeffersonian democracy rendered the judicial control of the common law less legitimate, and the populism of Jacksonian egalitarianism made elites of all kinds suspect, particularly legal elites.[67]

Popular discontent about lawyers, judges, and the common law showed in various ways. A majority of states legislatively required that judges be subject to election. Legislation also reduced the formerly active posture of judges in court. Efforts were made to simplify the law through restatement or codification (which were resisted mightily by lawyers and did not get far).[68] People were authorized to represent themselves in court. To break the monopoly of lawyers, standards for bar entry were reduced in many states;[69] New York legislated that any citizen of "good moral character" could be admitted to practice law, even without legal training[70] (later invalidated by the state high court). Open entry to legal practice was also legislatively mandated in New Hampshire, Maine, Wisconsin, and Indiana.[71] Members of the bar, in turn, blamed these legislatively lowered admission standards for the decline in the profession: "Very many become attorneys in order to profit by chicanery and trick. These injure the moral character of the bar and destroy its good name."[72] "The first half-century of the 1800s, then, gives evidence of a steady and resolute movement to whittle away at the power and autonomy of the legal profession."[73]

Throughout the nineteenth century and into the twentieth, law was repeatedly described by observers as a business.[74] "And although you have left no means unattempted to give you the appearance of *Officers*," said reformer Frederick Robinson about lawyers in 1832, "you are still nothing more than followers of a trade or calling like other men, to get a living . . ."[75] A speaker at the 1850 Indiana Constitutional

---

63 Gary B. Nash, "The Philadelphia Bench and Bar, 1800–1861," 7 *Comparative Studies in Society and History* 203,209 (1965).
64 Warren, *History of the American Bar*, supra 214.
65 Roscoe Pound, *The Lawyer From Antiquity to Modern Times* (St. Paul, Minn.: West 1953) 179–80.
66 Id. 227–9.
67 Id. 232–42. See also Wood, *Radicalism of the American Revolution*, supra 271–86.
68 Warren, *History of the American Bar*, supra Chap. XIX.
69 Nash, "Philadelphia Bench and Bar," supra 208.
70 See W. Raymond Blackard, "The Demoralization of the Legal Profession in Nineteenth Century America," 16 *Tennessee L. Rev.* 314 (1940).
71 Pound, *Lawyer From Antiquity to Modern Times*, supra 231.
72 Unidentified author, "Admission to the Bar, 4 *Albany L.J.* 309, 309 (1871).
73 Nash, "Philadelphia Bench and Bar," supra 213.
74 Maxwell Bloomfield, "Law vs. Politics: The Self-Image of the American Bar (1830–1860)," 12 *Am. J. Legal Hist.* 306 (1968).
75 Frederick Robinson, "Letter to the Hon. Rufus Choate Containing a Brief Exposure of Law Craft, and Some of the Encroachments of the Bar Upon the Rights and Liberties of the People" 14–15 (1832), quoted in Gawalt, "Anti-Lawyer Sentiment," supra 291.

Convention remarked that "the legal procedure was 'a cunningly devised machine to make money and deceive the people,'" apparently a common view at the time.[76] In a 1873 graduation address, Justice Ryan disputed the circulating view that law is "a business." In "The Lawyer To-day," published in 1904, a prominent lawyer remarked, "how often we hear that the profession is commercialized."[77] A 1912 article by a lawyer in the *Yale Law Journal*, entitled "The Passing of the Legal Profession," lamented that "The practice of law has become commercialized. It has been transformed from a profession to a business, and a hustling business at that."[78] Practicing law was no longer about the administration of justice, he wrote, but about doing the bidding of clients as a means to earn money. In a speech in 1914, "The Opportunity in Law," Louis Brandeis charged lawyers with "allowing themselves to become adjuncts of great corporations and have neglected the obligation to use their powers for the protection of the people."[79] An entry on the "Modern Legal Profession" in a leading encyclopedia published in the 1930s concluded: "The historic view was that a lawyer was an officer of the court and therefore an integral part of the scheme of justice. But the conception of the lawyer now obtaining is that he is the paid servant of his client, justified in using any technical lever that the law supplies in order to forward the latter's interest."[80]

Complaints by the public, or expressions of concern by lawyers, that the practice of law has become an unscrupulous business are apparently a constant of U.S. history. Friedman showed how, in all periods, American lawyers have hustled for business, scrambling to pick up and hold on to whatever fee-paying tasks they can find. Not everyone considered it lamentable to view law as a business. Oliver Wendell Holmes' famous "The Path of the Law," a graduation address, explicitly characterized the legal profession as a business in which lawyers are paid for advising people of the legal consequences of their prospective actions. Holmes urged a "business-like understanding of the matter"; and proudly proclaimed that "Law is the business to which my life is devoted."[81]

When the practice of law is taken as business, three additional senses of legal instrumentalism are uncovered. First, from the standpoint of a lawyer, the practice of law is a job like any other, a means to their own financial gain. Second, lawyers see their role as serving instrumentally as an advocate for their clients. Third, lawyers marshal, identify, interpret, and argue about legal rules in an instrumental manner to achieve their clients' and their own objectives.

Each of these senses of instrumentalism shows up in complaints about lawyers. Lawyers were easy targets for the charge of hypocrisy because the profession doggedly denied the evident business components of practice, and because lawyers collectively

76 Pound, *The Lawyer From Antiquity to Modern Times*, supra 240–1.
77 Lloyd W. Bowers, "The Lawyer To-Day," 38 *Am. L. Rev.* 823, 823 (1904).
78 G. Bristol, "The Passing of the Legal Profession," 22 *Yale L.J.* 590, 590 (1912–13).
79 Louis Brandeis, The Opportunity in Law, in Business – A Profession 337–9 (1933), quoted in Robert W. Gordon, "The Independence of Lawyers," 68 *Boston Univ. L. Rev.* 1, 2 (1988).
80 A.A. Berle, "Modern Legal Profession," *Encyclopaedia of the Social Sciences*, vol. 9, edited by Edwin R. A. Seligman (New York: MacMillan Co. 1933) 340–6.
81 Oliver Wendell Holmes, "The Path of the Law," 10 *Harvard L. Rev.* 457, 459, 473 (1897).

wielded public power, claiming to be public servants, while working to further their own and their clients' private interests. Lawyers ply a trade unique in possessing a public and a private side. A legal system occupies a special position in society as the coercive regime of governing rules; lawyers occupy a special position in the legal system by monopolizing the provision of legal services (lawyers) and by monopolizing the position of final decision-maker (judges). Lawyers use this monopoly to earn their livelihood and advance the agendas of those who pay them. Lawyers and judges keep reciting the public side of law in support of their activities, but their conduct suggests to critics that lawyers take advantage of the public power to enhance their private gains.

A justification derived from the adversary structure of the system is offered by lawyers and judges to smooth over these two faces of law. The connection between the two is explicit in Justice Ryan's 1873 address, which, in a kind of alchemy, weaves the instrumentalism of the lawyers to produce non-instrumental law:

> It is the business of a lawyer to consider well the merits of a controversy, before he takes a retainer to litigate it. But once he is retained, hesitation should give place to zeal. In forensic controversies, one of the parties is generally wrong; both may be. But that does not imply that the lawyer's retainer does wrong to the administration of justice. In doubtful cases, it is within neither the duty nor the power of a practicing lawyer to decide. That is for the court. It is only judgment, after litigation, which can settle right. In the selfish controversies of life, a practicing lawyer should generally accept all knowledge as uncertain, all aspects of truth as hypothetical, all opinion as doubtful, until tested by the ordeal of litigation. Even proximate justice is only to be secured, in the forensic contests of interest and feeling, by thorough presentation of both sides; by zealous advocacy of each as if it were the sure right. The counsel on both sides, within due professional limits, alike serve the cause of truth, alike contribute to the justice of the case. To this end, it is the duty of every retained lawyer to put his faith in his client's cause. The lawyer should believe in his retainer when he takes it; once taken, he should never mistrust nor betray it. The fidelity of our profession is a great moral lesson . . . . It is the wise policy of the law that the lawyer should be the legal *alter ego* of his client.[82]

Once a lawyer decides to take the case, Ryan said, a lawyer serves the interests of society, order, justice, and God through the expedient of single-minded advocacy of their clients' ends. The judge – possessing "the light of intelligence, purity of truth, love of right, firmness of integrity, singleness of purpose, candor of judgment"[83] – plays the crucial role within the system, serving as the sieve that processes the instrumentalism of the lawyers to produce justice. Through this reasoning, which after more than a century is still the primary rationalization of lawyer conduct, Ryan transforms a common complaint about the zealous conduct of lawyers into a virtue – "fidelity of the profession" – that serves as a mechanism for achieving justice.

82 Ryan, "Address to the Graduating Law Students of the University of Wisconsin," supra 155.
83 Id. 154.

Shared interest of the legal elite

There is a surface inconsistency between this chapter, which shows that instrumental views of legislation and of lawyers were circulating in the nineteenth century, and Chapters 1 and 2, which assert that non-instrumental views of law were expressed throughout this same period and must be taken seriously. They can be reconciled by paying attention to who is speaking and to what they are talking about. The first two chapters articulate the views of prominent judges, leaders of the bar, and legal academics (roles often filled by the same individuals). These were statements by the legal elite characterizing the nature of the common law, which until the late nineteenth century was thought of as *the* law. In contrast, this chapter focuses on legislation and on lawyers in daily practice.

The legal elite – leaders of the bar, judges, and academics – shared a confluence of interests that contributed to a unified front: Collectively they resisted the growth of legislation in the late nineteenth century and they distanced themselves from instrumentalism in legal practice, while promoting the view of law as science.

In the second half of the nineteenth century, legal education was being established in universities, seeking legitimacy as an academic course of study. It was not obvious that law was an appropriate or necessary subject for university study. Previously, law had been thought of as a craft best learned in an apprenticeship. David Dudley Field felt compelled to make the case at the 1859 opening of Northwestern Law School:

> How shall this science [of law] best be learned? There are three methods: the private study of books; the advice and aid of practitioners, amid the bustle and interruptions of practice; and the teaching of public schools. The inadequacy of the first is obvious; the disadvantages of the second are too painfully known to all of us who studied in that way; the third is beyond question the most efficient and complete. There is as much need of public schools for law as for any other science. There is more, for, the greater the science the greater the need. Above all others, this science, so vast, so comprehensive, so complicated and various in its details, needs to be studied with all the aids which universities, professors, and libraries can furnish.[84]

Discounting the hyperbole demanded by the occasion, it is revealing in the connections drawn between legal science and university education.

Many state and city bar associations formed in the 1870s, and worked to raise the standards for admission.[85] Universities were beneficiaries of the effort to raise bar standards because that would funnel more students to legal studies; this educational screening barrier, in turn, helped bar associations, raising the status of lawyers to

---

84 David Dudley Field, "Magnitude and Importance of Legal Science" (1859), reprinted in Stephen B. Presser and Jamil S. Zainaldin, *Law and Jurisprudence in American History* (St. Paul, Minn.: West Pub. 2003) 745.

85 Pound, *The Lawyer From Antiquity to Modern Times*, supra Chap. IX.

men learned in an academic science, and restricting the economic class of entering lawyers to those who could afford a university education (though admissions to the bar via apprenticeships would continue for decades).

Legislation threatened the autonomy of the common law and the power of judges who controlled it, and disrupted the domain of legal academics as the leading expositors and rationalizers of legal science. Judges and legal academics, therefore, both saw legislation as an interference in their important task. This resistance was often overt. According to historian Thomas Grey, "Langdell's Harvard colleagues and disciples Beale and Ames threatened to withdraw their offer to help the new University of Chicago Law School get started at the turn of the century, because its organizers proposed to teach a substantial number of public law [legislation-oriented] courses, thus violating the Harvard curricular dogma that students must be exposed only to scientific 'pure law' [common law] courses."[86]

All three agendas were thus served simultaneously by maintaining the non-instrumentalist portrayals of law as a matter of principle, reason, immemorial customs of the community, a body of specialized knowledge and a science. The prestige and autonomy of one was the prestige and autonomy for all. It must be emphasized that these assertions do not imply that the non-instrumental views of law were insincere. These centuries-old views were expressed with belief, commitment, and idealism, but they also matched the separate agendas of each group for enhancing their status and power. This confluence of interests offers a partial explanation for why non-instrumental veiws of law were maintained so doggedly for so long in the face of mounting contrary developments emerging from the legislative quarter and from legal practice.

Support for this argument can be found in the 1916 Presidential Address to the American Bar Association by Elihu Root, one of the most influential lawyers of the day. Root asserted that there were too many lawyers, too many of whom were incompetent and engaged in unnecessary legal activities, creating a "great economic waste in the administration of the law."[87] These lawyers were "loyally devoted to their client's interests," paying no heed to the interests of society.[88] A member of the corporate bar, critical of many in the practice, Root affirmed the unified elite stance in defense of the integrity of the law against these developments:

> There are indeed two groups of men who consider the interests of the community. They are the teachers in the principal law schools and the judges on the Bench. With loyalty and sincere devotion they defend the public right to effective service; but against them is continually pressing the tendency of the Bar and the legislatures and, in a great degree of the public, towards the exclusively individual view.[89]

86 Grey, "Langdell's Orthodoxy," supra 34.
87 Elihu Root, "Address of the President," 41 *Reports of American Bar Assoc.* 355, 358 (1916).
88 Id. 360.
89 Id.

Legal academics would later break away from this unspoken alliance, after the place of law schools in the university was secure. Political reasons provided one motivation for the break: Many law professors who would later be identified with Legal Realism supported Progressive reforms, which the recalcitrant stance of the judges inhibited.[90] Another reason for the break is that the values underlying the academic profession led law professors, over time, to assume a more distanced perspective on the law from that of judges and elite members of the bar.[91] Instead of seeing law itself as a science, which was Langdell's vision, legal academics, in tune with prevailing academic views of the time, came to believe that law should be *studied by* social science. That was the urging of the Legal Realists, taken up next.

90 Robert S. Summers, *Instrumentalism and American Legal Theory* (Ithaca, N.Y.: Cornell Univ. Press 1982) 29.
91 See Jerold S. Auerbach, *Unequal Justice: Lawyers and Social Change in Modern America* (New York: Oxford Univ. Press 1976) Chap. III.

4

Instrumentalism of the legal realists

The close of the nineteenth century and the opening of the twentieth was a period of great intellectual ferment. A burst of academic works spewed forth portraying law and politics as the battleground among competing groups;[1] their common theme was the "seemingly pervasive influence of economic interests" on government.[2] This was the core thesis of Arthur Bentley's *The Process of Government* (1908) and Charles Beard's controversial *An Economic Interpretation of the Constitution* (1913). Beard's book was notorious because he tossed mud on the national myth built around the iconic Founding Fathers, arguing that their primary motivation when constructing the Constitution was to advance the economic interests of merchants, large property owners, and creditors, groups in which they were members.[3]

A new intellectual radicalism emerged at the turn of the century, into which these works fit. Historian Christopher Lasch identified the various sources of this emergence:

> Everyone who has studied the history of American reform agrees that the reform tradition underwent a fundamental change around 1900. Some people identify the change with a changing attitude toward government, a new readiness to use government (particularly the federal government) as an instrument of popular control. Others associate it with an abandonment of the old populistic distrust of large-scale institutions, like corporations, and an acceptance of the inevitability of the concentration of wealth and power. Still others define the change as a movement away from the dogma of natural rights toward a relativistic, environmentalist, and pragmatic view of the world. All of these developments, in truth, were going on at the same time, and all of them contributed to the emergence of the new radicalism.[4]

Connected to these ideas, a general "revolt against formalism" was taking place across various fields of knowledge, observed historian Morton White. "American

---

1 See Hofstadter, *The Progressive Historians*, supra 181–206.
2 Herman Belz, "The Realist Critique of Constitutionalism in the Era of Reform," 15 *Am. J. Legal Hist.* 288,289 (1971).
3 Charles A. Beard, *An Economic Interpretation of the Constitution of the United States* (New York: Free Press 1986) 8–9.
4 Christopher Lasch, *The New Radicalism in America, 1889–1963: The Intellectual As a Social Type* (New York: W.W. Norton 1965) xiii.

intellectuals [were] ranging themselves, in the eighteen-nineties, against formalism, since they had been convinced that logic, abstraction, deduction, mathematics, and mechanics were inadequate to social research and incapable of containing the rich, moving, living current of social life."[5] Various streams of thought challenged formalist dogmas: "pragmatism, instrumentalism, institutionalism, economic determinism, and legal realism exhibit striking philosophical kinships."[6]

Both anti-formalism and the new radicalism were the products and concerns of intellectuals. They emerged against the backdrop of the intense economic conflict fought out at the turn of the century, as described in the preceding chapter. They fed the Progressive political movement, which urged reform of the economic, political, and cultural orders.

These leading intellectual tempers of the period, which construed law and government in instrumental terms, did not penetrate legal thinking immediately. Law is a conservative enterprise oriented to order and continuity with the past, and a practical activity that resists intellectual movements. Slowly at first but with irresistible momentum fed by different sources – the legal writings of Oliver Wendell Holmes, the work of the pragmatists, the influence of Bentham and Jhering, the growth of legislation, the general revolt against formalism, the Progressive movement, the new radicalism, political upheavals, and group conflict within law – the view that law is an instrument became ever-more explicit within the legal academy.

Pragmatism, Holmes, and Pound

Rudolph von Jhering's path-breaking book, *Der Zweck im Recht*, published in 1877, challenged Savigny's dominant historical school in Germany, a classic non-instrumental view that law has an immanent existence in the life of the community that is not to be declared at the will of the legislature. Jhering argued that law should be seen, not as an emanation from the common culture and not as a matter of abstract legal principles or concepts, but as an instrument utilized by individuals and groups to achieve their purposes. The content of legal rules and principles bear the mark of contests among interests. Jhering believed that society has common social purposes and shared social mores, and that well-functioning legal systems come to reflect and further these shared values and purposes.[7]

Jhering's book was translated and published in the United States in 1913 under the title *Law as a Means to an End*. The Editorial Preface to the book drew parallels between Bentham and Jhering and raised a plea for attention:

> American juristic thinking at the present time needs a von Ihering. Our jurists, our legislators and our courts, both bench and bar, are still holding fast to an historical

---

5 White, *Social Thought in America*," supra 11.
6 Id. 6.
7 These assertions are succinctly stated by Jhering in *Struggle for Law*, supra. A superb exposition in Jhering's ideas is Neil Duxbury, "Jhering's Philosophy of Authority," *Oxford J. of Legal Studies* (forthcoming 2005).

"Naturrecht" built up on the precedents of the Common Law. . . . All of our lawyers, judges and legislators who are trained in the traditions of the Common Law hold with characteristic and commendable professional conservatism to the good that is and has been in our legal system, insisting, too, upon the prime virtue of a system that is certain, but apparently forgetting that law is not an end in itself and as such to be brought to a state of formal and static perfection, but that the end is the good of society. The public is crying out against our crystallized and inelastic theory and practices of law.[8]

More than century after Bentham first promoted it, the time was finally ripe for an instrumental perspective on law. The emphasis within law on science helped pave the way for its reception: the social sciences in the late nineteenth century increasingly came to be seen in "social engineering" terms, which influenced legal thought.[9] As indicated earlier, the instrumental perspective spread generally, gaining strength on the belief that "human reason can guide and direct human life."[10]

In "Mechanical Jurisprudence," Roscoe Pound credited Jhering with pioneering the critique of conceptual jurisprudence.[11] Another source to which Pound referred several times was William James' *Pragmatism*, published the prior year. Pound credited James for articulating a modern "instrumental" view of theories and science.[12] As with so much in that abbreviated article, Pound had acutely identified at the very outset what would turn out to be an important influence on instrumental ideas about law.

The multiple close connections between pragmatism and reformist legal thought are a fascinating detail of American legal history. Pragmatic philosophy was presented and developed at a small elite gathering of Cambridge intellectuals in the final quarter of the nineteenth Century, called the Metaphysical Club, which included Charles Sanders Peirce, William James, Chauncey Wright, and Oliver Wendell Holmes, along with six additional lawyer members, including a disciple of Bentham named Nicholas St. John Green.[13] Louis Menand's study of the origins of pragmatism indicates that it was a joint affair, coalescing through contributions by different members, though the key philosophical writings were by Peirce and James.[14] Holmes, the most influential jurist in U.S. history, imbibed pragmatist views at their very inception.

"Instrumentalism" was another label for pragmatic philosophy, the label preferred by John Dewey (following Peirce and James, the most important early contributor to pragmatism), who for a time co-taught a seminar on jurisprudence at Columbia Law School and wrote several important articles that influenced Legal

---

8 Joseph H. Drake, "Editorial Preface to this Volume," in Rudolph von Ihering, *Law as a Means to An End* (Boston: Boston Book Co. 1913) xxii.

9 Ross, *Origins of American Social Science*, supra 94.

10 Id. 93.

11 Pound, "Mechanical Jurisprudence," supra 610–11.

12 Id. 608.

13 John P. Murphy, *Pragmatism: From Peirce to Davidson* (Boulder, Colo.: Westview 1990) 21.

14 See Louis Menand, *The Metaphysical Club: A Story of Ideas in America* (New York: Farrar, Straus and Giroux 2001).

Realism.[15] Pragmatism builds on the notion that truths are established in the course of the pursuit of collective projects in the world.[16] The pragmatists used the natural sciences as their model of successful knowledge acquisition. Truths work. They are created in the course of goal-oriented activities. They are understandings and ideas that are tested and prove successful and reliable when acted upon within a community of investigators. This does not mean that truths are whatever people desire or want to believe; to the contrary, people are up against a world not entirely malleable to their thoughts. Reality refutes and imposes constraints on beliefs, proving many of them unreliable or false. Pragmatism is thus experimental, empirical, action oriented, and social in bent. It denies the possibility of absolute truths outside of human experience. Ultimate truths can perhaps be found, but only through the confirmation of the universal community (at the end of time). Meanwhile, many reliable truths have already been established, especially by science, and more are constantly being added.

Pragmatism has less to say about moral values. Absolute moral values in the sense traditionally sought after by moral philosophers do not exist. Moral precepts are stated typically as general propositions ("do good and avoid evil," "never tell a lie," "always keep your promises"), but their meaning and implications become apparent only in specific contexts of application. Then choices must be made that take into consideration all of the competing values and goals and their concrete implications in the situation at hand. Moral precepts can be evaluated in terms of whether good or bad, desirable or undesirable, consequences follow when acted upon.[17] They can, and should, be evaluated as to whether satisfactory results follow from acting upon them in particular situations. But they cannot be adjudged true or false in the same sense as empirical claims; moral values operate in the realm of meaning. James wrote only one essay dedicated exclusively to the subject of moral values. Therein he observed that there is no morality in the nature of things.[18] Morality is an aspect of human social existence: "beyond the facts of his own subjectivity there is nothing moral in the world"[19] . . . "there are no absolute evils" . . . .[20]

In a 1914 article, Dewey regarded natural law principles (among which he included laissez faire notions of liberty) with open skepticism (although he granted that their invocation has sometimes helped prompt beneficial legal reform). His main criticism is "that one of the chief offices of the idea of nature [natural law and justice] in political and judicial practice has been to consecrate the existent state of

15 See Martin P. Golding, "Jurisprudence and Legal Philosophy in Twentieth Century America – Major Themes and Developments," 36 *J. Legal Educ.* 441, 467 (1986).
16 See William James, *Pragmatism and the Meaning of Truth* (Cambridge, Mass.: Harvard Univ. Press 1975).
17 See Elizabeth Anderson, "Dewey's Moral Philosophy," in *Stanford Encyclopedia of Philosophy* (Spring 2005 Edition) http://plato.stanford.edu/archives/spr2005/entries/dewey-moral/.
18 William James, "The Moral Philosopher and the Moral Life," in *Essays in Pragmatism* (New York: Hafner Press 1948) 69.
19 Id. 70.
20 Id. 83.

affairs, whatever its distribution of advantages and disadvantages, of benefits and losses; and to idealize, rationalize, moralize, the physically given."[21] Natural law ideas protect the status quo by suggesting that there is no choice in the matter. An instrumental view of law is superior, Dewey urged, because it is forward looking and requires consideration of desirable consequences. Dewey construed natural rights and principles in purely instrumental terms – "the question of the limits of individual powers, or liberties, or rights, is finally a question of the most efficient use of means for ends."[22]

An objection often lodged against pragmatic philosophy, owing to these skeptical views of absolute moral principles and natural law, is that it leads to moral relativism. A pragmatist apparently cannot argue, in other than instrumental terms, that one set of moral values is evil and another is good, only that it has good or bad consequences from the standpoint of the community or individual and their ends. This problem, as we shall see, also came to haunt the Realists.

Although Holmes viewed pragmatic philosophy, as everything, with a degree of skepticism, and did not credit it with influencing his ideas, core aspects of pragmatism show in his judicial decisions and his views of law, particularly his doubt that general propositions can unequivocally determine concrete cases, his assertion that experience rather than logic is at the heart of law, his endorsement of community-based standards, his experimentalism, his endorsement of attention to actual social consequences, and his instrumental view of law.[23]

Holmes called Langdell the "greatest living legal theologian,"[24] a crack about the latter's espoused faith in legal science. Although Holmes admired Langdell's achievement, he objected to the portrayal of law as a logically constructed system of rules and principles that could be deductively applied to produce answers in specific cases. "You can give any conclusion a logical form,"[25] Holmes wrote. Holmes was not against legal principles and logical consistency as such – indeed he vigorously promoted these aspects of law.[26] But he was against holding up systematic coherence as the ultimate end of law, and against the suggestion that judges reasoned in a purely logical, mechanical way. Holmes dismissed another often-cited support for the common law: "The time has long gone when law is only an unconscious embodiment of the common will."[27]

Holmes urged in instrumental terms that "a body of law is more rational and more civilized when every rule it contains is referred articulately and definitely to

21 John Dewey, "Nature and Reason in Law," 25 *Int. J. Ethics* 25, 30–1 (1914).
22 Dewey, "Force and Coercion," supra 366.
23 See Menand, *Metaphysical Club*, supra 337–47; James D. Miller, "Holmes, Peirce, and Legal Pragmatism, 84 *Yale L.J.* 1123 (1975).
24 O.W. Holmes, "Book Review (Of the Second Edition of Langdell's Casebook)," 14 *Am. L. Rev.* 233 (1880).
25 Holmes, "The Path of the Law," supra 466.
26 See Morris Cohen, *Law and the Social Order: Essays in Legal Philosophy* (New York: Harcourt 133) 165–83, 198–218.
27 Quoted in Wiecek, *Classical Legal Thought*, supra 180.

an end which it subserves, and when the grounds for desiring that end are stated or are ready to be stated in words."[28] "The language of judicial decision is mainly the language of logic. And the logical method and form flatter that longing for certainty and for repose which is in every human mind. But certainty generally is an illusion, and repose is not the destiny of man."[29] Judges must regularly weigh competing social interests, and base decisions on what best serves social policy. Holmes urged that judges engage in this process openly rather than by relying subconsciously or covertly upon social values. "[T]he result of the often proclaimed judicial aversion to deal with such [policy] considerations is simply to leave the very ground and foundation of the judgments inarticulate . . ."[30] That was his complaint about the *Lochner* decision. Holmes did not think it impossible for judges to decide cases in an objective fashion, it must be emphasized. He prided himself on his judicial capacity for "heroic disinterestedness."[31]

Roscoe Pound's remarkable "Mechanical Jurisprudence" article, in which he presaged many of the points later made by the Legal Realists, has been mentioned several times. Pound declared that "as a means to an end, [law] must be judged by the results it achieves, not by the niceties of its internal structure . . ."[32] "We do not base institutions upon deduction from assumed principles of human nature; we require them to exhibit practical utility, and we rest them upon a foundation of policy and established adaptation to human needs."[33] To support his critique of formalistic legal science and his proposed instrumental approach, Pound quoted William James' instrumental approach to philosophy:

> In the philosophy of to-day, theories are 'instruments, not answers to enigmas, in which we can rest.' The idea of science as a system of deductions has become obsolete, and the revolution which has taken place in other sciences in this regard must take place and is taking place in jurisprudence also . . .[34]

"The sociological movement in jurisprudence," wrote Pound, "is a movement for pragmatism as a philosophy of law."[35] He characterized jurisprudence as "a science of social engineering."[36]

The legal realists

Karl Llewellyn, Jerome Frank, Walter Wheeler Cook, Felix Cohen, and other Legal Realists, coming into their own in the 1920s and 1930s, assumed a more radical

28 Holmes, "The Path of the Law," supra 469.
29 Holmes, "The Path of the Law," supra 466.
30 Id. 467.
31 Menand, *Metaphysical Club*, supra 66.
32 Pound, "Mechanical Jurisprudence," supra 605.
33 Id. 609.
34 Id. 608.
35 Roscoe Pound, "The Need of a Sociological Jurisprudence," 19 *Green Bag* 607 (1907).
36 Roscoe Pound, *The Ideal Element in Law* (Indianapolis: Liberty Fund 2002) 234.

stance than Pound, but on the need for an instrumental understanding of law they were in complete agreement. According to Llewellyn, the Legal Realists "view rules, they view law, as means to end."[37] This "major tenet" of Legal Realism was supplemented by the insistence that law must be seen as it actually functions, not as an abstract body of rules, concepts, and principles.[38] Law can be understood and improved only by paying close attention to the actual conduct of legal officials in connection with legal rules, and the reactions of members of society to these legal actions. Cook put it succinctly:

> Underlying any scientific study of the law, it is submitted, will lie one fundamental postulate, viz., that human laws are devices, tools which society uses as one of the methods to regulate human conduct and to promote those types of it which are regarded as desirable. If so, it follows that the worth or value of a given rule of law can be determined only by finding out how it works, that is, by ascertaining, so far as it can be done, whether it promotes or retards the attainment of desired ends. If this is to be done, quite clearly we must know what at any given period these ends are and also whether the means selected, the given rules of law, are indeed adapted to securing them.[39]

Most law professors at the time paid attention only to legal doctrine. This is not the reality of the law, the Realists objected. Legal rules are dead letters when legal officials don't enforce them or the public doesn't comply with them. Hence Llewellyn's assertion, "What these officials do about disputes is, to my mind, the law itself."[40] Or as Cook put it, "This past behavior of the judges can be described in terms of certain generalizations which we call rules and principles of law."[41]

The Realists attacked conceptual formalism and rule formalism. Conceptual formalism, as indicated in the previous chapter, was the notion that legal rules, concepts, and principles have predetermined content and implications, and logical interrelations, forming a comprehensive whole, that must be discovered and worked out by judges. "Rule formalism" was the idea that judges mechanically apply the law to arrive at decisions. Cook remarked in 1927 that both remained the standard account of law in law schools, quoting a conceptual formalist statement that "The common law . . . is surely a philosophical system, a body of scientific principle . . . ," and a rule formalist statement that "Every judicial act resulting in a judgment consists of a pure deduction."[42]

---

37 Karl Llewellyn, "Some Realism About Realism – Responding to Dean Pound," 44 *Harvard L. Rev.* 1222, 1223 (1931). An excellent guide to Llewellyn's work, and to Legal Realism generally, is William Twining, *Karl Llewellyn and the Realist Movement* (London: Weidenfeld and Nicolson 1973).
38 M. McDougal, "Fuller v. The American Legal Realists: An Intervention," 50 *Yale L.J.* 827, 834–5 (1941).
39 Walter Wheeler Cook, "Scientific Method and the Law," 13 *A.B.A. Journal* 303, 308 (1927).
40 Karl Llewellyn, *The Bramble Bush* (New York: Oceana 1951) 3.
41 Walter Wheeler Cook, "Scientific Method and the Law," 13 *A.B.A. Journal* 308 (1927).
42 Cook, "Scientific Method and the Law," supra 303, 307 (1927).

Citing the pragmatist critique of abstract concepts, Felix Cohen derisively labeled conceptual formalism "transcendental nonsense" – the "theological jurisprudence of concepts."[43] The content of concepts is not indelibly predetermined but is a matter to be filled in by social choices. When asked whether he believed that legal principles existed, Arthur Corbin gave this realistic response: "Certainly I do. By this I don't mean something handed down from the sky. Instead I mean this: it is possible to group together a number of similar cases (decisions) on which to base a generalization that is usable, subject to change as new cases appear with varying facts."[44] The law as a whole, furthermore, is not a comprehensive, logically consistent system, but rather is a jumble of various influences, which has never been entirely rationalized.

Because the corpus of law, and its connection with facts, are untidy, argued the Realists, the idea that judging is a matter of deduction is false. There are conflicts and gaps among the rules, there are exceptions to every rule, general standards require judgments to be made, and principles can lead to more than one outcome in a given context of application – so judicial decision-making cannot be mechanical.[45] Moreover, the common law system of precedent accords judges wiggle-room when determining what binding rule of law is set forth in a given case, because that determination is often made in later cases.[46] Also, because every situation is unique, judges in later cases may claim they are not bound by an earlier case because the facts are different in crucial respects. Rather than starting from the rules and principles and deductively coming to a decision, the Realists suggested that judges begin instead with a rough sense of the decision and work backward to find supportive legal rules and principles,[47] revising the decision if necessary owing to constraints from the applicable body of rules.[48] Cohen remarked that judges' decisions "usually reflect the attitudes of their own income class on social questions."[49]

Most Realists saw law as a craft engaged in by lawyers and judges rather than as a scientific or philosophical activity. According to the Realists, to summarize, law is neither objectively filled in nor predetermined in any sense, nor is it completely determinate; judges do not reason mechanically, and the law is not a neutral presence standing above the conflict of interests within society. Echoing the legal positivists,

43 Felix Cohen, "Transcendental Nonsense and the Functional Approach," 35 *Columbia L. Rev.* 809, 820–21 (1935).
44 Quoted in *Laura Kalman, Legal Realism at Yale: 1927–1960* (Durham, N.C.: Univ. North Carolina Press 1986) 235, n. 13.
45 Karl Llewellyn, "A Realistic Jurisprudence – The Next Step," 30 *Columbia L. Rev.* 443 (1930).
46 See Herman Oliphant, "A Return to Stare Decisis," 14 *A.B.A. J.* 71 (1928).
47 See Joseph Hutcheson, "The Judgment Intuitive: The Function of a 'Hunch' in the Judicial Decision," 14 *Cornell L. Quarterly* 278 (1929); Jerome Frank, *Law and the Modern Mind* (New York: Doubleday & Co. 1963) 109, 114–21.
48 See Dewey, "Logical Method and Law," supra 23; Hutcheson, "The Judgment Intuitive: The Function of the 'Hunch' in Judicial Decision," supra.
49 Cohen, "Transcendental Nonsense and the Functional Approach," supra 845.

Cohen remarked: "Law commands obedience not because of its goodness, or its Justice, or its rationality, but because of the power behind it."[50]

The main affirmative proposal of early Realism was to urge close social scientific study of how legal institutions actually operate. Llewellyn observed that questions about the "ought" should be set aside temporarily until an adequate understanding what law "is" has been worked out.[51] Acquiring a better understanding of the reality of law is a prerequisite to improving the functioning and efficiency of law as an instrument of social engineering.

To understand Legal Realism, it is important to recognize that the ideas they promoted within law were also circulating more generally. As indicated earlier, a general revolt was taking place against formalist ways of thinking, urging greater attention to concrete reality. The instrumental perspective of the pragmatists found willing converts in many arenas of thought. Furthermore, the notion that judicial decisions were marked by bias did not originate with the Realists. A prominent political scientist in 1909 acknowledged the "popular criticism of the judicial branch of our government as unduly favorable to the so-called vested interests."[52]

Doubts about objectivity had penetrated many disciplines. Take, for example, Charles Beard's 1937 reflections on the objectivity of the historical method: "Every student of history knows that his colleagues have been influenced in their selection and ordering of materials by their biases, prejudices, beliefs, affections, general upbringing and experience, particularly social and economic."[53] Beard believed that historians could more closely approximate the goal of objectivity "if they acknowledged and stated their biases openly than if they imagined from the start that their commitment to science somehow made them free of bias."[54] Substitute "judge" for "historian" and "law" for "science," and these observations could have been written by the Realists about judges. These were the concerns of the day across the range of intellectual pursuits.

Even the notion that the social scientific study of law should concentrate on what *is* rather than on questions about *ought* was not unique to the Realists. A debate among political scientists occured in the 1930s and 1940s along identical lines, with many taking the position that "the study of politics can be or become scientific only when the study of means is divorced sharply from a consideration of ends."[55]

The Realists also reflected the bleak economic circumstances of the Depression era, according to historian G. Edward White, and the "whatever it takes to get it done" attitude of those endeavoring to remedy the situation. "In undertaking this task their environment was one of economic deprivation; their mood, cynicism; their fantasy

---

50 Id. 837.
51 Karl Llewellyn, "Some Realism About Realism," 44 *Harvard L. Rev.* 1234 (1931).
52 W.F. Dodd, "The Growth of Judicial Power," 24 *Pol. Sci. Quarterly* 193, 201 (1909).
53 Charles A. Beard, "Written History as an Act of Faith," 39 *Am. Hist. Rev.* 219, 220 (1934).
54 Hofstadter, *Progressive Historians*, supra 315.
55 John Hallowell, "Politics and Ethics," 38 *Am. Pol. Sci. Rev.* 639, 640 (1944).

heroes, hardboiled men of action; their academic tools, the behavioral sciences; their philosophy of government, experimentalist and pragmatic. The demythologizing tendencies of the Realists, their commitment to decision-making by experiment, their preference for empiricism rather than abstraction, even their questioning of moral absolutes, were in harmony with the spirit of the first New Deal."[56]

The realism of the legal establishment view

The Realists are generally regarded as radicals who raised a sharp challenge to the legal establishment. Many of their observations about judging were deliberately provocative (Holmes and Cardozo had said similar things earlier with less stridency). But consider this passage from Elihu Root's 1916 Presidential Address to the bar:

> The vast and continually increasing mass of reported decisions which afford authorities on almost every side of almost every question admonish us that by the mere following of precedent we should soon have no system of law at all, but the rule of the Turkish cadi who is expected to do in each case what seems to him to be right . . .

> The natural course for the development of our law and institutions does not follow the line of pure reason or the demands of scientific method.[57]

The thrust of the Realists' indeterminacy argument, and their denial that law is a matter of deduction and science, was stated by Root to a large gathering of lawyers a dozen years before the Realists. Root also recognized the gap between law in the books and social reality: "No matter what legislatures and congresses and publicists and judges may do, the people are making their own law today as truly as in the earlier periods of the growth of the common law. No statute can ever long impose a law upon them which they do not assimilate. Whether repealed or not it will be rejected and become a dead letter."[58]

Root recognized that modern mass society cannot be based on former individualist notions, and he perceived that the United States was inexorably "entering upon the creation of a body of administrative law quite different in its machinery, its remedies, and its necessary safeguards from the old methods of regulation by specific statutes enforced by courts."[59] Root saw, moreover, that law was being used instrumentally by legislatures to advance group interests and by lawyers to advance their own and their clients' interests. In one sense, Root was more realistic than the coming Realists. They advocated idealistically that law should be viewed as an instrument to advance the social good. Informed by insights gained from his own experiences (and perhaps conduct) as a corporate lawyer, Root lamented that

56 G. Edward White, *Patterns of American Jurisprudence* (Charlottesville, Va.: Michie 1978) 139.
57 Root, "Address of the President," supra 364.
58 Id. 269–70.
59 Id. 368.

legislation and lawyers frequently promoted private interests that did not serve the public good.

The realists' quest for certainty in law

In view of the relish with which the Realists lambasted conceptual and rule formalist bromides of judges and legal scientists, it is easy to think that their intention was to demonstrate the inherent indeterminacy of law and the inevitable influence that politics has on judicial decisions. A number of Realist works can be read in this way. But most Realists hoped that the social scientific study of law would lead to reforms that enhance the functioning of law.[60] They challenged conceptual and rule formalist accounts of the nature and extent of legal certainty, but not the proposition that law *should be* substantially certain. Holmes, their intellectual hero, energetically advocated objective tests to make the law more predictable, and insisted "that the efforts of law must always be directed to narrow the zone of uncertainty as far as possible."[61] Llewellyn urged that "What law needs is a manageable degree of certainty and predictability – enough to get on with."[62]

To get at the implications of this point, it is necessary to pry apart the Realists' critiques of formalism. As indicated earlier, classical non-instrumental views of law overlapped with conceptual formalism, which is an account of the content and logical interconnections of legal principles and concepts. But non-instrumental views of law did not espouse rule formalism, which is an account of judging. These two kinds of formalism, accordingly, must be considered independently. One may deny that legal rules and principles have any predetermined content yet believe that judges mechanically deduce the outcomes from a given set of legal rules and principles. Conversely, one may accept that legal rules and principles have predetermined content, yet admit that they cannot mechanically or deductively lead to outcomes in specific cases. Other permutations are possible, which need not be covered here.

The Realists were complete skeptics of conceptual formalism. They were adamant that there is no *necessary* content to legal rules, principles, and concepts. This argument directly bears upon, and denies, the central claim of classical non-instrumental views of law. The content of law is entirely open, a matter to be filled in or modified depending upon the social ends desired and the circumstances of their intended realization. The one aspect of conceptual formalism that survives the Realist critique is the common sense recommendation that when filling in content it is generally better that the rules and principles be logical and consistent with one another. "[L]ogical systematization with a view to the utmost generality and consistency of propositions is indispensable but is not ultimate," Dewey wrote. "It is an instrumentality, not an end. It is a means of improving, facilitating, clarifying, the inquiry

60 See Kalman, *Legal Realism at Yale*, supra Chap. 1.
61 M. Cohen, *Law and the Social Order*, supra 204.
62 Quoted in Kalman, *Legal Realism at Yale*, supra 8.

that leads up to concrete decisions. . . . It is most important that rules of law should form as coherent generalized logical systems as possible."[63]

With respect to rule formalism, although they did deny the mechanistic account of judicial decision-making, the Realists (except for rule skeptics like Jerome Frank) did not abjure the core kernel underlying rule formalism that legal rules can and should be binding upon legal officials and judges. The proposition that legal rules and principles had no binding effect owing to irrepressible and rampant indeterminacy would have been antithetical to their expressed faith in law. There is no point in advocating that legal concepts and rules be shaped instrumentally to serve social interests if every judge or public official will simply do whatever he or she desires regardless of what the legal rules say. An instrumental view of law, for this reason, presupposes the formal binding aspect of legal rules: Law is an effective tool for the achievement of social purposes when legal rules are consistently adhered to by those to whom it is addressed (legal officials and public). The Realists recognized that the utility of legal rules is enhanced when their applications are more predictable, which enables people to plan their activities with foreknowledge of their likely legal consequences. Dewey thus insisted that "There is of course every reason why rules of law should be as regular and definite as possible."[64]

A key implication of Dewey's observations is that a consistent legal instrumentalist can be led by instrumental considerations to adopt a formalist position on adhering to rules. There is no question that Holmes, for similar reasons, was committed to certainty and predictability in law, as was Pound, and both thought that legal rules possess a binding quality that ought to be respected by legal officials, especially judges.[65]

The intractable problem of ends in law

In an intra-family contretemps, in the 1930's, Pound attacked the Realists, with whom he had much in common,[66] for going too far in their critiques of judicial decision-making, exaggerating the freedom judges enjoy when rendering decisions.[67] He also came to believe that the Legal Realists had emptied the law of its moral resources.[68] A few Realists explicitly embraced moral relativism as an implication of modern scientific and philosophical views.[69]

---

63 Dewey, "Logical Method and Law," supra 19.
64 Id. 25.
65 See Duxbury, *Patterns of American Jurisprudence*, supra Chap. 1; Gilmore, *Ages of American Law*, supra.
66 See Summers, *Instrumentalism and American Legal Theory*, supra 19–38. It should also be noted that not all Realists were pragmatic instrumentalists and not all pragmatic instrumentalists were Realists. Duxbury, *Patterns of American Jurisprudence*, supra 70–1.
67 Roscoe Pound, "The Call for a Realist Jurisprudence," 44 *Harvard L. Rev.* 697 (1931).
68 Roscoe Pound, "The Future of Law," 47 *Yale L. J.* 2 (1937).
69 See Cook, "Scientific Method and the Law," supra 306; Underhill Moore, "Rational Basis of Legal Institutions," 23 *Columbia L. Rev.* 612 (1923). Purcell discusses this aspect of Realism in Purcell, *The Crisis of Democratic Theory*, supra 90–4.

A revealing irony for legal instrumentalism is that this very objection was earlier lodged against Pound. In "Pragmatism as a Philosophy of Law," published in 1925, Walter Kennedy noted that Pound rejected the concept of natural rights,[70] and promoted the satisfaction of social needs as "the final objective of law."[71] Kennedy quoted the following passage from Pound: " . . . if in any field of human conduct or in any human relation the law, with such machinery as it has, may satisfy a social want without a disproportionate sacrifice of other claims, there is no eternal limitation inherent in the nature of things, there are no bounds imposed at creation, to stand in the way of its doing so."[72] Kennedy responded that there are many "social wants," some of which are good and some not, and, furthermore, that there are conflicting social wants. Pound's answer: "I do not believe the jurist has to do more than recognize the problem and perceive that it is presented to him as one of securing all social interests so far as he may, of maintaining a balance or harmony among them that is compatible with the securing of all of them."[73]

Kennedy considered this inadequate: "Pragmatism has been frequently criticized because it is in a sense anarchistic and devoid of standards or principles . . . As a practical science, law requires an appreciable degree of uniformity, stability and certainty. It does not suffice to shuffle the mass of wants and claims of the litigants into a confused pile and then give effect to as many of them as we can in so far as harmony will permit."

The importance of Kennedy's point is more evident with the benefit of hindsight. A crucial shortcoming of Pound and of the Realists in his wake was a naïve or underdeveloped view of how to identify the social ends law was to serve. A number of Realists accepted utilitarianism; others thought social science could help provide answers;[74] others apparently thought, like Pound, that a happy balance among competing social interests could be arrived at; others said nothing on the subject. Promoting an instrumental understanding of law without attention to resolving the question of ends is woefully incomplete. On instrumentalist terms – that is, according to its own criteria – the question of whether it is wise to advocate an instrumental view of law cannot be answered without factoring in how it will work out in practice. If it turns out that law will not be used to achieve social ends or the common good, then an instrumental approach might work against the ends desired.

Kennedy continued:

> Pragmatism worships at the altar of social reform. The pages of the sociologist teem with the inequalities of our social, marital, and industrial relations. Ingenious remedies are poured forth which aim to make even the path of mankind. Inevitably these proposals

70 Walter B. Kennedy, "Pragmatism as a Philosophy of Law," 9 *Marquette L. Rev.* 63, 68 (1924–25).
71 Id. 69.
72 Id. 69, quoting R. Pound, *An Introduction to the Philosophy of Law* (1922) 97–8.
73 Id. 71, quoting Pound, *An Introduction to the Philosophy of Law*, 95–6.
74 See Martin P. Golding, "Jurisprudence and Legal Philosophy in Twentieth Century America – Major Themes and Developments," 36 *J. Legal Educ.* 441, 453 (1986).

are directed to the state as the effective instrument to give them effect. . . . If we accept the formula that law exists solely to give effect to 'claims' and 'wants,' it is difficult to question this sudden rush to state and federal Legislatures for relief against all real or imaginary pains and aches of the body politic, but there is grave doubt whether the law is capable of absorbing the tasks of social and religious reformation. . . . If there is weight in this criticism of the present day tendency to legislate society into a state of perfection, to erase the shortcomings of human relations by government intervention, the pragmatic jurist must bear a goodly part of the responsibility; they are the tangible results of the endeavor to infuse into statutes all the demands of the people without the stabilizing influences of Constitutional principles or the dictates of natural rights.[75]

Kennedy was wrong if he meant to blame Pound's pragmatic instrumentalist approach for causing the rush to legislatures by groups seeking relief. This practice, incited by events external to legal thought, was already well underway in the late nineteenth century before Pound first suggested it. Kennedy was correct, however, that pragmatic instrumentalist legal theory was consistent with this practice and provided it with theoretical underpinnings and respectability.

Kennedy's article presaged the firestorm of opposition raised against Realism (and pragmatic philosophy) in the mid-to-late 1930s and 1940s. World War II and its aftermath prompted a collective reaffirmation that U.S. society and values were good and right, morally superior to the evils of Nazism (and Communism).[76] Many of the most horrific actions of the Nazi regime were committed by the government in the name of law. It became urgent to confirm that U.S. law was nothing like Nazi law. The Legal Realists were roundly chastised for suggesting – uncharitably interpreted that way by opponents – that law was a matter of power, with no integrity unto itself, and for their moral relativism.[77] Robert Hutchins, the former Dean of Yale Law School and later the President of the University of Chicago, an early exponent of Realist views, became a severe critic, concluding that science had little to offer to law.[78] He advocated a return to natural law thought: "We know that there is a natural moral law," Hutchins affirmed in 1943, "and we can understand what it is because we know that man has a nature, and we can understand it. The nature of man, which is the same everywhere, is obscured but not obliterated by the differing conventions of different cultures. . . . [M]an is a rational and spiritual being."[79] Subject to this withering attack, several of the Realists publicly repented. "I for one am ready to do open penance," wrote Llewellyn, "for any part I may have played for giving occasion for the feeling that modern jurisprudes or any of them have ever lost sight of this

---

75 Kennedy, "Pragmatism as a Philosophy of Law," supra 72–3.
76 Purcell, *The Crisis of Democratic Theory*, supra Chaps. 7, 8, 9, 10. Purcell's book is an outstanding intellectual history of the Realists.
77 See Lucey, "Natural Law and American Legal Realism: Their Respective Contributions to a Theory of Law in a Democratic Society," 30 *Georgetown L. J.* 493 (1942) (suggesting that the pragmatism and relativism of Legal Realism encourages absolutism).
78 Purcell, *Crisis of Democratic Theory*, supra Chap. 8.
79 Quoted in John Dewey, "Challenge to Liberal Thought," 30 *Fortune* 155, 180 (1944).

[ethical component of law]."[80] Other Realists suggested that they had been unfairly mischaracterized.[81]

Legal Realism was effectively silenced.

These are formidable difficulties for legal instrumentalism, which Pound grappled with valiantly. But proponents of non-instrumental views of law suffer from their own critical defect. Kennedy inadvertently demonstrated this when he (progressively) argued, citing a Papal encyclical among other sources, that natural law doctrines support the legislative enactment of a minimum wage to provide for living necessities. Kennedy surely knew that others believed that a legislated minimum wage infringed upon the liberty of contract, and, furthermore, that Papal encyclicals were not universally authoritative. Given the manifold complexities of modern social life, how are the contents and implications of liberty of contract, right to property, due process, and so on, to be determined in any given situation? Especially intransigent complications arise when a community is heterogeneous or the culture or society consists of alternative or conflicting circulating principles, values, or interests. It is no solution to place faith in judges because they disagree among themselves over such questions. Jurists committed to a non-instrumental approach to law are thus put to the test at precisely the same spot that they skewer instrumentalists. They dismiss the instrumentalists for lacking limits on the uses of law; the instrumentalists respond that said limits will always be controversial.

The root source of this shared dilemma is not unique to law – it is the modern condition, the culmination of streams of ideas set in motion with the seventeenth-century scientific revolution and the eighteenth-century Enlightenment (and before that, with the Protestant Reformation, which broke the centuries-long intellectual domination of Europe by the Roman Catholic Church). The pragmatists and the Realists were merely taking note of developments across all fields of knowledge, in which objectivity, universal values, and absolute truths were losing their former grounding. The invention of non-Euclidean geometry shook the formerly unquestioned dominance of Euclidean geometry as objectively and exclusively correct; Einstein's theory of space–time relativity dethroned Newton's mechanistic laws and raised questions about the status of scientific theories, which theretofore were thought to discover unshakable truths; Heisenberg's uncertainty principle suggested that the very act of observation shapes and alters what is seen; anthropological studies revealed for academic and popular consumption the abundance of diverse moral systems. Cultural meaning systems and individual subjectivity appeared to color everything. In his 1927 essay, "Scientific Method and the Law," Walter Wheeler Cook pointed to several of these developments to predict that "The reign of relativity thus inaugurated by the basic sciences, is destined to work a corresponding

---

80 Karl Llewellyn, "On Reading and Using the Newer Jurisprudence," 40 *Columbia L. Rev.* 593, 603 (1940)
81 See Purcell, *The Crisis of Democratic Theory*, supra 172–4. This discussion is indebted to Purcell's account.

revolution, deep, noiseless it may be, but inevitable, in all the views and institutions of man."[82]

Logical positivism also contributed to the deepening the crisis over values. This school of philosophy argued that all true or correct judgments are either analytic – a judgment is correct owing to the meaning of the terms – or empirical – a judgment is correct if it can be verified in relation to facts. Questions of value, which fit neither category, cannot be adjudged correct or true.[83] A critic protested in 1944 that "The effect of this trend toward positivism was to undermine all belief in transcendental truth and value. Value judgments were considered to be expressions of subjective preference rather than of objective truth."[84]

Another contributor to the mix of ideas that undermined confidence in values was Marxist theory, especially popular among Leftist intellectuals in the 1920s through 1940s. Engels wrote:

> We . . . reject every presumptuous attempt to impose upon us any dogmatic morality whatever as eternal, final, immutable ethical laws under the pretext that also the moral world has its permanent principles which stand above history and national differences. We maintain, on the contrary, that all past theories of morality are the product, in the last instance, of the contemporary economic conditions of society. And just as society hitherto has moved in class antagonisms, so has morality always been a class morality.[85]

The Marxist notion of ideology undercut moral argument in a pernicious way. By suggesting that entire complexes of beliefs, including *sincerely held* political ideals and moral values, mask specific class interests unbeknownst to (behind the backs of) the people who hold those beliefs, all moral positions are rendered suspect. "What people say they believe cannot always be taken at face value, and one must search for the structure of interests beneath the ideas; one looks not at the *content* of ideas, but their *function*."[86] This skeptical view spread well beyond adherents of Marxism.

Owing to ideas and forces beyond the control of the Realists, therefore, the dynamic that provides the centerpiece of this book – the rise of instrumental thinking about law, coinciding with the penetration of relativist views that would undercut the notion of the social good – was set in motion before the 1940s. The Realists' sanguine attitude toward the problem of the proper ends of law was a failing, but it was not theirs alone, as it was a quandary for which no one had answers. Although they have been saddled with some of the blame for subsequent events, an argument can be made that the Realists had a belated role in these affairs: An instrumental

---

82 Cook, "Scientific Method and Law," supra 306.
83 Brand Blanshard, "The New Subjectivism in Ethics," 9 *Philosophy and Phenomenological Research* 504 (1949).
84 Hallowell, "Politics and Ethics," supra 643.
85 Friedrich Engels, translated and quoted in Daniel Bell, *The End of Ideology* (Cambridge, Mass.: Harvard Univ. Press 2001) 448.
86 Id. 397.

approach was a fact of law, at least with respect to legislation, well before the Realists advocated it, and moral relativism was a society wide dilemma not unique to law.

Pound, in his later years, expressed regret about his earlier espousal of a purely instrumental approach to law. To locate restraints, he called for a "revived natural law of today." "Today the role of the ideal element in law and the need of a canon of values and technique of applying it are recognized by all. . ."[87] But Pound could not forget that courts had thrown up reactionary barriers to social reform in the name of protecting natural rights and the integrity of the common law. To guard against this, he proposed that a theory of judicial decision must be developed which recognizes "that the legal order has always been and is a system of practical compromises between conflicting and overlapping human claims or wants or desires in which the continual pressure of these claims and of the claims involved in civilized social life has compelled lawmakers and judges and administrators to seek to satisfy the most of the scheme of claims as a whole with the least sacrifice."[88] Pound was at war with himself: the reformist legal instrumentalist, on the one hand, and the jurist dedicated to the integrity of law and worried about the excesses of legal instrumentalism, on the other. Pound's final major work was a search for *The Ideal Element in Law* (1958) to provide some kind of restraint on legal instrumentalism.[89] He came up empty.

87 Roscoe Pound, *The Formative Era of American Law* (Boston: Little Brown 1938) 28–9.
88 Id. 125–6.
89 Roscoe Pound, *The Ideal Element in Law* (Indianapolis: Liberty Fund 2002 [1958]).

5

Twentieth-century Supreme Court instrumentalism

A 1909 article on the courts by political scientist W.F. Dodd observed that "In this field [public policy] decisions of the courts necessarily depend not upon any fixed rules of law but upon the individual opinions of the judges on political and economic questions; and such decisions, resting, as they must, upon no general principles, will be especially subject to reversal or modification when changes take place in the personnel of the courts."[1] Dodd presciently encapsulated what became the standout theme surrounding the twentieth-century Supreme Court. This chapter conveys how judging and judges on the Supreme Court in several different ways came to be perceived in instrumental terms. The events covered are the 1937 Court Packing Plan and its aftermath, the reforms brought by the Warren Court, and the backlash against those reforms as they played out in connection with later Supreme Courts, leading up to the present.

Court packing plan

President Franklin D. Roosevelt's failed 1937 "court packing plan" has been characterized as a "great constitutional war,"[2] which culminated in a "constitutional revolution."[3] It was the closest the country had come to a genuine constitutional crisis since the Civil War and Reconstruction.

Roosevelt's New Deal legislative program was an attempt to find solutions to the ongoing economic crisis and to ameliorate the most desperate social and economic consequences that continued to linger from the recent Depression. Key pieces of legislation in this effort were the Railroad Retirement Act, which mandated that pensions be created by railroad companies for their employees, the National Industrial Recovery Act (NIRA), which authorized rulemaking powers in the Executive branch to handle all sorts of economic issues, the Agricultural Adjustment Act,

---

1 Dodd, "Growth of Judicial Power," supra 198.
2 Marian C. McKenna, *Franklin Roosevelt and the Great Constitutional War: The Court Packing Crisis of 1937* (New York: Fordham Univ. Press 2002).
3 Constitutional law scholar Edwin Corwin is credited with coining this phrase in the 1941 book with that title. See also William E. Leuchtenburg, *The Supreme Court Reborn: the Constitutional Revolution in the Age of Roosevelt* (New York: Oxford University Press 1995).

which authorized price and production controls to support the recovery of farmers, and the Bituminous Coal Act, aimed at helping the crippled coal industry by setting prices and establishing labor regulations that would lessen strikes. All four of these New Deal statutes were invalidated by the Supreme Court in its 1935–6 term.[4] The specific grounds cited by the Court for invalidation were different in each case, but they collectively served as a warning that the New Deal would not pass through the Supreme Court unscathed. As if to belligerently underscore its opposition to social welfare legislation, the Court ended the term by invalidating New York's enactment of a minimum wage law for women.[5]

Except for the unanimous striking of the NIRA as an impermissible delegation of power, these decisions were by split votes, confirming for observers their tenuousness. Justices Louis D. Brandeis, Harlan Fiske Stone, and Benjamin N. Cardozo could generally be counted on to support social welfare legislation; Justices Willis Van Devanter, James McReynolds, George Sutherland, and Pierce Butler were steadfastly against it; Chief Justice Charles Evans Hughes and Justice Owen J. Roberts were swing votes.[6] Hughes was more inclined to line up with supporters, so the tendency of the Court was a four-to-four split, leaving Roberts as the determinative vote.

Roosevelt was incensed by these decisions, but said little publicly about the Court in the year leading up to the election, perhaps not to add fuel to the Republican campaign theme that he was determined to have his way, even at the expense of the Constitution.[7] Roosevelt won by a historic margin, taking all but two small states. Democrats obtained huge majorities in the House and Senate, leading some to speculate about demise of the Republican Party. It was seen not just as a great victory for Roosevelt but also as a resounding rebuke of the Court. "Although they appeared on no ballot, the justices plainly lost the election. The election, commented one newspaper, yielded 'a roar in which cheers for the Supreme Court were drowned out.' Voters overwhelmingly validated what the Supreme Court had invalidated."[8]

Two-and-a-half weeks after his inauguration for a new term, with no advance warning to the Congress and apparently little consultation with his circle of advisors,[9] Roosevelt announced his plan: Congress should enact a law to create an additional position for every judge in the federal judiciary over the age of seventy. Roosevelt justified the plan as a way to solve the backlog in the processing of cases, which he attributed to the slower working pace of aged judges. He said not a word

4 Invalidating these statutes, in respective order: *Railroad Retirement Board v. Alton R.R.Co.*, 295 US 330 (1935); *Schechter Poultry Corp. v. United States*, 295 US 495 (1935); *United States v. Butler*, 297 US 1 (1936); *Carter v. Carter Coal Co.*, 298 US 238 (1936).

5 *Morehead v. New York ex rel Tipaldo*, 298 US 587 (1936).

6 A fascinating account of the individual justices and their votes in this period is in Fred Rodell, *Nine Men: A Political History of the Supreme Court from 1790 to 1955* (New York: Random House 1955) Chap. 7.

7 Donald Grier Stephenson, *Campaign and the Courts: The US Supreme Court in Presidential Elections* (New York: Columbia Univ. Press 1999) 149–53.

8 Id. 154.

9 See Leuchtenburg, *Supreme Court Reborn*, supra 82–3.

(until over a month later) about what was evident to all – that he would be able to immediately appoint six compliant justices to the Supreme Court, increasing its size to fifteen, effectively ending the Court's opposition to his New Deal legislative program.

The idea was a disaster, a terrible stumble for this usually adroit politician. Historians who have studied the event remain mystified about his strategic misreading in the preparation and presentation of the plan. Roosevelt was roundly accused of duplicity for failing to disclose his true purpose. It was painted in the press as a frontal attack on the Court by an overreaching dictator and a threat to the nation's historic tradition of an independent judiciary.[10] Even members of his party in Congress came out vocally against the plan. Polls showed a majority of the public against the plan.[11] Most of the opposition was not based upon support for the Court's recent decisions,[12] but rather on the grounds that the proper way to deal with the Court was through the unwieldy but more legitimate process of seeking an amendment to the Constitution. When explaining to the public why that alternative was insufficient, Roosevelt observed, with a strong dose of realism, that "An amendment, like the rest of the Constitution, is what the Justices say it is rather than what its framers or you might hope it is."[13] Another preferred solution, said opponents, would have been to use the acknowledged power of Congress to restrict the Court's appellate jurisdiction, lessening its opportunities to invalidate economic legislation. Roosevelt's attempt to tamper with the institutional structure of the Court itself just went too far. The plan was killed in the Senate in July of 1937.

Less than two months after the plan was announced, the Supreme Court upheld a Washington minimum wage law that was identical to the New York legislation it had invalidated just ten months prior.[14] The decision was widely perceived as a hasty, almost unseemly retreat by the Court prompted by the plan, though in fact (unknown at the time) the case was voted upon by the Justices prior to Roosevelt's announcement of the plan.[15] In subsequent months, the Court upheld the National Labor Relations Act,[16] which protected labor organizing, and the Social Security Act, which created unemployment and old-age benefits.[17] These decisions were patently contrary to the letter and spirit of the anti-New Deal cases decided just the previous term. And the Court made no real attempt to distinguish the earlier

10 McKenna, *Franklin Roosevelt and the Great Constitutional War*, supra 303–11.
11 Stephenson, *Campaigns and the Court*, supra 157 cites a Gallup Poll that shows public opposition at 50 percent against to 35 percent for.
12 The Court decisions were not universally unpopular. See Barbara A. Perry and Henry J. Abraham, "Franklin Roosevelt and the Supreme Court: A New Deal and a New Image, in *Franklin D. Roosevelt and the Transformation of the Supreme Court*, edited by Stephen K. Shaw, William D. Pederson, and Frank J. Williams (Armonk, NY: M.E. Sharp Pub. 2004) 13–35.
13 Roosevelt's fireside chat, quoted in Bruce Ackerman, *We the People: Foundations* (Cambridge, Mass.: Harvard Univ. Press 1991) 417.
14 *West Coast Hotel v. Parrish*, 300 US 379 (1937).
15 Bernard Schwartz, *A History of the Supreme Court* (New York: Oxford Univ. Press 1993) 235.
16 *National Labor Relations Board v. Jones & Laughlin Steel Corp.*, 301 US 1 (1937).
17 *Steward Machine Co. v. Davis*, 301 US 538 (1937); *Helvering v. Davis*, 301 US 619 (1937).

cases or to explain the change in tack. Primarily responsible for the reversal was a switch in sides by Roberts, along with more consistent support by Hughes. Justice Van Devanter announced his retirement effective in June of that summer. Four new appointments came in the next two years. The Supreme Court would not again strike economic legislation for impinging upon constitutional limits.

"A switch in time saved nine." So went a popular saying that captured the widespread perception about what was behind this sudden and complete turnabout in the Court's jurisprudence.[18] Roosevelt observed that "It would be a little naïve to refuse to recognize some connection between these decisions and the Supreme Court fight."[19] For many observers, these events confirmed that judges respond to political influences, whether pressure from the President or reading the election returns.[20]

Justices who later spoke about the event denied that they had caved to pressure. A few scholars support their assertion.[21] Barry Cushman has argued that the origin of the shift lies in the earlier collapse of the unstable public/private doctrine – the notion that businesses affected with a public interest (like railroads) could be regulated solely with respect to those interests – which the court had used to distinguish legitimate from illegitimate legislation.[22] In *Nebbia v. New York*, decided in 1934, the Court upheld price regulation of private milk producers, marking a major change in approach. Justice Roberts wrote for the majority that "a state is free to adopt whatever economic policy may reasonably be deemed to promote the public welfare, and to enforce that policy by legislation adapted to its purpose. The courts are without authority either to declare such policy, or, when it is declared by the legislature, to override it."[23] This rationale discarded the stricter "businesses affected with the public interest" test in lieu of a broader "promote the public welfare" standard, to be applied by courts with a deferential posture toward the judgment of legislatures.

Whether it was the pressure of the plan or the internal development of constitutional doctrine that prompted the 1937 decisions upholding social welfare legislation is of secondary significance for the purposes of this book. The critical point is the nigh universal *perception* that the external pressure on the Court did the trick. The deeper message for observers from this event was that judicial interpretations

---

18 The reality is that, prior to these events, the Hughes Court already had been progressively more lenient toward social welfare legislation, upholding a far greater proportion of this legislation than the predecessor Taft Court. See Roger W. Corley, "Was There a Constitutional Revolution in 1937," in *Franklin D. Roosevelt*, supra 36–59.

19 Quoted in Schwartz, *History of the Supreme Court*, supra 237.

20 See Robert A. Dahl, "Decision-making in a Democracy: The Supreme Court as a National Policymaker," 6 *J. Public Law* 283 (1957), arguing that the Court generally remains in step with dominant public opinion.

21 See G. Edward White, "Constitutional Change and the New Deal: The Internalist/Externalist Debate," 110 *Am. Hist. Rev.* 1094 (2005).

22 Barry Cushman, *Rethinking the New Deal Court: The Structure of a Constitutional Revolution* (New York: Oxford Univ. Press 1998) Chap. 1.

23 *Nebbia*, 291 U.S. at 537 (McReynolds, dissenting).

of the Constitution were, beyond doubt, a product of the views of the individual Justices, demonstrating this more convincingly than all the Realist articles put together. Roberts formalistically stated in one of the 1936 cases striking legislation that the sole duty of the Court in constitutional challenges was "to lay the article of the Constitution which is invoked beside the statute which is challenged and to decide whether the latter squares with the former."[24] Yet this laying of the texts side-by-side yielded radically contrasting results from one year to the next. Justices could no longer credibly claim that they were legal oracles merely pronouncing on the written words of the document. According to historian G. Edward White, by the mid-1930s, *before* the court packing plan, many commentators believed that judging could be "infused with ideological presuppositions";[25] what transpired subsequent to the announcement of the plan clinched this view.

Witnessing these events, Roosevelt's Attorney General, Robert Jackson, wrote that "the spectacle of the Court that day frankly and completely reversing itself and striking down its opinion but a few months old was a moment never to be forgotten."[26] Jackson marveled at the fact that "many of the old precedents which so restricted the Constitution were overruled by the identical Court which had previously invoked them."[27] This drove home the lesson that a change of mind, or membership, of one or two individuals on the Supreme Court could have political and legal consequences affecting millions of people.

Implications for an instrumental view of law

Following the rapidly altered composition of the Court, a string of cases issued overruling longstanding precedent. *Lochner,* which had been silently abandoned by the Court in 1917,[28] then revived in 1923,[29] then silently abandoned again in *Nebbia,* was finally explicitly repudiated.[30] Judges would no longer pass on the wisdom of economic legislation. A case famous among lawyers, *Erie R.R. Co. v. Tompkins,* decided in 1938, overruled a century-old precedent, Justice Story's *Swift v. Tyson,* mentioned in Chapter 2 as a classic example of a non-instrumental understanding of law. The Court held that there is no such thing as a general federal body of common law, notwithstanding the fact that federal courts had rendered decisions based upon this nonexistent law for the preceding hundred years.[31]

The downfall of *Swift* represents the official death knell of the once-dominant non-instrumental view of law. To the New Deal–friendly Court, this classical

---

24 *United States v. Butler,* 297 U.S. 1, 62 (1936).
25 White, "Constitutional Change and the New Deal," supra.
26 Robert H. Jackson, *The Struggle for Judicial Supremacy: A Study of Crisis in American Power Politics* (New York: Vintage 1941) 207–8.
27 Id. 235.
28 Bunting v. Oregon, 243 U.S. 426 (1917), upholding a maximum hour law for factory workers.
29 *Adkins v. Children's Hosp.,* 261 U.S. 525 (1923), striking minimum wage law.
30 See *Lincoln Federal Labor Union v. Northwestern Iron and Metal Co.,* 335 US 525, 535 (1949).
31 *Erie R.R. Co. v. Tompkins,* 304 US 64 (1938), overruling *Swift v. Tyson,* 41 US 1 (1842).

understanding was a threatening aspect of *Lochner* and its ilk's attempt to constitutionalize common law principles. "Within this traditional framework, the common law of property, contract and tort was not the outcome of political will, but the product of judicial reason . . . "[32] In *Erie*, however, "Brandeis exposed the 'common law' as another name for the exercise [by courts] of sheer political will."[33] The implication of this recognition was to reaffirm that the presumptive locus of law-making power was not in courts but in legislatures. "Henceforward, it was unconstitutional for the Court to indulge rationalist fantasies about the common law . . . ; these common law frameworks were merely judicial expedients that could be revised at will by democratic majorities."[34]

With no constitutional amendment, the Court's interpretation of the Constitution on issues of fundamental importance was altered; in particular, federal legislative authority over the economy expanded dramatically. Before joining the Court, when still Governor of the state of New York, Chief Justice Hughes had observed that "We are under a Constitution, but the Constitution is what the judges say it is."[35] Events during his tenure proved this point to a certainty.

The radical change in the meaning of the Constitution was tantamount to a set of constitutional amendments, much like the Reconstruction Amendments (13th, 14th, 15th) that emerged from the Civil War. Bruce Ackerman, a prominent constitutional scholar, has pressed exactly this argument – that the overwhelming electoral support for Roosevelt's New Deal initiatives, and the enduring alteration in constitutional doctrines that resulted, represent a de facto amendment of the constitution.[36] Not only are the changes in constitutional doctrine therefore legitimate, according to Ackerman, but they should be secure from a reinterpretation by a more conservative Supreme Court, at least until an equally overwhelming popular uprising demands a conservative counterrevolution.

Set aside the merits of Ackerman's argument, and contemplate instead what it says about the U.S. legal culture that prominent constitutional theorists would seriously propose that changes in court interpretations of law are functionally and normatively *equivalent* to amending the words of the Constitution. This is a dramatic assertion of the interpretive power judges possess to fill in the words of a legal provision with meaning, basically equivalent to the power to write the words to begin with. Ackerman is cognizant that there are major differences between legislatures writing on a blank slate and judges writing on an already engraved slate, but in the end both get to write. Under this view, law is an empty vessel that can be determined by will (legislative or judicial), even when its terms have already been filled in.

---

32 Ackerman, *We the People*, supra 370.
33 Id. 371.
34 Id. 371–2.
35 Hughes, *Charles Evans, Addresses* (New York 1908) 139, quoted in Sidney Ratner, "Was the Supreme Court Packed by President Grant," 1 *Pol. Sci. Quarterly* 343 (1935).
36 Bruce Ackerman, *We the People*, supra.

Recognition of the power held by judges to import new meaning through interpretation compels combatants engaged in the struggle over law to carry the struggle into the judicial arena as well. If the only stage that matters is writing the law, the battles would remain centered on the legislatures. If victories in the legislative process can be defeated through court rulings, or if the meaning of a law can be rewritten (or narrowed or twisted) by judges, then the battle is not won until the courts are secured. Ackerman recognized that one of the continuing consequences wrought by the 1937 revolution was "the self-conscious use of *transformative judicial appointments* as a central *tool* for constitutional change."[37]

A separate development that would have relevance for legal instrumentalism was the disavowal by the Court of the power to scrutinize the wisdom or sincerity of legislative decisions. As indicated earlier, a standard view of the nineteenth century was that the legislative power was limited to the enactment of legislation that furthered the common good. "[T]he underlying philosophy held that the only legitimate goal of government in general, and of the police power in particular, was to protect individual rights and otherwise enhance the *total* public good; if they were to be upheld, governmental regulations thus had to promote 'the general welfare' and not be 'purely for the promotion of private interests.'"[38] Pursuant to this philosophy, courts evaluated the propriety of the ends of legislation, striking those that failed to meet this standard. Dissenting in *Nebbia*, Justice McReynolds openly claimed this power: "But plainly, I think, this Court must have regard to the wisdom of the enactment."[39] *Nebbia* repudiated this position. If a given piece of legislation was enacted pursuant to an acknowledged legislative power, like the thereafter broadly read Commerce Clause, the Court would not presume to reexamine the Congressional determination of the public interest purportedly advanced.[40] Although this judicial abdication of oversight stopped short of announcing that there need be no general public interest objective behind legislation,[41] the effect of nigh total judicial deference was to eliminate any real check – other than in the conscience of individual legislators – against legislation that favored particular groups. It is but a half step from there to devolve to the position that the identification of the public good served by a piece of legislation would be satisfied by a few perfunctory words in the preamble of a statute.

In the aftermath of the court packing plan, several major advancements for legal instrumentalism took place in the legal culture. The (non-instrumental) conceptual formalist view of the common law criticized by the Realists was repudiated by the Supreme Court in *Erie*. The skepticism of the Realists was given support by the sweeping alteration in constitutional jurisprudence that followed from a change in

---

37 Id. 26 (first emphasis in original, second emphasis added).
38 Tribe, *American Constitutional Law*, supra 571 (emphasis in original).
39 *Nebbia*, 291 U.S. at 556 (McReynolds, J., dissenting).
40 The initial case on this was *United States v. Darby*, 312 US 100 (1941).
41 Tribe, *American Constitutional Law*, supra 582.

views and membership of the Justices. And judgeships came to be seen as a tool for effecting legal change.

Warren Court reforms, and the backlash

The deferential stance assumed by the Supreme Court following the court packing event did not last for long, although the Court would continue to grant a free pass to economic legislation. A new, unprecedented level of judicial assertiveness, particularly in the area of individual rights, was ushered in by the 1953 appointment of Chief Justice Earl Warren. Aside from taking up a different set of concerns, the Warren Court's actions were qualitatively different from the obstructionist court that capitulated in 1937. The latter mainly blocked legislative initiatives. A number of important Warren Court constitutional rulings, in contrast, laid out rules and procedures to be followed by the government in a manner tantamount to legislation. These two courts had different thrusts: The pre-1937 Court put the brakes on legislative initiatives designed to deal with social conditions, whereas the Warren Court took as its mission to issue rulings that prompted social change. Notwithstanding these differences, by the end of its tenure, one of the charges commonly leveled by critics against the liberal Warren Court was that it represented the second coming of the discredited, conservative *Lochner* court.

The landmark *Brown v. Board of Education* (1954) case was the coming-out announcement of the Warren Court. The Court invalidated legally imposed segregation in education, common throughout the South at the time, finding that it violated the Equal Protection Clause of the 14th Amendment. Few would quarrel today with the proposition that legalized segregation was deeply immoral (although a sizable majority Southerners at the time disagreed); it stands with slavery as an indelible stain on the nation's history. But the *Brown* decision has always been dubious from a legal standpoint.[42] The historical record, although not certain, supports the conclusion that the ratifiers of the 14th Amendment did not understand it to prohibit legalized segregation.[43] Racial segregation was a way of life, thought by many to reflect God's natural order; during the ratification period, a number of the states that approved the amendment also sanctioned segregation in schools and elsewhere.[44] Also standing in the way of *Brown* was *Plessy v.*

---

42 A recent collection by leading constitutional theorists proposes alternative ways to have written the decision. Jack M. Balkin, *What Brown v. Board of Education Should Have Said* (New York: NYU Press 2001). This very exercise, five decades later, is compelling testimony of the weakness of the legal reasoning, as well as of the importance of the decision. As their various struggles show, the decision is hard to justify within the terms of standard constitutional discourse. The best way to have issued Brown and Bolling, in my view, would have been as a "one off" case compelled by the unique moral impropriety of legally imposed segregation within our modern constitutional system – a once-in-an-epoch evil of government coercion that could not be tolerated in a system committed to the rule of law.

43 See Alexander M. Bickel, "The Original Understanding and the Segregation Decision," 69 *Harvard L. Rev.* 1 (1955).

44 Charles Hyneman, *The Supreme Court on Trial* (Westport, Conn.: Greenwood Press 1974) 189–94.

Ferguson,[45] a half-century-old precedent which held that the Equal Protection Clause was not offended by legalized segregation because separate facilities can still be equal.

For the legal establishment, a glaring flaw of *Brown* is that it was strikingly devoid of the normal trappings of constitutional analysis. It contains no significant case analysis or citation to constitutional principles. At bottom, the opinion appears to be based upon psychological and sociological assertions that the legalized segregation imposes a badge of servitude on blacks, and is therefore constitutionally impermissible. "A lawyer reading *Brown* was sure to ask, 'where's the law?'" wrote Lucas Powe, detailing the reaction to the decision in his study of the Warren Court.[46] Adding to the impression that *Brown* had a shaky legal quality is a companion case issued the same day, *Bolling v. Sharpe,*[47] which struck legalized segregation in the District of Columbia. Because the 14th Amendment Equal Protection Clause, by its terms, applies to the states only, and D.C. is not a state, *Bolling* was pinned instead on the Due Process Clause of the 5th Amendment, resting on the weak assertion that the two clauses are not "mutually exclusive."

While many in the nation welcomed *Brown,* an outcry of protest and open defiance was raised against the decision and others that followed, especially from the South. Several Southern state legislatures declared that the decision was an unconstitutional "usurpation of power" by the Court and accordingly "null, void, and of no effect."[48] Nineteen Senators and seventy-seven members of the House entered a statement into *The Congressional Record* in 1956, which read, in part:

> We regard the decision in the Supreme Court in the school cases as a clear abuse of judicial power. It climaxes a trend in the Federal Judiciary undertaking to legislate, in derogation of the authority of Congress, and to encroach upon the reserved rights of the States and the people....
>
> ... the Supreme Court of the United States, with no legal basis for such action, undertook to exercise their naked judicial power and substituted their personal political and social ideas for the established law of the land....[49]

The 1958 Conference of State Chief Justices issued a set of resolutions with an accompanying report, approved by thirty-six of the forty-three Chief Judges present:

> ... the Supreme Court too often has tended to adopt the role of policy maker without proper judicial restraint.

---

45 *Plessy v. Ferguson,* 163 US 537 (1896).
46 Lucas A. Powe, *The Warren Court in American Politics* (Cambridge, Mass.: Harvard Univ. Press 2000) 40.
47 *Bolling v. Sharpe,* 347 U.S. 497 (1954).
48 Collected and quoted in Hyneman, *Supreme Court on Trial,* supra 21. Hyneman's book, first published in 1963, is a sustained criticism of the Warren Court.
49 *The Congressional Record,* March 12, 1956, vol. 102, pp. 4460, 4515–16, set out in Hyneman, *Supreme Court on Trial,* supra 19.

.... It has long been an American boast that we have a government of laws and not of men. We believe that any study of the recent decisions of the Supreme Court will raise at least considerable doubt as to the validity of that boast.[50]

Considering the comity that judges typically extend one another, this is a searing condemnation by the Chief Judges of the states of their brethren sitting on highest court in the nation. Even liberal law professors who considered legally imposed segregation to be morally repugnant expressed concerns that the Warren Court's decision lacked sufficient grounding in constitutional precedent and principle.[51]

Brown was only the beginning. The Warren Court went on to impose various constitutional protections in policing and criminal prosecutions. Evidence obtained in improper searches could no longer be used in trials;[52] confessions obtained by coercive techniques were disallowed;[53] people in police custody had to be advised of and waive their rights before they could be interrogated;[54] indigent defendants were entitled to lawyers at public expense;[55] and more. The Court ordered that voting districts must be drawn in a way proportional to population – the "one person, one vote" formula – a matter that was previously considered to be a political decision at the discretion of legislatures.[56] It increased protection for pornography,[57] and disallowed prayers in schools.[58] The Court found that a constitutional right of "privacy" existed, notwithstanding the fact that it was nowhere stated in the document.[59]

The effect of the Warren Court's jurisprudence was to greatly expand the parameters of the political and civil rights held by individuals and to enforce these rights against the state and federal governments. The range of Warren Court reforms was much broader than the changes brought by the New Deal Court, which centered mainly on economic legislation and the expansion of national power. Moreover, the Warren Court's penchant for overturning precedent was unparalleled. In the entire history of the Court until Warren, eighty-eight precedents had been overruled; the Warren Court dispatched forty-five precedents, thirty-three of them between 1963 and 1969, seven in a single term.[60]

---

50 Id. 23.
51 See Herbert Weschsler, "Toward Neutral Principles of Constitutional Law," 73 *Harvard L. Rev.* 1 (1959).
52 *Mapp v. Ohio,* 367 U.S. 643 (1961).
53 *Escobedo v. Illinois,* 378 U.S. 478 (1964).
54 *Miranda v. Arizona,* 384 U.S. 436 (1966).
55 *Gideon v. Wainwright,* 372 U.S. 335 (1963).
56 *Baker v. Carr,* 369 U.S. 186 (1962); *Reynolds v. Sims,* 377 U.S. 533 (1964).
57 *Kingsley International Pictures Corp. v. Regents,* 360 U.S. 684 (1959); *Jacobellis v. Ohio,* 378 U.S. 184 (1964).
58 *Engel v. Vitale,* 370 U.S. 421 (1962); *School District of Abington Township v. Schempp,* 374 U.S. 203 (1963).
59 *Griswold v. State of Connecticut* 381 U.S. 479 (1965).
60 Powe, *Warren Court and American Politics,* supra 486; Philip Kurland, *Politics, the Constitution, and the Warren Court* (Chicago: Univ. Chicago Press 1970) Introduction.

With seemingly little restraint, the Warren Court flexed its power to change the law in the name of constitutional values in the mid-1960s, at at time "when a consensus over public values was disintegrating."[61] Voicing the opinion of many critics, in one dissent, Justice John Marshall Harlan objected to a decision granting new protections to welfare recipients on the grounds that it "reflects to an unusual degree the current notion that this Court possesses a peculiar wisdom all its own whose capacity to lead this Nation out of its present troubles is contained only by the limits of judicial ingenuity in contriving new constitutional principles to meet each new problem as it arises."[62]

Supporters of the Court argued that it stood up for moral (constitutional) principle to combat legal and social ails at a vital transformational moment in the history of the country. The Court was said by some to have hearkened back to a classical natural principles approach – Justice William O. Douglas, for one, occasionally wrote this way. The problem with this claim, however, is that to many observers these moral (cum constitutional) principles appeared to be policy and value preferences the individual judges imposed on everyone else by fiat.[63]

The noble ambition of the Warren Court was not just to reform the law, but to use the law as a means to *reform society* for the better.[64] This is the grandest expression that an instrumental view of the judicial power can take. Critics saw this ambition as the Warren Court's hubris, assuming a role inappropriate for courts, doomed ultimately to failure.

It is impossible today to appreciate the seething hatred the Warren Court evoked from conservative quarters and the South, although one sign of this is that mention of the Court still gets a rise from conservatives more than four decades later. Critics charged the Warren Court with coddling criminals, encouraging immorality, stomping on community (or Southern) values, and being anti-religious. They appended the "activist" label to the Warren Court, spitting out the term as an epithet.

Even those who applauded the Warren Court were uneasy about the dubious legal groundings for the decisions, fearing that later conservative courts might gut the reforms and, what's worse, utilize the same techniques to move constitutional jurisprudence rightward. After all, if the Warren Court can do it, what is there to stop later Courts from advancing an opposing set of values in a similar manner?

Burger Court continues trend

In the 1968 presidential election, Richard M. Nixon made a major campaign issue of the Warren Court and its liberal decisions. Just days before the election, Nixon promised that his appointees would not be judicial activists: "[N]ominees to the high Court . . . would be strict constructionists who saw their duty as interpreting

61 Id. 496.
62 *Shapiro v. Thompson*, 394 U.S. 618 (1969).
63 Kurland, *Politics, the Constitution, and the Warren Court*, supra.
64 See Powe, *Warren Court and American Politics*, supra 486–7.

law and not making law. They would see themselves as caretakers of the Constitution and servants of the people, not super-legislators with a free hand to impose their social forces and political viewpoints on the American people."[65] President Nixon appointed Chief Justice Warren E. Burger to fill the vacancy left by Warren's retirement, and in the next few years he appointed Harry A. Blackmum, Lewis F. Powell, and William H. Rehnquist. The Court was substantially remade, but Nixon's expressed wish was frustrated.

After a dozen years of the Burger Court, constitutional scholar Vincent Blasi concluded that "By virtually every meaningful measure . . . the Burger Court has been an activist court."[66] Using the propensity to invalidate federal and state legislation as a measure of "judicial activism," which was the original coinage of the term and the meaning alluded to by Nixon,[67] the Burger Court was *more* activist than the Warren Court. In fifteen years, the Warren Court struck 23 federal statutes and 186 state statues on constitutional grounds; in seventeen years, the Burger Court struck 32 and 309, respectively.[68]

The Burger court was activist in other respects as well, especially in asserting power against other organs of state and federal government and in constructing new constitutional doctrines. *United States v. Nixon* was an landmark ruling – requiring Nixon to comply with a subpoena from a special prosecutor to turn over tapes and documents – that boldly asserted the authority of the Court over the President.[69] In *Furman v. Georgia,* the Court erased all state death penalty laws as unconstitutional.[70] The court officially sanctioned compulsory busing as a remedy for desegregation,[71] and it recognized the constitutionality of affirmative action in *Bakke.*[72]

Burger's tenure brought *the* watershed event of contemporary Supreme Court history. Three of Nixon's appointees voted with the majority in *Roe v. Wade* to invalidate state statutes that prohibited abortion on the grounds that they constituted an impermissible infringement upon a woman's constitutional right of privacy to control her body.[73] The opinion set out a trimester scheme in which the

---

65 E. E. Kenworthy, "Nixon Scores Indulgence," *New York Times,* November 3, 1968, p. 1, 79, quoted in Stephenson, *Campaign and Courts,* supra 181.
66 Vincent Blasi, "The Rootless Activism of the Burger Court," in *The Burger Court: The Counter-Revolution That Wasn't* (New Haven: Yale Univ. Press 1983) 208.
67 The first use of "judicial activism" is in Arthur M. Schlesinger, "The Supreme Court: 1947," *Fortune,* January 1947, Volume XXXV, 201. It refers to a willingness to strike legislation.
68 Congressional Research Service, "The Constitution of the United States of America: Analysis and Interpretation," and 2000 Supplement (Washington, D.C.: Government Printing Office, 1996, 2000) reproduced in Thomas M. Keck, *The Most Activist Supreme Court in History: The Road to Modern Judicial Conservatism* (Chicago: Univ. Chicago Press 2004) 40–1. See also Bernard Schwartz, *The Ascent of Pragmatism: The Burger Court in Action* (Reading, Mass.: Addison Wesley Pub. 1990) 398–413.
69 *United States v. Nixon,* 418 U.S. 683 (1974).
70 *Furman v. Georgia,* 408 U.S. 238 (1972).
71 *Swann v. Charlotte-Mecklenburg Board Of Education,* 402 U.S. 1 (1971).
72 *Regents of University of California v. Bakke,* 438 U.S. 265 (1978).
73 *Roe v. Wade,* 410 US 113 (1973).

state would gain increased power to regulate abortions as the fetus matured. It was unlike any constitutional opinion ever written. For opponents, *Roe* reigns as the unmatched example of judicial arrogation of legislative power, of justices imposing their personal views on the populace in the name of interpreting the Constitution.

The continued activism of the Supreme Court was a surprise to many observers of the Court, who expected (or hoped for) more judicial modesty. Adding to the dismay of conservative critics of the Supreme Court, although it issued many decisions favored by conservatives, many Burger Court decisions, especially in its early years, lined up on the liberal side.[74] The triumvirate of *Roe*, *Furman*, and *Bakke* would be on every list of Supreme Court decisions despised by conservatives, ranking higher than many Warren Court decisions. One partial explanation for this is that liberal holdovers from the Warren Court remained during much of Burger's tenure, including Justices Douglas, William J. Brennan, and Thurgood Marshall; it takes five votes to make a court ruling, and each Justice counts for only one.

Two additional partial explanations are the legal commitment to precedent, and the legal craft of working out the implications of existing doctrines, which helped hold in place the liberal decisions of the Warren Court. "Legal conservatism" requires doctrinal consistency and respect for precedent. Even when a precedent might be objectionable on legal grounds, Justices feel some obligation to honor it. Rapid or radical alterations in doctrine that follow from changes in court membership suggest that rulings are politics rather than law, to the discredit of the Court. To the chagrin of conservatives, Warren Court decisions, accused of being political in nature, were accorded a measure of protection by legal values against a counter-revolution by a conservative majority.

Another explanation for the mixed legacy of the Burger Court, one consistent with the themes of this book, is that many Burger Court decisions reflected pragmatic decision-making and ad hoc balancing among competing interests,[75] in contrast to the broad value-based Warren Court decisions. The origins of balancing in constitutional analysis trace directly back to the pragmatic instrumentalism of Pound and the Realists.[76] Justice Stone, the reliable New Deal supporter on 1930's Supreme Court, gave an address at Harvard in 1936 that endorsed balancing pursuant to an instrumental view of law: "We are coming to realize more completely that law is not an end, but a means to an end – the adequate control of those interests, social and economic, which are the special concern of government and hence of law. . . . [The judicial] choice will rightly depend upon the relative weights of the social and economic advantages which will finally turn the scales of judgment in

---

74 For a strong argument about the left-lean of the Burger Court decisions, see Earl M. Maltz, *The Chief Justiceship of Warren Burger, 1969–1986* (Columbia, S.C.: Univ. of South Carolina Press 2000).

75 See Blasi, "Rootless Activism of the Burger Court," supra; Schwartz, *The Ascent of Pragmatism: The Burger Court in Action*, supra.

76 T. Alexander Aleinikoff, "Constitutional Law in the Age of Balancing," 96 *Yale L.J.* 943, 955–63 (1987).

favor of one rule rather than another."[77] Balancing showed up in selected constitutional contexts from the late 1930s through the 1960s, but it spread throughout
constitutional analysis in the 1970s and 1980s. *Roe*, for example, is a balancing decision. Despite the frequent use of balancing in constitutional analysis, however, "[n]o
system of identification, evaluation, and comparison of interests has been developed."[78] In the absence of such a system, although they purportedly weigh social
values by some standard measure, when engaging in balancing it often appears that
Justices rely upon their own sense of the values at issue.

The balancing decisions and tailored holdings of the Burger Court emerged in
uncertain patterns scattered around a moving center, apparently the product of
whichever side could cobble together enough votes to form a majority in a given
case.[79] It looked like politics. A 1981 study of Supreme Court decisions over the
previous three decades gave concrete support to this impression by revealing a
strikingly high correlation between the votes of certain Justices and their political
attitudes. Justice Douglas, for example, voted on the liberal side in 94.3 percent of
the civil liberties cases and 82.1 percent of the economic cases studied; in the same
pool of cases, at the opposite end of the spectrum, Justice Rehnquist voted liberal in
4.5 percent of the civil rights cases and 15.6 percent in the economic cases.[80] Thus,
one could predict the Justices' legal decisions based upon their political views with
a high degree of reliability without knowing anything about the law applicable to a
given case. Court watchers recognized these correlations before the study. Many
court decisions appeared to be the product of political alliances or overlapping ends
among justices, with the Justices interpreting the law instrumentally to achieve
preferred ends.

Rehnquist Court activism

Perhaps the most confounding aspect of this tale is the record of the Rehnquist
Supreme Court, dominated by appointees of Republican Presidents who vocally
opposed "government by judiciary" and vowed to select judges who would respect
the authority of the legislative branches of government as the primary law-making
body in a democracy. President Ronald Reagan elevated Rehnquist to Chief Justice, and appointed Justices Sandra Day O'Connor, Antonin Scalia, and Anthony
Kennedy; President George H.W. Bush added Justices David Souter and Clarence
Thomas. Yet, using the same measure – the propensity to invalidate legislation –
the activism of the Court continued unabated. The Rehnquist Court, lasting four
years longer, struck *twice* the number of federal statutes as Warren Court (47 to 23,

---

77 Harlan Fisk Stone, "The Common Law in the United States," 50 *Harvard L. Rev.* 4, 20 (1936).
78 Aleinikoff, "Constitutional Law in the Age of Balancing," supra 982.
79 See Maltz, *Chief Justiceship of Warren Burger*, supra.
80 C. Neal Tate, "Personal Attribute Models of Voting Behavior of United States Supreme Court
    Justices: Liberalism in Civil Liberties and Economics Decisions, 1946–1978," 75 *Am. Pol. Sci. Rev.*
    355 (1981).

respectively), and ample though fewer state statutes (132 to 186, respectively).[81] The annual average of federal statutes struck on constitutional grounds by the Rehnquist Court is the highest in the history of the Supreme Court. Based on these and other measures, one study concluded that the Rehnquist Court was "the most activist Supreme Court in history."[82] Like the Burger Court, the Rehnquist Court managed to provoke the ire of both the right and the left of the political spectrum.

In the closely watched *Casey* case, the majority upheld *Roe*, owing in part to its reluctance to overturn settled precedent. The decision outraged Christian conservatives, who vowed that they would not rest until Supreme Court support for abortion rights was halted. Opening the Court up to ridicule from opponents, the *Casey* opinion waxed romantically that "At the heart of liberty is the right to define one's own concept of existence, of meaning, of the universe, and of the mystery of human life."[83] In *Lawrence v. Texas*, the Court overruled a recent precedent (notwithstanding its refusal to do so in *Casey*) to invalidate state statutes that criminalized homosexual sodomy as an unconstitutional infringement upon privacy.[84] The court also struck an anti–gay-rights initiative as a violation the Equal Protection Clause.[85] The Court invalidated a "males only" admission policy at a Virginia military academy as an impermissible discrimination against women.[86] The Court allowed consideration of race as a factor in the admissions decision of Michigan Law School.[87] And the Court declared unconstitutional the imposition of the death penalty for juveniles and the mentally retarded.[88]

Reminiscent of the attacks on the Warren Court, enraged conservatives decried these actions as a "judicial usurpation of politics" by an imperial Court: "the judiciary has in effect declared that the most important questions about how we ought to order our life together are outside the purview of 'things of [the people's] knowledge.'"[89] Critics fumed that these decisions were the views of the intellectual, cultural elite. Justice Scalia wrote apoplectic dissents in several of these decisions, charging that the majority "has embarked on a course of inscribing one after another of the current preferences of the society (and in some cases only the counter-majoritarian preferences of the society's law-trained elite) into our Basic Law."[90]

---

81 Numbers updated to the end of Rehnquist's tenure can be found at http://faculty.maxwell. syr.edu/tmkeck/Book_1/Research_Updates.htm; see also Keck, *Most Activist Supreme Court in History*, supra 40–1.

82 Id.

83 *Planned Parenthood of Southeastern Pennsylvania v. Casey*, 505 US 833, 851 (1992).

84 *Lawrence v. Texas*, 539 US 558 (2003), overruling *Bowers v. Hardwick*, 478 US 186 (1986).

85 *Romer v. Evans*, 517 US 620 (1996).

86 *United States v. Virginia*, 518 US 515 (1996).

87 *Grutter v. Bollinger*, 539 US 306 (2003).

88 *Roper v. Simmons*, 543 US 551 (2005); *Atkins v. Virginia*, 536 US 304 (2002).

89 Michael S. Muncie, ed., *The End of Democracy: The Judicial Usurpation of Politics, The Celebrated First Things Debate with Arguments Pro and Con* (Dallas: Spence Pub. 1997) 5. This book compiles the symposium issue of the conservative journal *First Things*, which sharply criticized the Rehnquist Court.

90 *United States v. Virginia*, supra at 567.

Although relieved at some of its holdings, liberals were also unhappy with the Court, holding their collective breath in trepidation at the announcement of each ruling. The Rehnquist Court struck certain state and federal affirmative action policies as violations of the 14th Amendment.[91] It struck as a violation of the freedom of association a state statute that prohibited discrimination against gays in public groups (supporting the Boy Scouts' decision to ban homosexual scout leaders).[92] It invalidated various federal statutes as beyond the power of the Commerce Clause,[93] scrutinizing the purported ends of the legislation after six decades of deference, generating concerns from the left that New Deal-type legislation might be under threat. This latter cluster of decisions, along with others that found new protections for the states under the previously dormant 11th Amendment[94] and 10th Amendment,[95] marked what has been labeled the "federalism revolution," in which the Supreme Court set about to restrict the legislative power of the federal government in favor of the states, drawing new constitutional lines of authority based on vague notions like "sovereignty."[96] Topping off these cases for liberal outrage was *Bush v. Gore*,[97] a brazen, apparently political decision by the majority to seat George W. Bush as president.

Liberal constitutional law scholar Cass Sunstein asserted that the Rehnquist Court has engaged in "illegitimate judicial activism," in which it has been "exceedingly willing to strike down congressional (and also state) enactments, not when the Constitution is clear, but when it is unclear and when reasonable people can disagree about what it means."[98] Many of these invalidations, he observed, "fit the agenda of extreme elements of the Republican Party."[99] At the opposite pole of the political spectrum, avidly conservative Judge Robert H. Bork has been scathing in his criticism:

> . . . the Supreme Court brought home to us with fresh clarity what it means to be ruled by an oligarchy. The most important moral, political, and cultural decisions affecting our lives are steadily being removed from democratic control. . . . A majority of the court routinely enacts its own preferences as the command of our basic document.[100]

91 *Adarand Constructors Inc. v. Pena*, 515 U.S. 200 (1995). In *Gratz v. Bollinger*, 539 U.S. 244 (2003), the Court struck Michgan's undergraduate affirmative action policy.
92 *Boy Scouts of America v. Dale*, 530 U.S. 640 (2000).
93 *United States v. Lopez*, 514 U.S. 549 (1995); *United States v. Morrison*, 529 U.S. 598 (2000).
94 *Seminole Tribe of Florida v. Florida*, 517 U.S. 43 (1996); *City of Boerne v. Flores*, 521 U.S. 507 (1997); *Board of Trustees of the University of Ala. V. Garrett*, 531 U.S. 356 (2000).
95 *New York v. United States*, 505 U.S. 144 (1992); *Printz v. United States*, 521 U.S. 898 (1997).
96 See Jack M. Balkin and Sanford Levinson, "Understanding the Constitutional Revolution," 87 *Virginia L. Rev.* 1045 (2001); Timothy Zick, "Are the States Sovereign?" 83 *Wash. U. L.Q.* 229 (2005).
97 *Bush v. Gore*, 531 U.S. 98 (2000).
98 Cass Sunstein, "A Hand in the Matter," *Legal Affairs*, March–April, 27–30, http://www.legalaffairs.org/printerfriendly.msp 2, 3.
99 Id. 2.
100 Robert H. Bork, "Our Judicial Oligarchy," in *The End of Democracy*, supra 10.

After twelve years of Presidents Reagan and Bush, each of whom made a determined effort to appoint Justices who would abide by the Constitution as originally understood, we seem farther than ever from a restrained Court...A majority of the Justices has become more arrogantly authoritarian than ever.[101]

Conservative constitutional law scholar Mary Ann Glendon asked melancholically: "How did it come about that 'conservative,' 'moderate' justices on today's Supreme Court are often more assertive and arrogant in their exercise of judicial power than the members of the 'liberal,' 'activist' Warren Court?"[102]

This mystery can be explained. The conservative Presidents who appointed the Justices responsible for these decisions had two separate agendas: first, to halt "government by judiciary,"[103] the practice of Justices vetoing legislation and presuming to legislate their personal views; and second, to implement a socially and economically conservative vision of the law.[104] When the Warren Court made its liberal reforms, these two agendas appeared to coincide: The activism of the court advanced a liberal political vision, so calls for a restrained court furthered the conservative political vision. But these two agendas can easily be at odds.

The latent conflict between them surfaced when conservatives came to control the Court and hoped to use this position to implement their substantive political agenda. Under these circumstances, practicing judicial restraint hampers the achievement of conservative political goals. For example, to cut back on the regulatory power of the federal government, economic conservatives would like to revive pre-New Deal views of the Commerce Clause,[105] which requires leaping backward over more than a half century of the Court's jurisprudence, and would entail vigorous policing of economic legislation enacted by Congress. Pursuing this agenda thus implicates the Court in two different forms of judicial activism: overruling longstanding precedent and invalidating Congressional legislation. The "states rights" initiative favored by conservatives is advanced by striking federal statutes. Whether conservatives seeking to advance their agenda desire or oppose activism is a function of the underlying legislative position at issue. When a state legislature enacts a liberal policy – say, prohibiting discrimination against gays or promoting affirmative action in education – conservatives urge courts to invalidate the offending provision, calling for judicial activism. When a state supports a conservative policy – criminalizing homosexual sodomy, restricting abortion, or enacting anti-gay rights legislation – conservatives want the courts to lay off, denouncing judicial activism.

---

101 Id. 16.
102 Glendon, *A Nation Under Lawyers: How the Crisis in the Legal Profession is Transforming American Society* (New York: Farrar Strauss 1994) 117.
103 See Raoul Berger, *Government By Judiciary: The Transformation of the Fourteenth Amendment* (Cambridge, Mass.: Harvard Univ. Press 1997).
104 Thomas Keck's superbly researched book, *Most Activist Supreme Court in History*, supra unpacks these two agendas and shows what happens when they come into conflict.
105 See Richard Epstein, "The Proper Scope of the Commerce Power," 73 *Virginia L. Rev.* 1387 (1987).

The left engages in a different version of the same inconsistency, one that focuses on the politics of the Justices: favoring court activism when the Justices were liberal but increasingly against it as the bench has become more conservative, with some on the left now proposing that the power of judicial review be abolished or curtailed.[106] For anyone who views law as a means to advance their political ends, flipping positions for or against "judicial activism" in this manner is inevitable. A consistent opponent of this kind of judicial activism would want the court to abstain from striking legislation except in the most blatant instances of clear constitutional violations, regardless of the underlying political orientation of the legislation or the political make-up of the judiciary.

It should be recognized that there is always the potential for a problem to arise between "judicial activism" and adherence to *any* particular substantive theory of constitutional interpretation. If a given piece of legislation contravenes what the particular constitutional theory dictates, the legislation will be struck; Congressional authority be damned. Justices Scalia and Thomas, for example, have urged that judges should interpret constitutional provisions by adherence to the original meaning these provisions had for those who framed and ratified them. This approach, they claim, would be truer to the democratic constitutional system. A 2005 study found that in cases raising a constitutional challenge to the validity of federal legislation, Justice Thomas voted to invalidate the statute 65.63% of the time, and Scalia 56.25% of the time, which ranked first and third highest among the Justices (Justice Kennedy was second at 64.06%).[107] They were far more "activist," by this measure, than their liberal colleagues: Justices Stephen Breyer (28.13%), Ruth Bader Ginsburg (39.06%), and John Paul Stevens (39.34%), who exhibited much greater deference to Congress than the conservative stalwarts. Had Scalia and Thomas been able to carry the majority in the cases, the Court would have invalidated well over half of federal legislation that was challenged, telling Congress that it has dismal judgment about the proper constitutional exercise of its powers, which is hard to reconcile with respect for a democratic system.

The two swing votes on the Court, Justices O'Connor and Kennedy, sometimes lined up with the more liberal wing to support liberal positions, and sometimes lined up with conservatives to support conservative positions. Hence the presence of "activist" decisions on both sides of the political spectrum, to the dismay of liberals and conservatives alike, but in different categories of cases.[108] In reality and in perception, there was so much "activism" overall because both sides got their victories, and because both sides tended to characterize their losses as the product of judicial activism favoring the other side. A high proportion of decisions fell along predictable political lines (swung this way or that by O'Connor and Kennedy), such that it smacked of constitutional politics rather than law.

106 Mark Tushnet, "Democracy Against Judicial Review," *Dissent* (Spring 2005).
107 See Paul Gerwith and Chad Golder, "So Who Are the Activists?" *New York Times*, A 19, July 6, 2005.
108 Keck, *Most Activist Supreme Court*, supra Conclusion.

At the outset of the twenty-first century, the Supreme Court displayed, in its willingness to strike legislation, an unusual lack of regard for the authority of the political branches and an unusual willingness to vote their personal preferences. It is as if, owing to the cumulative impact of the Legal Realists, the 1937 revolution, the Warren Court reforms, the Burger Court continuation, and the *Roe* singularity, an essential component of judging on the Supreme Court *snapped*, an intangible but no less real sense of self-restraint. Scalia and Thomas have directed this very complaint at their colleagues, but vehemently deny that they are doing the same, claiming that their originalist theory limits judicial discretion, and attributing their high rate of voting to strike statutes as a consequence of the Constitution. Many observers, however, have noted the high frequency with which their decisions line up with their personal views.[109]

This was not the original constitutional design. In *Federalist* 78, Alexander Hamilton, who supported judicial review, anticipated precisely this problem and made plain its impropriety: "It can be of no weight to say, that the courts on the pretence of a repugnancy, may substitute their own pleasure to the constitutional intentions of the legislature. . . . The courts must declare the sense of the law; and if they should be disposed to exercise WILL instead of JUDGMENT, the consequence would equally be the substitution of their pleasure to that of the legislative body."[110]

Some will say that Supreme Courts have always engaged in instrumental manipulation of the law for ideological purposes, though they may have better concealed it. Perhaps, but a distinction exists between thinking that a practice is inappropriate, so it must be resisted or concealed, versus thinking that it is acceptable. Chief Justice Rehnquist wrote that "a President who sets out to 'pack' the Court seeks to appoint people to the Court who are sympathetic to his political or philosophical principles. There is no reason in the world why a President should not do this."[111] Earlier sitting Justices would not have so baldly endorsed this proposition, even if it was engaged in by presidents unspokenly. Public outrage at this proposition shouted down Roosevelt's attempt in 1937 to do precisely that.

Five types of instrumentalism

Five related types of Supreme Court instrumentalism show up in this chapter. The first type is the belief that courts have the power to direct social change through their decisions. Justice Brennan explicitly asserted that the Supreme Court possesses this power: "The main burden of my twenty-nine terms on the Supreme Court has thus been to wrestle with the Constitution in this heightened public context [involving

---

109 Robert M. Howard and Jeffrey A. Segal, "An Original Look at Originalism," 36 *Law & Soc'y. Rev.* 113, 133 (2002).
110 Alexander Hamilton, James Madison, and John Jay, *The Federalist Papers* (New York: Bantam Classic 2003) Federalist 78, p. 476.
111 William H. Rehnquist, "Presidential Appointments to the Supreme Court," 2 *Constitutional Commentary* 319 (1985).

issues over which society is "most deeply divided"], to draw meaning from the text in order to resolve public controversies. . . . The course of vital social, economic, and political currents may be *directed*."[112] The same belief was reflected in the Court's suggestion in *Casey* that people in society must accept *Roe* and move on. This first sense of legal instrumentalism is faith in the power of judicial decisions to change society according to its dictates.

The second type of instrumentalism is the general approach applied by the Court, as put by Steven D. Smith:

> In its most visible aspect, constitutional law presents reason in instrumentalist or "means–end" terms. Scholars have pointed out that most of the doctrinal formulas articulated by the Court, whether under the First Amendment of the Fourteenth or the commerce clause, are presented in essentially the same monotonously instrumentalist terms. So laws are viewed as means to social ends, and a law's constitutionality is said to depend on how important the law's ends are and how effective and necessary the law is as a means to achieving those ends.[113]

The triumph of the view that law is a tool to advance ends is evident in this passage.[114]

The third type of instrumentalism, connected to what Smith describes, is the increasingly common balancing analysis applied by the Supreme Court. "[B]alancing now dominates major areas of constitutional law."[115] Rejecting "formalistic" distinctions as unrealistic, the Supreme Court renders decisions that purport to strike the proper balance among the competing interests at stake. When attaching weights to and comparing the various interests at stake, judges inevitably render social policy choices; balancing, moreover, involves "black box" decisions – presenting conclusions that certain interests outweigh others, but without justifying or providing specific weights – that allow Justices to arrive at outcomes they personally prefer in a manner that cannot be checked or evaluated.[116] Balancing is nothing like rule application.

The fourth type of instrumentalism relates to the pervasive skepticism with which the Court's doctrinal analysis is viewed. It is increasingly difficult to take the

---

112 William J. Brennan, "The Constitution of the United States: Contemporary Ratification," in *Interpreting Law and Literature: A Hermeneutic Reader*, edited by Sanford Levinson and Steven Mailloux (Evanston, Ill.: Northwestern Univ. Press 1988) 14–15 (emphasis added).

113 Steven D. Smith, "The Academy, the Court, and the Culture of Rationalism," in *That Eminent Tribunal: Judicial Supremacy and the Constitution*, C. Wolfe, ed. (Princeton: Princeton Univ. Press 2004) 105. Smith cites Robert F. Nagel, "Rationalism in Constitutional Law," 4 *Constitutional Commentary* 9 (1987).

114 See Albert W. Alschuler, *Law Without Values: The Life, Work, and Legacy of Justice Holmes* (Chicago: Univ. Chicago Press 2000).

115 Aleinikoff, "Constitutional Law in the Age of Balancing," supra 965.

116 See Christopher Wolfe, "The Rehnquist Court and 'Conservative Judicial Activism,'" in *That Eminent Tribunal: Judicial Supremacy and the Constitution*, edited by Christopher Wolfe (Princeton: Princeton Univ. Press 2004) 224.

Justices' articulation of the legal grounds for their decisions at face value. Court watchers routinely predict and parse decisions in relation to the political views of the Justices. Many contemporary political scientists, legal scholars, students in constitutional law classes, legal journalists, and members of the public at large who pay attention to the Court, flatly assume that Justices instrumentally utilize Constitutional doctrines to dress up personally favored outcomes.[117] Constitutional law is seen as mostly politics. Constitutional theories, doctrines, and language are tools Justices invoke and manipulate to get where they want to go.

The fifth type of instrumentalism relates to how people came to see judgeships. For the purposes of encouraging the public to perceive judges in instrumental terms, *Roe* had no peer, at least until *Bush v. Gore* came along. The public was and remains sharply divided on the issue of abortion. The decision came against a backdrop of two decades of the Supreme Court pulling one after another unanticipated finding in whole cloth out of the Constitution. After *Roe*, the Court would become a target of specific groups with an overarching aim in mind: Seat individuals who share their particular agenda on the bench in order that their views can become the law. This is the effort to stock judicial positions as the key strategy for seizing the law to instrumentally further one's agenda.

Owing to the preeminent standing (institutional and symbolic) of the Supreme Court, the aforementioned forms of instrumentalism permeate the entire judiciary. At the outset of the twenty-first century, many judges apparently believe that they have the power to direct social change, much legal analysis is means–ends oriented, widely used balancing tests enable judges to engage in unconstrained instrumental reasoning, judges' decisions are viewed skeptically by observers as manipulation of legal rules to come to ends they desire, and groups endeavor to populate the judiciary with like-minded people under the assumption that they will shape the law in support of their position. Each of these senses of instrumentalism plays out in the contemporary legal culture, as following chapters show.

"Partisan entrenchment" is the name of a theory of constitutional law developed by two of the most eminent contemporary constitutional scholars, Jack Balkin and Sanford Levinson.[118] Balkin's and Levinson's argument is that the meaning of the Constitution is shaped by social movements and political parties, in interaction with prevailing understandings and practices within the legal tradition. Shared interpretive conventions of the legal tradition set limits on plausible readings of the law, but various interpretations of constitutional provisions may be possible at any given moment, and the constraining conventions change over time owing to social

---

117 Harold J. Spaeth and Jeffrey A. Segal, *Majority Rule or Minority Will: Adherence to Precedent on the US Supreme Court* (Cambridge: Cambridge Univ. Press 1999); Harold J. Spaeth and Jeffrey A. Segal, The *Supreme Court and the Attitudinal Model Revisited* (New York: Cambridge Univ. Press 2002).

118 See Jack M. Balkin and Sanford Levinson, "Legal Historicism and Legal Academics: The Roles of Law Professors in the Wake of *Bush v. Gore*," 90 *Georgetown L.J.* 173 (2001).

and political pressures. Through this process, an interpretation of a constitutional text that once seemed absurd may, at a later date, become the standard view. They assert "that legal materials are a site of struggle between various groups in society, so that 'legal materials and conventions are open to alternative interpretations . . . '"[119] Under the theory of partisan entrenchment, the struggle for law as a means to an end is a descriptive account of how the Constitution obtains its meaning.

119 Jack M. Balkin, "'Wrong the Day it Was Decided:' Lochner and Constitutional Historicism," supra 714.

Part 2

Contemporary legal instrumentalism

6

Instrumentalism in legal academia in the 1970s

An instrumental view of law is so taken for granted today that it rarely evokes comment, but in the 1960s and 1970s its novelty in legal education was recognized and prompted expressions of concern. A brief discussion of the legal process school will set the stage for this pivotal period in legal academia. Legal process thought represented the mainstream consensus view of law within the legal academy in the period from the Realists through the 1970s. Although it fell into rather sudden disfavor decades ago, for reasons that will be recounted, it has been claimed, with justification, that legal process thought "has dominated legal scholarship for the last fifty years."[1]

The legal process approach accepted many of the insights of Legal Realism while offering answers to its most threatening implications. Legal Realism was silenced by the collective reaffirmation during World War II of the goodness of the American legal system in contrast to the evil legal regime of Nazi Germany. Law in the United States is more than raw state power, many argued. The need for moral and legal legitimacy was equally pressing at the height of the Cold War, faced with the threat of Soviet communism. For the reasons elaborated at the end of Chapter 4, however, relativist views had spread within intellectual circles during the 1930s and 1940s, making it difficult to identify and defend universal or objective moral or legal principles.

Democracy became *the* defining characteristic that distinguishes a free society from a totalitarian one. Leading theorists went so far as to argue that democracy is more compatible with moral relativism than with natural law ideas. Hans Kelsen, a legal philosopher of Jewish descent who fled Nazi Germany, argued that natural law is historically correlated with and has an affinity with absolutist governments: "If one believes in the existence of the absolute, and consequently in absolute values, in the absolute good . . . is it not meaningless to let a majority vote decide what is politically good?"[2] Relativist views, Kelsen asserted, are a superior fit for democracies. Because relativism acknowledges that one's position on fundamental value choices might

---

1 Edward L. Rubin and Malcolm M. Feeley, "Judicial Policy Making and Litigation Against Government," 5 *U. Penn. J Const. L.* 617, 635 (2003).
2 Hans Kelsen, "Absolutism and Relativism in Philosophy and Politics," 42 *Am. Pol. Sci. Rev.* 906, 913 (1948).

prove wrong, it recognizes the need for an open and continuous discussion that respects all opinions. That is what democracy promotes.

John Dewey also paired belief in absolute principles with absolutism in politics; he contrasted this combination with the methodology of modern science. "At bottom the issue is drawn between dogmas (so rigid that they ultimately must appeal to force) and recourse to intelligent observation guided by the best wisdom already in our possession, which is the heart of the scientific method."[3] Absolutist governments that claim adherence to objective principles are detrimental to modern science because their all-encompassing ideology squelches or distorts inquiry – witness the Nazi denigration of "Jewish physics" – whereas science thrives on open exchange of ideas. Dewey drew parallels between democracy and the pragmatic view of modern science, both open to discussion and experimentation, both suited to a rapidly changing world: "The democratic faith is the extension of the ethic of scientific method . . . to all other human undertakings and institutions."[4] Dewey thereby rehabilitated the pragmatist understanding of knowledge by identifying it with democracy, and set up both as partners against absolute principles and absolutist governments.

These arguments were countered by supporters of natural principles, of course, but the inconclusive debate was, in a sense, beside the point.[5] Legal theorists had no choice but to reconcile their understandings of law to the presence of relativism, which was here to stay. In the absence of the ability to identify or agree upon objective moral or legal principles, the only obvious alternative source of legitimacy for law requires a shift in emphasis from content to procedures. That was the orientation of the legal process school.

The legal process response to legal realism

Legal process thought gestated within a web of relationships at Harvard Law School, going back to the 1940s, among law professors and their top students, many of whom enjoyed prestigious clerkships and then became legal academics, passing on legal process understandings to the next generation of students. Of primary influence were the academic writings and judicial opinions of Harvard professor and later Supreme Court Justice Felix Frankfurter, who emphasized judicial restraint and the purposive interpretation of statutes, and the jurisprudential work of Lon Fuller, who emphasized the procedural aspects of law and legal processes, and argued that by its nature, law is imbued with social purposes. The main vehicle for the spread of this school of thought was *The Legal Process* (1958) materials, compiled by Henry Hart and Albert Sacks for use in their class at Harvard. For almost two decades,

3 Dewey, "Challenge to Liberal Thought," supra 182.
4 Id. 188.
5 Felix Oppenheim, "Relativism, Absolutism, and Democracy," 44 *Am. Pol. Sci. Rev.* 951 (1950).

this manuscript was copied and utilized as teaching material in many law schools around the country, though it was not actually published until 1994, by then long out of date and hardly used. This peculiar history – that it was a widely used teaching material but remained unpublished – says volumes about the fate of legal process thought.

The legal process material set out a distinctively modern view that law is an instrument to serve social needs. Hart wrote that "every legal problem is a problem of purpose, of means to an end . . . "[6] "Not even jurists have always appreciated the sweep of the concept of policy in the law, and its bearing both in the interpretation of statutes and other enactments and in the development of the unwritten law."[7] This is what Holmes, Pound, and the Realists had argued. When statutes, administrative regulations, and the common law are interpreted and applied, taught the legal process school, the underlying social purpose should have controlling influence. "Thus a court . . . interpreting common law precedents has a responsibility to figure out what purposes those precedents serve, in order to pull out some rule, principle, or standard. Similarly, a judge interpreting a statute must first identify the purpose of the statute, what policy or principle it embodies, and then should reason toward the interpretation most consistent with that policy or principle."[8] A purposive approach, both in judicially developed common law and in the judicial interpretation of statutes, allows the law to evolve to meet changing social circumstances while remaining true to underlying purposes.

Recall that by the close of the nineteenth century, legislation was already largely seen in instrumental terms, but not the common law. The Holmes-Pound-Realist criticism of traditional views was aimed at breaking down the understanding that kept apart the common law as a non-instrumental realm unto itself. As these statements show, the legal process approach accepted that the common law and legislation were, at bottom, alike in functioning to serve social needs. Like the Realists, proponents of legal process thought rejected conceptual formalist ideas about the inherent or necessary content of legal concepts and principles, and substituted, in its place, a loose utilitarianism. Hart and Sacks affirmed that "The Constitution of the United States and the various state constitutions commit American society, as a formal matter, to the goal of the general welfare, judged on the basis that every

6 Quoted in William Eskridge and Philip Frickey, "An Historical and Critical Introduction to *The Legal Process*," in Henry M. Hart and Albert M. Sacks, *The Legal Process*, edited by William Eskridge and Philip Frickey (Westbury, N.Y.: Foundation Press 1994 [1958]) lxxxii. Eskridge and Frickey's essay provides an excellent introduction to this school of thought. My account also draws from G. Edward White, "The Evolution of Reasoned Elaboration: Jurisprudential Criticism and Social Change," in *Patterns of American Legal Thought*, supra; Jan Veter, "Postwar Legal Scholarship on Judicial Decision Making," 33 J. Legal Educ. 412 (1983); Neil Duxbury, "Faith in Reason: the Process Tradition in American Jurisprudence," 15 *Cardozo L. Rev.* 601(1993); Gary Peller, "Neutral Principles in the 1950's," *21 U. Mich. J. L. Reform* 561 (1988).
7 Hart and Sacks, *The Legal Process*, supra 148.
8 Eskridge and Frickey, "An Historical and Critical Introduction to *The Legal Process*," supra xcii.

human being counts one – which seems only another way of expressing the objective of maximizing the total satisfactions of valid human wants, and its corollary of a presently fair division."[9]

The basic problem, legal process theorists recognized, was the presence of legitimate disagreement about the goods and wants of society, and issues of fair distribution. Choices must be made, and discretion is unavoidable. Their central insight was that social policies should be determined and principles identified by funneling the decision to appropriate institutions, which then utilize fair procedures when rendering decisions. This was "*the principle of institutional settlement*," which "expresses the judgment that decisions which are the duly arrived at result of duly established procedures of this kind ought to be accepted as binding upon the whole society unless and until they are duly changed."[10]

Each legal institution has its own characteristic strengths and weaknesses, its own unique capabilities – problems should be channeled toward or away from these institutions accordingly. Legislatures are able to gather information and enact comprehensive programs relating to large social problems. As democratic bodies, legislatures have final say on all debatable questions of social policy. But overarching consistency is not a strength of the legislative process. Courts resolve disputes between parties, with a special capacity to engage in reasoned analysis grounded in the recognition and development of legal concepts. But judges are generalists who lack expertise in particular subjects, they have limited information gathering and monitoring ability, they have no special insight or legitimacy to make policy choices that have complex social ramifications, the binary structure of court cases does not work well with polycentric issues, and their piecemeal, case-specific decisions are not suitable for the declaration of comprehensive legal regimes. Administrative agencies compile expertise in particular subjects, they monitor situations, they can flexibly adjust their actions to better achieve general policy directives in specific contexts, and they possess the unique advantage of being able to operate in rule-making, enforcement, and adjudicative modes to effectuate policy. But they should not make fundamental policy decisions that entail matters of choice rather than expertise, especially when the decision goes beyond, or conflicts with, the implementation of legislatively determined policies.

Legal process thought thus accorded priority to legislatures, designating courts and administrative agencies as important collaborators, but subordinate institutions that carry out legislative purposes.[11] Judges must interpret statutes, and fill gaps in statutes, guided by legislative purpose. Furthermore, judges produce common law doctrines as facilitators of the legislature in the development of law, consistent with legislative regimes and with preexisting principles within the law, always subject to legislative overruling.

9 Hart and Sacks, *Legal Process*, supra 105.
10 Id. 4 (emphasis in original).
11 See Eskridge and Frickey, "An Historical and Critical Introduction to *The Legal Process*," supra xcii–xciv.

The resonance of these ideas today is an indication of how deeply the legal process understanding has penetrated the U.S. legal culture. In that broad sense, it continues to live on. It is also an indication of how adeptly legal process thinkers refined and articulated previously inchoate understandings of the increasingly formidable bureaucratic legal apparatus of modern legislative and administrative institutions. Prior to the legal process school, the emphasis within legal academia was still on courts and the common law. Courses on legislation and administrative law were not widely taught in law schools until after the 1930s. Legal process thinkers broke this mold by according equal attention and standing to the legislative and administrative institutions as law-producing bodies. This acknowledgment of public law was a belated recognition of the massive shift in law-making impetus that had taken place in favor of legislation and administration away from the common law. Felix Frankfurter noted that "as late as 1875 more than 40% of the controversies" before the Supreme Court were common law litigation, but this had dropped "almost to zero" by 1947.[12]

Given the legal process endorsement of the superior authority of the legislature to declare the law, it is an odd, yet consistent, implication of the legal process emphasis on purposes of the law that judicial interpretations may legitimately be *contrary to the language of a statute* and sometimes even contrary to the expectations and understandings of the legislators. Hart and Sacks approved of the recent "overthrow" of the "plain meaning" rule of statutory interpretation,[13] which held that the plain meaning of a statute must be applied without regard to consequences. Fidelity to purpose can trump clear statutory language when the statute is poorly written or when the language fails to allow for or anticipate certain eventualities. The leading case for this proposition was *United States v. American Trucking Co.*, in which the Supreme Court held that "even when the plain meaning did not produce absurd results but merely an unreasonable one 'plainly at variance with the policy of the legislation as a whole' this Court has followed that purpose, rather than the literal words."[14]

Courts can arrive at interpretations of statutes that are contrary to the intentions of the legislators under the legal process approach for another reason as well. Hart and Sacks suggested that the purpose of a given statute can be found by "a court trying to put itself in imagination in the position of the legislature which enacted the measure." Immediately following this suggestion, however, they articulated a quite different approach:

> The court, however, should not do this in the mood of a cynical political observer, taking account of the short-run currents of political expedience that swirl around any legislative session.

12 Felix Frankfurter, "Some Reflections on the Reading of Statutes," 47 *Columbia L. Rev.* 527, 527 (1947).
13 Hart and Sacks, *Legal Process*, supra 1235–47.
14 *United States v. American Trucking Assoc.*, 310 U.S. 534, 543–4 (1940).

It should assume, unless the contrary unmistakably appears, that the legislature was made up of reasonable persons pursuing reasonable purposes reasonably.

It should presume conclusively that these persons, whether or not entertaining concepts of reasonableness shared by the court, were trying responsibly and in good faith to discharge their constitutional powers and duties.[15]

The legislative purpose to be discovered in this manner is not oriented at uncovering what purposes the legislators *actually* intended, but is instead what a court determines *reasonable legislators* under the circumstances *would have* intended when enacting reasonable legislation. Besides the obvious retort that these two ways of understanding legislative purpose can produce divergent findings, the "reasonableness" test creates an opportunity for judges to substitute their own judgment of what is reasonable for the judgment of the legislature.

The opening to depart from statutory language is further expanded in so far as judges were required by Hart and Sacks to satisfy the immediate purposes behind the legislation *and* also to fit this within the general purposes (the "general fabric") of the legal system taken as a whole.[16] Even if one grants that the legal system manifests general purposes, which is a questionable proposition, the idea that judges should identify and reconcile them with specific purposes when interpreting legislation assigns judges a complex task and accords them a great deal of room to maneuver. Although Hart and Sacks asserted that purposive interpretation by judges would assist the legislature in discharging its function, they also acknowledged the "danger that a judge who lets himself think this way will tend to arrogate to himself the functions of the legislature . . ."[17]

Legal process thought offered a reassuring response to the suggestions by the more radical Realists that judicial decisions were the products of the personal views of judges. Judges operate within institutional constraints. They have a duty to render decisions in an unbiased fashion following full consideration of reasoned arguments on both sides. The decision is (or should be) delivered in a written opinion supported by logical explanations based on authoritative legal doctrines.[18] It is the role of courts, Hart wrote, "to be a voice of reason, charged with the creative function of discerning afresh and of articulating and developing impersonal and durable principles . . ."[19] Judging, at least when done properly, involves the collaborative "reasoned elaboration" of legal principles. Personal bias and mistakes can be corrected through the appeals process, in which groups of judges are engaged in dialectical decision-making – back and forth exchanges over the proper interpretation of applicable legal rules. The error of the radical Realists, according to this

15 Hart and Sacks, *Legal Process*, supra 1378.
16 See Duxbury, "Faith in Reason," supra 664–5.
17 Hart and Sacks, *Legal Process*, supra 1148.
18 See Lon L. Fuller, "The Forms and Limits of Adjudication," 92 *Harvard. L. Rev.* 253 (1978). This posthumously published article had circulated since 1957.
19 Henry Hart, "The Supreme Court, 1958 Term – Forward: The Time Chart of the Justices," 73 *Harvard L. Rev.* 84, 99 (1959).

view, was their failure to appreciate that these institutional constraints restricted untrammeled judicial discretion.

Through reasoned elaboration, judicial decisions participate in "the maturing of collective thought."[20] Legal principles refined by judges, reflecting common social aims, emerge as the reasonable implications of existing rules and doctrines. Lon Fuller wrote that these principles are not the subconscious effusion of shared cultural values and not principles in the natural law sense; rather, judges develop these principles as "an active participant in the enterprise of articulating the implications of shared purposes."[21] The gradual development of these principles by judges is the process of "the law 'working itself pure.'"[22]

Social consensus underpinnings

The legal process school was the manifestation in legal academia of the consensus view that saturated American intellectual thought and popular culture in the golden 1950s. Society basked in the afterglow of victory in World War II, the lengthy economic boom, Levittown-style suburban communities, popular television, mass consumer culture, and the status of America as a first-order global power and leader of the West. It was, as Daniel Bell put it in his study of the period, "the apathy of the fat fifties."[23]

The defining elements of this consensus were the rejection of ideologies – fascism, communism, utopianisms of any kind – and a collapse of radicalism in the political sphere.[24] Too much bad had come of grand ideologies of late. "In the Western World," Bell wrote at the time, "there is today a rough consensus among intellectuals on political issues: the acceptance of a Welfare State; the desirability of decentralized power; a system of mixed economy and of political pluralism."[25] The prevailing sensibility was that differences could be worked out within shared parameters. "Postwar political scientists . . . regarded American democracy as a rational phenomenon, the product of widespread rational consensus."[26] Legal process thought partook of the same assumptions. "Fuller and Hart and Sacks had seen American institutions as fundamentally benign and had been optimistic about the prospects for reform within a context of general agreement on social goals."[27]

The comforting legal process arguments provided a middle position that absorbed the critiques of the Realists while preserving the integrity of law, now

20 Id. 100.
21 Fuller, "Forms and Limits of Adjudication," supra 378.
22 Id. 377.
23 Bell, *The End of Ideology*, supra 308.
24 Judith N. Shklar, *After Utopia: The Decline of Political Faith* (Princeton: Princeton Univ. Press 1957).
25 Bell, *End of Ideology*, supra 402–3.
26 Duxbury, "Faith in Reason," supra 651.
27 Veter, "Postwar Legal Scholarship on Judicial Decision Making," supra 420.

perceived in procedural rather than substantive terms. Good procedures – as opposed to good or necessary legal principles (which could no longer be confidently identified) – render the law good. A legal system that conforms to these procedures, as the U.S. system does, promises to produce socially beneficial results, and gives rise to a duty of citizens to obey the law. Judging operates within legal constraints; any decisions that come down to pure questions of social expediency should be rendered by legislatures rather than judges. Legislatures, courts, and administrative agencies work together in the joint formulation and achievement of beneficial social policies.

At the same time that legal process ideas were being worked out, however, they were already being undermined by percolating social and legal events. The consensus view of the time was secured by an unreflective blindness toward the dreadful conditions of blacks in American society, excluded from the mainstream. Civil rights protests would soon shatter the veneer of a self-satisfied society.

More immediately, the reformist decisions of the Warren Court could not be squared with basic legal process tenets. This conflict was all the more painful for legal process theorists because most were liberals who shared in the substantive aims of the Court.[28] By legal process criteria, however, the Court's decisions appeared to be result-oriented, more the product of the personal moral views or policy preferences of the judges than legal analysis. Legal process scholars abhorred the pre-1937 Supreme Court as result-oriented judging gone amok, and found it no more acceptable when perpetuated by the Warren Court.

The beginning of the end for the legal process school was Herbert Weschler's 1959 article, "Toward Neutral Principles of Constitutional Law,"[29] which criticized the Warren Court's civil rights decisions as unsupported by constitutional principle. Weschler acknowledged that *Brown* was a momentous decision that could bring about positive social change, but he challenged it as inappropriately based upon sociological and psychological notions. His argument was that legislatures have the power to legislate on social issues however they please (and however misguided) unless constitutional principles are obviously contravened – Weschler could find no such principles. Separate educational facilities can be equal, in theory at least, and the principle of freedom of association equally supports segregation or integration. Not all legal process scholars agreed with his argument, but it was consistent with legal process thought. The massive thousand-plus pages of the *Legal Process* materials conspicuously failed to mention *Brown* – the most controversial case of the time – an omission which said a great deal.

Law students who were sympathetic to the plight of blacks and disgusted by legally imposed segregation recoiled from the argument. The "neutral principles" of legal

---

28 This conflict is described in Eskridge and Frickey, "An Historical and Critical Introduction to *The Legal Process*," supra.
29 Herbert Weschler, "Toward Neutral Principles of Constitutional Law," 73 *Harvard L. Rev.* 1 (1959).

process thought appeared to be set against the vindication of moral principles; in *Brown* and other Warren Court decisions, adherence to the former would seem to prohibit the law from doing what is right. The student editors of the *Harvard Law Review* made this agonizing dilemma explicit: "The compelling logic of the Frankfurter–Hart school has often appeared to impose a deadening hand; one has felt impelled to choose between rejecting progressive judicial positions for lack of coherent, principled rationales and abandoning the commitment to principle in frank or disguised result-orientedness."[30]

Supporters of the Warren Court offered a variety of criticisms against legal process thought. One set of arguments challenged the legal process attempt to sidestep questions of substance: The idea of "neutral principles" is impossibly narrow or incoherent; the Constitution contains or invokes substantive principles, so courts cannot avoid making substantive decisions about what is right; legal institutions and their procedures must be morally or substantively evaluated and justified, so the substance/procedure dichotomy breaks down.[31] A separate critique was that the legal process school has a naïve view of legislative processes. Legislation does not merit deference when certain groups are systematically excluded from participation[32] – whether through gerrymandering of voting districts or by erecting barriers to voting such as prohibitive poll taxes or literacy tests – or when legislation targets disfavored groups for ill treatment, or when legislation and administrative actions are dictated by special interests.[33] Under such circumstances, the procedures are *not* fair and they produce bad results, calling into question the legal process presumption that legislative purposes are reasonable and entitled to deference. Doubts were also raised about the plausibility of "reasoned elaboration" as an explanation for how legal principles are developed and cases are decided. The law of torts, for instance, contains several sometimes-conflicting sets of legal ideas, one of which emphasizes moral responsibility, another of which emphasizes compensation for injury, another of which emphasizes deterrence, and another of which emphasizes maximizing social wealth or economic efficiency.[34] These different streams of thought cannot all be reconciled through "reason." Judges must choose from among equally available alternatives.

Later refinements by process theorists accommodated several of these objections, for example, giving greater attention to perversions in the democratic process that disadvantage selected minorities.[35] By the end of the 1960s, however,

---

30 "With the Editors," 83 *Harvard L. Rev.* xxv, xxvi (1970).
31 See J. Skelly Wright, "Professor Bickel, the Scholarly Tradition, and the Supreme Court, 84 *Harvard L. Rev.* 769 (1971); Laurence Tribe, "The Puzzling Persistence of Process-Based Constitutional Theories," 89 *Yale L.J.* 1063 (1980); Richard Davies Parker, "The Past of Constitutional Theory – And its Future," 42 *Ohio St. L.J.* 223 (1981).
32 See Peller, "Neutral Principles in the 1950's," supra.
33 Eskridge and Frickey, "An Historical and Critical Introduction to *The Legal Process*," supra cxxiv.
34 See Duxbury, "Faith in Reason," supra 665–6.
35 See John Ely, *Democracy and Distrust* (Cambridge, Mass.: Harvard Univ. Press 1980).

further developments in the theory were all but irrelevant. The era of consensus was over.

Conflict penetrates the legal academy

The 1960s and 1970s witnessed a massive social upheaval in the United States: civil rights marches and boycotts; violent protests against the Vietnam War; public resistance to school busing; assassinations of President John F. Kennedy and his heir apparent Robert Kennedy; the murders of Martin Luther King, Jr., and Malcolm X; political terrorism and bombings and bank heists of the Weathermen, the Black Panthers, and the Symbionese Liberation Army; sexual revolution and drugs; corruption of Watergate; economic fears wrought by oil shortages, and an intransigent combination of high inflation and high unemployment.

Law was caught up in the middle of this social schism, castigated from all sides. People on the left saw law too often line up on the side of power and privilege, answering peaceful marches and sit-ins with police brandishing night sticks and snapping dogs. People on the right thought that defiant public displays of civil disobedience threatened social order, which was encouraged by the meek response of law enforcement. Progressives cheered the Warren Supreme Court as the one legal institution doing the right thing, while the right despised the Court as activist usurpers writing their own personal liberal views into the Constitution. All sides thought it evident that a "crisis of legal liberalism" was at hand.[36]

A vivid sense of the time, with obvious implications for the legal process school, leaps off the pages of the "With the Editors" statements prepared by the student editors of the *Harvard Law Review*, cited earlier on the dilemma posed by the Warren Court. The officers of the law review were the anointed *ultra* elite – the best of the brightest, on a royal path to an assured future as leading law professors, judges, lawyers, and government officials. In a marked departure from the past practice of using the column to issue mundane housekeeping observations, in the 1969–70 volume, the Editors set forth a series of radicalized comments, prompted by events that came to their very doorstep – literally:

> On the night of April 15, a conflagration raged between police and demonstrators in Harvard Square. Its destructive effects, however, spread far beyond the original participants and area. Stationing themselves just a block from Gannett House [the home of the law review], scores of helmeted police cordoned off the Square from the north. Many students stood in small groups outside the police barricade, silently watching and wondering about the events occurring a few blocks away. Suddenly, and without any observable provocation from the bystanders, the police advanced, soon running and swinging their riot clubs wildly. Students fled from the charging policemen and sought refuge in Gannett House or other nearby buildings. Others were less fortunate. An officer of the *Review*, trying to avoid the onrushing police, had his key in the lock of

36 Lestor Mazor, "The Crisis of Legal Liberalism," 81 *Yale L.J.* 1032 (1972).

the Gannett House door when he was clubbed from behind by one of the two officers running by. Neither stopped; the blow on the head was merely a gratuitous gesture by the guardians of the law.

... Police here, as in so many other cities, added recruits to the radical cause by their misguided attempts to bludgeon that very ideology.[37]

As matters worsened, Harvard law students, including a number of the editors, took time away from school to engage in anti-war activities:

Like so many other institutions, the *Law Review* has discovered in recent weeks that it is increasingly difficult to function normally in the current national climate. The invasion of Cambodia and the official murders at Kent State, Jackson State and elsewhere have evoked an impassioned response from countless concerned citizens who now feel the need to act directly to change current national policy.

. . .

Thus the events which have made national headlines in recent weeks have had a profound personal cost for all of us at Gannett House, whether or not we chose the route of direct political action. All of us prefer our former roles as full-time law students and *Law Review* editors to our presently imposed positions as political protesters and institutional crisis managers. Yet as long as the country remains in its present precarious state, we may all be forced to continue to fight battles in a contest we do not seek. And the result will surely be continuing frustration and even despair, as agonizingly slow progress is made toward the uninspiring goal of restoring ourselves and our institutions to where we thought we were only a short time ago.[38]

Inevitably, this white hot envelope of events, especially the discredited authoritarian face of the law and government, affected how law students perceived their legal education and the law:

At a time when so many venerable traditions are being skeptically scrutinized, if not harshly attacked, it is hardly surprising that legal reasoning is also attracting increasing criticism. Growing numbers of students are questioning whether lawyer-like logic and analysis are indeed proper tools for contemporary problem solving. Such students believe that the Law School and the method of analysis it teaches deliberately obscure rather than clarify relevant issues. In assessing legal logic, at least one disgruntled student has termed it a "cerebral trickbag," which is presumably manipulated by the malevolent masters of the Establishment.

It is true that what passes for logic in some judicial opinions (and in many classrooms) is a little more than finely spun sophistry. It is also important to note that pure logic does not offer a solution to all problems. In reaching a great many solutions, a value

37 "With the Editors," 83 *Harvard L. Rev.* xxxiii (1970). The "With the Editors" statements were included in individual issues of the law review, but removed when the issues were bound into a single volume. They are available in the HeinOnLine law review archives.
38 "With the Editors," 83 *Harvard L. Rev.* xxxv, xxxv–xxxvi (1970).

judgment or aesthetic choice becomes inevitable, no matter how much the decision-maker may isolate and clarify the relevant issues by means of careful analysis. Indeed, in some cases the 'logical' solution may even be inappropriate because certain emotional or other supposedly illogical factors are proper considerations.[39]

Moderating their skeptical stance, the editors urged that legal logic still had value and was not entirely deserving of "the contempt it has recently received." Yet they returned several times to their core point: "When problems are properly reducible only to issues which transcend the logical method, it is a misuse of legal reasoning to obscure a value judgment with a flourish of supposed analysis."[40]

Harvard Law School was the home of the legal process school. Its doctrines filled the halls. Little imagination is required to interpret these statements by the editors of the law review, in conjunction with their earlier-cited observation that legal process thought appears to require that moral principle be sacrificed on the altar of legal reasoning, as a decided turn away from legal process thought. On the first page of the volume, the editors left no doubt about where their sympathies lay (on the occasion of his retirement): "To Chief Justice Warren, who with courage and compassion led a reform of the law while the other branches of government delayed, the editors respectfully dedicate this issue."[41]

A number of the 1969–70 law review members would go on to distinguished careers at top law schools around the nation, including Lewis Sargentich, James Gordley, Richard Parker, Ira Lupu, Martin Redish, Ronald Rotunda, and Louis Seidman. Harvard, it should be emphasized, was less radicalized than Columbia, Yale, Wisconsin, and Berkeley, and many other college and law school campuses. The main theories of law circulating today within the U.S. legal culture, the views of law professors, judges, and practicing lawyers, took root in this period of turmoil, formulated by law students or new law professors in the 1960s and 1970s. Whichever side one was on, it was nigh impossible for one's views of law to remain untouched by contemporary events. Views of law today bear the indelible imprint of this fateful time.

Legal instrumentalism and moral relativism in the academy

Legal historian Calvin Woodward wrote in 1968 that prevailing attitudes within the legal academy were thoroughly Legal Realist. Although the legal process school was partially successful in domesticating the Realists' most radical arguments, the resonance of its incisive critiques of conceptual and rule formalism continued like a subterranean river. "At least in the better law schools," Woodward remarked, "'functionalists' and 'realists' are no longer lonely aliens in a hostile world. In truth

---

39 "With the Editors," 83 *Harvard L. Rev.* xxxi (1970).
40 Id.
41 Dedication, 83 *Harvard L. Rev.* 1 (1969).

they probably outweigh in influence, if not in numbers, the Langdellians."[42] Graduates from the better law schools, he might have added, would become professors at law schools across the land, carrying with them and further propagating these views. Given that the functional/purposive aspects of Realist thought were also adopted by legal process adherents, one could comfortably hold both understandings, up to a point.

Woodward recognized that responsibility for the triumph of instrumental views of law could not be laid on the Realists alone:

> ...the society-wide trend toward secularization is the culmination of a centuries-long development that has transformed the Law from a "brooding omnipresence in the sky" into a down-to-earth instrument of social reform and, at the same time, translated...the lawyer from a quasi-priestly figure into a social engineer. Legal education...has both reflected and contributed to this long-term trend.[43]

In the course of the twentieth century, society at large underwent a general loss of belief in objectively existing principles.[44] With a seemingly irresistible momentum, in each passing decade "the knowledge of good and evil, as an intellectual subject, was being systematically and effectively destroyed."[45] Political thinker Walter Lippmann worriedly remarked in 1955 that "the school of natural law has not been able to cope with the pluralism of the later modern age – with the pluralism which has resulted from the industrial revolution and the enfranchisement and the emancipation of the masses of the people."[46] The spectacular evil and suffering inflicted by all sides on all sides in two World Wars, followed by the rise of Soviet totalitarianism, pummeled the faith in reason and human progress that informed so much of eighteenth and nineteenth century political thought.[47] The collapse of non-instrumental views of law described in Part 1, which paved the way for the takeover of the instrumental view of law, was a piece of this broader trend.

On the positive side, the newly accepted instrumental understanding of law offered important advantages. The New Deal was constructed entirely through legal initiatives and mechanisms, confirming that law can be used effectively as an instrument of social policy; the Warren Court had advanced the cause of social justice (in the eyes of supporters); the common law was slowly being wrested by state judges into the modern age with more attention to ameliorating the social risks brought by mass society. But Woodward sounded a cautionary note: "Predictably,

---

42 Calvin Woodward, "The Limits of Legal Realism: An Historical Perspective," 54 *Virginia L. Rev.* 689, 732 (1968).
43 Id. 733.
44 An unparalleled historical exploration of the ideas that led to this state can be found in Richard Tarnas, *The Passion of the Western Mind: Understanding the Ideas that Have Shaped our World View* (New York: Harmony Books 1991).
45 Arthur Allen Leff, "Economic Analysis of Law: Some Realism about Nominalism," 60 *Virginia L. Rev.* 451, 454 (1974).
46 Walter Lippmann, *The Public Philosophy* (New York: Mentor Books 1955) 85.
47 See Robert A. Nisbet, *Social Change and History* (New York: Oxford Univ. Press 1969).

the result [of these ideas] is a generation of law teachers who find it difficult to believe – by this I mean profoundly believe – in the existence of law beyond what fallible courts say it is; a generation of law students who consequently do not learn to be restrained in any essential way by the law . . . "[48]

A decade later, the Dean of Cornell Law School, Roger C. Cramton, wrote that legal instrumentalism had become "the ordinary religion of the law school classroom."[49] This "orthodox" wisdom, conveyed daily by law professors to their students, is "an instrumental approach to law and lawyering," along with "a skeptical attitude toward generalizations, principles, and received wisdom."[50] Cramton credited (or blamed) Holmes, the Legal Realists, and pragmatism for these attitudes about law:

> Today law tends to be viewed in solely instrumental terms and as lacking values of its own, other than a limited agreement on certain 'process values' thought to be implicit in our democratic way of doing things. We agree on methods of resolving our disagreements in the public arena, but on little else. Substantive goals come from the political process or from private interests in the community. The lawyer's task, in an instrumental approach to law, is to facilitate and manipulate legal processes to advance the interest of his client.[51]

Cramton captured the prevailing view of law as an empty vessel, matched by a vision of the lawyer who instrumentally utilizes legal rules and processes for clients.

In the hands of Realist-influenced law professors, Langdell's case method for the study of law underwent a complete inversion, from upholding the principled nature of law to subverting it. Realist Max Radin described the original purpose of the case method:

> The case method was, of course, a method of dialectic. But its principal purpose was not that of training students in method but of inculcating in their minds certain legal propositions which were regarded as valuable. They constitute the 'right doctrine,' the 'true doctrine' or the 'right theory,' the 'true theory,' – no one said the 'orthodox theory' – and if the student remembered the propositions and assumed them to be irrefutable, he had been well taught.[52]

In the skeptical atmosphere of the 1970s and thereafter, many law professors taught *against* the cases – training students to critically scrutinize judicial reasoning, demonstrating that the court's reasoning in nearly every case can be undercut. A favorite pedagogical technique is to require students to articulate equally solid

48 Woodward, "Limits of Legal Realism," supra 734.
49 Roger C. Cramton, "The Ordinary Religion of the Law School Classroom," 29 *J. Legal Educ.* 247 (1978).
50 Id. 248.
51 Id. 257.
52 Max Radin, "The Education of a Lawyer," 25 *Cal. L. Rev.* 676, 681 (1937).

arguments for opposing sides, or to build up one side then proceed to break it down. The lesson brought home by this use of the case method is that there is no unchallengeable "right doctrine" or "right theory" – that everything is up for argument.

There is a temptation to shrug "so what" at this purely instrumental characterization of law, so routine is it now. Woodward and Cramton found it worthy of comment precisely because, although it had been creeping up for decades, it was contrary to earlier ways of teaching law, the memory of which had not yet been extinguished. They openly worried about the unknown implications of a purely instrumental view of law being purveyed in law schools. At no previous time in U.S. history had law been seen by the entire legal culture in a consummately instrumental way.

Cynicism about government was also in full bloom. Another prominent legal historian, G. Edward White, observed in 1973 that a feature of contemporary life was "an acknowledged gap between the goals of officeholders and those of their constituents, as well as a widespread judgment that those same officeholders are furthering their own goals while merely paying lip service to their constituents' needs."[53] Administrative agencies, for example, "charged with the duty of regulating the activities of industrial enterprises in the public interest," regularly "define 'public interest' to be synonymous with the needs of their regulatees."[54] Critics of government were "linked in their perception that terms such as 'public interest' and 'social welfare' have lost their meaning: the terms are capable of such wide, divergent, and contradictory interpretations that they are useless as standards of performance."[55]

"A final and possibly the most significant aspect of American culture in the 1970's," White observed, "is the disintegration of common values or goals. In the place of consensual values around which members of American society can cohere stand sets of polar alternatives ... "[56] Beyond the fact of the sharp disagreement over values was the bleak prospect that without access to absolute moral standards these disputes could not be resolved. "[T]here is no way of deciding these matters," Robert Bork wrote in 1971, "other than by reference to some system of moral or ethical values that has no objective or intrinsic validity of its own and about which men can and do differ."[57] Arthur Leff remarked in 1974 that the absence of objective moral foundations "is a fact of modern intellectual life so well and painfully known as to be one of the few which is simultaneously horrifying and banal."[58]

---

53 G. Edward White, "The Evolution of Reasoned Elaboration: Jurisprudential Criticism and Social Change," 59 *Virginia L. Rev.* 280, 295 (1973).
54 Id.
55 Id.
56 Id. 296.
57 Robert H. Bork, "Neutral Principles and Some First Amendment Problems," 47 *Indiana L.J.* 1, 10 (1971).
58 Leff, "Economic Analysis of Law," supra 455.

In legal academia, the public climax of this realization was Leff's 1979 article, "Unspeakable Ethics, Unnatural Law," which raised a hopeless plea for some source of moral and legal grounding in an apparently groundless world. Confident that objective principle could be better secured in reason or science, moderns had banished God and natural law only to arrive at an unanticipated and apparently insurmountable destination: "*There is no such thing as an unchallengeable evaluative system*. There is no way to prove one ethical or legal system superior to any other, unless at some point an evaluator is asserted to have the final, uncontradictable, unexaminable word."[59] His essay memorably left off with the words "God help us."[60] Roberto Unger's highly influential (among the radical left) *Knowledge and Politics* (1975) argued that the modern belief in the subjectivity of values planted deep contradictions into liberal legal systems with no evident solution. It ended "Speak, God."[61] In the air at the time was a palpable awareness that society and law had been cut adrift irretrievably from their old moorings with no new anchorage in sight.

The abhorred moral relativism that was used to bludgeon the Legal Realists into silence in the 1940s had become a way of life in the conflict of the 1960s and 1970s. For many, it was an accepted article of the faith that "in a pluralistic and tolerant society it is impossible to expect that individuals or groups will agree about many basic values."[62] The legal process school, which relied heavily on assumptions about social consensus, lost its reassuring quality; the answers it provided implausiblely patched over the hard questions.

By the 1970s, then, the two streams that underlie the dynamic driving the contemporary legal culture were set in place. The view that law is in essence an instrument had won over the legal academy. This took place in a context of sharp, society-wide, group-based disagreement over moral values and over the public good, coinciding with a loss of belief in the availability of objective standards by which to resolve such disputes.

This combination, to draw out the broader point, has implications not sufficiently contemplated by early advocates of an instrumental view of law. When the instrumental view of law was promoted, it was unfailingly urged that law is an instrument to achieve social ends, and it was assumed that disputes over social ends could be worked out As events transpired, the first half of the proposition gained strength while confidence in the second half waned. Without the second half, however, the import of an instrumental view of law turns from benign to ominous. Woodward raised the crucial question back in 1968: "does the functional approach

---

59 Arthur Allen Leff, "Unspeakable Ethics, Unnatural Law," 1979 *Duke L. J.* 1229, 1240 (1979) (emphasis in original).
60 Id. 1249.
61 Robert M. Unger, *Knowledge and Politics* (New York: Free Press 1975) 295.
62 Cramton, "The Ordinary Wisdom of the Law School Classroom," supra. 252.

not teach all manner of men to look to law as an instrument for *their* private or personal disposal?"[63]

Since the 1970s, when the instrumental view of law infused the legal academy, law students have been trained to see law as purely an instrument. These are the lawyers of today, who permeate society and its structures of power, corporate lawyers, cause lawyers, law professors, judges, legally trained legislators and their staffs, administrative agency officials, executive branch officials, and lawyer-lobbyists. The implications of this for law and society are displayed in the following chapters.

63 Woodward, "The Limits of Legal Realism," supra 735 (emphasis in original).

7

Instrumentalism in theories of law

Almost all of the major theoretical and empirical perspectives toward law that circulate today developed during the 1960s and 1970s, or have roots in that period, and characterize law in fundamentally instrumental terms. The economic analysis of law, critical legal studies and their progeny, the law and society movement, legal pragmatism, and the formal version of the rule of law, each in central respects builds its understanding around the proposition that law is a means to an end. Many of these schools of thought also take an instrumental view toward their own scholarship and toward the scholarship of others. That is, as a consequence of general skepticism about the capacity to achieve objectivity, there is a widespread sense that theories of law, and knowledge about law, are inevitably colored by politics, akin to the assumption that politics influences judging.

These various schools of thought are given an abbreviated sketch, in the order just set out, limited to revealing their core instrumental components. This narrowly focused survey shows how instrumentalist views permeate theoretical understandings of law. At the close of the chapter is a brief mention of the non-instrumental theories of law that hang on against the tide.

Economic analysis of law

The starting assumption of economic analysis of law is "that the people involved with the legal system act as rational maximizers of their satisfaction."[1] Armed with this assumption, practitioners of law and economics, foremost among them Judge Richard A. Posner, set forth to examine the entire gamut of legal subjects, practices, and institutions; tort, property, and contract law; criminal law, tax law, corporations law, securities law, antitrust law, family law, procedural rules, enforcement behavior, administrative rule making, legislation; virtually every conceivable aspect of law. The analysis is monotonously instrumental, examining in every context whether law is an efficient means to designated ends.

Adherents of law and economics proffer a descriptive and a prescriptive claim. The *descriptive* claim is that the law – common law rules in particular – operates by and large (though not completely) to maximize social wealth, even when judges

---

1 Richard A. Posner, "The Economic Approach to Law," 53 *Texas L. Rev.* 757, 61 (1975).

do not explicitly or consciously identify that as their objective. Maximizing wealth in this context means that legal rules facilitate the transfer of activities, goods and services to those who value them the most (hypothetically measured by their willingness to pay). The twofold explanation offered by Posner for how this came about is that many of the current common law doctrines were put into place in the late nineteenth century, when laissez faire views were dominant among judges, and, furthermore, that when rendering their decisions, judges often aim to further social welfare,[2] which amounts to maximizing wealth. Practitioners of law and economics are generally skeptical of judicial accounts of judging and legal rules, and they reject the notion that law has autonomy or integrity onto itself.

The *prescriptive* claim is that law *should* be oriented toward maximizing wealth. One rationale offered in support of this proposition is that few people would object to a legal regime that strives to make society as wealthy as possible. Another rationale is that our liberal culture has a general utilitarian orientation toward government and law, and wealth maximization provides a way to operationalize utilitarianism. People have different desires and goods which are difficulty to quantify, so valuing desires in terms of willingness to pay is a convenient and universally applicable surrogate measure of value. If activities, goods, and services go to those who value them the most, society is better off overall.

In the mid-1970s, as its influence was spreading, Arthur Leff observed that a major aspect of the appeal of the economic approach to law is that it offers an apparent solution to irresolvable disagreements over the ends that law should serve.[3] Law must simply maximize the ability of people (in the aggregate) to get what they want, obviating the need to come to an agreement. Maximizing wealth is the social end – law is the means to achieve that end.

With the arrival of law and economics, the Realist program of using law as an instrument to achieve social ends can finally be realized, claim adherents. Lending credence to this claim is the often-cited remark of Oliver Wendell Holmes, "For the rational study of the law the black-letter man may be the man of the present, but the man of the future is the man of statistics and the master of economics."[4] Economic analysis purports to consist of a small set of easily mastered ideas that offer a way to check the objectivity of legal decisions, and to produce predictable legal results. Legal rules and judicial decisions can be evaluated against a clear, common standard – maximizing wealth – based upon calculations that can be reproduced.[5] This is a new kind of formalism that claims mathematical precision and objectivity.

Many criticisms have been lodged against the economic approach to law, which need not be covered exhaustively here.[6] A criticism often made is that maximizing

---

2 Richard A. Posner, *The Problems of Jurisprudence* (Cambridge, Mass.: Harvard Univ. Press 1993) 354–9.
3 Leff, "Economic Analysis of Law," supra 456–9.
4 Holmes, "Path of the Law," supra 469.
5 See Posner, "Economic Approach to Law," supra.
6 Leff's early criticism, "Economic Analysis of Law," supra still stands as a sound one.

efficiency is neither the only nor the most important end of law;[7] but many adherents are willing to retreat from this extreme claim,[8] content to assert that it is among the most important concerns of law. Another criticism is the charge that, whereas law and economics claims to be an objective science, concealed behind its ubiquitous tables and mathematical calculations is a built in conservative bias.[9] Willingness to pay is a function of ability to pay, which raises issues of fair distribution, but distributional questions are usually bracketed as outside its domain.[10] Another common objection is that, in practice, economic analysis requires a multitude of contestable, simplifying assumptions, which shape the results produced, so findings cannot be applied to real-world conditions; moreover, the calculations required are so complicated as to be beyond the capacity of most judges and legal scholars to utilize or evaluate.

Despite these limitations, in the past three decades, the economic analysis of law has had a greater influence on legal doctrine and judicial analysis, particularly in antitrust and torts, than any other theoretical approach to law covered in this chapter, although this can be confidently asserted partly because other schools of thought have had hardly any discernable impact (perhaps legal pragmatism aside). "Part of the power of economic analysis," legal theorist Brian Bix observed, "is that it presents a largely instrumental approach, which fits well with the analysis and evaluation of law: it forces the question, do these legal rules achieve the objectives at which they aim, and would alternative rules do any better?"[11]

Critical approaches to law

The 1970s also ushered in the Critical Legal Studies Movement (CLS), which was the radical-left counterpart to law and economics. Arriving on the scene together, these schools of thought were siblings, the good and bad – depending upon one's sensibilities and politics – offspring of the Legal Realists.[12] Law and economics absorbed the critical lessons of the Realists and took up the consequentialist (utilitarian), science-oriented aspects of constructive Realist thought, whereas CLS pressed the critique further, took up the politically progressive aspects, and discarded as naïve the Realists' promotion of social scientific studies of law. Owing to the skeptical perspective on legal doctrine common to both, many mainstream legal scholars were dismayed at both schools of thought.[13] Despite these commonalities, their fates have diverged: Economic analysis of law is a thriving field of legal analysis and has

---

7 See Anthony T. Kronman, "Wealth Maximization as a Normative Principle," 9 *J. Legal Studies* 227 (1980).
8 Even Posner has acknowledged lately that "wealth maximization" is "unsatisfactory as a universal norm." Posner, *Problems of Jurisprudence,* supra 373.
9 Morton J. Horwitz, "Law and Economics: Science or Politics?" 8 *Hofstra L. Rev.* 905 (1981).
10 See generally Thomas Cotter, "Legal Pragmatism and the Law and Economics Movement," 84 *Georgetown L.J.* 2071, 2012–2138 (1996).
11 Brian Bix, *Jurisprudence: Theory and Context* (Durham, N.C.: Carolina Academic Press 2004) 190.
12 See Joseph Singer, "Legal Realism Now," 76 *California L. Rev.* 465 (1988)
13 See Owen Fiss, "The Death of the Law," 72 *Cornell L. Rev.* 1 (1986).

been incorporated by judges in selected areas of law, whereas CLS no longer exists as a concrete movement and has had no evident impact on legal doctrine, though it continues to influence academics. Sympathizers of CLS explain these contrasting receptions by the conservatism of the U.S. legal tradition, which favors the conservative tilt of law and economics; another explanation is that law and economics offers a usable formula, whereas CLS mainly criticized.

Although CLS consisted of many strands, at its core were three main ideas,[14] all captured by the movement's rallying mantra: "Law is politics." First, picking up a Realist theme, the body of legal rules is so indeterminate that law does not inevitably produce a single correct answer in cases:

> ... indeterminacy stems from the reality that the law usually embraces and legitimizes many or all of the conflicting interests involved in controversial issues and a wide and conflicting array of 'logical' or 'reasoned' arguments and strategies of argumentation, without providing any legally required hierarchy of values or arguments or any required method for determining which is most important in a particular context. Judges then make choices, and those choices are most fundamentally value based, or political.[15]

The second point is that the political aspects of law are hidden under a guise of neutrality and objectivity conveyed by phrases like "the rule of law, not man" or grand terms like "liberty" or "rights." The third point is that the law favors the dominant class. First-hand observers of the social turmoil of the 1960s and 1970s, the "Crits" (as they were called) saw "all the myriad ways in which the legal system was not a set of neutral techniques available to anyone who could seize control of the levers and switches but a game heavily loaded in favor of the wealthy and powerful."[16] They were determined to expose the hidden bent and bias of the system.

CLS portrayed law in thoroughly instrumental terms. On the invitation to the inaugural CLS conference, held in May 1977, it was declared that "law is an instrument of social, economic, and political domination, both in the sense of furthering the concrete interests of the dominators and in that of legitimating the existing order."[17] This was not the crude instrumentalism of "vulgar" Marxism, which construes law as a direct weapon of elite domination; instead, law displays a degree of autonomy that serves to enhance its credibility as standing above the fray of sectional clashes in society. "[B]ut over the long term, the law taken as a whole will take its shape from the interests of socially powerful groups."[18] Theories of democratic interest-group pluralism, by this account, are delusory. Every now and

14 An informative overview of CLS is Joseph W. Singer, "The Player and the Cards: Nihlism and Legal Theory," 94 *Yale L.J.* 1 (1984).
15 David Kairys, "Introduction," in *The Politics of Law: A Progressive Critique*, 3rd ed. (New York: Basic Books 1998) 2. This book contains an excellent set of essays reflecting the critical approaches covered in this section. See also Critical Legal Studies Symposium, 30 *Stanford L. Rev.* 1 (1984).
16 Robert W. Gordon, "Some Critical Theories of Law and Their Critics," in *Politics of Law*, supra 644.
17 Quoted in Louis B. Schwartz, "With Gun and Camera Through Darkest CLS-Land," 36 *Stanford L. Rev.* 413, 417 (1984).
18 Mark Tushnet, "Perspectives on the Development of American Law: A Critical Review of Friedman's 'A History of American Law,'" 1977 *Wisconsin L. Rev.* 81 (1977).

then scraps are parceled out to various competing groups to keep them appeased and to make the system appear honest, but, on the whole, there is "a built in tilt toward reproduction of existing power relations."[19]

Two other critical schools of thought, critical feminist theory and critical race theory, which still exist, have independent roots in the 1960s in feminism and the civil rights movements, respectively, but they also developed in conjunction with and out of CLS. They, too, hold an instrumental view of law. Critical feminists paint law as an instrument that "enforces and maintains a male supremacist social order."[20] Critical race theorists emphasize that law is an instrument that "reproduce[s] the structures and practices of racial domination."[21] The underlying theory of both is much the same as that of CLS. "Long ago, empowered actors and speakers enshrined their meanings, preferences and views of the world into the common culture and language. Now their deliberation within that language, purporting always to be neutral and fair, inexorably produces results that reflect their interests."[22] Adherents point to ample evidence in support of their claims. Women had to overcome stiff resistance to secure the right to vote, their legal standing was subsumed under their husband upon marriage, and until recently, men inflicted domestic violence upon women with impunity. Slavery was enshrined within the Constitution and was viciously enforced by the law.[23] Slavery's demise brought legally imposed segregation, enforcing white domination; blacks were kept from voting by targeted, prohibitive voting requirements,[24] and black defendants have always been and continue to be treated more harshly than whites in various contexts of the criminal justice system.[25] Up through the 1960s, furthermore, few women and minority law students were admitted into law schools, and were almost nonexistent as partners in elite law firms, or as judges or law professors. The numbers in all of these categories have since improved – women and men now attend law school in equal numbers – but women and minorities continue to disproportionately lag white males in achieving elite professional positions.[26]

In addition to their contrasting targets, the main distinction between these critical schools is that CLS tended to present the legal system as deeply corrupt and perhaps irredeemable – a position that led intemperate opponents to castigate Crits as legal

19 Gordon, "Some Critical Theories of Law and Their Critics," supra 464.
20 D. Polan, "Toward a Theory of Law and Patriarchy," in *Feminist Legal Theory*, edited by D. K. Weisberg (Philadelphia: Temple Univ. Press 1993) 419.
21 Kimberly Crenshaw, et. al., "Introduction," in *Critical Race Theory*, edited by K. Crenshaw, et al. (New York: New Press 1995).
22 Richard Delgado and Jean Stefancic, "Hateful Speech, Loving Communicates: Why Our Nation of 'A Just Balance' Changes So Slowly," 82 *California L. Rev.* 851, 861 (1994).
23 A wrenching summary of this legal oppression is in Friedman, *History of American Law*, supra 218–29.
24 Id. 504–10.
25 A recent overview of the studies that demonstrate one aspect of this is Shawn D. Bushway and Anne Morrison Piehl, "Judging Judicial Discretion: Legal Factors and Racial Discrimination in Sentencing," 35 *L. & Soc. Rev.* 733 (2001)
26 See ABA Commission on Women in the Profession, A Current Glance at Women in the Law 2005, at www.abanet.org/women/ataglance.pdf.

nihilists who do not belong in the legal academy[27] – whereas critical feminists and critical race theorists are willing to utilize the tools that law offers, such as antidiscrimination laws and rights claims, as a means to further their agendas.

Law and society movement

The thriving Law and Society Movement (Law & Society), also known as sociolegal studies, is the third of the three distinct approaches toward law to emerge in the 1960s and 1970s claiming descent from the Legal Realists.[28] The banner of Law & Society is the social scientific study of law and society, a broad umbrella that includes legal historians, political scientists who study judicial decision-making, legal sociologists of various stripes (researching the legal profession, public attitudes about law, legal issues relating to women and minorities, death penalty, etc.), criminologists, legal anthropologists, behavioral economists, comparativists, law and development scholars, and various other approaches, united by an empirical orientation to law. It may seem odd to include empiricists in a chapter on Theories of Law, but many participants are highly theoretical, all posit a full set of theoretical assumptions about law in their work, and in essential respects these scholars overlap with two approaches covered earlier.

Law & Society shares the critical and skeptical stance of law and economics and CLS toward legal doctrine and about the nature and effects of legal activities. Like law and economics, Law & Society takes up the social scientific agenda promoted by the Realists, but it rejects the former's association with conservative positions and it rejects as non-empirical the emphasis in (early) law and economics on abstract modeling. Like CLS, many leading members of Law & Society openly align themselves with the political left. Past presidents of the Law and Society Association have proudly identified Law & Society with "progressive politics," claiming that their work is a form of "left-liberal scholarship."[29] Like CLS, a recurring theme of sociolegal studies has been the exposure of law's hegemonic ideological domination.[30] A complete embrace of the two was never possible, however, because CLS was hostile to social science as objectivist mystification that supports the status quo.[31] And many sociolegal scholars, although personally sympathetic to liberal politics, consider the politicization of sociolegal scholarship to be inappropriate and detrimental to their efforts to produce reliable knowledge about law. Nonetheless, there was a significant overlap of individuals in the early membership of these two groups.[32]

27 Paul D. Carrington, "Of Law and the River," 34 *J. Legal Educ.* 222 (1984).
28 An overview of the Movement is provided in Brian Z. Tamanaha, *Realistic Socio-Legal Studies: Pragmatism and a Social Theory of Law* (Oxford: Clarendon Press 1997).
29 Sally Engle Merry, "Resistance and the Cultural Power of Law: 1994 Presidential Address," 29 *L. & Soc. Rev.* 11, 12 (1995); Kitty Calavita, "Engaged Research, 'Goose Bumps,' and the Role of the Public Intellectual," 36 *L. & Soc. Rev.* 5 (2002).
30 See Special Issue, "Law and Ideology," 22 *L. & Soc. Rev.* (1988).
31 See David Trubek, "Where the Action is: Critical Legal Studies and Empiricism," 36 *Stanford L. Rev.* 575 (1984).
32 Duxbury, *Patterns of American Jurisprudence*, supra 435–50.

Sociolegal scholars adopt a thoroughly instrumental understanding of law that shows up in different forms. An already mentioned theme is the idea that law is an instrument of domination, whether by the elite, by males, or by whites. Core early themes of Law & Society, explicitly taken from the Realists, include the study of the gap between the printed legal rules and the actual activities of legal officials, the gap between legal rules and the behavior of people in society,[33] and the influence of non-legal sources of social order that are inconsistent with and more effective than the law.[34] This focus aims at discerning the actual efficacy of law as an instrument of social ordering and social change.[35] A constant refrain in these studies is a reminder about the complexity of social life and the many barriers it erects to law. Consequently, law is often a surprisingly impotent instrument of social change. "Years of instrumentalist effectiveness research had led only to the monotonous conclusion that legal rules, so considered, rarely produce the intended results and are therefore apparently of little social significance."[36] An instrumental perspective on law is manifested in Law & Society in other ways as well. Within the sociology of law, a leading approach (consistent with the themes of this book) focuses on the conflicts among interests in society. The "hallmark of the conflict approach was its instrumentalist conception of law;" the "content (and form) of law [was] seen as an epiphenomenon of the balance of power within society."[37] Political scientists who conduct studies of judicial decision-making locate their inspiration in Realist insights;[38] many of these studies, which demonstrate statistical correlations between the attitudes of judges and their decisions, set out to establish that judges are "politicians in black robes" who instrumentally manipulate legal rules to arrive at outcomes that match their personal predilections.[39]

One theoretical work that emerged from Law & Society has particular relevance to the themes in Part One of this book. Philippe Nonet and Philip Selznick explicitly situated their 1978 book *Law and Society in Transition* in the tradition of pragmatism, Pound, and the Realists. They argued that modern law is in the process of evolving to a higher legal form through a greater orientation toward instrumentally achieving social purposes. They labeled this new stage "responsive law" in which "there is a renewal of instrumentalism . . . for the achievement of public ends."[40] This

---

33 See Tamanaha, *Realistic Socio-Legal Theory*, supra 101–3.
34 The classic study is Stewart Macaulay, "Non-Contractual Relations in Business: A Preliminary Study," 28 *Am. Soc. Rev.* 55 (1963); see also Robert Ellickson, *Order Without Law: How Neighbors Settle Disputes* (Cambridge, Mass.: Harvard Univ. Press 1991).
35 See Richard Abel, "Law Books and Books About Law," 26 *Stanford L. Rev.* 175 (1973).
36 John Griffits, "The Social Working of Legal Rules," 48 *J. Legal Pluralism* 1, 14 (2003).
37 David Nelken, "The Gap Problem in the Sociology of Law; A Theoretical Review," 1 *Windsor Yearbook of Access to Justice* 35, 46 (1981).
38 C. Herman Pritchett, "The Development of Judicial Research," in *Frontiers of Judicial Research*, edited by J.B. Grossman and J. Tanenhaus (New York: J. Wiley 1968) 28–9.
39 H. R. Glick, *Courts, Politics, and Justice* (New York: McGraw Hill 1983) 243.
40 Phillippe Nonet and Philip Selznick, *Law and Society in Transition: Toward Responsive Law* (New York: Octagon Books 1978) 15. Another book which laid out a similar evolutionary framework, though less optimistic, was Roberto M. Unger, *Law in Modern Society: Toward a Criticism of Social Theory* (New York: Free Press 1976).

is an advance, they claimed, over the previous formalistic stage of "autonomous law" in which law is seen as separate from politics, and decisions are made strictly according to legal rules with no attention to consequences. In this new higher stage, "the logic of legal judgment becomes closely congruent with the logic of moral and practical judgment."[41] Several other important legal theorists in the 1970s also noted the apparent ongoing shift in style of judicial decision-making, away from strict rule application toward more instrumental reasoning to achieve social purposes, though few were as sanguine about this development.[42] The timing of Nonet's and Selznick's prescriptive argument was poor, at least from the standpoint of liberal scholars. The Rehnquist Court and a plethora of conservative judicial appointees to the bench lay ahead just around the bend. The suggestion that judges should render moral and policy decisions is unappealing to liberal scholars when the judiciary is filled with conservatives.

Another relevant aspect of Law & Society is the struggle by participants to mediate a direct clash between two cherished ideals. On the one hand, many participants are committed to empirical social science, which involves the pursuit of knowledge. On the other hand, many are committed to leftist politics and want their work to advance the progressive vision of social justice. The obvious question this raises is whether, or to what extent, a leftist political agenda taints the knowledge produced. Are their research findings merely leftist dogma delivered in scientific packaging? Conservative commentators, who regularly point out the numerical dominance of liberal professors in universities and law schools, have said as much.

The dilemma that confronts sociolegal scholars runs deeper than merely conflicting motivations – at base it is an epistemological one that doubts the very possibility of unbiased knowledge. Richard Tarnas, a historian of ideas, summarized the uncertain state of affairs that plagues knowledge today, what he labels the "post-modern condition," a product of the ideas traced in earlier chapters:

> Reality is in some sense constructed by the mind, not simply perceived by it, and many such constructions are possible, none necessarily sovereign. . . . There is no empirical 'fact' that is not already theory-laden, and there is no logical argument or formal principle that is a priori certain. All human understanding is interpretation, and no interpretation is final. . . .
>
> Hence the nature of truth and reality, in science no less than in philosophy, religion, or art, is radically ambiguous. The subject can never presume to transcend the manifold predispositions of his or her subjectivity.[43]

Sociolegal scholars have debated the apparently debilitating implications of these ideas for social scientific research. "Critical-empiricists" urge fellow sociolegal scholars to drop the hollow residual scientism and embrace the implication that their

---

41 Nonet and Selznick, *Law and Society in Transition*, supra 89.
42 See Unger, *Knowledge and Politics*, supra; Patrick S. Atiyah, *From Principle to Pragmatism: Changes in the Function of the Judicial Process and the Law* (Oxford: Clarendon Press 1978).
43 Tarnas, *Passion of the Western Mind*, supra 396–7.

work is political.[44] In response, "Post-empiricists" acknowledge that old standards of validity and reliability, and the stance of neutrality, are no longer plausible, and that social scientists cannot escape their "backgrounds and biographies," but continue to hold out that they are producing knowledge that is not entirely political, though they do not explain precisely how or in what sense.[45] Although these epistemological issues remain unresolved, conscientious sociolegal researchers carry on with their studies, doing the best they can to get the facts right, holding in abeyance doubts about the social scientific enterprise – doubts which, if accepted, would lead to paralysis.[46]

Ironically, the commonplace contention of social scientists that judges' personal views influence their legal decisions circles back to sting the scholars themselves. The complex of ideas summarized by Tarnas undermines *all* claims to knowledge and objectivity. There appears to be no escaping the web of subjectivity, whether by a judge or a social scientist, or a legal academic, or anyone else. Everything is perceived, according to this view, in a manner colored by group and individual interests and ideas. If judging is mere instrumental manipulation to arrive at preconceived ends, so too, it seems, social scientific studies of law are mere instrumental manipulation of study design, methodology, choice of subjects, and interpretation of results to arrive at preconceived ends. This reflexive sting should give sociolegal scholars pause in their assumption that judging is just politics; if sociolegal scholars insist that their own work is not pure politics, they should be receptive to the identical claim by judges, given that the objectivity of both endeavors have been challenged by the same set of ideas.

Legal pragmatism

In the late 1980s and early 1990s came a veritable eruption of work by theorists who touted "legal pragmatism."[47] Although pragmatic approaches to law had seeped into the legal culture for generations, it had not been thought of or discussed as a particular theoretical approach (with a few exceptions).[48] Its meteoric rise to prominence in legal scholarship is partially attributable to the brilliant writings on the subject of philosopher Richard Rorty,[49] who brought philosophical pragmatism back into vogue after a period of relative neglect.

44 See David M. Trubek and J.P. Esser, "From 'Scientism Without Determinism' to 'Interpretation Without Politics': A Reply to Sarat, Harrington, and Yngvesson," 15 *L. & Soc. Inquiry* 171 (1990).
45 See Austin Sarat, "Off to See the Wizard: Beyond Validity and Reliability in the Search for a Post-Empiricist Sociology of Law," 15 *L. & Soc. Inquiry* 155 (1990).
46 For an argument that the lack of foundations does not undercut social scientific studies, see Tamanaha, *Realistic Socio-Legal Theory*, supra Chap. 2.
47 The literature on this subject is massive. An excellent early collection is Symposium, On the Renaissance of Pragmatism in American Legal Thought, 63 *S. Cal. L. Rev.* 1569 (1990).
48 The main exception to this assertion is Robert S. Summers, *Instrumentalism and American Legal Theory*, supra.
49 See Richard Rorty, *Philosophy and the Mirror of Nature* (Princeton: Princeton Univ. Press 1979); Richard Rorty, *Consequences of Pragmatism* (St. Paul: Univ. of Minn. Press 1982).

A peculiar feature of this rush to pragmatism was the participation of scholars from across the spectrum of political views, including law and economics guru Richard Posner, CLS veterans Morton Horwitz and Martha Minow, critical feminist Margaret Radin, critical race theorist Mari Matsuda, and a multitude of scholars from the mainstream who identify with no particular school of thought.[50] Theorists who have demonized one another – Crits and Posner – found themselves touting the same program. Judge Benjamin Cardozo, by all accounts the model of pragmatic judging, was held up as a shared icon.[51] This remarkable convergence on pragmatism – though there were dissenters[52] – was not the product of reconciliation. These scholars remained as far apart as ever in their substantive visions of what the law should be. The very fact of this convergence among sworn foes confirms what has been a constant source of criticism: Pragmatism is empty with respect to ends, offering no particular guidance on values. Dewey claimed that pragmatism has an affinity with democracy,[53] but otherwise pragmatism does not say what the good is, how to live, what kind of economic system to develop, or anything else of that nature. Pragmatism is a theory about how knowledge is produced that says nothing about specific content.

Another peculiarity of the rush to pragmatism is that it is not evident what insight, if any, it offers to contemporary law. The pragmatic philosophy of James, Peirce, and Dewey was primarily a negative critique of absolutist theories of truth. Their core argument was that knowledge is contextual and instrumental, derived through our activities in the world within a community of inquirers. Whatever proves consistently reliable in the pursuit of these projects is true. When Pound, Dewey, and the Realists invoked pragmatist thought in the early twentieth century, they were combating prevailing non-instrumental views of law as consisting of abstract principles, applied in a logical blinkered fashion that paid little heed to social consequences. Pragmatism had bite then. By the 1960s and 1970s, however, legal instrumentalism was "the ordinary religion of the classroom." Judges have for decades routinely considered social policy and the social consequences of their decisions. Conceptual formalist judges are now rare or nonexistent; judges continue to espouse aspects of rule formalism, but not in the mechanistic terms of yesteryear. When most everyone sees law in the terms espoused by the Realists, there is little reason to call for legal pragmatism.[54]

With the notable exception of Posner, the promotion of pragmatism within legal theory quieted down almost as suddenly as it had erupted. Rorty asserted that

---

50 For an exhaustive list from across the political spectrum, Cotter, "Legal Pragmatism and the Law and Economics Movement," supra n. 1.
51 See Tamanaha, *Realistic Socio-Legal Theory*, supra 43–7.
52 See Steven D. Smith, "The Pursuit of Pragmatism," 100 *Yale L.J.* 409 (1990); Ronald Dworkin, *Law's Empire* (Cambridge, Mass.: Harvard Univ. Press 1986) 161.
53 See Michael Sullivan and Daniel Solove, "Can Pragmatism be Radical? Richard Posner and Legal Pragmatism," 113 *Yale L.J.* 687 (2003).
54 A fuller argument to the effect that pragmatism has little to offer to legal theory is set forth in Tamanaha, *Realistic Socio-Legal Theory*, supra Chap. 2.

pragmatism in law today is "banal" because its insights had long ago been absorbed by the legal culture.[55] Legal scholars also quickly came to realize that a pragmatic style of judging would not necessarily advance their political vision of what law should be. Here is a representative characterization of the pragmatic attitude:

> Pragmatism in the sense that I find congenial means looking at problems concretely, experimentally, without illusions, with a full awareness of the limitations of human reason, with a sense of the 'localness' of human knowledge, the difficulty of translation between cultures, the unattainability of 'truth,' the consequent importance of keeping diverse paths of inquiry open, the dependence of inquiry on culture and social institutions, and above all the insistence that social thought and action be evaluated as instruments to *valued human goals* rather than as ends in themselves.[56]

Most legal pragmatists would find this description congenial. They would agree that judges "must come up with the decision that will be best with regard to present and future needs,"[57] and that "Judges often must choose between rendering substantive justice in the case at hand and maintaining the law's certainty and predictability."[58]

But an unpalatable catch is lurking behind those words. The aforementioned characterizations of pragmatism were penned by Posner, leading promoter of law and economics, a long-time judge on the federal appellate court. Imagine that the pragmatic judge tasked in a case with deciding what are "present and future needs" or "substantive justice" or "valued human goals" is Posner himself. Many legal scholars on the left would be repelled by this thought. Posner has repeatedly argued that a central goal of law should be wealth maximization. Many left legal scholars advocate a more egalitarian distribution of wealth as a primary goal, which they would seek to implement if they were pragmatic judges. Such potentially divergent results are what you get with pragmatism in judging.

Posner is a marvel of productivity who churns out books promoting legal pragmatism, lately deemphasizing but still firmly committed to law and economics. Endorsing Judge Cardozo's assertion that the end of law "is the welfare of society,"[59] Posner has declared again and again that "Legal rules should be viewed in instrumental terms."[60] "All that pragmatic jurisprudence really connotes ... is a rejection of the idea that law is something grounded in permanent principles and realized in logical manipulations of those principles, and the determination to use law as an instrument for social ends."[61] Pragmatic judging "is resolutely antiformalist."[62]

---

55 Richard Rorty, "The Banality of Pragmatism," 63 *S. Cal. L. Rev.* 1811 (1990).
56 Posner, *Problems of Jurisprudence*, supra 465 (emphasis added).
57 Richard A. Posner, *The Problematics of Moral and Legal Theory* (Cambridge, Mass.: Harvard Univ. Press 1999) 242.
58 Id.
59 Benjamin N. Cardozo, *The Nature of the Judicial Process* (New Haven: Yale Univ. Press 1921) 66.
60 Richard A. Posner, *Overcoming Law* (Cambridge, Mass.: Harvard Univ. Press 1995) 391.
61 Id. 405.
62 Richard A. Posner, *Law, Pragmatism, and Democracy* (Cambridge, Mass.: Harvard Univ. Press 2003) 85.

In a recent book on the subject, Posner attempted to lend more specificity to what pragmatic judging entails, flushing out a list of twelve generalizations. The bottom line generalization is this: "the ultimate criterion of pragmatic adjudication is reasonableness."[63]

> There is no algorithm for striking the right balance between rule-of-law and case-specific consequences, continuity and creativity, long-term and short-term, systematic and particular, rule and standard. In fact, there isn't too much more to say to the would-be pragmatic judge than make the most reasonable decision you can, all things considered.[64]

If the ultimate criterion for a decision is "reasonableness," Posner is correct that there isn't much more to say about the matter beyond "be reasonable," though he fails to heed his own insight and continues to engage in an elusive quest to nail this down.

A crucial point must be made, acknowledged by Posner, though easily lost sight of amidst the overflowing stream of words delivered in his supremely able style. Pragmatic philosophy does not necessarily endorse pragmatic judging (Posner's or any version). An evaluation of the consequences that would follow from this style of judging might lead to the conclusion that the "be reasonable" standard provides too much leeway to judges, or results in too much variation among judges owing to their different judgments about reasonableness, to the detriment of legal certainty and predictability. Posner is well aware of this:

> It would be entirely consistent with pragmatism the philosophy not to want judges to be pragmatists, just as it would be entirely consistent with utilitarianism not to want judges to conceive their role as being to maximize utility. One might believe that overall utility would be maximized if judges confined themselves to the application of rules, because discretionary justice, with all the uncertainty it would create, might be thought on balance to reduce rather than to increase utility. Similarly a pragmatist committed to judging a legal system by the results the system produced might think that the best results would be produced if the judges did not make pragmatic judgments but simply applied the rules.[65]

Certainty is one of the most important social benefits conferred by a legal system. It allows individuals to plan their activities and coordinate their behavior. In a pragmatic judging system, however, it could not be known in advance whether the legal rules would later be applied or set aside. This decrease in certainty would be magnified when the pool of judges entrusted with making these decisions adhere to a range of different views of social goals or justice. The outcomes of cases will differ as a function of which judge happens to be assigned the case. The principle of the equality of application of the law would, thus, also be a casualty. Considering these

63 Id. 59.
64 Id. 64.
65 Posner, *Problematics of Moral and Legal Theory*, supra 241.

consequences, a pragmatist might well decide that the high cost incurred by adopting a system of pragmatic judging leads to the (pragmatically arrived at) conclusion that judges should operate in a formalist fashion. It all depends, a consistent pragmatist would say, on the valued goals of a legal system and how they can best be served in practice. As Posner put it, it may be the case that "the pragmatic judge would think the pragmatic thing to be would be a formalist."[66]

Formal rule of law

"The rule of law" is the preeminent political ideal of contemporary Western liberal democracies, notwithstanding disagreement about what this ideal means.[67] Most legal theorists adopt the "formal" version of rule of law, the essence of which is that the government must abide by legal rules set out publicly in advance. A fleshed out version of the formal rule of law was offered by legal theorist Lon Fuller (one of the main contributors to legal process thought) in the 1960s. Law, according to Fuller, must be stated in general terms, and be clear, certain, public, and stable; the conduct of legal officials should be consistent with the rules; the rules cannot be retroactive, contain contradictions, and require the impossible.[68] As long as it satisfies these formal requirements, the law can consist of any content whatsoever. Fuller asserted that the substantive emptiness of the formal rule of law enhances law's instrumental capacity: It is "indifferent toward the substantive aims of the law and is ready to serve a variety of such aims with equal efficiency."[69] This is unadulterated legal instrumentalism. Law is an empty vessel, a tool that can serve any ends.

The most influential single essay on the rule of law was written by legal theorist Joseph Raz in the 1970s, articulating characteristics similar to Fuller's. An instrumental understanding of law is on full display in Raz's elaboration:

> A good knife is, among other things, a sharp knife. Similarly, conformity to the rule of law is an inherent value of law, indeed it is their most important inherent value. It is of the essence of law to guide behavior through rules and courts in charge of their application ... Like other instruments, the law has a specific virtue which is morally neutral in being neutral as to the end to which it the instrument is put.[70]

The law is a tool like a knife, which can be used to slice vegetables or to kill people. Thus has an instrumental understanding of law become an integral part of the most widely adopted formulation of the rule of law ideal, which serves as a defining characteristic of the U.S. legal and political systems.

---

66 Posner, *Overcoming Law*, supra 401.
67 See Brian Z. Tamanaha, *On the Rule of Law: History, Politics, Theory* (Cambridge: Cambridge Univ. Press 2004).
68 Lon L. Fuller, *The Morality of Law*, 2nd ed. (New Haven: Yale Univ. Press 1969) Chap 2.
69 Id. 153.
70 Joseph Raz, "The Rule of Law and its Virtue," in *The Authority of Law* (Oxford: Clarendon Press 1979) 225–6.

Remaining non-instrumental views of law

Several varieties of natural law thought continue to have lively expositors.[71] John Finnis has revived the Catholic natural law thought of Aquinas.[72] Ernest Weinrib has argued in support of a formalist understanding of law backed by classical natural law.[73] Michael Moore has articulated a theory of moral realism in which there are objectively existing legal and moral entities that provide correct answers to legal questions.[74] Ronald Dworkin has argued that there are single correct answers to legal questions in every case, answers that can be discerned by judges through consideration of the immanent moral and political principles of the community.[75]

Although each of these theorists elaborates a non-instrumental approach to law, they also allow a substantial range for the application of an instrumentalist view of law. None would deny that law should advance the ends of society. Natural law theory typically operates at a high level of generality, on large issues like justice, the good, and rights, with little to say about parking regulations, securities and banking regulations, and so forth. Using law instrumentally to deal with mundane and complex situations is a fact of modern life, which these theories acknowledge.

Ronald Dworkin has offered a full-blown theory of the common law, the Constitution, and legislation, which comes the closest to former non-instrumental views that law consists of principles that are an immanent product of the community. He rejects the notion that law is empty vessel subject to the untrammeled will of the law-maker. The main difficulty faced by Dworkin, shared by all the others, is that there is no agreement on how these principles are to be identified and filled in. As moral philosopher Alastair MacIntyre observed in a book on natural law, "no fact seems to be plainer in the modern world than the extent and depth of moral disagreement, often enough disagreement on basic issues."[76] Dworkin's analyses of legal issues are consistently liberal, prompting the suspicion that his own political views are being hoisted to a higher standing (likewise, Finnis's natural law account matches Catholic positions). Large, unanswered questions remain over how to move from general principles to application in specific cases, and over what to do when competing principles are invoked – such as protecting the life of the fetus and the woman's right to control her body. There is also the burning question

---

71 An excellent overview of natural law theory is Brian Bix, "Natural Law Theory: The Modern Tradition," in *The Oxford Handbook of Jurisprudence and Philosophy of Law*, edited by Jules Coleman and Scott Shapiro (Oxford: Oxford Univ. Press 2002).
72 John Finnis, *Natural Law and Natural Rights* (Oxford: Clarendon Press 1980).
73 Ernest J. Weinrib, *The Idea of Private Law* (Cambridge, Mass.: Harvard Univ. Press 1995); Ernest J. Weinrib, "Legal Formalism: On the Immanent Rationality of Law," 97 *Yale L.J.* 949 (1988).
74 Michael S. Moore, *Educating Oneself in Public: Critical Essays in Jurisprudence* (Oxford: Oxford Univ. Press 2000).
75 Dworkin, Law's Empire, supra; Ronald Dworkin, *A Matter of Principle* (Cambridge, Mass.: Harvard Univ. Press 1985).
76 Alastair MacIntyre, "Theories of Natural Law in the Culture of Advanced Modernity," in *Common Truths: New Perspectives on Natural Law* edited by E.B. McLean (Wilmington, Del.: ISI Books 2000) 93.

of *who* should render these decisions. Dworkin anoints judges to undertake this Herculean (his metaphor) task, which promises to remove hotly contested political issues from democratic arenas and hand them over to unaccountable judges who disagree among themselves over such questions.

It is late in the day of the exhausted skeptical modern age for constructing a plausible, functional non-instrumental view of law.

Getting by without a theory of law

Although there is no poll to confirm it, it is fair to assert that a majority of legal academics do not identify with any one of the theoretical approaches to law discussed above. Many law professors teach and incorporate into their scholarship aspects of law and economics without endorsing its more extreme claims. CLS no longer exists. The works of critical feminists and critical race theorists are located at the margins of the legal academy. Being a "legal pragmatist" does not appear to mean much that is different from how people already think about law (although a pragmatic approach to judging is a real option, the implications of which will be taken up further in Chapter 13). Many law professors refer to empirical material in their scholarship without participating in Law & Society. Natural law theories of all stripes are a tough sell. Although sometimes partaking in aspects of one or more of these approaches, many legal academics nonetheless find each to be overly narrow or extremist. If there is a general theoretical perspective on law, though not a specific school of thought as such, that can claim a consensus, it is the emphasis on the procedural aspects of law – due process, fair hearings, consistency, etc. – along with residual survivals of the legal process school. The formal rule of law comports with this understanding.

Legal academics, whose primary task is to train law students to become lawyers, can function without adhering to any particular theoretical approach, and many do precisely that. This does not make the forgoing survey superfluous. The underlying point is that, aside from natural law schools that remain on the fringes, when the differences in attitude, orientation, theoretical presuppositions, and politics among these various approaches and ideas about law are stripped away, they share a common component: All construe law in fundamentally instrumental terms. Legal academics who do not adopt any particular legal theory also share this baseline.

8

Instrumentalism in the legal profession

The first sentence of the rules governing the legal profession declares that the core of lawyering is a means (lawyer)–ends (client) relationship: "a lawyer, as a member of the legal profession, is a representative of clients."[1] It mandates that "a lawyer shall abide by a client's decisions concerning the objectives of representation."[2] Confirming this avowedly instrumental connection, the rules caution that "A lawyer's representation of a client ... does not constitute an endorsement of the client's political, economic, social or moral views or activities."[3] The implicit point is that serving as a tool to advance a client's perhaps immoral ends does not make the lawyer immoral. Legal practice is infused with an additional sense of instrumentalism: lawyers take an instrumental attitude toward law itself, wielding and manipulating legal rules and processes to advance their clients' goals. Legal rules and mechanisms are the tools of their craft, what they operate with to get things done. Furthermore, many lawyers see the practice of law instrumentally as a means to their own enrichment and wield and manipulate legal rules and processes to further their personal ends.

Practicing lawyers have long acted instrumentally in the three respects just mentioned. The shift away from non-instrumental views of law chronicled in earlier chapters relates specifically to views expressed the legal elite: leaders of the bar, prominent judges, and legal academics. That does not mean these developments had no effect on legal practice. Ideals affect how people conduct themselves, so presumably a change in legal ideals will have consequences of some kind in lawyer behavior. Moreover, lawyers are socialized by legal education, so the entrenchment of an instrumental view in legal academia in the 1960s and 1970s must have had some effect in the practice of law. It is not purely coincidental that, as historian Robert Gordon remarked, "Since the 1970s, [the older] conception of the wise-counselor-lawyer-statesman has been in decay."[4]

---

1 *American Bar Association Model Rules of Professional Conduct* (2002), Preamble: A Laywer's Responsibilities [1].
2 Id. Rule 1.2 (a).
3 Id. Rule 1.2 (b).
4 Robert W. Gordon, "A New Role for Lawyers? The Corporate Counselor After Enron," in *Lawyers' Ethics and the Pursuit of Justice*, edited by Susan D. Carle and Robert W. Gordon (New York: NYU Press 2005) 381.

There are manifold indications that the legal profession today is in a dire state. Highly publicized books in the early 1990s warned about *The Lost Lawyer*, *The Betrayed Profession*, and the *Crisis in the Legal Profession*.[5] Their common theme was that lawyers had, perhaps irrevocably, lost their former ideals and positions as pillars of the community, as lawyer–statesmen, as public leaders, as individuals of rectitude, as preservers of the public good. Watergate in the 1970s and the Savings and Loan debacle in the 1980s, both lawyer infested, were cited as excrescence of the decline. Worriers lamented that lawyers have become "amoral technicians" who do whatever their clients require, no matter how morally repugnant or socially harmful, pressing against the outer limits of legality (and sometimes beyond). Surveys conducted in the early 1990s found a low level of public confidence in lawyers' ethics and honesty (equal to auto mechanics, substantially lower than accountants and doctors).[6]

In the late 1990s and early 2000s came another wave of worries about the worsening state of the legal profession. Rampant fraudulent billing practices in law firms were exposed, involving systematic padding of hours.[7] Attention was placed on the plight of young associates, demoralized and depressed, who routinely worked in excess of sixty hours a week on mind-numbing drudgery to meet inhumanly high billing expectations.[8] Lawyers were key facilitators in the massive corporate fraud that transpired at Enron, and in other corporate scandals. Lawyer partners in accounting firms and in major corporate law firms created and marketed illegal tax shelters.[9] Lawyers at the respected Department of Justice's Office of Legal Counsel wrote the infamous "torture memo," twisting the applicable law in an effort to authorize torture.[10]

Just about every other week, it seems, brings a new report of lawyers involved in unethical or criminal conduct related to their practice. A prominent defense lawyer was convicted of aiding a terrorist. A lawyer who represented members of a criminal syndicate was charged with carrying messages about proposed executions, including hits on the sons of two cooperating witnesses in a trial.[11] A lawyer was

---

5 See Anthony Kronman, *Lost Lawyer: Failing Ideals of the Legal Profession* (Cambridge, Mass.: Harv. Univ. Press 1993); Sol Linowitz, *The Betrayed Profession: Lawyering at the End of the Twentieth Century* (New York: Knopf 1994); Glendon, *Nation Under Lawyers*, supra.

6 John P. Heinz, et. al., *Urban Lawyers: The New Social Structure of the Bar* (Chicago: Univ. of Chicago Press 2005) 77.

7 See Lisa G. Lerman, "Blue-Chip Bilking: Regulation of Billing and Expense Fraud by Lawyers," 12 *Georgetown J. Legal Ethics* 205 (1999).

8 See Patrick J. Schiltz, "On Being a Happy, Healthy, and Ethical Member of an Unhappy, Unhealthy, and Unethical Profession," 52 *Vanderbilt L. Rev.* 871 (1999); Susan S. Fortney, "Soul for Sale: An Empirical Study of Associate Satisfaction, Law Firm Culture, and the Effects of Billable Hour Requirements," 69 *UMCK L. Rev.* 239 (2000).

9 See Paul Braverman, "Helter Shelter," *American Lawyer*, December 2003; Paul Braverman, "Evicted from the Shelter," *American Lawyer*, January 2004.

10 For an excellent exploration of the issues involved, including a review of the literature, see Robert K. Vischer, "Legal Advice as Moral Perspective," 19 *Georgetown. J. Legal Ethics* 223 (2006).

11 Robert Worth, "Mob Boss's Lawyer Charged With Aiding Murder Plot," *New York Times*, June 25, 2005, B4.

indicted for receiving over $2 million in kickbacks from a top securities litigation firm in exchange for serving as a named plaintiff in stockholder class actions suits over a twenty-year period that netted the law firm $44 million in settlements.[12] The law firm and two of its senior partners were indicted on charges of racketeering, conspiracy, and money laundering.[13]

When evaluating the implications of these events, keep in mind that similar concerns about lawyers have been expressed for centuries, as recounted in Chapter 3.[14] A year before Watergate, the President of the American Bar Association (ABA) began his annual address with the observation that "It is a matter of common knowledge that today more Americans are concerned with lawyers and legal processes than ever before in history."[15] This statement had been uttered before, and would be again.

It must also be recognized that things were not all that great in the good old days, when the legal profession was restricted to a small elite segment of society – White Anglo-Saxon Protestant males – excluding Jews, Catholics, the unkempt lower orders (the working classes and whatever the latest group of immigrants and their offspring), women, and blacks. Women and minorities were not admitted into the profession in significant numbers until the 1970s. Local bar associations were elite preserves. The upper echelon of the U.S. legal profession has always worked closely with corporate interests.[16] The entire professionalism agenda, some have argued, has a dark self-interested underside, operating primarily to enhance the status and income of lawyers, elite lawyers in particular.[17] Corporate lawyers drafted the first professional rules to target the conduct of low status ethnic urban lawyers.[18] Lawyers fought for self-regulation to stave off external oversight and interference. The profession collectively set fees, imposed a monopoly over many activities that could have been provided more cheaply by nonlawyers (enforced by criminal penalties against "the unauthorized practice of law"), and restricted competition by limiting entry and prohibiting advertising. These activities, conducted in the name of protecting the public by ensuring quality, enabled lawyers to artificially prop up fees at the expense of the public.

In light of this background, it is prudent to ask whether this latest round of complaints about the profession marks anything new; and to maintain an open

12 John Broder, "Ex-Lawyer is Indicated on Kickbacks in Lawsuits," *New York Times*, June 25, 2005, A10. Timothy L. O'Brien and Jonathan D. Glater, "Robin Hoods or Legal Hoods? The Government Takes Aim at a Class-Action Powerhouse, *New York Times*, July 17, 2005, B1.
13 Stephanie Kirchgaessner, "Prosecutors Indict Milberg Weiss," *Financial Times*, May 19, 2006, 15.
14 A study documents the regularity with which the bar declared a crisis just in the period from 1925 to 1960: Rayman L. Solomon, "Five Crises or One: the Concept of Legal Professionalism, 1925–1960," in *Lawyers' Ideals/ Lawyers' Practices: Transformation in the American Legal Profession*, edited by Robert L. Nelson, David M. Trubek, and Rayman L. Solomon (Ithaca, N.Y.: Cornell Univ. Press 1992).
15 Edward L. Wright, "Self-Discipline of the Bar: Theory or Fact?" 57 *A.B.A.J.* 757, 757 (1971).
16 See Geoffrey C. Hazard, "The Future of Legal Ethics," 100 *Yale L.J.* 1239 (1991).
17 See Richard Abel, *American Lawyers* (New York: Oxford Univ. Press 1989); Jerold Auerbach, *Unequal Justice: Lawyers and Social Change* (New York: Oxford Univ. Press 1976).
18 Jerold S. Auerbach, "A Stratified Profession," in *Lawyers' Ethics and the Pursuit of Social Justice*, supra 79–84.

mind on whether the changes that have prompted these complaints are detrimental to the public. Marc Galanter, who has produced decades of leading research on the legal profession, observed that "We are surely living in the literary Golden Age of nostalgia for the Golden Age of lawyering."[19] Many of these exercises in professional hand-wringing hold up revered icons like Abraham Lincoln, Louis Brandeis, and Archibald Cox, and compare them against the harried and overworked (albeit handsomely paid) corporate lawyers or criminal defense lawyers of today. Galanter suggested that the current sense of crisis may be exacerbated by the fact that there is now more information and publicity about the foibles and dubious conduct of lawyers.

The brutish conditions of contemporary legal practice

We have a fair idea of the problems confronting the legal profession today, but lack reliable knowledge about whether things were much better before. At least four concrete transformations in the circumstances of legal practice are beyond dispute. There are many more lawyers today, in raw terms as well as per capita, tripling from 1960 to 1983 alone, going from about 200,000 to about 650,000.[20] The number of lawyers has risen steadily ever since, now admitting approximately 40,000 new lawyers every year, far exceeding the rate of departure, reaching a total of 1,116,967 lawyers in 2006;[21] in 1951 there was 1 lawyer for every 695 persons, compared with 1 per 572 persons in 1970, 1 per 313 persons in 1991, and 1 per 264 persons in 2001.[22] Most of this increase went to the service of corporate clients rather than individual clients, so more lawyers are chasing the same pool of well-paying clients.

The second change is that private lawyers, in major law firms as well as in smaller firms[23] (though not government lawyers), work more hours. Prior to the 1950s, lawyers did not utilize a billable hour system to charge clients. Adoption of this system created an irresistible incentive for expending more time on legal work (and for *claiming* to have spent more time on work). The median for billable hours among corporate law firms in the 1960s was 1,500; by the late 1990s, it was 2,000 hours, with a sizable group of lawyers billing up to 2,400 hours.[24] To calculate actual time spent at work, these numbers must be adjusted upward by 20% or more, at least for honest billing, given that not all work done is billable to a client. Partners divide among themselves every dollar brought in above office expenses and the salaries

19 See Marc Galanter, "Lawyers in the Mist," supra 553.
20 Hazard, "The Future of Legal Ethics," supra 1259 (citing the Census).
21 Lawyer Demographics, ABA Market Research Department, at http://www.abanet.org.
22 Barbara Curran and Clara N. Carson, *Lawyer Statistical Report: The Legal Profession in the 1990's* (Chicago: American Bar Foundation 1994); Clara N. Carson, *Lawyer Statistical Report: The Legal Profession in 2000* (Chicago: American Bar Foundation 2004).
23 See Carroll Seron, "Managing Entrepreneurial Legal Services: the Transformation of Small-Firm Practice," in Nelson, et al., *Lawyers' Ideals*, supra.
24 See Fortney, "Soul for Sale", supra 247–8; Schiltz, "On Being a Happy," supra 891.

and bonuses of associates, giving them a direct interest in prodding associates to bill ever more hours.

The third change is that the cost of becoming a lawyer has gone up astronomically, beginning in the 1970s. From 1992 to 2002, law school tuition increased in private schools by 76% and in public schools by 134%, compared with a cost-of-living increase of 28%.[25] The median annual tuition for private law schools is marching toward $30,000. A "vast majority" of students graduate with a combined undergraduate and law school debt "of sixty to one hundred thousand dollars,"[26] facing monthly loan payments of a thousand dollars or more. This debt burden puts pressure on graduates to seek the highest paying jobs available. Salaries for beginning lawyers in top corporate law firms went up significantly in this period, now over $130,000, but pay for solo or small firm practitioners and in the government has not kept pace, remaining half to two-thirds lower.[27] Except for graduates from elite schools with meaningful loan forgiveness programs, or for graduates from wealthy families, government jobs and public service positions are unaffordable for young lawyers, who increasingly take such jobs only as a last resort (though many are happy to have *any* job that pays a decent salary).

The fourth change has been a transformation in the internal culture of corporate law firms and their relationships with their clients.[28] Unlike in the past, when lawyers shared in the firm's profit, under the current "eat what you kill" system, partners must perpetually hustle to bring in clients because that determines their income. Laggard partners are let go or become salaried employees ("of counsel") rather than equity partners. Egged on by trade publications that annually rank firms by partner pay scales, rainmaking partners who bring in business threaten to leave if their pay is below the level of peers.[29] Unlike in the past, furthermore, corporate clients are no longer held tightly by firms. Corporate clients are sophisticated consumers, using their own in-house legal departments to deal with outside law firms. They require law firms to engage in "beauty contests" to compete for work.[30] Many corporations spread their work among a number of leading firms, giving credence to the threat to take work away from one law firm and hand it to a more compliant competitor. There is now substantially less loyalty and stability within law firms among the lawyers and between law firms and their clients. Although many of these developments initially

---

25 See *Lift the Burden: Law Student Debt as a Barrier to Public Service, Final Report of the ABA Commission on Loan Repayment and Forgiveness* (Chicago: American Bar Association 2003) 9–11.

26 Lerman, "Blue-Chip Bilking," supra 221. See NALP, *From Paper Chase to Money Chase: Law School Debt Diverts Road to Public Service* (Washington, D.C.: Equal Justice Works, NALP, Partnership for Public Service 2002).

27 See NALP, *From Paper Chase to Money Chase*, supra 14–15. See also John P. Heinz, et al., *Urban Lawyers: The New Social Structure of the Bar* (Chicago: Chicago Univ. Press 2005) Chap. 7.

28 See generally Marc Galanter and Thomas Palay, *Tournament of Lawyers: The Growth and Transformation of the Large Law Firms* (Chicago: Univ. of Chicago Press 1991).

29 See Linowitz, *Betrayed Profession*, supra 32.

30 See Ronald J. Gilson, "The Devolution of the Legal Profession: A Demand Side Perspective," 1990 *Maryland L. Rev.* 869 (1990).

took place in corporate law firms, they have affected the entire legal profession, which is typified by a high degree of lawyer mobility.

There are many more lawyers today in absolute numbers and per capita; more of them are competing for the best paying jobs; they compete intensely for the best paying clients; more of them are working longer hours; more of them carry heavy debts that constrain their options; and within the legal profession, a sharp differentiation has developed along the lines of pay and status, with some doing very well (corporate lawyers) and others doing okay (government lawyers and lawyers serving individuals).[31] Under these onerous conditions, it cannot be lightly assumed that the current talk of crisis is just the latest exercise in a time-honored ritual of the legal profession. Granting that there have always been struggling lawyers, and that competition for work and money is a constant of the profession, the combined effect of these factors is a set of debilitating structural conditions for lawyers engaged in the practice of law. The lives of many lawyers appear to be more brutish today than in the past. In ways that will be indicated shortly, these conditions have added pressure on lawyers to behave more instrumentally.

While instrumentalism in the three variants set out in the first paragraph of this chapter may well have been common among practicing lawyers a century ago or longer, there is *no doubt* that it is dominant today, more so than ever. Any restraints that previously operated to hold back legal instrumentalism have all but fallen away, owing to the consequences of the developments described in earlier chapters, enhanced by the pressures from the trying conditions that practicing lawyers now operate under. Instrumentalism has been fully unleashed in the practice of law.

The lawyer's two devotions: clients and the public good

To perceive the sense in which this has happened, one must begin with the longstanding dualistic ideal of the legal profession, as defined by the 1986 ABA's Commission on Lawyer Professionalism: "devotion to serving both the client's interest and the public good."[32] This combination has been utilized by the legal profession throughout its history to justify its special autonomous status. Law is essential to social order and justice: it requires specialized knowledge that only lawyers possess; the public needs lawyers to facilitate their intercourse with one another, and to protect them from harm by others and from the government; lawyers have a special role in the state as guardians of the legal order.

Notice that these accounts say nothing about the lawyer's interests. Lawyers, in this professional ideal, earn a decent living and achieve status in the community as a *by product* of their service to clients and the public good. This is not a selfless claim, as it was thought entirely proper that fulfilling this valuable role should be

---

31 See Abel, *American Lawyers*, supra Chap. 9.
32 American Bar Association, *In the Spirit of Public Service: A Blueprint for the Rekindling of Lawyer Professionalism* (Chicago: American Bar Association 1986) 10.

handsomely rewarded, but the pursuit of money was not to be a lawyer's immediate or primary aim. This explains why, a century ago, complaints that law was becoming a "business," which is unabashedly about making money, had so much import. "Law is a profession, not a trade, and success in it consists in more that money getting," insisted the President of the ABA in 1915.[33] Lawyers who pursue money above all else have always existed, everyone admits, but from the standpoint of the bar they have been a small minority, atypical greedy sorts who unfairly besmirch the reputation of all.

Although service to the client was always clear, ambiguity has continuously surrounded the idea that lawyers served the public good. In a minimalist sense, this is accomplished simply by being a lawyer, as the law itself is essential to order and justice and the law is the product of the activities of lawyers. In a similarly minimalist sense, which collapses the devotion to the public good into the devotion to the client, the lawyer serves the public good by virtue of serving clients – who collectively *are* the "public"; everyone is entitled to a lawyer and that's the public service lawyers provide. Another variation involves the often-repeated slogans that lawyers are "officers of the court" or "handmaidens of the law," both of which suggest that lawyers have special duties. But even these notions lack substance beyond a stricture against lying to judges and against engaging in illegal behavior, duties that ordinary citizens share. Another way lawyers have been said to serve the public good was set out by Tocqueville, who observed that lawyers as a group are inclined toward order and tend to act in a measured fashion, which helps temper the excesses of democracy.[34] This understanding also adds little by way of concrete obligation, however, because lawyers purportedly accomplish this by virtue of their bearing and sensibilities. Lawyers also serve the public good, it has been said, in the sense that many become politicians, judges, and public servants, or some are public interest lawyers and legal aid lawyers, but that does not entitle all lawyers to make the claim. Many lawyers also engage in civic activities outside their practice, and some take on special causes or pro bono work, but these are side or external activities.

None of the above understandings of the devotion to the public good ideal, all of which have been recited by lawyers to lend it meaning,[35] amounts to very much, if anything, in the daily practice of law. Nor is it obvious that the legal profession lives up to, or has ever lived up to, these understandings about serving the public good. In the late 1990s, fewer than one-third of the five hundred largest law firms reached the ABA's suggested level of pro bono service, and more than four-fifths of the legal needs of the poor and one-third of the legal needs of the middle class were unmet.[36] Everyone might, in theory, be entitled to a lawyer, but many people are not being served by lawyers.

33 Peter W. Meldrim, "Address of the President," 40 *Reports of American Bar Assoc.* 313, 323 (1915).
34 Alex de Tocqueville, *Democracy in America* (New York: Mentor Books 1900) 122. See Charles F. Liddy, "Address of the President," 35 *Reports of the American Bar Assoc.* 331 (1910).
35 The *ABA Model Rules of Professional Conduct* (1983) recite a number of these in its Preamble.
36 See Deborah L. Rhode, "Pro Bono Can't Fill the Gap," *National Law Journal*, September 6, 1999.

The strongest sense of this ideal hearkens to the Republican, aristocratic image of lawyers rendering independent judgments about morality, justice, and the public good, which they incorporate into their daily practice. This version of the lawyer ideal as promoter of the public good once had salience within the legal profession.[37] "In the early years of the republic," according to Robert Gordon, "the upper bar was dominated by gentlemen who thought of law not only as a living, but as a branch of statesmanship and high culture;" this view among elite lawyers survived into the early twentieth century (although whether or in what sense it was lived up to remains unclear).[38] Today, it is the version *least* held by practicing lawyers, and many would disavow it as improper. Legal education has long sent a strong contrary signal. In 1937, Max Radin observed that "There is scarcely any teacher of law who has not been confronted at some time with a student who objected to a decision because he thought it unjust. The approved method of dealing with a student of this sort is to pour contempt on him and to treat his objection as not merely irrelevant, but slightly stupid."[39]

A note of realism was sounded in a 1938 speech at an ABA meeting by Supreme Court Justice Stanley Reed:

> Whether we like it or not, law has become in many of its aspects a business. Does a duty higher in character or more weighty in its burden rest upon such lawyers to contribute of their energies to public welfare, than rests upon other well trained members of the community? I cannot say that it does. The historical concept of the dual character, public and private, of the lawyer's career must give way to actualities.[40]

Legal elites continued for some time to spout the claim that a lawyer owed a duty to the public good (albeit of an unspecified nature), but it would not hold up.

The gradual falling away of this view is openly visible in successive changes in the code of professional ethics. The first code, the 1908 Professional Canons, held that the lawyer "advances the honor of the profession and the best interests of his client when he renders service or gives advice tending to impress upon the client and his undertaking exact compliance with the strictest principles of moral law."[41] It added that in the conduct of the case the lawyer "must obey his conscience and not that of his client."[42] The next version, the 1969 ABA Model Code of Professional Responsibility, noticeably used more hedged language: "In assisting his client to reach a proper decision, it is often desirable for a lawyer to point out those factors which may lead to a decision that is morally just as well as legally permissible."[43]

---

37 See Gordon "The Independence of Lawyers," supra 14–15.
38 Gordon, "The Independence of Lawyers," supra 68.
39 Radin, "Education of a Lawyer," supra 690.
40 Stanley Reed, "The Bar's Part in the Maintenance of American Democratic Ideals," 63 *Reports of American Bar Assoc.* 710, 713 (1938).
41 *ABA Canons of Professional Ethics*, supra Canon 32, 14.
42 Id. Canon 15, 9.
43 *ABA Model Code of Professional Responsibility* (1969), Ethical Consideration 7–8.

This modest advice was immediately followed with "In the final analysis... the lawyer should always remember that the decision whether to forego legally available objectives or methods because of non-legal factors is ultimately for the client and not for himself."[44] The current version, the 1983 ABA Model Rules of Professional Conduct, is the least demanding of all: "In rendering advice, a lawyer may refer not only to law but to other considerations such as moral, economic, social and political factors, that may be relevant to the client's situation."[45] Informing lawyers that, when advising clients, they *may* raise moral among other considerations (today), is a far cry from the assertion that it is desirable to point out to clients what is morally just (1969), which was already a retreat from impressing upon clients exact compliance with the strictest principles of moral law (1908).[46] Lawyers who find their client's desires unacceptable are free to withdraw, but, again, the question remains: in what sense can it be said that the lawyer serves the public good?

As is familiar to all lawyers, there is a latent, easily triggered conflict between the lawyer's purported two devotions. What happens when the client's interest in a particular situation is detrimental to the public good? Slum lords require lawyers when buying property, evicting troublesome tenants, or defending their minimal or borderline legal/illegal upkeep of buildings against the weak enforcement actions of understaffed agencies. Lawyers who represent churches sued for facilitating sexual abuse by their priests have aggressively invoked statutes of limitations, religious privileges, privacy, and nondisclosure agreements. Corporations and wealthy individuals hire tax lawyers to exploit every possibility within the regulations in order to fork over less money, siphoning away enormous sums from the public treasury. How ought the lawyer to proceed if the client's chances of prevailing are enhanced by hardball tactics, or by delay, or by showering an opponent with discovery requests to drive up the price they must pay for persevering with their claim? Tobacco and chemical companies utilize lawyers to fight in these ways against impending suits; large corporations have done this against the government in antitrust suits.[47] What are lawyers to do when an insurance company they represent has legal grounds to avoid paying on a claim that, in fairness, ought to be paid? What are lawyers to do when they think adverse witnesses are likely telling the truth, but it would be an easy matter to trip them up to give the impression that they are wrong or dissembling? This is standard operating procedure for litigators. In all of these situations, the clients expect, and often demand, that their lawyer take the morally dubious or socially detrimental course of action, so long as it is not strictly prohibited by the law.

44 Id.
45 *ABA Model Rules of Professional Conduct* (1983) Rule 2.1.
46 A fascinating study of the negotiating processes surrounding the enactment of the latest code shows how the trial lawyers lined up against the bar elite and the academics in a way that led to greater protection for their activities. Theodore Schneyer, "Professionalism as Politics: The Making of a Modern Legal Ethics Code," in Nelson, et. al., *Lawyers' Ideals*, supra.
47 See Glendon, *Nation Under Lawyers*, supra Chap. 3; Linowitz, *Betrayed Profession*, supra Chap. 5.

Those who pine for the honorable legal profession of yore insist that formerly lawyers would have said "No!" To give credence to this claim a pithy statement by Elihu Root is trotted out: "about half the practice of a decent lawyer consists in telling would-be clients that they are damned fools and should stop."[48] Those upstanding lawyers, we are told,[49] would not have used dilatory tactics, or have driven up fees of opponents to force them to submit, or have failed to disclose adverse case law on a contested legal point, or have failed to hand over a document in discovery that might sink their case, or have made a truthful witness look like a liar. The 1908 Canons declared that nothing fosters "popular prejudice against lawyers as a class" as much as the view that "it is the duty of the lawyer to do whatever may enable him to succeed in winning his client's cause."[50] Earlier generations of lawyers, steadfast servants of the public good, purportedly would have insisted that their clients do the right thing.

It is impossible to know how true to reality these characterizations of past lawyers are. A lawyer-historian has shown that the above quote from Root was taken out of context – it was about keeping clients from getting themselves into trouble rather than about counseling clients to engage in conduct that supports the public good.[51] In another context, Root said almost the opposite of the above quote: "The client never wants to be told he can't do what he wants to do; he wants to be told how to do it, and it is the lawyer's business to tell him how."[52] Historian Gordon showed that Root and his fellow leaders of the New York City Bar, including James C. Carter, whose speech was cited in Chapter 1 as a classic articulation of a non-instrumental view of law, indeed dedicated efforts *outside their practice* to developing the law and the legal profession. Gordon also showed, however, that they eagerly accommodated the growing, lucrative corporate legal practice, representing trusts, banks, and railroads at a time when law was often treated by large corporations and their leaders as a hindrance.[53] In 1899, economist Thorstein Veblen offered this colorful characterization of corporate lawyers: "The lawyer is exclusively occupied with the details of predatory fraud, either in achieving or in checkmating chicane, and success in the profession is therefore accepted as marking a large endowment of that barbarous astuteness which has always commanded men's respect and fear."[54]

For present purposes, the truth of these accounts is not what matters. Assertions about the duty of lawyers to serve the public good were often repeated then, but are seldom uttered now. Lawyers of the past, certainly at least the legal elite, consistently

48 See Glendon, *Nation Under Lawyers,* supra 37; Linowitz, *Betrayed Profession,* supra 4.
49 See Id. Chap. 1.
50 *ABA Canons of Professional Ethics,* supra Canon 15, 9.
51 Stuart M. Speiser, "Sarbanes-Oxley and the Myth of the Lawyer-Statesman," 32(1) *Litigation* 5 (2005).
52 Statement quoted in David Luban, "Making Sense of Moral Meltdowns," in *Lawyers' Ethics and the Pursuit of Social Justice,* supra 362.
53 Robert W. Gordon, "'The Ideal and the Actual in the Law': Fantasies and Practices of New York City Lawyers, 1870–1910" in Gerard W. Gawalt, *The New High Priests: Lawyers in Post-Civil War America* (Westport, Conn.: Greenwood Press 1984).
54 Quoted in White, *Social Thought in America,* supra 60.

claimed to aspire to both ideals – service to the client *and* service to the public good. In contrast, most lawyers today see their role as instruments for their clients, plain and simple. The "servant of the public good" ideal is still occasionally affirmed, to be sure, but mostly by judges and legal academics who enjoy the luxury of being liberated from the trying conditions of law practice (and many are privately thankful for having escaped these conditions). Today it would be considered almost in poor taste for a practicing lawyer to proclaim the lawyer's "devotion to the public good" before other lawyers in any sense beyond a ceremonial repetition of words that no one listening is expected to take seriously. Judges are excused when they repeat this ideal because it is expected of them, and they *are* doing a public service. Legal ethics academics are dismissed as engaging in high minded preaching when they urge this ideal, as they are wont to do. "Join us in the trenches and let's see what you would do or how long you would last," a lawyer would retort.

Even if no other conditions surrounding the practice of law had changed, it is difficult to image any other way things could now be, given that by the late 1960s and 1970s, the "ordinary religion of the classroom" was legal instrumentalism, and there was a pervasive sense that the "public good" and correct moral values could not be identified with confidence. The demand in the 1908 Canons that lawyers should comport themselves in exact compliance with the "strictest principles of moral law" can be traced directly back to mid-nineteenth-century writings that were steeped in non-instrumental views of law.[55] This exhortation rang hopelessly out of date by the late 1960s, when the language was removed. The dominant message conveyed to law students in the latter period was that "Moral commitment, or the lack thereof, was superfluous. What counted was one's ability to 'think like a lawyer.'"[56] As Karl Llewellyn enthusiastically put it, students were taught to "knock your ethics into temporary anesthesia.... You are to acquire the ability to think precisely, to analyze coldly, to see, and see only, and *manipulate the machinery of law*."[57] Even morally conscientious lawyers, given the moral relativism of the age, could see it as an inappropriate act of arrogance to impose their own views of morality and the public good on their clients (while less conscientious ones can invoke this as a handy excuse to pursue a reprehensible course of action).

More to the point, conditions surrounding the practice of law have dramatically changed, in ways that make it almost demand heroic behavior to expect lawyers to comply with an independent duty to serve the public good. A corporate lawyer who does less than the utmost in pursuit of a client's ends, within the outer bounds of the law, will risk losing the client to a competitor next door who does not suffer from

---

55 See Russell G. Pearce, "Rediscovering the Republican Origins of the Legal Ethics Codes," and Norman W. Spaulding, "The Myth of Civic Republicanism: Interrogating the Ideology of Antebellum Legal Ethics," in *Lawyers' Ethics and the Pursuit of Social Justice*, supra.
56 Walter Bennett, *The Lawyer's Myth: Reviving Ideals in the Legal Profession* (Chicago: Univ. Chicago Press 2001) 15.
57 Karl Llewellyn, *The Bramble Bush: On Our Law and Its Study* (Dobbs Ferry, N.Y.: Oceana 1960) 84 (emphasis added).

similar moral qualms. Even if that risk is not imminent owing to a bank of trust that
has developed between the lawyer and client, the lawyer will still fear it. Judge Jed
Rakoff observed that the current atmosphere of "price competition among lawyers"
has "led lawyers to feel the need to say 'yes,' rather than 'no,' to whatever a business
executive who had influence over their hiring or firing wanted to do. This was, if
anything, even more true in the case of the in-house lawyer, who could, in effect,
be fired, or ostracized, at will."[58]

If the client insists on forging ahead after a lawyer has raised moral concerns, it
is naïve to think that many lawyers today would feel free to tell the client she "is
a damned fool and should stop." The unreality of this suggestion is apparent, not
just with corporate lawyers, who stand to lose millions of dollars in billings from a
single client, but with small firms and solo practitioners, for whom every case is a
precious revenue source that can walk down the street to find a competitor eager
to comply. In small practices, almost in reverse to corporate practices, it is often
more accurate to say that the lawyers make all the decisions and run the clients, one
shot deals who are less wealthy and often uninformed; thus any immoral course
of action or immoral goals are at least as much the result of the lawyer's dictated
course of action, guided by what is in the lawyer's financial interest as much what is
in the client's interest. But the bottom line in both situations is money, and clients
spell money.

Lawyers can and do still refuse an odious case or refrain from a legally permissible
but morally questionable course of action. Although concrete evidence on this point
is scarce, it would seem fair to surmise, extrapolating from studies of the behavior of
corporate lawyers, that lawyers seldom exercise such restraint when lots of money
is at stake. Cynics say this is about excessive lawyer greed. A fairer assessment is that
it is also about financial survival in a relentlessly competitive environment driven
by its own momentum, which forces lawyers to do things they might not otherwise
do if they felt they had more of a choice.

The line most lawyers will not cross in advocacy for clients is engaging in illegal
conduct. Stopping at this limit may reflect loyalty to the legal system, but it is also
about not risking loss of livelihood and freedom. The old "servant of the public
good" ideal of lawyering once meant more than not engaging in illegal behavior.
Lawyers had a special duty as an officer of the court "to help in securing justice."[59]
This old ideal was backed up by former non-instrumental views of "inherently
correct principles of law."[60] When law was thought to consist of such principles,
lawyers could hold themselves to standards that transcended a particular client's
interests; a law emptied of such principles leaves nothing but service to the client
and the lawyer's own interests.

58 Jed S. Rakoff, "Corporate Ethics in an Age of Steroids," 60 *The Record* 236, 240 (2005).
59 Statement of Moorfield Storey, *The Reform of Legal Procedure* (New Haven: Yale Univ. Press 1911)
   6, quoted in Susan D. Carle, "From Buchanan to Button: Legal Ethics and the NAACP (Part II),"
   8 *U. Chi. L. Sch. Roundtable* 281, 292 (2001).
60 Carle, "From Buchanan to Button," supra 293.

Instrumental manipulation of legal rules and processes

The entrenchment of instrumentalism extends to the very way in which legal rules and processes are perceived and utilized by practicing lawyers. Lawyers can satisfy their duty to clients while remaining within the spirit of the law, treating the law as binding dictates that require compliance. There are practicing lawyers who view the law this way, perhaps most prevalent among idealistic government lawyers who see themselves as serving the public. A contrasting approach, however, considers legal rules and processes in purely instrumental terms. When serving clients, these lawyers stretch to the outer limits of the law, no matter how far away from or contrary to its underlying spirit. Both mindsets are recognized approaches toward lawyering.[61]

They may sound similar, but pushed to each extreme, they are as far apart as this: do what the law requires when pursing the client's end, versus do whatever it takes when pursuing the client's end, including manipulating or circumventing the law, stopping only at clear illegality. The first one is oriented toward the binding quality of legal rules; the second is oriented toward the indeterminate quality of legal rules. The essential difference is that in the second orientation, the lawyer treats legal rules and processes in an unreservedly instrumental manner while serving the client, in contrast to the first orientation, which accepts that law has binding content and values that must be respected when serving the client. Many lawyers in private practice today take an attitude closer to the second than the first.

The second attitude toward law is ingrained in students in law school. Below is a characterization of what, since the 1960s and 1970s, became a widely practiced method of teaching law:

> Most important of all, [lawyers] must have the ability to suspend judgment, to see both sides of a case that is presented to them, for they may be called on to argue either case. The task of the law professor is often to change a student's mind, and then change it back again, until the student and the class understand that in many situations that will come before them professionally they can with a whole heart devote their skills to either side. Then they have to block out much of that part of their mind that saw the other side, finding ways to diminish and combat what they once considered the strong points of the opponent's argument.[62]

Students entering law school often think that law consists of "black letter" rules. Through the standard pedagogical technique described, however, students are taught to ignore the binding quality of law. The indeterminacies of rules and their applications to fact situations are played up, along with the flexibility of purpose

---

61 Excellent explorations of the different models of lawyering can be found in Rob Atkinson, "A Dissenter's Commentary on the Professionalism Crusade," 74 *Texas L. Rev.* 259 (1995); Stephen L. Pepper, "Counseling at the Limits of the Law: An Exercise in the Jurisprudence and Ethics of Lawyering," 104 *Yale L. J.* 1545 (1995).
62 Linowitz, *The Betrayed Profession*, supra 116.

and policy analysis. Law is all about making arguments, is the message, and there is *always* some argument to be made. After three years of exposure to this, graduates departing law school understandably think that legal rules are simply tools lawyers utilize on behalf of whichever side they represent. They have learned, to repeat Llewellyn's fitting phrase, to "manipulate the machinery of law."

Consistent with a purely instrumental attitude toward legal rules and processes, lawyers "are expected and even encouraged to exploit every loophole in the rules, take advantage of every one of their opponents' tactical mistakes or oversights, and stretch every legal or factual interpretation to favor their clients."[63] Inevitably, this instrumental attitude extends not just to the legal rules that relate to the clients' situation and goals, but also to lawyers' views of the professional ethics rules that regulate their own conduct. With respect to both, the binding quality of the rules is minimized in favor of allowing the greatest leeway to the lawyer and the client. Robert Gordon connected these two in his characterization the advocate model:

> Lawyers should not commit crimes or help clients to plan crimes. They should obey only such ethical instructions as are clearly expressed in rules and ignore vague standards. Finally, they should not tell outright lies to judges or fabricate evidence. Otherwise they may, and if it will serve their clients' interest must, exploit any gap, ambiguity, technicality, or loophole, any non-obviously-and-totally-implausible interpretation of the law or facts.[64]

This manipulative attitude toward legal rules and processes knows few bounds. To offer one devious example, a firm circulated internal messages discussing questionable activity to their legal counsel, not for the purpose of seeking legal advice, but rather with the aim of cloaking the messages in the protection against discovery offered by the attorney–client privilege.[65] Reports have detailed how the lawyers engaged in the frauds perpetrated at Enron structured transactions or issued opinion letters in ways that met formal legal requirements while disguising the underlying substance.[66] When a "true sale" of assets was required, for example, the lawyers created shell entities through which a purely paper transaction was routed for the purposes of making it *look as if* a "true sale" had occurred. The lawyers accomplished what the client wanted with awareness that the transaction did not meet the spirit – and probably the letter – of the applicable legal rules. The rampant practice of selling questionable tax shelters provides another example. After its lawyers strenuously attempted to impede a Justice Department investigation,[67] KPMG finally admitted criminal culpability in creating and selling illegal tax shelters. The scheme was devised by KPMG lawyer-partners, and was endorsed through opinion letters

---

63 Gordon, "Independence of Lawyers," supra 10.
64 Id. 20.
65 See Lynnley Browning, "KPMG Had Doubts About its Tax Shelters, Memos Show," *New York Times*, October 3, 2005, C2.
66 See Milton C. Regan, "Teaching Enron," 74 *Fordham L. Rev.* 1139 (2005).
67 See Calvin H. Johnson, "Tales From the KPMG Skunk Works: The Basis-Shift of Defective-Redemption Shelter," Special Report, *Tax Notes* 431, July 25, 2005.

by the Brown & Wood law firm. Using a complex paper transaction run through a straw Cayman Island entity, the scheme generated artificial losses against which capital gains could be offset, thereby eliminating or substantially reducing the tax bill. The entire transaction was a sham disallowed by tax laws. Other law firms have engaged in similar conduct. Three lawyers from the prominent law firm Jenkens & Gilchrist are under criminal investigation for selling hundreds of opinion letters at $75,000 a piece blessing dubious tax shelters, generating over $200 million in fees for the firm.[68]

It is a mistake to dismiss these as unrepresentative instances of extremely bad lawyer behavior. The consensus of those who have closely examined these situations is that their opprobrious conduct is symptomatic of a broad culture among lawyers, especially among corporate lawyers and tax lawyers. Lawyers have been the "main players" in the huge, lucrative industry to evade taxes.[69] Tax lawyers as a group routinely manipulate legal rules to reduce tax burdens, constantly pushing the boundary of legality.[70] A committee investigating the Enron fraud found that "the lawyers were proud of their work, not ashamed."[71] "Vinson & Elkins has defended its work for Enron by arguing that lawyers have a duty to exploit 'loopholes,' in the law, and it has found many defenders."[72] "[C]orporate lawyers today want to be seen as creative business problem-solvers and team players, not obstructionists who tell the client what it can't do."[73] In-house corporate lawyers are literally a part of the team, often seeing themselves in "entrepreneurial terms";[74] they are unlikely to risk their livelihood by stamping a business initiative as illegal. The Sarbanes-Oxley Act of 2002, passed in the wake of the frauds at Enron and Worldcom, sought to counter this mentality by imposing a requirement on corporate lawyers to report to the General Counsel and/or the Board of Directors of a corporation whenever they learn of illegal conduct by corporate officers; the corporate bar fought the enactment of this mandatory reporting requirement, preferring that it be kept optional.

In the examples just cited, the lawyers instrumentally manipulate legal rules to advance the clients' ends and to maintain a lucrative practice. In class action consumer and shareholder lawsuits, lawyers do the same, but often exclusively or mainly in their own financial interests. Consumer class action cases usually involve small claims by a multitude of individuals. Because of the limited potential recovery, many of these kinds of cases would not be brought by individuals, so

---

68 Lynnley Browning, "3 Lawyers Face Scrutiny in Tax Inquiry," *New York Times*, January 25, 2006, C1.
69 Tannina Rostain, "Travails in Tax: KPMG and the Tax Shelter Controversy," in *Legal Ethics Stories*, edited by Debora Rhode and David Luban (New York: Foundation Press 2006) 90.
70 See Alvin D. Lurie, "Toward a Trusty Test to Track and Tax Shelters," Viewpoints, *Tax Notes* 1041, May 24, 2004.
71 Luban, "Making Sense of Moral Meltdowns," supra 358.
72 William H. Simon, "Introduction: The Post-Enron Identity Crisis of the Business Lawyer," 74 *Fordham L. Rev.* 947, 953 (2005).
73 Id. 71.
74 Robert L. Nelson and Laura Beth Nielson, "Cops, Counsel, and Entrepreneurs: Constructing the Role of Inside Counsel in Large Corporations," 34 *L. & Soc. Rev.* 457 (2000).

class action suits can constitute a useful mechanism of corporate accountability. Often, however, law firms that specialize in class action claims troll for actions, find nominal clients, file claims, and quickly settle for nice payoffs. The real winners are the lawyers, who obtain hefty fee awards, and the corporations, who are pleased to settle claims for coupons toward future purchases, unlikely to be redeemed, of scant value to consumers.[75] Leading lawyers involved in shareholder class action suits file numerous and repeated claims against corporations, sometimes based on little more than a drop in stock price (until a change in the law made this more difficult), with the expectation of wringing a settlement from the corporations. These types of claims can have merit, but that is not what motivates them. William Lerach, the acknowledged king of such suits, said unapologetically, "We're no angels. We're driven by the profit motive just like everyone else."[76]

The claim here is not that all lawyers take such an unrestrained instrumental attitude toward legal rules all the time, either in the service of clients and/or their own financial rewards, but that many lawyers do much of the time. In the practice of law there are a range of attitudes that shade from seeing law as a set of binding dictates to be complied with to seeing law as tools to be manipulated to achieve ends. Individual lawyers sometimes shift along this continuum depending upon the situation. But many lawyers remain at the manipulative end. That is what they were taught, and the constraints of practice encourage it.

This characterization is not limited to private lawyers. All types of lawyers in all kinds of positions have this orientation to the law. The U.S. Justice Department Office of Legal Counsel's infamous "torture memo" is a supreme example of lawyers exploiting "any gap, ambiguity, technicality, or loophole, any non-obviously-and-totally-implausible interpretation of the law or facts." It is an everyday lawyerly exercise in selective reading of the applicable body of legal rules to arrive at the desired result of identifying an extraordinarily high threshold to define torture: "the level that would ordinarily be associated with a sufficiently serious physical condition or injury such as death, organ failure, or serious impairment of bodily functions..."[77] Lots of pain and suffering can be inflicted before engaging in torture, by that legal interpretation, which is precisely what the Bush Administration wanted. The lawyers got there in a transparently simple move. The statute that prohibited torture described it as "severe" pain and suffering, without defining what was "severe." The lawyers searched for the most stringent definition of "severe pain" they could find, which happened to come in an insurance-related statute defining emergency medical conditions that talked about organ failure and death.[78] The overarching orientation of these lawyers was not to figure out what the law was

---

75 See Richard Zitrain and Carol M. Langford, *Moral Compass of the American Lawyer: Truth, Justice Power, and Greed* (New York: Ballantine Books 1999) Chap. 10.
76 O'Brien and Glater, "Robin Hood or Legal Hoods," supra b–4.
77 Memorandum from Jay S. Bybee, Assistant Attorney General, to White House Counsel Judge Alberto Gonzales, August 1, 2002, 6.
78 See Vischer, "Legal Advice as Moral Perspective," supra.

trying to prohibit ("torture"), but instead was to produce an arguable interpreta-tion of the law that would allow them to accomplish what they desired: apply as high a level of pain as possible to make prisoners talk, and to have legal cover if the torture was discovered.

When this memo came to light, on the heels of disclosure of torture at Abu Ghraib prison, the outcry was intense. What is most revealing for the purposes of this exploration was the relatively unruffled response of lawyers, summarized by a legal scholar:

> Much of the legal profession ... met the news with a dramatically different take. Charles Fried, for example, defended the OLC's work, asserting that '[t]here's nothing wrong with exploring any topic to find out what the legal requirements are.'.... Eric Posner and Adrien Vermeule characterized the analysis as 'standard lawyerly fare, routine stuff.' Those lawyers who did criticize the memoranda concerned themselves with the deficiencies of the legal analysis ...[79]

Although the subject of torture is anything but routine, the memo is indeed routine stuff in the sense that every lawyer who reads it will find intimately familiar the style of instrumentally manipulating the law to reach the end desired. It is what lawyers do. Fried's observation was disingenuous in one sense – lawyers know the difference between an even-handed exploration of the law on both sides of an issue (oriented to law in its binding sense) to identify the applicable legal requirements, in contrast to a purely instrumental analysis for the purpose of advocacy. All capable lawyers pay strict attention to this distinction, for only then can they reliably estimate the likelihood that their advocacy will succeed, which is a crucial lawyer skill. The tor-ture memo is plainly an example of advocacy. Or more accurately, it is an example of advocacy couched in the guise of an even-handed exploration (also a common practice). But Fried was correct in his broader point that lawyers see nothing wrong with offering a legal analysis that instrumentally stretches the law as far as possible to reach the desired result.

The routine normalcy of this instrumental orientation toward rules is evident when one considers the players involved. One author of the memo, Jay Bybee, is an accomplished lawyer who now sits on the federal appellate court. Another author, John Yoo, is a professor of law at Berkeley. The recipient of the memo was Alberto Gonzales, a former judge on the Supreme Court of Texas, who was White House Counsel at the time and later (after the flap over the memo) was promoted to U.S. Attorney General, the highest legal officer of the federal government. Fried is a Harvard professor, a former judge on the Massachusetts Supreme Court, and former Solicitor General of the United States. Vermeule and Posner are professors at Chicago. These are distinguished lawyers all.

Lawyers at every level in every type of job, from solo general practitioners barely getting by, to prosecutors and defenders, to in-house lawyers at corporations, to

79 Vischer, "Legal Advice as Moral Perspective," supra.

partners in elite firms, to the Attorney General, have been taught to see and treat legal rules and processes in purely instrumental terms.

It is perhaps soothing to think that such lawyers will get their comeuppance, that non-manipulative lawyers prevail in the end. The President of the ABA made this Pollyannaish claim in 1915, asserting that the lawyer "should remember that a good cause requires no abuse, and that a bad one is not helped by it."[80] But it is naïve to think that a lawyer who manipulates legal rules and processes without restraint gains no advantage over a more principled opponent. It is as if a combatant abiding by the Marquis of Queensbury rules for boxing goes up against others who kick, bite, and choke, strike from behind the back, anything short of using guns and knives. The skilled but nonmanipulative lawyer will, at most, win those cases that should be won on the merits, whereas the purely instrumental lawyer will extract victories or earn draws in certain cases that should have been lost on the merits. There is another problem. When most lawyers are manipulating legal rules and processes, a presumption arises that every lawyer is doing so – playing it straight is dismissed as a manipulative ploy – so no special credibility points are earned by the conscientious lawyer. If even top lawyers at the Justice Department grossly manipulate legal rules while pretending to engage in a dispassionate exploration of legal issues, with the endorsement of elite law professors and judges, it is difficult to trust any legal analysis put forth by lawyers.

The design of the U.S. legal system was built on lawyers exercising a degree of autonomy from the wishes of their clients, a degree of integrity in their own conduct, a minimum of respect for the binding quality of legal rules and not abusing legal processes, and some sense that being a lawyer involves a duty of some kind toward the public good. Even if actual lawyer behavior regularly fell short of these aspirations, the aspirations themselves were widely espoused as the unquestioned standards for proper conduct. That has changed. It is not yet clear what the consequences will be to a legal system that is pervasively characterized by lawyers who ignore the binding quality of rules to instrumentally manipulate legal rules and processes without restraint on behalf of their clients' ends or their own interests. There are manifold indications that the U.S. legal profession has traveled far in this direction.

Breakup of the legal elite

A factor that affects the growth and spread of legal instrumentalism is a widening schism among the legal elite – the leaders of the bar, judges, and legal academics. In the nineteenth century, law schools were staffed mainly by practitioners and judges who taught part time. Toward the end of the century, after Langdell's case method was introduced, law schools began to hire more full-time teachers, although practitioners continued to carry much of the teaching load. By the late 1950s,

80 Meldrim, "Address of the President," supra 323.

however, full time faculty taught about 90% of the classes, over half of whom had less than five years of practice experience.[81]

Throughout this period, legal academics, leading lawyers, and judges enjoyed a bond of solidarity.[82] West Publishing Company began to publish judicial opinions in the late nineteenth century, creating an unmanageable profusion of cases. Law professors wrote treatises that cut this overflow down to an organized presentation of rules and doctrines, authoritatively synthesizing areas of law, producing essential legal material for judges and practitioners. Treatise writers and their texts, such as Wigmore on evidence, Williston and Corbin on contracts, and Prosser on torts, became legendary sources of law within the legal academy and among lawyers. Writing a treatise was the peak achievement of a legal academic. Another joint enterprise was the various restatements of law produced by the American Law Institute, prepared by committees composed of distinguished academics, prominent practitioners, and judges – experts in the various fields of law covered. The most successful of these, such as the Restatement on Torts, were often cited by courts, helping the law become more uniform among jurisdictions. Llewellyn had a major role in preparing the Uniform Commercial Code, adopted in almost every state. Legal academics saw themselves as key participants in the creation of the legal order, training students to become able lawyers and engaging in scholarship that contributed directly to the development of law.

Law professors have long been members of two professions simultaneously, law and academia, with one foot inside and one foot outside of each: producing law free from the constraints on lawyers and judges, and producing directly useful doctrinal scholarship that was avowedly less abstract than most work created in the university setting. A dramatic transformation of legal academia began in the 1960s and 1970s. Law school enrollment doubled in that period, boosted by an influx of many entrants not particularly interested in practicing law.[83] The next generation of law professors was drawn from elite law schools, many with little or no experience as lawyers. Many identified themselves as scholars, as social and legal theorists, as philosophers, as sociologists or anthropologists, as legal economists, as critical theorists, as people who produce knowledge *about* law, as anything but lawyers by proclivity, interest, and occupation. Law was their object of study.

This is the generation that gave rise to the critical theoretical approaches to law conveyed in the preceding chapter. Recall that these theoretical approaches do not take legal doctrine seriously on its own terms. Doctrinal scholarship, once the proud craft of law professors, was denigrated as unworthy of legal scholars. Yale law professor George Priest observed in 1983 that "The treatise is no longer a credit to those competing on the leading edge of legal thought."[84] Twenty years later

---

81 See Abel, *American Lawyers*, supra 172–5.
82 Glendon conveys this relationship well in Chapters 9 and 10 of *Nation Under Lawyers*, supra.
83 See Glendon, *Nation Under Lawyers*, supra 199–215.
84 George L. Priest, "Social Science Theory and Legal Education: the Law School and the University," 33 *J. Legal Edu.* 437, 441 (1983).

two prominent scholars confirmed that "legal writing whose audience is lawyers is simply not considered scholarship."[85]

Federal judge Harry T. Edwards, in 1992, declared his frustration at the "Growing Disjunction Between Legal Education and the Legal Profession."[86] Edwards lacerated law professors for producing volumes of highfalutin scholarship largely for one another's edification, which is all but useless for judges and lawyers. Another judge derisively asked "Who Gives a Hoot About Legal Scholarship?"[87] Consistent with these assertions, studies have documented a marked decline since the 1970s in the citation of law review articles by courts.[88] A comprehensive study of the law review database, covering about 385,000 articles, found that 43% of published articles are not cited *at all* – not by courts or law reviews – and 79% of articles are cited fewer than ten times; a mere 1% of law review articles account for 96% of all citations.[89] Acknowledging that scholarship not cited might still be *read*, these dismal numbers nonetheless raise serious questions about the relevance and value of much legal scholarship.

Law professors, a bevy of critics claim, are abdicating their former role as leading participants in the development of legal doctrine, and, furthermore, appear distressingly uncommitted to the task of properly training new lawyers. Indulging the interests of the faculty, law schools are offering more "law and ... [literature] or [sociology] or [film]," with no apparent relevance to preparing students for their future as practicing lawyers. A critical study by the ABA concluded that law schools must do a better job of teaching students the basic skills of being a lawyer. It proposed the expansion of clinical programs to give law students more practical experience and better training.[90] Law schools obliged by hiring separate clinical professors, meeting the students' needs while allowing professors to happily continue their scholarly pursuits. A prominent Yale professor asserted defiantly that "law professors are not paid to train lawyers, but to study the law and to teach their students what they happen to discover."[91]

This portrait of the rupture between legal academia and the practice of law should not be too overdrawn. Elite law schools are at the center of these changes. Law schools outside this orbit still have professors who see their primary task as training lawyers, and who are engaged in doctrinal scholarship. Within the legal

---

85 Rubin and Feeley, "Judicial Policy Making and Litigation Against Government," supra 628.
86 Harry T. Edwards, "The Growing Disjunction Between Legal Education and the Legal Profession," 91 *Michigan L. Rev.* 34 (1992).
87 Alex Kozinksi, "Who Gives a Hoot About Legal Scholarship?" 37 *Houston L. Rev.* 295 (2000).
88 See Michael D. McClintock, "The Declining Use of Legal Scholarship by Courts: An Empirical Study," 51 *Oklahoma L. Rev.* 659 (1998).
89 Tom Smith, "A Voice Crying in the Wilderness, and Then Just Crying," The Right Coast, at http:therightcoast.blogspot.com/2005/07/voice-crying-in-wilderness-and-then.html.
90 See "McCrate Report," A.B.A. Section on Legal Education and Admissions to the Bar, *Legal Education and Professional Development – An Educational Continuum, Report of the Task Force on Law Schools and the Profession: Narrowing the Gap* (1992).
91 Owen Fiss, "Owen M. Fiss to Paul D. Carrington," 35 *J. Legal Educ.* 1, 26 (1985).

academy, there is a significant gap between the conditions and orientation of the elite schools and the rest, with the former much more academic in orientation.

Nonetheless, elite schools set the model emulated by the rest. Their law professors tend not to produce doctrinal work, and their law reviews tend not to publish it. And substantial numbers of law professors who teach at non-elite schools are graduates of elite schools. Harvard and Yale graduates together supplied one third of all newly hired law professor across the nation in 2005; add graduates from Columbia, New York University, and Chicago, and the total is one half of all law professors hired.[92] In recent years, furthermore, law schools have increasingly hired teaching candidates who hold doctorates in other subjects in addition to (and sometimes without) a law degree, almost invariably with limited legal practice experience, furthering the academic orientation of law faculties.[93] Becoming more academic is their goal. The conventional wisdom is that candidates who practice law for more than a handful of years will harm their chances of obtaining a teaching position, as if they are somehow tainted (or insufficiently academic oriented) by a lengthier practice experience. Clearly there is a "growing chasm between practitioners and the academy."[94]

The disintegration of unity among the legal elite, although most advanced in the disconnect between academics, and judges and practitioners, goes beyond that. In the past generation, as Geoffrey Hazard observed, "the relationship between the profession and the courts became more distant and less politically sympathetic."[95] The bar was vocally critical of the Warren Court's reforms,[96] and continues to be critical of the assertiveness of courts. The critical sniping goes in both directions. As the corporate bar hurtled headlong into commercialization, and the rest of the private bar followed, courts responded by more aggressively regulating lawyer behavior[97] and by issuing more biting remarks about the decline of lawyers' ethics. Courts in the past assumed a protective stance toward the bar. Now judges appear less sympathetic to their practicing brethren.

It perhaps contributes to the growing rift that the pay of judges and law professors today is a fraction of that of partners in law firms. Young associates at major corporate law firms can earn salaries in excess of judges and professors. As the profession relinquished the aspiration of being more than a business, becoming wealthy increasingly came to be seen as the height of career success, shifting status

---

92 See Lawrence Solum, "2005 Entry Level Hiring Interim Report," April 26, 2005. Legal Theory Blog, http://Solum.blogspot.com. According to Solum's figures as of this writing, there were 153 new hires, with 35 from Harvard, 21 from Yale, 11 from Columbia, 10 from NYU, and 8 from Chicago.

93 See Lawrence Solum, "Hiring Trends at Top American Law Schools," July 19, 2004, Legal Theory Blog, http://Solum.blogspot.com/archives/2004_07_01.

94 Stephen M. Feldman, "The Transformation of an Academic Discipline: Law Professors in the Past and Future (or Toy Story Too)," 54 *J. Legal Educ.* 471 (2004).

95 Hazard, "Future of Legal Ethics," supra 1260.

96 See John C. Satterfield, "Lawyers and Law in a Changing World," Presidential Address, 87 *Reports of American Bar Assoc.* 516.

97 See Id.; also Schneyer, "Professionalism as Politics," supra showing how the professional code has become more legalistic over time.

away from judges and legal academics to corporate law partners earning $2 million a year. A growing number of federal judges have, for financial reasons, resigned their lifetime judicial commissions to return to private practice (fifty-nine judges since 1990),[98] which was unusual in the past.[99]

Among practicing lawyers, there has also been a breakup of the legal elite; or more correctly, the elite no longer speak for the profession.[100] The leadership of the bar has long urged professional behavior on the part of the mass of lawyers.[101] Already by 1932, however, the leaders of the bar recognized that the profession was differentiated in ways that limited their influence.[102] Most practicing lawyers didn't join the ABA or local bar associations. The expansion and opening up of the profession in the 1960s and 1970s resulted in further stratification among lawyers. New associations of lawyers – practice groups, women's associations, minority groups, Christian groups, young lawyers, conservative lawyers, liberal lawyers, trial lawyers, defense lawyers, in-house counsel lawyers, etc. – were formed to reflect and defend tighter communities of interest. More importantly, the prestige, practice circumstances, and economic gap between types of lawyers today are so great that in many respects they can hardly be said to be engaging in the same activity. The pay of corporate lawyers has gone up substantially in the past few decades, while the pay of government attorneys and of practitioners who serve individuals has *decreased* in real terms.[103] Corporate law partners, city child services attorneys, insurance defense lawyers, cause lawyers, solo practitioners, legal aid lawyers, and the rest have little in common beyond their similar law school indoctrination. There is no single group that speaks for the legal profession.

The aforementioned ruptures will never be complete, as there is a great deal of movement and overlap among legal academics, judges, and the practice of law. The subject has been raised here because a theme of earlier chapters was the solidarity among the legal elite in upholding non-instrumental approaches to law and lawyering. Not only has the espousal of non-instrumental views of law diminished in all of these arenas in the past century; the elite groups that formerly championed these views are no longer united. The main critics of unbridled instrumentalism in the practice of law remain, to be sure, judges and legal academics. But judges and legal academics are just as critical of one another.

---

98 Linda Greenhouse, "A New Justice, and Old Plea: More Money for the Bench," *New York Times*, January 1, 2006, A13.

99 See William Rehnquist, "2002 Year-End Report on the Federal Judiciary," January 1, 2003, 3, edited by Shelley L. Dowling (Buffalo, N.Y.: William S. Hein & Co. 2000), citing "Insecure About Their Future: Why Some Judges Leave the Bench," *The Third Branch*, vol. 34, no. 2, February 2002.

100 Schneyer's fascinating study over the Code, "Professionalism as Politics," supra nicely illustrates how the bar now consists of many different groups with varying interests.

101 See Earle W. Evans, "Responsibility and Leadership," Annual Address, 59 *Reports of American Bar Assoc.* 278 (1934).

102 Guy A. Thompson, "The Lawyer, the Layman, and the Public Good," 57 *Reports of American Bar Assoc.* 255 (1932).

103 See Heinz, Nelson, et. al., *Urban Lawyers*, supra Chap. 7.

Furthermore, the steady drift of legal academics away from the practice of law comes at the cost of credibility that the law professoriate has anything relevant to say to lawyers. The legal academy has always assumed the role as "keepers of the professional conscience."[104] As law professors identify themselves more within the academic profession and less within the legal profession, however, they look increasingly like lecturing outsiders rather than relevant role models.[105] Under these circumstances, the unified stance among the legal elite that once nurtured non-instrumental views of law cannot be recovered easily.

104 Hofstadter, *Age of Reform*, supra 158.
105 For example, among the loudest critics of the legal profession, David Luban of Georgetown Law School, is a trained philosopher with no law degree.

9

Instrumentalism of cause litigation

Cause litigation involves lawyers instigating legal actions to obtain decisions that further the particular agenda they support. It represents a "commitment to litigation as a tool for social change."[1] As one cause lawyer put it, "The law has always been an instrument of change, of course, but in recent decades it has become, through the deliberate, indeed passionate, efforts of a new breed of lawyer-activists, a favored engine of change."[2] "Since the early 1950s, the courts have been the most accessible and, often, the most effective instrument of government for bringing about the changes in public policy sought by social protest movements."[3]

The attempt to change society through court rulings is among the most ambitious forms of legal instrumentalism. It utilizes litigation in a manner that was actually prohibited a century ago. The standard paradigm of litigation envisions an unresolved dispute between parties. An injury or harm has occurred and the injured person seeks the assistance of a lawyer to obtain redress against the purported wrongdoer. Litigation is a last resort. The 1908 Canons declared firmly that "It is unprofessional for a lawyer to volunteer advice to bring a lawsuit.... Stirring up strife and litigation is not only unprofessional, but it is also indictable at common law."[4] Stirring up strife and litigation, then known as "barratry," is precisely what public interest litigators do in pursuit of a cause.

Public interest litigation involves a further major departure from the traditional model in that the lawyers bringing suits have clients in only a nominal sense. Clients are required because there must be an injured party to institute a suit (in legal parlance, the "standing" requirement). In cause litigation, however, the clients, who often have been solicited by the lawyers, are secondary to the primary purpose of securing rulings that further the lawyer's broader agenda. "At its core, cause lawyering is about using legal skills to pursue ends and ideals that transcend client

---

1 Michael McCann and Helena Silverstein, "Rethinking Law's 'Allurements': A Relational Analysis of Social Movement Lawyers in the United States," in *Cause Lawyering*, edited by Austin Sarat and Stuart Scheingold (New York: Oxford Univ. Press 1998) 263.
2 Thomas B. Stoddard, "Bleeding Heart: Reflections on Using the Law to Make Social Change," 72 *NYU L. Rev.* 967, 973 (1997).
3 Aryeh Neier, *Only Judgment: The Limits of Litigation in Social Change* (Middletown: Conn.: Wesleyan Univ. Press 1982) 9.
4 *ABA Canons of Professional Ethics*, supra No. 28, 12.

service."[5] Cause lawyers "tend to see client service as a means to their moral and political ends."[6] In ordinary cases, the lawyer is the instrument to advance the client's interests; in cause litigation, the named client is mainly an accoutrement to advance the lawyer's goals. In these cases, the *real* "client" is the cause the lawyer aims to promote; sometimes this greater objective is inconsistent with what might be best for the named client, raising significant ethical concerns.[7] Cause lawyers stand at the opposite pole from the "amoral technician" model of lawyering covered in the previous chapter: They are morally committed crusaders wielding litigation in pursuit of their cause.

Modern public interest litigation took off in the 1970s. Mostly liberal causes were involved in the first wave. Conservative interest group litigation emerged in full force by the early 1980s. Now there are a multitude of groups who litigate to further a range of interests and objectives, all in the name of the "public good." The consequence of this consummately instrumental use of law in a context of sharp group conflict is that "The courts have become the battlefield for the supremacy of ideas in this country."[8]

Origins of public interest litigation

Interest groups have brought test cases to advance their cause at least as far back as the economic battles of the late nineteenth century. In his study of the role of interest groups in government, David Truman offered the example of the Edison Electricity Institute, a trade association of private utilities that fought enactment of the Tennessee Valley Authority Act. Immediately following the passage of the Act, the Institute laid out its intended course of action in a memo:

> Utility executives were uncertain ... how soon the court action would be started or which particular section or sections of the law would be chosen to bear the brunt of the attack. Until the attorneys had an opportunity to decide which company would lend itself most readily as the complainant there would be no decision.[9]

Interest groups also participated in litigation by filing *amicus curiae* ("friends of the court") briefs in support of a party in an ongoing case. In the 1936 *Butler* case in which the Supreme Court struck the Agricultural Adjustment Act, mentioned in Chapter 5, *amicus* briefs were submitted by groups against the Act

5 Stuart A. Scheingold and Austin Sarat, *Something to Believe In: Politics, Professionalism, and Cause Lawyering* (Stanford, Calif.: Stanford Univ. Press 2004) 3.
6 Id. 7.
7 See Karen L Loewy, "Lawyering for Social Change," 27 *Fordham Urban L.J.* 1869 (2000); Dean Hill Rivkin, "Reflections on Lawyering for Reform: Is the Highway Alive Tonight?" 64 *Tenn. L.Rev.* 1065 (1997).
8 Daniel J. Popeo, "Public Interest Law in the 80's" *Barron's*, March 2, 1981, 28 (Popeo was the General Counsel of Washington Legal Foundation, a conservative public interest firm); see Karen O'Conner and Lee Epstein, "Rebalancing the Scales of Justice: Assessment of Public Interest Law," 7 *Harv. J.L. & Pub. Pol'y* 483, 484 (1984).
9 Quoted in Truman, *Government Process*, supra 495.

(National Association of Cotton Manufacturers, Farmers' Independence Council, etc.) as well as by groups for the Act (League for Economic Equality, American Farm Bureau Federation, etc.).[10] During this period, trade associations were unabashed about the fact that they were promoting the specific interests of their members.

Robert Jackson, in a 1941 book discussing the court packing plan, included a chapter entitled "Government by Lawsuit,"[11] outlining the harmful implications of the common practice of groups challenging in court every significant piece of legislation. "[Judicial justice] is inherently ill-suited, and never can be suited, to devising or enacting rules of general social policy. Litigation procedures are clumsy and narrow, at best; technical and tricky, at their worst."[12] "Each success in thwarting Congressional power, or each effort that comes to near success as to lack but a vote or two," Jackson observed, "stimulates competing lawyers and aggrieved interests to new attack."[13] This is no way to conduct government policy, Jackson argued, and he urged that judges should recognize the limitations of their position and exercise self-restraint. In hindsight, his sensible counsel amounted to suggesting that a bucket of water be tossed at an oncoming tsunami to slow it down.

The birth of cause litigation in its modern form is widely attributed to the National Association for the Advancement of Colored People (NAACP) and its Legal Defense Fund.[14] In the 1930s, the NAACP developed a plan to launch legal actions to dismantle segregation.[15] Two decades later, this plan culminated in *Brown* and its progeny. Hired to carry out the plan was Charles Hamilton Huston, a 1922 graduate of Harvard Law School. His law school notes reveal that he had thoroughly absorbed Roscoe Pound's jurisprudential thought. "Houston took the ideas he gained through his elite law school training, including his immersion in the new sociological jurisprudence that took improved social policy as the goal and law as the means or instrument to attain that goal, and applied them to create a vision of African-American lawyers as 'social engineers.'"[16] Thurgood Marshall, who would later become lead counsel in *Brown* and subsequently a Supreme Court Justice, was one of Houston's students and protégées.

The initial strategy of the NAACP, in the late 1930s and 1940s, was to bring litigation challenging segregation in universities and challenging unequal pay for black

---

10 Truman, *Governmental Process*, supra 495.

11 Jackson, *Struggle for Judicial Supremacy*, supra Chap. IX.

12 Id. 288.

13 Statement of Robert H. Jackson, Judiciary Committee of the Senate on Reorganization of the Federal Judiciary, March 11, 1937.

14 Earlier public interest litigation, mainly in a defensive mode, was brought by the National Consumer's League and the American Civil Liberties Union. See O'Conner and Epstein, "Rebalancing the Scales of Justice," supra 484–5.

15 A detailed historical account of the NAACP's actions is Mark V. Tushnet, *Making Civil Rights Law: Thurgood Marshall and the Supreme Court, 1936–1961* (New York: Oxford Univ. Press 1994).

16 See Carle, "From Buchanan to Button," supra 296; see also Tushnet, *Making Civil Rights Law*, supra 6.

public school teachers. The organization scored a string of successes, chipping away at the "separate but equal doctrine" by showing in various contexts that blacks, while separate, were not in fact being treated equally. The NAACP also challenged primaries that were limited to white voters, labor union discrimination, and covenants that restricted blacks from purchasing land, and they defended blacks wrongfully imprisoned or defended civil rights protesters from criminal prosecution. In 1939, the Legal Defense Fund (LDF) was created as a separate entity to handle legal work for the NAACP. It was, in effect, a small law firm dedicated to furthering the goals of the organization.

The legal activities of the LDF were spread around the mid-Atlantic and Southern states. LDF attorneys served as counsel in some cases or found local attorneys to handle cases, and worked together with local attorneys. In the 1950s, building on earlier successes, the NAACP took on school segregation. Presentations were made at local sites to inform blacks of their legal rights, inviting individuals willing to serve as plaintiffs to contact them. After the shock of *Brown*, southern states began to target the LDF and its local attorney cohorts. Criminal investigations were initiated by local officials into whether the lawyers were improperly "stirring up litigation" by soliciting clients to bring cases. Such activities were prohibited by professional ethics standards, and in many states were a common law crime.[17] Virginia, along with several other states, enacted legislation designed to shut down the NAACP's litigation efforts; the statute prohibited non-parties from soliciting funds to support litigation, and it prohibited paying for someone else's litigation expenses. The NAACP challenged the validity of the Virginia statute, arguing that it infringed upon the organization's First Amendment freedom to engage in litigation as a form of political speech.

In *NAACP v. Button*, decided in 1963, the Supreme Court agreed. Writing for the majority, Justice Brennan observed:

> In the context of NAACP objectives, litigation is not a technique of resolving private differences;...It is thus a form of political expression. Groups that find themselves unable to achieve their objectives through the ballot frequently turn to the courts. Just as it was true of the opponents of New Deal legislation during the 1930's, for example, no less is it true of the Negro minority today.[18]

Longstanding prohibitions against barratry were valid when applied to restrain lawyers who stir up litigation "for private gain, serving no public interest."[19] Lawyers bringing suits in pursuit of the public interests, however, enjoy constitutional protection.

Draped in this constitutional protection, public interest litigation would become a major feature of modern U.S. legal culture.

17 See Tushnet, *Making Civil Rights Law*, supra Chap. 19.
18 *NAACP v. Button*, 371 US 415, 429–30 (1963).
19 *NAACP v. Button*, 371 US at 440.

Contemporary public interest litigation

From the mid-1960s through the 1970s, a host of new organizations, primarily from the left of the political spectrum, were formed specifically to bring litigation on behalf of causes they supported.[20] Like the LDF, these were mini law firms that consisted of a small cadre of dedicated lawyers. Created during this period were the Sierra Club Legal Defense Fund, the Environmental Defense Fund, and the Natural Resources Defense Council, all to support environmental interests; the Committee on Law and Social Action of the American Jewish Congress; Ralph Nader's consumer advocacy litigation groups; Lambda Legal for gay and lesbian issues; the Lawyer's Committee for Civil Rights Under the Law; Children's Defense Fund; the National Organization for Women's Legal Defense and Education Fund; and the Mexican-American Legal Defense and Educational Fund. Many of these groups received substantial funding from large foundations, especially the Ford Foundation.[21] A 1976 study by the Ford Foundation found that there were more than seventy public interest law firms "litigating in areas as diverse as consumer and environmental protection, political reform and mental health."[22]

Cases were brought seeking reform of prisons, foster care, special education programs, access for disabled, public housing, air, water and noise pollution, and more. It was a heady time for liberal advocacy groups who saw strides being made in their agenda through litigation, and also for judges, who found themselves in the middle of major social and political issues being invited to render far-reaching decisions. Courts on the whole encouraged these actions, loosening standing requirements to allow suits to be more easily brought by interest groups, and occasionally finding "implied" causes of action to allow private suits for violations of statutory schemes that did not explicitly provide for such suits.[23]

Courts were by no means responsible for this development on their own, however. Beginning in the 1960s and 1970s, Congress enacted dozens of statutes that encouraged the bringing of law suits by private citizens to advance public goals, many providing awards of attorneys' fees for successful "private attorneys general."[24] Public interest litigation firms obtained a significant amount of funding through these fee-awarding provisions. A de facto partnership was formed in the endeavor to use law to change society: The Congress set out the general reform goals in statutes; it invited interested groups (as well as regulatory agencies) to effectuate and monitor them through litigation; and it left it to courts to supervise and work out the details.

20 For a retrospective on this, see Gary Bellow, "Steady Work: A Practitioner's Reflections on Political Lawyering," 31 *Harv. C.R.–C.L. L. Rev.* 297 (1996).
21 See O'Conner and Epstein, "Rebalancing the Scales of Justice," supra 486–7.
22 Id. 489, citing Center for Public Interest Law, *Balancing the Scales of Justice* (1976).
23 See *Cort v. Ash*, 422 US 66 (1975).
24 See Ross Sandler and David Schoenbrod, *Democracy by Decree: What Happens When Courts Run Government* (New Haven: Yale Univ. Press 2003).

The novelty of public interest litigation, beyond its tension with professional ethics, was recognized at the time. An influential 1976 article in the *Harvard Law Review* by Abraham Chayes took stock of the new phenomenon. So unprecedented are these suits, he asserted, that "the proceeding is recognizable as a lawsuit only because it takes place in a courtroom before an official called a judge."[25] There are more parties involved than the old bilateral litigation structure. The remedy is not aimed at a past injury, but instead is forward looking, with the ambition of changing an existing social or legal situation. Decisions turn less on interpretations of legal rights and more on public policy questions, and remedies are not simple awards for damages or injunctions but are legislative-like detailed decrees. Although these actions take place in the name of public interest litigation, Chayes recognized that they are driven by organized interest groups using litigation to further their agendas.

Typical of mainstream legal academics who believed in the instrumental capacity of law, Chayes was generally positive about the potential benefits of such litigation, although he worried about the consequences for groups not able to participate owing to a lack of funding or poor organization. Because his article was written at a relatively early stage in the emergence of public interest litigation, Chayes failed to anticipate the full parameters of the problems that would eventuate. In many instances, the cases remain open under the supervision of courts (or appointed special masters) for decades or indefinitely; courts make policy decisions and render judgments on highly complex and specialized subjects about which they have no particular expertise; judges issue orders that direct substantial expenditures from state officials, constraining legislative discretion over the allocation of resources; many cases are resolved through consent agreements worked out by the parties with little input from outsiders, a process that accords significant power to plaintiffs' lawyers to establish the details of public policies.[26]

Inevitably, the successes of cause litigation by the left prompted the emergence of conservative interest group litigation. In 1971, just prior to his nomination to the Supreme Court, Lewis F. Powell urged the U.S. Chamber of Commerce:

> Other organizations and groups ... have been far more astute in exploiting judicial action than American business. Perhaps the most active exploiters of the judicial system have been groups ranging in political orientation from the 'liberal' to the far left.... It is time for American business ... to apply their great talents vigorously to the preservation of the system itself.[27]

Powell added that "the Judiciary may be the most important instrument for social, economic and political change."[28] He proposed that supporters of American

---

25 Abraham Chayes, "The Role of the Judge in Public Law Litigation," 89 *Harvard L.Rev.* 1281, 1303 (1976).

26 These problems are detailed in Sandler and Schoenbrod, *Democracy by Decree*, supra.

27 Quoted in O'Conner and Epstein, "Rebalancing the Scales of Justice," supra 494.

28 Quoted in Jeffrey Rosen, "The Unregulated Offensive," *New York Times Magazine*, April 17, 2005, 46.

business should form their own groups and engage in their own brand of cause litigation.

The Pacific Legal Foundation was established in 1973, funded by corporations and corporate-friendly foundations, including the Lilly Endowment and Olin Foundation. Edwin Meese, Ronald Reagan's Attorney General, later characterized the Pacific Legal Foundation as "the first of what I call the *real* public-interest law firms – the ones that represented taxpayers, the parents, the law-abiding citizens."[29] A host of additional conservative public interest litigation firms were formed across the country in the mid-1970s and 1980s, including the Southeastern Legal Foundation, Mountain States Legal Foundation, Atlantic Legal Foundation, and Washington Legal Foundation, funded directly or indirectly by major American corporations and their foundations, including General Motors, Gulf Oil, Sears, U.S. Steel Foundation, Scaife Family Foundation, and the Coors Foundation, among others.[30]

Economic issues dominated the first wave of groups on the right, focusing on regulation and other matters of corporate interest.[31] The subsequent generation of conservative public interest law firms, forming in the 1980s and 1990s, came in two broad categories. Civil libertarians such as the Center for Individual Rights and the Institute for Justice opposed affirmative action, promoted school choice, advocated the sanctity of private property, and urged less regulation by and less power in the federal government.[32] Religious conservatives such as the American Center for Law and Justice formed by Pat Robertson and the Liberty Counsel formed by Matt Stover fought gay marriage, took on legalized abortion, sought to include creationism (or Intelligent Design) in the public school science curriculum, and promoted and defended the erection of religious symbols (the Ten Commandments and Christmas creches) on public property and prayer in public contexts.

Conservative cause lawyers unabashedly borrowed litigation strategies pioneered by the LDF, taking care to find appealing clients, and searching around the country for opportunities to bring test cases that are likely to prevail. The Center for Individual Rights (CIR), for example, brought its successful challenge of affirmative action against the University of Texas in the Fifth Circuit, known to have a bevy of conservative judges.[33] In its attack against the University of Michigan's affirmative action admissions policy, CIR lawyers interviewed a number of candidates and picked as the plaintiff a sympathetic daughter of a policeman.[34] Ironically, when the CIR took out an advertisement in fourteen college newspapers encouraging students to sue

---

29 Interview with David Wagner, "Legal Activism – When Conservatives Lay Down the Law," *Insight Magazine*, August 10, 1998, 1, available at http://www.insightmag.com.

30 O' Conner and Epstein, "Rebalancing the Scales of Justice," supra 494–501.

31 An excellent study of the lawyers involved is John P. Heinz, Anthony Paik, and Ann Southworth, "Lawyers for Conservative Causes: Clients, Ideology, and Social Distance," 37 *L. & Soc. Rev.* 5 (2003).

32 See Terry Carter, "On a Roll(back)," *ABA Journal*, February 1, 1998.

33 See *Hopwood v. Texas*, 78 F.3rd 932 (5th Cir. 1996), cert. denied, 518 US 1033 (1996).

34 See David Segal, "D.C. Public Interest Law Firm Puts Affirmative Action on Trial," *Washington Post*, February 20, 1998; W. John Moore, "A Little Group Makes Big Law," November 15, 1998.

colleges for racial discrimination in affirmative action programs, the Editor of the "Journal of Blacks in Higher Education" wrote that CIR's activities raised "serious questions of legal ethics."[35] That was, of course, precisely the charge lodged against LDF in its attack on segregation.

The proliferation in the past two decades of conservative cause litigation correlates with the increasingly conservative judiciary that resulted from the judicial appointments by Presidents Reagan, George H. W. Bush, and George W. Bush; judges sent signals that litigation by conservative groups would be favorably received.[36] Reflecting this enhanced likelihood of success, beginning in the mid 1980s, "While funds for conservatives have increased rapidly, those earmarked for liberal public interest law are in decline."[37] The mostly liberal-supporting Ford Foundation scaled back its funding of public interest litigation. Reagan's de-funding of the Legal Services Corporation (and Congressionally imposed restrictions on types of cases) inflicted a blow to leftist cause litigation. Money flowed toward those groups that were successful and away from those that were not. A remaining active source of liberal public interest litigation are law school-sponsored clinical programs,[38] which do not depend entirely on fundraising for their existence.[39]

By the early 1990s, with diminishing funding and perceiving a less friendly reception in courts, liberal groups slowed a bit their use of public interest litigation while conservative groups embarked on an increase.[40] Now, conservative groups are committed to "using whatever tools of law are available to pursue their own visions of the public interest,"[41] and see a "lawsuit as a tool for reform."[42] Liberals, formerly enthusiastic proponents, have begun to reevaluate the merits of public interest litigation in advancing their causes. One leftist cause lawyer in 1996 bemoaned, "In field after field – mental health, death penalty defense, welfare – the paradigms of reform that we thought we had constructed have crumbled."[43] Liberals have painfully learned that instruments can be used in your favor, or against you, with equal facility. The tide has turned against liberals so much that a once-favored tool – cause litigation – has come to look like a fearsome weapon for the other side.

---

35 Statement of Theodore Cross, quoted in Nikhil Aziz, "Colorblind: White Washing America," 16 *The Public Eye* 1, 9 (2002).
36 See Andrew Jay Kosner, *Solving the Puzzle of Interest Groups Litigation* (Westport, Conn.: Greenwood Press 1998); Karen O'Conner and Lee Epstein, "The Rise of Conservative Interest Group Litigation," 45 *Journal of Politics* 479 (1983).
37 O'Conner and Epstein, "Rebalancing the Scales of Justice, supra 502.
38 See Stephanie M. Wildman, "Democracy and Social Justice: Founding Centers for Social Justice in Law Schools," 55 *J. Legal Educ.* 252 (2005).
39 See Heather MacDonald, "Clinical, Cynical: You'll Never Believe What Left-Wing Law Profs Consider 'Mainstream,'" *Wall Street Journal*, January 11, 2006.
40 Lee Epstein, "Interest Group Litigation During the Rehnquist Era," 9 *J. Law & Pol.* 639, 682 (1992–93).
41 Statement of Michael Horowitz advocating conservative public interest litigation, quoted in Id. 503.
42 David Wagner, "Legal Activism – When Conservatives Lay Down the Law," *Insight Magazine*, August 10, 1998, 2, available at http://www.insightmag.com
43 Rivkin, "Reflections on Lawyering for Reform," supra 1069.

The propensity of interest groups to utilize litigation to advance their agenda is now a set piece of contemporary U.S. law. Numbering fewer than a hundred in the mid-1970s, by 1989, there were more than 250 cause litigation firms.[44] A quantitative sign of this increase has been the rise in *amicus curiae* briefs in Supreme Court cases: in 13% of the cases in 1953, compared with 92% in 1993.[45] In the 1993 term, 550 briefs were filed in 92 cases, averaging almost 6 per case.[46] Some of the participation in high-profile cases, especially when duplicating arguments made by other parties, can be explained by an ulterior motive – providing a fund-raising item prominently displayed in marketing material.[47] A few of the partners in these small law firms, especially those with ample corporate funding, are not just doing good, they are doing well.

Robert Kagan's *Adversarial Legalism*[48] details how, to a degree unmatched anywhere else in the world, government policies in the United States today, often at great expense and delay, are subject to review and determination "by means of lawyer-dominated litigation."[49] Encouraged by the Warren Court reforms, "an American political activist in the 1960's . . . grabbed the 'instrument' that best seemed to address his dilemma – adversarial legalism."[50] Cause litigation occupies a large area of this adversarial landscape.

Consequences of the battles of interest groups

Five decades of experience with cause litigation have brought a few lessons. It is now evident that obtaining a favorable court decision is a long way from achieving the desired social change.[51] *Brown* is a prominent example. After the Count invalidated legally imposed segregation, integration did not follow. Southern states resisted for more than a decade. Not until national politicians (enacting the Civil Rights Act) and local officials got behind the effort did real change take place. Even then, owing to seemingly impregnable patterns of residential segregation (and to "white flight," the departure en masse of white residents from cities to suburbs) in many urban areas, schools in the 2000s are as segregated as they were in the 1950s. *Roe* is another example. Abortion opponents have effectively restricted access to abortion in many locations by applying direct social pressure (including physical threats) on abortion providers, and by securing restrictive state legislation.[52] "A study in 2000 found that

44 See Epstein, "Interest Group Litigation," supra 647.
45 Kosner, *Solving the Puzzle of Public Interest Group Litigation*, supra 7.
46 Id. 8.
47 Epstein, "Interest Group Litigation," supra 656, 675–6.
48 Robert A. Kagan, *Adversarial Legalism: the American Way of Law* (Cambridge, Mass.: Harvard Univ. Press 2001).
49 Id. 3.
50 Id. 42.
51 See Neier, *Only Judgment*, supra.
52 See Karen Tumulty, Where The Real Action Is . . . " *Time*, January 30, 2006, 50.

94% of counties in the Midwest and 91% in the South had no abortion provider and that 34% of all women live in counties that do not have one."[53]

A study by Gerald Rosenberg of efforts to use court decisions as a vehicle of social change in the areas of civil rights, abortions rights, the environment, voting rights, and criminal procedures, concluded that "U.S. courts can almost never be effective producers of significant social change."[54] Because courts lack the coercive power or financial resources to enforce their decisions, they rely upon the support of other branches of government. When that is not forthcoming, courts are impotent to effect social change. Rosenberg argued, furthermore, that in the cases of *Brown* and *Roe*, social forces already underway were bringing about the desired change; these court decisions arguably proved to be setbacks for proponents of the changes, which had the effect of galvanizing opposition while draining resources and commitment from the underlying political movements. Supporters saw the court decisions as great victories, prematurely softening their sense of urgency and determination to engage in political action.

Sociolegal scholars have repeatedly pointed out that law, including court decisions, legislation, and enforcement actions, has a limited capacity to effectuate a desired social change. Legal institutions, individually and collectively, exist within an environment composed of other (social, economic, political) institutions, entrenched customs and social practices, and material conditions, which constrain the efficacy of legal output. Society is thick with various forms of normative regulation – law being only one, and not necessarily the most powerful one – that passively or actively throw up barriers to the dictates of law.[55] Judicial rulings, even when all of the legal institutions are united behind them, do not easily or automatically translate into the desired social actions. Often what follows are unanticipated consequences (such as white flight) in which social actors alter their behavior to avoid the dictates of the law. This was another point first made by Pound and the Legal Realists, who highlighted the often large gap between what legal officials order and what people in society do.

Naysayers like Rosenberg, while issuing a valuable cautionary reminder, are too sweeping in their declarations of the impotence of the law to prompt social change. Law matters, though not always in the ways immediately intended. Contemporary U.S. culture and society would look unimaginably different had *Brown* not been decided when it was. Considering the massive backlash the case evoked, there is little reason to be confident that without *Brown* segregation laws would have been dismantled throughout the South for decades. *Brown* in a single swoop disallowed legally imposed segregation, a monumental change to the law itself with

---

53 Posner, "Forward: A Political Court," supra 78, n. 131.
54 Gerald N. Rosenberg, *The Hollow Hope: Can Courts Bring About Social Change* (Chicago: Univ. of Chicago Press 1991) 338.
55 See Antony Allott, *The Limits of Law* (London: Butterworth 1980).

supreme symbolic import, expelling a poison within the law, with social consequences that extend beyond the specific subject of school segregation. Furthermore, certain litigation-driven initiatives can claim successes, such as prison reform, which forced the improvement of sometimes shocking conditions in many prisons across the country.[56] Though it is correct that successful reforms hinge upon overt support or tacit complicity of local officials, it is not the case that reforms would have taken place in the time and manner they did without the involvement of the courts.

Having said that, the record of public interest litigation in achieving the desired social change is a checkered one, and its myriad untoward costs (beyond financial) are becoming more apparent. A number of former participants in cause litigation have expressed reservations about this activity in recent years, pointing out the questionable record of success in achieving desired goals, and highlighting the negative consequences of asking unaccountable courts to manage complex situations and render policy decisions in specialized areas beyond their legal expertise.[57] The disturbing reality behind many of these situations, given the limited time and expertise of judges, is that lawyers (particularly plaintiffs' lawyers) act as technocrats who determine policies and the details of remedial plans, often without fully consulting the various parties – including their nominal "clients" – who will be affected. Public interest lawyers operate "in a narrowly instrumentalist mode" of thought which "neglects [complex interrelated] issues and fosters overconfidence in predicting the future."[58] "Many class members and/or their allies and guardians either have no idea of what is transpiring on their behalf, or feel that the institutional workings of public interest class actions ignore, marginalize, or suppress their concerns."[59]

One result of public interest litigation that few observers deny is nasty back-and-forth battles in judicial and legislative arenas, reminiscent of events in the late nineteenth and early twentieth centuries. Then, the fights were over economic issues, whereas today there are many more groups and the fights cover a gamut of religious, social, economic, and political issues.

Gay marriage is an example much in the news. In 1993, the Hawaii Supreme Court held in *Baehr v. Lewin* that the Equal Protection Clause of the Hawaii Constitution requires that gays and lesbians be allowed to marry.[60] Lambda Legal, a gay cause litigation firm, helped bring the case. Initially, *Baehr* was celebrated by gay organizations as a momentous victory, the first ever of its kind. However, the decision rallied religious conservatives across the country to successfully prompt state legislatures to enact bills that prohibited same-sex marriages. Hawaii passed a constitutional amendment to the same effect, as did Nebraska. The federal Defense

---

56 See Malcolm M. Feeley and Edward L. Rubin, *Judicial Policy Making and the Modern State: How the Courts Reformed America's Prisons* (Cambridge: Cambridge Univ. Press 1998).
57 See Sandler and Schoenbrod, *Democracy by Decree*, supra.
58 Peter Margulies, "The New Class Action Jurisprudence and Public Interest Law," 25 *NYU Rev. L. & Soc. Change* 487, 512 (1999).
59 Id. 502.
60 *Baehr v. Lewin*, 852 P.2d 44 (Haw. 1993).

of Marriage Act was enacted in 1996, recognizing only marriages between a man and woman. A former Lambda Legal lawyer summed up the effect of Baehr: "In short, one encouraging judicial decision in only one of the fifty states...touched off a national political and legal avalanche with horrifying consequences for gay people."[61]

This event was replayed according to script following the 2003 Massachusetts Supreme Court holding that under the Massachusetts Constitution gays are entitled to rights equivalent to those conferred in marriage.[62] Gays nationwide again were jubilant. Officials in San Francisco and a few other cities conducted gay marriages; national news programs broadcast newlywed celebrations on the steps of city halls. Predictably, in the following election, eleven states passed constitutional amendments that flatly banned gay marriage. Burned once again, gay rights litigation groups openly contemplated whether winning in court may ultimately lead to greater losses,[63] but they persisted. In a challenge brought by Lambda Legal and the American Civil Liberties Union's (ACLU) Lesbian and Gay Rights Project, a federal district judge invalidated Nebraska's constitutional amendment as a violation of the U.S. Constitution,[64] a ruling that is currently under appeal.[65] This decision, in turn, was cited by conservative Christian groups as more compelling evidence that President George W. Bush's conservative slate of judicial nominees must be confirmed in order to remake the liberal bench.[66] On the opposing side of each of these cases have appeared Christian cause litigation firms urging courts to rule that marriage be restricted to a man and woman. Constitutional amendments banning gay marriage have been placed on the ballot for the November 2006 elections in seven additional states. There is no end in sight to this spiraling conflict fought within and through law.

A cause favored by Christian conservatives, the attack on Darwin's theory of evolution, has had similarly dubious results. Lawyers from the Thomas More Law Center, a Christian cause litigation firm, traveled to school boards around the country to find one willing to defend the teaching of intelligent design (ID) in biology courses. The president of the More Center "says its role is to use the courts 'to change the culture.'"[67] After being turned down by a number of school boards, the lawyers finally persuaded the Dover school board in Pennsylvania, which by resolution mandated mention of intelligent design theory in science class. This policy was immediately challenged in court by the ACLU as a poorly disguised attempt to

61 Stoddard, "Bleeding Heart," supra 988.
62 *Goodridge v. Massachusetts Department of Public Health*, 798 N.E.2d 941 (Mass. 2003).
63 Adam Liptak, "Caution in Court for Gay Rights Groups," *New York Times*, November 16, 2004, A16.
64 "Judge Voids Same-Sex Marriage Ban in Nebraska," *New York Times*, May 13, 2005, A14.
65 *Citizens for Equal Protection, et al. v. Attorney General Jon Bruning, et al.*, Case No. 05–2604, Eighth Circuit Court of Appeals.
66 Carl Hulse, "Senate Republicans to Open Filibuster War Next Week," *New York Times*, May 14, 2005, A9.
67 Laurie Goodstein, "In Intelligent Design Case, a Cause in Search of a Lawsuit," *New York Times*, November 4, 2005 (quoting Richard Thompson, President and Chief Counsel).

bring religious views into the science curriculum. The Supreme Court had already ruled that teaching "creation science" in science class violates the Establishment Clause by indoctrinating religious views in public education.[68] After a trial, Federal Judge John E. Jones struck the policy, concluding that intelligent design is religion wrapped in science and therefore impermissible. Judge Jones squarely blamed the defendant's cause lawyers: "this case came to us as the result of the activism of an ill-informed faction on a school board, aided by a national public interest law firm eager to find a constitutional test case on ID, who in combination drove the Board to adopt an imprudent and ultimately unconstitutional policy."[69] Apparently undaunted by the fact that the Dover school board is potentially liable for plaintiffs' attorneys fees of a million dollars, variations of this policy are being considered by legislatures and school boards across the country. Religious proponents of teaching intelligent design are defiant of the decision and vow to continue their efforts to to use law to inject their religious views into science classes around the country, expressing confidence that they will ultimately prevail. "This decision is a poster child for a half-century secularist reign of terror that's coming to a rapid end with Justice Roberts and soon-to-be Justice Alito," said Richard Land, President of the Religious Liberty Commission of the Southern Baptist Convention.[70]

An extraordinary example of excess in these battles surrounded Terry Schiavo, a brain-dead woman whose husband had obtained a court order to remove her feeding tube. The American Center for Law and Justice, a Christian cause litigation firm, represented Schiavo's parents in their quest to overturn the court's order, unsuccessfully taking the case about a dozen times in all to the Florida Supreme Court, the Federal Court of Appeals, and the U.S. Supreme Court. Congress got into the act, hurriedly passing an unprecedented law directing the federal courts to take jurisdiction over the case to reconsider the state court order to remove the feeding tube; the federal courts refused. After Schiavo died, House Majority Leader Tom DeLay issued an inflammatory threat against the judges involved. In response, the President of the American Bar Association, Robert Grey, sent a letter to the entire membership calling for the bar to defend the judiciary. The heart of the problem, he observed, is the unrestrained instrumental perspective on the judiciary and the law: "Too often judges are characterized as political tools and the justice system merely an offshoot of politics..."[71]

Turning a politicized eye on judges is precisely where cause litigation, which uses courts to advance political ends and requires judges to render policy decisions, leads. Chayes recognized this implication already in 1976: "Litigation inevitably becomes

68 *Edwards v. Arkansas*, 482 U.S. 578 (1987).
69 *Tammy Kitzmiller, et al. v. Dover Area School District, et al.*, Case No. 04cv2688, Memorandum Opinion, at 137–8.
70 Quoted in Michael Powell, "Advocates of 'Intelligent Design' Vow to Continue Despite Ruling," *Washington Post*, December 22, 2005, A03.
71 Robert J. Grey, "Message From ABA President," April 1, 2005.

an explicitly political forum and the court a visible arm of the political process."[72]
How could judges not be seen as political tools under these circumstances?

Looking past this scene, Supreme Court Justice Ruth Bader Ginsburg, formerly
a liberal cause lawyer on women's issues, offered a positive appraisal of cause litigation and the political battles it incites in court. "Our system of justice works
best when opposing positions are well represented and fully aired. I therefore greet
the expansion of responsible public-interest lawyering on the 'conservative' side
as something good for the system, not a development to be deplored."[73] This is a
conspicuously complacent view of the rancorous battle now taking place amongst
political interests in the judicial arena.

Justice Ginsburg's assertion is a patched together amalgamation taken from two
contexts. One idea comes out of the traditional adversarial litigation model involving
two private parties in a dispute over a claimed legal injury; courts are thought to
benefit when two sides fully air the contesting legal merits of each side. This refers
to how courts can best make informed decisions about the application of legal rules
to the facts in a case. The second idea comes from the political arena, in which it
is often said that a contest among competing factions – a political marketplace of
ideas – leads to the best political decision, either through finding a compromise
among competing ideas or by one or more ideas proving more persuasive than the
others. This is about how to best make a political decision. Ginsburg's description
hovers between these two justifications, partaking of each.

This might seem fitting given that cause litigation embroils judges in mixed
legal/political decisions. But a less benign view can be taken that this combination
operates to the detriment of both aspects: Political fights distort the application
and interpretation of legal rules, whereas legal rules and the parameters of litigation
pervert political disagreements, inhibiting their proper resolution.

Judicial decisions in cause litigation cases, as much as they involve political
issues, remain legal decisions – authoritative legal rules and processes shape how
the questions are presented and handled. Judges are limited to issues framed by the
parties and to information provided by the parties, and often lack expertise in any
particular subject. The participants are instrumentally motivated lawyers dedicated
to furthering their cause, which leaves the judge without any independent source
of information or advice. The overtly political combat in the case can overwhelm
the legal decision-making aspects of the judge's role, encouraging judges to make
decisions based upon their political preferences rather than the legal merits.

The political process suffers as well. Cause litigation can worsen political fights
between groups in a way that precludes cooperative attempts to locate a solution.
The adversarial structure of a legal case sets groups at odds and calls for winners and
losers. Judges often pressure parties to settle, but this does not in itself encourage

---

72 Chayes, "Role of the Judge in Public Law Litigation," supra 1304.
73 Ruth Bader Ginsburg, "In Pursuit of the Public Good: Access to Justice in the United States,"
   7 *Wash. U.J.L. & Pol'y* 1, 8 (2001).

antagonists to relinquish their original positions and arrive at agreement on a truly shared position. Winners move to a new legal arena to consolidate their gains, while losers try their luck in a different legal institution (an appeal, the legislature, federal and state levels) to overturn or chip away at the loss. Whether battles are won or lost, the respite is only temporary, a moment to gather resources and retool strategies, but the war never ends. Victory and losses are alike useful in the sense that both support fundraising requests by the cause litigation firm to subsidize its next endeavor.

Debasing the notion of "the public interest"

Cause litigation also threatens to debase the notion of "public interest." The mere existence of such nasty battles between groups, all of which carry the banner of the "public interest," breeds cynicism about the notion. Participants also routinely denigrate their opponents' "special interests." Ubiquitous assertions of this type convey the impression that "public interest" is whatever any particular group says it is, which makes the claim devoid of meaning.

Lambda Legal declares that it "pursues litigation in all parts of the country, in every area of law that affects lesbians, gay men, bisexuals, transgender people and those with HIV."[74] One can be sympathetic to the issues and positions taken by Lambda Legal, while at the same time recognizing that these activities further the particular interests of gays. Their web site claims that "Lambda Legal's work ultimately benefits all people, for it helps to fashion a society that is truly diverse and tolerant." It is a contestable assertion – which they do not attempt to demonstrate – that the positions they support and the means they apply in fact help fashion a diverse and tolerant society. The pushing of gay marriage through litigation on a resistant public, for example, may have increased social divisiveness and provoked greater intolerance than would have resulted following a more gradual change in public attitudes. This is not to say that the members of Lambda Legal are insincere about their desire to vindicate public norms, or even that they are wrong in their claim, only that they have not fully articulated the sense in which their activities indeed advance the public interest, taking seriously and responding to the views of the many people who disagree. Putting greater effort into persuading others about the public interest merits of their position, furthermore, might be more effective in achieving their long-term goals than litigation.

Washington Legal Foundation, which claims to be the "nation's preeminent center for public interest law," raises identical doubts, again without questioning the sincerity of the lawyers involved. For almost three decades, it has been a leading economically conservative litigation firm. "Litigation is the backbone of the Washington Legal Foundation's (WLF) public interest programs." "WLF has shaped public policy through aggressive litigation of over 900 court cases," boasts its web

74 Lambda Legal, at http://www.lambdalegal.org/cgi-bin/iowa/about.

site, claiming that it litigates to protect "freedom and justice."[75] However, all of the litigation activities listed on its web site – reducing government regulation, tort reform, opposition to price controls, etc. – reflect positions favored by major American corporations: pharmaceuticals, insurance companies, manufacturers, oil, mining and logging companies, utility companies, and so forth. It should come as no surprise, therefore, to discover that Washington Legal Foundation is substantially funded by corporate interests, including foundations set up by Pfizer, Procter and Gamble, and Eli Lilly.[76]

The items on their agenda may indeed offer benefits for the public, *if* approached in a manner that takes into consideration all interests and concerns. But their motivations and their litigation strategies do not have that as their objective, which is plainly to reduce regulation, costs, and suits against business as much as possible. Their position does not acknowledge well-supported arguments on the opposing side; the tort reform agenda, for example, and particularly the attack on medical malpractice, has been demonstrated to be built on myths about the harmful and costly effects of frivolous litigation, when the fact is that insurance premiums are driven by other factors.[77] Only an unapologetic ideologue could assert that what's good for corporate America and its shareholders automatically furthers the public interest. Yet that is, in effect, Washington Legal Foundation's litigation platform. If Pfizer went around the country instigating lawsuits on behalf of the precisely the same objectives, it would be disallowed as pursuit of its own private interest, not protected by *Button*. The same activity conducted under the aegis of a "public interest" litigation firm is magically transformed into efforts for the public good. In the early days of this type of litigation, it was called "interest group" litigation, not "public interest" litigation, and the idea was that, assuming standing requirements could be met, groups were entitled to pursue and defend *their* interests through litigation like everyone else. Now (encouraged by *Button*) these interests claim to be representing the public interest, which is a very different claim.

This phenomenon is another symptom of a general loss of confidence in the capacity to distinguish groups that are truly acting in the public interest from those that are merely making this claim to cover the pursuit of selfish interests. Every claim to be acting to further the public interest is as good as any other.

---

75 See Washington Legal Foundation, at http://www.wlf.org/Litigating/litprojects.asp.
76 See Anne Mulkern, "Watchdogs or Lap Dogs?" *Denver Post*, May 23, 2004.
77 See Tom Baker, *The Medical Malpractice Myth* (Chicago: Univ. of Chicago Press 2005).

10

Instrumentalism and the judiciary

Political scientist Nathan Glazer, in 1975, asked whether the U.S. polity had permanently shifted "Towards an Imperial Judiciary?" The "Court is committed to an activist posture, with great impact on various areas of life.... [and the Court is] simply legislating its views on difficult problems."[1] In the quarter century since Glazer posed his question, the assertive stance of courts has increased, according to many observers. Armed with the power of judicial review, and prompted by cause litigation, by rights cases, and by the interpretation of far-reaching legislation, judges increasingly make decisions that penetrate all aspects of social life. At the end of the twentieth century, said Robert Bork, "It is arguable that the American judiciary – the American Supreme Court, abetted by the lower federal court and many state courts – is the single most powerful force shaping our culture."[2] There are reasons to doubt that courts are as efficacious in this effort as Bork suggests, but there is no doubt that his view is widely shared.

Conservatives have been exercised at courts for decades for these actions. To the delight of conservatives,[3] of late, liberals have also begun to protest the assertiveness of courts. Since the 1960s, liberals have reposed faith "in the courts as vehicles for social change."[4] Now that conservative appointments appear likely to dominate the federal judiciary for the coming generation, prominent liberals have begun to join conservatives like Bork in proposing that the power of judicial review be curtailed or abolished.[5] Conservatives, meanwhile, are engaging in their own reversal. While assiduously mouthing the mantra of judicial restraint, conservatives urge conservative judges to render decisions consistent with *their* ideological views, eschewing restraint if necessary to achieve these outcomes. Christian conservatives want judges

---

1 Nathan Glazer, "Towards an Imperial Judiciary," *Public Interest*, Fall 1975, 115.
2 Robert Bork, *Slouching Toward Gomorrah* (New York: Regan Books 1996) 96.
3 See Mark Kozlowski, *The Myth of the Imperial Judiciary: Why the Right is Wrong About the Courts* (New York: NYU Press 2003) Introduction.
4 Mark Tushnet, "Democracy Versus Judicial Review: Is it Time to Amend the Constitution?" *Dissent*, Spring 2005, 59.
5 Id.; see also Larry Kramer, *The People Themselves: Popular Constitutionalism and Judicial Review* (New York: Oxford Univ. Press 2004).

to issue decisions that reflect Christian values; libertarian conservatives urge judges to sweep away New Deal economic legislation.[6]

The logic of this collection of ideas about judges and judging *must* culminate in pitched ideological battles over who is seated as judges. If judges wield inordinate power to shape social life and have decisive say over major political and economic issues, if a judge has substantial scope to inject personal views into legal decisions, then it is imperative to populate the judiciary with individuals who share your ideological views. This strategy is more expedient than participating in the vagaries of the political process to secure legislation. Political coalitions for legislation come and go, but achieving a critical mass of like-minded judges can lock in the dominance of a set of ideological views for a generation. Furthermore, judges can trump or constrain the political process though judicial review or by eviscerating statutes and regulations with narrow interpretations.

This battle is precisely what we see today at all levels of federal and state courts. In the spring of 2005, a nasty controversy erupted over the use of the filibuster by Democratic Senators to prevent President George W. Bush's most conservative judicial nominees from coming to a floor vote. This was the latest episode in a decade-long escalating fight over the appointment of judges. Republicans who complained about outrageous Democratic obstructionism of judicial appointments conveniently forgot "the acrimonious judicial selection politics of the Clinton years and what many would characterize as unprecedented mistreatment of Clinton's nominees."[7] When President Clinton left office, forty-two of his nominees were unconfirmed, thirty-eight of whom never received a hearing.[8] During the final six years of Clinton's presidency, Republicans engaged in "a highly politicized, partisan, and divisive judicial confirmation process for lower federal court judges."[9] Republicans, in response, point to the earlier outrage of the ideologically motivated dumping of Ronald Reagan's impeccably qualified nominee for the Supreme Court, Robert Bork.

Equally heated ideological contests have been taking place at the state level. A sampling of reports from across the country show: "the bitterest state judicial races in memory" (Wisconsin); "angriest and most expensive" (West Virginia); "wildest results" (Texas); "surprising and extraordinary" (Nevada); judicial elections

---

6 Roger Pilon of the Cato Institute argues, along with Richard Epstein, that much of the legislation since the New Deal has been unconstitutional and should be invalidated by courts. Thus the correct stance is not judicial restraint but activism. Roger Pilon, "How Constitutional Corruption Has Led to Ideological Litmus Tests for Judicial Nominees," *Policy Analysis*, No. 446, August 6, 2002. See also Jeffrey Rosen, "Justice Thomas's Other Controversy," *New York Times Magazine*, April 17, 2005.

7 Sheldon Goldman, et al., "W. Bush Remaking the Judiciary: Like Father Like Son?" 86 *Judicature* 282, 294 (2003).

8 John Anthony Maltese, "Confirmation Gridlock: The Federal Judicial Appointments Process Under Bill Clinton and George W. Bush," 3 *Journal of Appellate Practice and Process* 1, 21 (2003).

9 Sheldon Goldman, et al., "Clinton's Judges: Summing Up the Legacy," 84 *Judicature* 228, 254 (2001).

everywhere have become "noisier, nastier, and costlier."[10] In addition to the afore-mentioned states, Oklahoma, Tennessee, Alabama, Ohio, California, Mississippi, Idaho, South Carolina, Florida, Idaho, Louisiana, and Michigan, all experienced caustic and expensive judicial election campaigns since the early 1990s, worsening over time.[11] "The 2000 judicial elections were unprecedented, with campaigns far more costly than ever, and outside groups' participation far more active and nasty than ever, even 'sleazy,' 'a national disgrace,' 'rotten to the core.'"[12]

At both federal and state levels, battles surrounding the appointment or election of judges have been over judicial treatment of abortion, toughness on crime, tort reform, gun control, friendliness or hostility to business, family values (anti-gay rights), affirmative action, the place of religion in public life, and the death penalty, among other issues. At both federal and state levels, leading participants in the battles are "public interest" groups on the left and right of the political spectrum – environmental groups, women's groups, advocates for business, Christian groups, etc. – including many of the groups mentioned in the preceding chapter.[13] Many of the very same groups bringing cause litigation are also vigorously attempting to shape the ideological profiles of the judges who will hear their cases, operating on the assumption that their efforts to use courts to achieve their objectives will be more successful if the judges share their underlying ideological views.

A few observers suggest that what is happening today is not novel, that throughout the history of the United States, judges have been appointed for ideological reasons.[14] This point is partially correct – the ideological views of judges have taken on prominence in appointments decisions at past intervals in U.S. history – but it is also misleading. In previous generations, judicial appointments were mainly matters of patronage, and state judicial elections were quiet affairs. The focus on ideology and the attempt to seat like-minded judges has never before been of such duration, so systematic, so extreme, so widespread, so single-minded and unrelenting. As with the subjects covered in earlier chapters, this situation reflects a marked worsening, deepening, coarsening, owing to the spread and entrenchment of instrumental views of law in a context of sharp disagreement over the social good.

---

10 Steven P. Croley, "The Majoritarian Difficulty: Elective Judiciaries and the Rule of Law," 62 *Chicago L. Rev.* 689, 734 (1995) (citations omitted).

11 Anthony Champagne, "Interest Groups and Judicial Elections," 34 *Loyola L.A. L. Rev.* 1391 (2000–01); Stephen J. Ware, "Money, Politics and Judicial Decisions: A Case Study of Arbitration Law in Alabama," 15 *Journal of Law and Politics* 649 (1999); John D. Echeverria, "Changing the Rules by Changing the Players: The Environmental Issue in State Judicial Elections," 9 *NYU Environmental L.J.* 217 (2000–01).

12 Roy A. Schotland, "Financing Judicial Elections, 2000: Change and Challenge," 2001 *L. Rev. Mich. St. U. Det. C.L.* 849, 850 (2001).

13 See Anthony Champagne, "Interest Groups and Judicial Elections," 34 *Loyola L.A. L. Rev.* 1391 (2000–02).

14 Erwin Chemerinsky, "Ideology and the Selection of Federal Judges," 36 *U.C. Davis L. Rev.* 619 (2003).

"Until now," Robert Bork observed, "such battles [over judicial appointments on ideological grounds] had not extended to nominations to the lower courts."[15]

The primacy of ideology in judicial appointments

Much of the debate surrounding judicial appointments is couched in terms of "judicial activism" versus "judicial restraint." Many observers, however, consider this a false debate, a rhetorical war of words in which "activist" serves as an insult lodged against opponents regardless of the underlying reality. Contributing to the confusion, different meanings are attached to "activism." Sometimes it means a penchant for striking legislation;[16] sometimes it means deciding cases according to personal preferences; sometimes it means a willingness to overturn longstanding precedent; and sometimes it means interpreting court power expansively with respect to other branches of government. These different forms of activism do not necessarily line up together: Justice Scalia, for example, claims to be against activism; he castigates the importing by judges of personal preferences into their judicial decisions, but votes to strike federal legislation at a comparatively high rate, thus committing one kind of activism while defending against another.

Given the rampant rhetorical uses of this term, there is a great deal of skepticism about the sincerity of avowed opponents of activism (in any of these senses). Staying with the same example, commentators have remarked that Scalia "has an uncanny ability to reach the result that happens to coincide with his own preferences in case after case,"[17] and he appears much less wedded to the text and original meaning of the Constitution when his personal political views require otherwise.[18] Political scientists who have conducted statistical studies of the voting patterns of the Supreme Court have concluded that Justices "appear to use [judicial] restraint ... as a means to rationalize, support, and justify their substantive policy concerns. If they support a policy, ... restraint serves as a useful cloak to conceal the nakedness of a barefaced statement of substantive preferences."[19] Skepticism about the avowal of judicial restraint is not the exclusive preserve of behaviorist social scientists and

15 Robert Bork, "Adversary Justice," *The New Criterion*, May 2002, 4.
16 This was the original meaning of the term. See Schlesinger, "The Supreme Court: 1947," supra.
17 Jeffrey Rosen, quoted in Keck, *The Most Activist Supreme Court in History*, supra 269; see also Kozlowski, *The Myth of the Imperial Judiciary*, supra Chap. 1; Adam Cohen, "Psst ... Justice Scalia ... You Know, You're an Activist Judge, Too," *New York Times*, April 20, 2005, A20.
18 See Sunstein, "A Hand in the Matter," supra 3; Keck, *Most Activist Supreme Court in History*, Chap. VII. An empirical study of the Justices' voting patterns concluded that "Justices might speak about following an 'originalist' jurisprudence, but they only appear to do so when arguments about text and intent coincide with the ideological position they prefer." Robert M. Howard and Jeffrey A. Segal, "An Original Look at Originalism," 36 *L. & Soc. Rev.* 113, 133 (2002).
19 Keck, "The Most Activist Supreme Court in History," supra 269, quoting Jeffrey A. Segal and Harold Spaeth, *The Supreme Court and the Attitudinal Model Revisited* (Cambridge: Cambridge Univ. Press 2002). See also Howard Gilliam, "What's Law Got to Do With It? Judicial Behavioralists Test the 'Legal Model' of Judicial Decision Making," 26 *Law and Social Inquiry* 465, 466 (2001) (emphasis added).

liberal critics of the Supreme Court. Conservative legal scholar Douglas Kmiec, a former official in the Reagan–Bush Justice Department, candidly acknowledged that President Reagan's judicial selection team was well aware that "there is often a striking confluence of conservative outcomes and the methods employed by a restrained judge."[20]

When legal explanations for decisions are dismissed as cover for political decisions, ideological considerations inevitably loom large in judicial appointments for all levels, not just the Supreme Court. Prominent liberal constitutional law scholar Erwin Chemerinsky unflinchingly drew out the implications of these views:

> [C]onfirmation fights occur when there is the perception of deep ideological divisions over issues likely to be decided by courts. . . . It is widely recognized that the outcome of cases concerning these questions will be determined by who is on the bench. Therefore, senators know, and voters recognize, that the confirmation process is enormously important in deciding the content of law. Interest groups on both sides of the ideological divide have strong reasons for making judicial confirmation a high priority because they know what is at stake in who occupies the federal bench.[21]

Citing the Legal Realists, Chemerinsky suggests that the written words of the law matter less than what the judge wants the law to say, and that this cannot be prevented:

> [S]ome suggest that using ideology [in appointments] is undesirable because it will encourage judges to base their rulings on ideology. The argument is that ideology has to be hidden from the process to limit the likelihood that once on the bench judges will base their decisions on ideology. This argument is based on numerous unsupportable assumptions: it assumes that it is possible for judges to decide cases apart from their views and ideology; it assumes that judges do not already often decide cases because of their views and ideology; it assumes that considering ideology in the selection process will increase this in deciding cases. All of these are simply false. Long ago, the Legal Realists exploded the myth of formalistic value-neutral judging. Having the judicial confirmation process recognize the demise of formalism won't change a thing in how judges behave on the bench.
>
> . . .
>
> Ultimately, disputes over confirmation are battles over the content of the law. . . . Of course ideology should and must be considered in the judicial selection process.[22]

Ideology determines how judges interpret the content of law, so fight to ensure that the judges share your ideology, is the message conveyed by Chemerinsky.

---

20 Douglas W. Kmiec, "Judicial Selection and the Pursuit of Justice: the Unsettled Relationship Between Law and Morality," 19 *Catholic U. L. Rev.* 1, 13 (1989–1990).
21 Chemerinksy, "Ideology and the Selection of Federal Judges," supra 626.
22 Id. 630–1.

The rise of ideology in federal judicial appointments

What makes the contemporary situation of judicial appointments unique is not to be observed at the level of the Supreme Court, for which ideological considerations have always mattered. Federal appellate and district court appointments, however, have not always been dominated by ideology. Judicial appointments traditionally served as a reward for friends or supporters of presidents, as a favor for powerful Senators or other allies, or to build political capital or shore up party or constituency support.[23] Federal judgeships were highly coveted positions and accordingly were treated by presidents as a valuable form of patronage to be dispensed for maximum political gain.

President Franklin D. Roosevelt is an exception to the general presidential practice who paid close attention to the appointment of lower court judges. He ensured that prospective appointees supported New Deal legislation, so ideology mattered, but he also strategically used appointments for political purposes.[24] President Harry S. Truman was less involved with appointments, which he did not see as essential to his policy agenda. A notable innovation during Truman's presidency was the creation by the American Bar Association of the Standing Committee on Federal Judiciary, in 1946, which thereafter conducted evaluations of the professional qualifications of judicial nominees. The stated goal of the ABA was that "judicial appointments should be completely removed from the area of political patronage and made only from those lawyers and judges, irrespective of party affiliation and political consideration, who possess the highest qualifications."[25] Like Truman, President Dwight D. Eisenhower was peripherally involved in judicial appointments, and did not see it as essential to his policy agenda.

Presidents John F. Kennedy and Lyndon B. Johnson paid closer attention to judicial appointments, but again used them mostly for political purposes rather to advance a specific policy agenda.[26] Their main ideological concern was that judges support civil rights. They also showed some concern about gender, ethnic, racial, and religious representation in judicial appointments. In the 1964 election, Johnson's opponents Barry Goldwater and George Wallace repeatedly attacked the Warren Court's liberal decisions, but Johnson did not treat judicial appointments as an election issue.[27]

President Richard M. Nixon, in the 1968 election campaign, ran as a law and order candidate, and made a major issue of the Warren Supreme Court, promising to appoint judges who would "be strict constructionists who saw their duty as

23 See Sheldon Goldman, *Picking Federal Judges: Lower Court Selection from Roosevelt Through Reagan* (New Haven: Yale Univ. Press 1996) Chapter One.
24 Id., has provided an unmatched historical study of lower court appointments from Roosevelt to Reagan, which provides the primary source for the following summary observations.
25 Id. 140.
26 Id. Chap. Five.
27 William G. Ross, "The Role of Judicial Issues in Presidential Campaigns," 42 *Santa Clara L. Rev.* 391, 427–34 (2002).

interpreting and not making law."[28] Despite his often-heated rhetoric about courts usurping power, neither Nixon nor his successor President Gerald R. Ford paid much attention to the appointments of lower court judges, and neither made especially ideologically driven appointments.[29]

In an effort to shift from patronage considerations to merit, President Jimmy E. Carter attempted a meaningful reform of the judicial appointments system by creating a number of independent nominating commissions. In addition, Carter was determined to appoint more women and minorities to the federal bench. Beyond those general concerns, he was not closely involved in the process, and did not use appointments to advance his policy agenda.[30]

The election of President Ronald W. Reagan ushered in the modern era in the ideological screening of lower court judges. The Republican Platform for the 1980 election affirmed the desirability of:

> women and men ... whose judicial philosophy is ... consistent with the belief in the decentralization of the federal government and efforts to return decisionmaking power to state and local elected officials ... who respect traditional family values and the sanctity of human life.[31]

This language drew sharp criticism as the inappropriate use of a "litmus test" for appointments. The ABA issued a resolution protesting judicial selections "on the basis of particular political ideological views or philosophies."[32]

Sheldon Goldman, a close follower of judicial appointments for decades, concluded that "the Reagan administration was engaged in the most systematic judicial philosophical screening of judicial candidates ever seen in the nation's history, surpassing Franklin Roosevelt's administration."[33] Reagan disbanded Carter's judicial selection commissions, and created the Office of Legal *Policy* – a telling name – in the Justice Department to manage a selection process tightly controlled by a small circle of close Reagan advisors: Counselor Edwin Meese, Attorney General William French Smith, and White House Counsel Fred Fielding. The selection team insisted publicly that the primary criterion was to select judges who would exercise restraint, but according to one detailed study they screened for judges who were social and economic conservatives – pro business, anti-regulation, unfriendly to welfare claims and unions, against racial preferences (affirmative action), against civil rights claims, supportive of religion (and of voluntary civic associations generally), and less solicitous of criminal defendants.[34]

---

28 Richard Nixon, quoted in Ross, Id. 436.
29 Goldman, *Picking Federal Judges*, supra Chap. Six.
30 Id. Chap. Seven.
31 1980 Republican Platform, reprinted in 38 *Cong. Q. Weekly Rep.* 2030, 2046 (1980).
32 Quoted in Ross, "Role of Judicial Issues in Presidential Campaigns," supra 439.
33 Sheldon Goldman, "Reagan's Judicial Legacy: Completing the Puzzle and Summing Up," 72 *Judicature* 318, 319–20 (1989).
34 Herman Schwartz, *Packing the Courts: The Conservative Campaign to Rewrite the Constitution* (New York: Charles Scribner 1988).

This screening program commenced a still-continuing, decades-long conservative effort to turn back the tide of progressive decisions in the Supreme Court and the lower federal courts from the 1960s and 1970s through the expedient of judicial appointments.[35] Those involved in this effort recognize that the overwhelming bulk of legal decisions are rendered in lower courts, only a miniscule fraction of which are ever reviewed by the Supreme Court. If a wholesale change in the law is to occur, it must be effectuated by judges positioned throughout the court system. The Federalist Society was formed in 1982, with a specific commitment to fill the federal judiciary with conservative judges as a means to "reorient the federal courts toward a view of the Constitution much closer to its 18th-century authors' intent, including a much less expansive view of its application to individual rights and federal power."[36]

Reagan's second-term appointments were especially ideologically driven, managed by Meese, who pointedly sought: "younger, vigorous, more aggressive supporters of the Administration's judicial philosophy."[37] Meese admitted that his intention was to "institutionalize the Reagan revolution so that it can't be set aside no matter what happens in future presidential elections."[38] The overwhelming majority of Reagan's judicial appointments were not obstructed by Democrats.

Bork's failed nomination to the Supreme Court bears special mention because it represents a signal moment for both the right and the left. Bork was a judge on the U.S. Court of Appeals, a former Yale Law Professor and Solicitor General, a recognized constitutional scholar, and by all accounts a brilliant thinker. Nonetheless, five out of fifteen members of the ABA evaluation committee did not give him a "qualified" rating. His nomination was rejected fifty-eight to forty-two by the Senate. Bork's defeat was perceived by conservatives as a great injustice.

> Judge Bork had been "lynched" by what Reagan called "an ugly spectacle, marred by distortions and innuendos and casting aside the normal rules of honesty and decency. The *Wall Street Journal* railed against a "bloody campaign" of "brazen lies," "smears," "distortions," and "McCarthyism." Bork's opponents had politicized what should be apolitical and had misled the American people.[39]

Conservatives placed high hopes in Bork as a formidable intellectual force who would provide the leadership necessary to move away from the Warren and Burger Court mistakes. His defeat was a bitter disappointment that has not yet been forgotten.

35 See Nancy Scherer, *Scoring Points: Politicians, Activists, and the Lower Federal Court Appointment Process* (Stanford: Stanford Univ. Press 2005).
36 David Kirkpatrick, "Team Fueled Effort to Shift Court to Right," *New York Times*, January 30, 2006, A18.
37 Goldman, "Reagan's Judicial Legacy," supra 327.
38 Statement of Ed Meese, quoted in Maltese, "Confirmation Gridlock," supra 9; see also "Judges With Their Minds Right: The President Pushes for Conservative Control of the Bench," *Time*, November 4, 1985, 77–8.
39 Schwartz, *Packing the Courts*, supra 125–6.

The left saw Bork as a dangerous right-wing zealot. His defeat was an inspiring victory that showed what can be accomplished with sufficient will and political organization. More than three hundred groups came out against Bork, including environmental groups, women's groups, Common Cause, Planned Parenthood, and the ACLU. "It may well have been the first and only time the entire liberal and public-interest community joined together on a single issue."[40]

Similar to what occurred in the cause litigation context, conservatives learned from the success of liberal groups. From this moment forward, conservative as well as liberal groups would exist with the singular purpose of monitoring and participating in judicial appointments at all federal levels, springing into action to support or oppose particular appointments based entirely on ideological concerns.[41] No previous generation had standing groups involved in lower court appointments on an ongoing basis.

President George H.W. Bush had his own highly controversial Supreme Court nominee, Clarence Thomas, accused in the confirmation hearings of sexual harassment by law professor Anita Hill. He was ultimately confirmed by a close fifty-two to forty-eight vote. The Bush Administration also engaged in careful screening of judges' philosophies, and developed a contentious relationship with Democrats on the Senate Judiciary Committee.[42]

The combined legacy of Reagan's and Bush's twelve years of judicial appointments was significant. Reagan alone appointed 47% of the sitting federal judges.[43] At the end of this twelve years, Republican appointees outnumbered Democratic appointees by more than three to one. Empirical studies, although not conclusive, detected a measurable conservative tilt in the decisions of these judges.[44]

There is disagreement about the ideological character of President William Jefferson Clinton's judicial appointments. A conservative group charged that his appointments "have been drawn almost exclusively from the ranks of the liberal elite."[45] Most scholars have concluded, however, that many of his nominees were moderates (matching his centrist political stance). As an indication of this moderation, a number of left groups were displeased with his appointments.[46] To these groups, Clinton seemed distressingly uninterested in judicial appointments. Like Carter, he was more concerned with adding women and minorities to the bench than with screening for ideology.

40 Id. 132.
41 See Scherer, *Scoring Points*, supra Chap. 5.
42 See Sheldon Goldman, "Bush's Judicial Legacy: The Final Imprint," 76 *Judicature* 282 (1993)
43 Goldman, "Picking Federal Judges," supra 336.
44 Id. 296. See Timothy Tomasi and Jess Velona, "All the President's Men? A Study of Ronald Reagan's Appointments to the US Courts of Appeals," 87 *Columbia L. Rev.* 766 (1987); see Scherer, *Scoring Points*, supra.
45 Quoted in Maltese, "Confirmation Gridlock," supra 15.
46 See id.; Goldman, et al., "Clinton's Judges: Summing up the Legacy," 84 *Judicature* 228, 354 (2001).

The lower court judicial confirmation process during Clinton's second term was the most acrimonious ever. Republican control of the Senate over the last six years of Clinton's presidency was a major contributing factor in this clash. During one period, Republican Senator Orin Hatch, Chair of the Senate Judiciary Committee, held up *all* judicial nominations until Clinton agreed to appoint a judge favored by conservatives; in a separate episode, Republican Senator James Inhofe held up consideration of thirty judicial nominees in protest of Clinton's appointment of a gay man as Ambassador to Luxembourg.[47] A pattern of lengthy delay became entrenched, especially in connection with Clinton's appointments to the appellate courts. During George H.W. Bush's tenure and during Clinton's first term, the average period between the President's nomination and the Senate Judiciary Committee's hearing on appellate court nominees ranged between seventy-seven and eighty-one days. After Clinton's reelection, hearings on nominees were scheduled an average of 231 days after nomination (105th Congress), later increasing to 247 days after nomination (106th Congress).[48] After a successful nomination made it out of the Judiciary Committee, further lengthy delays followed before a full Senate vote was taken, taking an average of forty-two additional days in the 105th Congress and an additional sixty-eight days in the 106th Congress. A number of judges waited between two to four years for confirmation.[49] "[T]he average court of appeals judge waited more than three hundred days to be confirmed – ten times as long as when Carter was president."[50] These lengthy delays don't count the three dozen of Clinton's nominees who never received a hearing at all.

So bad was the delay that Chief Justice Rehnquist, in his 1997 Report on the State of the Judiciary, issued a rare rebuke of the Republican-controlled Senate. He observed that there were eighty-two judicial vacancies, almost one tenth of the judiciary, twenty-six of which had been vacant for at least eighteen months. "The Senate," Rehnquist wrote, "is surely under no obligation to confirm any particular nominee, but after the necessary time for inquiry it should vote him up or vote him down."[51]

Ideology in contemporary federal judicial appointments

The subject of judicial appointments was "more prominent in the 2000 election than in any election since 1968."[52] President George W. Bush revived the Office of Legal Policy, and his Administration conducted careful ideological screening

47 Stephanie K. Seymour, "The Judicial Appointment Process: How Broken is It?" 39 *Tulsa L. Rev.* 691, 702 (2004).
48 See Goldman, et. al., "Clinton's Judges," supra 235–6.
49 Seymour, "Judicial Appointments Process, "supra 707.
50 Scherer, *Scoring Points*, supra 136.
51 William Rehnquist, 1997 Annual Report of the Chief Justice of the Supreme Court of the United States, supra 9.
52 Ross, "Role of Judicial Issues in Presidential Campaigns," supra 460.

of judges.[53] Breaking a fifty-year tradition, the Bush Administration excluded the ABA from any official role in evaluating judicial candidates. White House Counsel Alberto Gonzales explained this action by characterizing the ABA as a politically active "interest group," suggesting that it was inappropriate for any such group to have a "quasi official role" in the selection process.[54] It was widely reported, however, that Gonzales and Attorney General John Ashcroft were soliciting judicial nominations from conservative groups.[55] According to one account, the Federalist Society recommended seventeen to twenty of Bush's first seventy nominations.[56]

At the outset of Bush's presidency, with the Senate evenly divided, Democrats had control of the Senate Judiciary Committee. They proceeded to engage in their own slow down. Although moderate appointments were confirmed, Democrats rejected a number of very conservative nominees. When control of the Senate was regained by Republicans, Bush renominated several previously rejected candidates. Democrats threatened a filibuster to halt their consideration (which requires sixty votes to break). This time, the Republicans indignantly complained that "every judicial nominee deserves an up or down vote."[57] Senate Majority Leader Bill Frist threatened to enact a rule change that would prohibit filibusters on judicial nominations, a serious action, given that the filibuster is a time-honored practice that protects minority parties in Congress. Democrats promised to shut down the Senate if the filibuster was eliminated. A compromise was brokered at the final hour by moderate Senators from both parties.

In yet another reversal of positions, conservatives who previously urged that Clinton's liberal appointments be rejected for ideological reasons now objected to the rejection by Democratic Senators of Bush nominees on ideological grounds. A rejection on such grounds, observed one conservative commentator, "politicizes and degrades the judiciary by sending the implied message that judges are biased and make decisions based on their personal will instead of the rule of law ... Americans must resist it by strongly asserting the requirement that judges selflessly set aside their political philosophy when rendering judgments."[58] This argument, of course, also bears against the unprecedented systematic vetting for two decades by conservatives of judicial nominees on ideological grounds. Judicial appointments are marked by hypocrisy on all sides.

---

53 Sheldon Goldman, et al., "W. Bush Remaking the Judiciary: Like Father Like Son?" 86 *Judicature* 282 (2003).

54 See Gonzales' Letter to ABA President Martha W. Barnett, reprinted as Appendix 1, in Laura E. Little, "The ABA's Role in Prescreening Federal Judicial Candidates: Are We Ready to Give Up on the Lawyers," 10 *William & Mary Bill Rights J.* 3771–3 (2001).

55 See Robert S. Greenberger, "ABA Loses Major Role in Judge Screening," *Wall Street Journal*, March 23, 2001, B8.

56 Neil A. Lewis, "Bush to Reveal First Judicial Sources Soon," *New York Times*, April 24, 2001, A17. See also Little, "ABA's Role in Prescreening Federal Judicial Candidates," supra n. 4.

57 Associate White House Counsel Brett Kavanaugh, quoted in Goldman, et al., "W. Bush Remaking the Judiciary," supra 300.

58 Douglas Hibbard, "To Advise and Consent: The Senate's Role in Evaluating Judicial Nominees," Issue 237, *Family Research Council*, 4, http://www.frc.org/get.cfm?i.

The debacle surrounding the Bush nomination and the subsequent withdrawal of Harriet Miers for the Supreme Court removed any doubt about the primacy of ideological considerations for conservatives. Her nomination was sunk by vicious opposition from conservatives that she lacked confirmed conservative credentials (and had weak qualifications to boot).[59] The White House attempted to appease religious conservatives by emphasizing her churchgoing convictions. Influential Republican Senator Sam Brownback was nonplussed about her nomination, telling reporters after an hour-long meeting that she "had done little to assure him that she would be open to revisiting or overturning [Roe v. Wade]."[60] Miers' nomination was all but done.

Unlike the Federalist Society, which has worked behind the scenes on judicial appointments, conservative evangelical Christian leaders, including Tony Perkins of the Family Research Council and James Dobson of Focus on Family, have been among the most vocal and committed groups in the effort to secure the appointment of conservative judges. They take substantial credit for Bush's electoral victory for organizing a strong voter turnout in pivotal states among Christian voters who went overwhelmingly for Bush. By their lights, conservative judicial appointments are their due reward. At a private conference held in March 2005, attended by Senate Majority Leader Bill Frist and then House Majority Leader Tom DeLay, evangelical leaders discussed a plan to "work with congressional Republicans to achieve a judiciary that sides with them on abortion, same sex marriage, and other elements of their agenda."[61] Tony Perkins stated "For years activist courts, aided by liberal interest groups like the A.C.L.U., have been quietly working under the veil of the judicial bench, like thieves in the night, to rob us of our Christian heritage and our religious freedoms."[62] Now evangelicals are bent on seizing control of the judiciary and using judicial activism for their own ends. Conservative evangelicals often assert that they are defending natural law and moral principle (in a non-instrumental sense), but in the pursuit of this mission they take a consummately instrumental approach to litigation, judicial appointments, legislation, and legal rules and processes.

Conservative and liberal groups leapt into action with the announcement of Justice O'Connor's retirement and upon Justice Rehnquist's death. Progress for America announced that it planned to spend $18 million in support of a Bush nominee (whoever it might be), and the group preemptively spent $700,000 to

59 See Elizabeth Bumiller, "White House Tries to Quell A Rebellion On the Right," *New York Times*, October 7, 2005, A20; David Kirkpatrick, "New Questions from the Right on Court Pick," *New York Times*, October 6, 2005, A1.
60 Sheryl Gay Stoleberg, "Foe of Abortion Senator is Cool to Court Choice," *New York Times*, October 7, 2005, A1.
61 See Peter Wallsten, "2 Evangelicals Want to Strip Courts' Funds," *Los Angeles Times*, April 22, 2005.
62 Tony Perkins' statement, quoted in David Kirkpatrick, "First Set to Use Religious State on Judges Issue," *New York Times*, April 15 2005, A14.

discredit liberal attacks *before* any had been aired.[63] Christian conservative Dobson said that "the confrontation is coming with a vengeance."[64] War-like rhetoric dominated the media characterizations of the looming "Battle Over Court."[65] "In fight to Confirm New Justice, Two Field Generals Rally Their Troops Again."[66]

Despite resistance from liberal groups, John Roberts was handily confirmed as Justice by a seventy-eight to twenty-two vote, though the number of no's was relatively sizable compared to other confirmations. The vote on Samuel Alito, which hewed closely to party lines, was closer (fifty-eight to forty-two), but never really in doubt.[67] Objecting to the party-line voting on Alito, prominent Republicans threatened future retaliation. "So I say to my Democratic friends," said Senator Jon Kyle, "think carefully about what is being done today. Its impact will be felt well beyond this particular nominee."[68] On the very day Alito was confirmed, hardly pausing to savor the victory, the combatants were already looking ahead. Gary Bauer, president of the conservative group American Values, stated, "I do believe there may be close to five votes [on the Supreme Court] to at least move church-state issues a little more toward the conservative perspective.... The next vacancy, depending on who it is, will really be the *mother of all battles*."[69]

In a disconcertingly swift follow-up, a month after Alito's ascension to the Supreme Court the South Dakota legislature overwhelmingly approved an almost total ban on abortion (permissible only if the life of the mother is at risk). This ban was explicitly put forth by supporters to generate a test case for overturning *Roe*. With a $1 million dollar pledge already in hand, efforts began immediately to raise funds to defray the cost of defending the ban against the constitutional challenge they hope will follow. "'I'm convinced that the timing is right for this,'" said a state representative who sponsored the bill, "noting the appointments of Chief Justice John G. Roberts Jr. and Samuel A. Alito."[70] Roberts and Alito were openly screened and sold to supporters for their conservative ideological views; now comes the expected pay off in their judicial decisions.

Ideology has played a role in federal judicial selections in the past, certainly at the level of the Supreme Court, and for the lower courts with Roosevelt. It is also true that periodic political attacks on the courts are a staple of American

63 Jason DeParle, "In Battle to Pick Next Justice, Right Says Avoid a Kennedy." *New York Times*, June 27, 2005, A 12.

64 Id.

65 Headline, "O'Connor to Retire, Touching Off Battle Over Court," *New York Times*, July 2, 2005.

66 David E. Rosenbaum and Lynette Clemetson, *New York Times*, July 3, 2005.

67 See Lois Romano and Juliet Eilperin, "Republicans Were Masters in the Race to Paint Alito," *Washington Post*, Feb. 2, 2006, A1.

68 David Kirkpatrick, "On Party Lines, Panel Approve Alito for Court," *New York Times*, Jan. 25, 2006, A1.

69 Quoted in Charles Babington, "Alito Is Sworn in on High Court," *Washington Post*, Feb. 1, 2006, A1 (emphasis added).

70 Monica Davey, "South Dakota Lawmakers Set to Vote on a Bill Banning Nearly All Abortions," *New York Times*, February 22, 2006, A14; Monica Davey, "Ban on Most Abortions Advances in South Dakota," *New York Times*, February 23, 2006, A14.

history. Justice Samuel Chase was impeached, though not convicted; courts have been temporarily shut and their jurisdiction occasionally limited. But it is wrong to think that the present controversies hold nothing new and represent nothing uniquely harmful. The duration, comprehensiveness, and single-minded dedication toward this ideological screening, monitored and urged on by committed groups eager to fight, and the high-stakes battles this has engendered, are contemporary innovations.

State judicial elections

A "crisis of integrity" is brewing in state judicial elections.[71]

Judges must stand for elections in thirty-eight states, either for their initial appointment or in periodic retention votes. At the formation of the country, most state judges were appointed. In the wake of President Jackson's populism, a number of states converted to elective judiciaries; most new states thereafter followed this model. A historical study of this shift found surprisingly little discussion of the issue beyond the broad sentiment that people should have a say in who becomes judges.[72] Enthusiasm for judicial elections waned in the early twentieth century, with the growing perception that inept or corrupt judges were securing positions owing to voter ignorance. After calls for reform, a number of states adopted versions of the "Missouri Plan," in which professional groups nominate several candidates based upon merit, one of whom is then appointed by the Governor; after serving far an initial term, these judges stand in unopposed retention elections. Today there is a mix of systems among and within states, with more than 80% of judges facing a vote of some kind.

"Inspired by the role model of the Warren Court,"[73] in the 1960s and 1970s, state high courts became more assertive in a range of areas. Far-reaching decisions were issued by judges on school financing, zoning, tobacco regulation, gun control, products liability, the right to die, the death penalty, gay marriage, and more, sometimes in a "freewheeling" manner that departed from the preexisting case law or understandings of statutes and state constitutional provisions.[74]

Prior to the 1970s, judicial elections were sleepy events garnering little attention and involving relatively small sums of money. By the late seventies and early eighties, prompted by the growing judicial assertiveness, money began to flow into judicial election races. The escalation in amounts was rapid. Texas held the first judicial election campaign in the million-dollar range in the 1980s. A multimillion-dollar campaign followed in 1986 that resulted in the recall of three justices of the California

71 Paul D. Carrington, "Judicial Independence and Democratic Accountability in Highest State Courts," 61 *Law & Contemp. Probs.* 79, 126 (1998).
72 Steven P. Croley, "The Majoritarian Difficulty: Elective Judiciaries and the Rule of Law," 62 *U. Chicago L. Rev.* 689, 714–24 (1995).
73 Carrington, "Judicial Independence and Democratic Accountability," supra 99.
74 See Id. 99–107.

Supreme Court. "Between 1986 and 1996, the cost of running for Alabama Supreme Court rose 776%."[75] In campaigns for positions on the Texas Supreme Court in the mid-1990s, seven justices collectively raised in excess of $9 million.[76] In the late 1990s, election spending for the Wisconsin Supreme Court reached $1.3 million, double the record set two years earlier.[77] In 2000, candidates collectively raised more than $45 million for Supreme Court elections in twenty states, a 61% increase over the previous record set in 1998; in five of those states, independent interest groups spent an additional $16 million.[78] Three candidates in the 2000 elections for the Illinois Supreme Court spent over a million dollars each.[79] Four years later, two candidates in Illinois raised a total of $5 million.[80] As these numbers suggest, "The sums of money being spent to capture [state high court] seats is growing exponentially."[81]

The nasty tone of recent campaigns has far exceeded anything previously seen. A favorite tactic is to misleadingly twist past decisions of a judge. The typical campaign media spot makes it impossible for false impressions to be effectively corrected.[82] An insidious aspect of these efforts is that many groups do not openly campaign in terms of their agenda, but instead level charges that the targeted judge engages in "judicial activism" or "coddles criminals." In the 2004 West Virginia election, for example, an organization known as "And For the Sake of Kids," dedicated solely to defeating sitting Judge Warren McGraw, ran advertisements claiming that the judge "cast the deciding vote" to set free a child molester. This was a distortion of the judge's decision, which was part of a panel decision, and related to the release of a juvenile involved in consensual statutory rape who was eligible for release upon turning eighteen. Of the $2.5 million raised by the group, $1.7 million was contributed by Don L. Blankenship, the CEO of a coal mining company, who admitted that his objective was to elect a pro-business justice.[83]

The forces behind the dramatic rise in sums spent and the harsh tones of the campaigns are evident: "political interest groups and parties began in about 1980 to take a heightened interest in judicial elections."[84] Initially, the main contributors to judicial elections were trial lawyers and the defense bar, lawyers who routinely brought cases before the judges they contributed to; later, contributions were made by business associations such as the Chamber of Commerce and individual corporations

75 Anthony Champagne, "Interest Groups and Judicial Elections," 34 *Loyola L.A. L. Rev.* 1391 (2001).
76 See "Payola Justice: How Texas Supreme Court Justices Raise Money from Court Litigants," available at http://www.tpj.org/docs/1998/02/reports/payola/toc.html.
77 Champagne, "Interest Groups and Judicial Elections," supra 1403.
78 Schotland, "Financing Judicial Elections, 2000," supra 850–1.
79 Campagne, "Interest Groups and Judicial Elections," supra 1397.
80 Adam Liptak, "Judicial Races in Several States Become Partisan Battlegrounds," *New York Times*, October 24, 2004, A1.
81 Id. A30.
82 See Vincent R. Johnson, "Ethical Campaigning For the Judiciary," 29 *Texas Tech L. Rev.* 811 (1998).
83 Liptak, "Judicial Races in Several States Become Partisan Battlegrounds," supra A30.
84 Carrington, "Judicial Independence and Democratic Accountability," supra 105.

or business people. For example, the Vinson and Elkins law firm alone gave seven justices on the Texas Supreme Court a total of $244,018 in the mid-1990s; political action committees (PACs) and executives from a number of corporations with cases on the court's docket – including Enron, Coastal Corp., Texas Utilities, Dow Chemical, and Exxon – contributed an additional $1.4 million.[85]

An odor of impropriety is created by this practice. "There have been celebrated occasions . . . when very large contributions were made by lawyers or parties who thereafter secured large favorable judgments or remunerative appointments such as receiverships."[86] Polls confirm a high level of suspicion among the public about the integrity of judicial decisions:

> A recent national survey of public opinion and the court system found that eighty-one percent of respondents believed that "judges' decisions are influenced by political considerations." Seventy-eight percent believed "elected judges are influenced by having to raise campaign funds." These national survey findings are supported by state surveys. In Texas, eighty-three percent of respondents thought judges were influenced by contributions in their decisions. A Pennsylvania poll showed that eighty-eight percent thought judicial decisions were influenced by contributions made to judicial campaigns. An Ohio poll found that ninety percent of Ohioans believed political contributions affected judicial decisions. A Washington poll found that seventy-six percent of the respondents believed judges were influenced by political decisions and sixty-six percent by having to raise campaign funds.[87]

One study concluded that this new age of multimillion-dollar judicial campaigns "works to the advantage of relatively well-heeled, cohesive interest groups, such as the business community, and to the disadvantage of the general public."[88] Members of the general public usually have little interest in or knowledge about judicial candidates, and judicial campaigns are rarely backed by grassroots support. Campaigns by interested business groups, in contrast, are well-organized, funded, and targeted. Some campaigns, like those by the United States Chamber of Commerce or the Christian Coalition, have a national reach involving multiple state contests.[89]

Most of the big-money campaigns have taken place at the level of state supreme courts, which have final say on issues of state law. Recently this same phenomenon has shown up in lower court elections as well. According to one survey, a trial court race in Sacramento cost a combined total of $750,000; a candidate for the Court of Common Pleas in Lackawanna County, Pennsylvania, spent $1 million.[90]

---

85 "Payola Justice," supra Summary.
86 Carrington, "Judicial Independence and Democratic Accountability," supra 92.
87 Champagne, "Interest Groups and Judicial Elections," supra 1407–8.
88 John D. Echeverria, "Changing the Rules by Changing the Players: The Environmental Issue in State Judicial Elections," 9 *NYU Environmental. L.J.* 217, 224 (2001).
89 See Id.; Kara Baker, "Is Justice For Sale in Ohio? An Examination of Ohio Elections and Suggestions For Reform Focusing on the 2000 Race for the Ohio Supreme Court," 35 *Akron L. Rev.* 159 (2001).
90 Champagne, "Interest Groups and Judicial Elections," supra 1403.

The commitment of such large sums of money raises the question of whether contributors are getting what they pay for. Several instances have been identified in which strategically funneled campaign financing was subsequently followed by the desired change in court decisions.[91] Judges, of course, deny that contributions have any effect on their decisions, although a few have admitted that in the period leading up to elections they approach criminal cases with trepidation, concerned that a decision favorable to a defendant will be used against them.[92]

A study of the Alabama Supreme Court found a "striking" correlation between campaign financing and decisions. Justices funded by businesses overwhelmingly rule in favor of businesses, and justices funded by plaintiffs' lawyers overwhelmingly rule against business. With no hint of irony, the author matter-of-factly concluded that "From the data presented in this article . . . it appears that contributing to a judicial campaign can be a sound investment. The money invested yields consistent returns, i.e., judicial candidates who, if elected, vote the contributor's way, day-in, day-out. Those who believe that law, especially law made by elected judges, is nothing more than interest-group politics can find confirmation of their belief in these cases."[93]

A high correlation alone does not provide a basis to assert that the judges voted in favor of or against businesses *owing to* the financial support they received. That would be corruption. Interest groups put their money behind preferred judges in anticipation – based upon the expressed views or past actions of the justices – that the justices' interpretation of the law will coincide with their desires. The interest groups might not be buying the judges, but they are buying interpretations and applications of the law they want. This is an unrepentantly instrumental attempt to control the law, accomplished through the judicial appointment process.

Caught in a cycle of distrust

The project to shape the law in a desired direction by controlling judicial appointments is a slow one with few obvious signs. It occurs by accretion in the cumulative multitude of judicial decisions, and is constrained by the legal respect for precedent. The twenty-plus-year effort of conservatives at the federal and (more recently) state levels appears to have borne some fruit. Particularly in the common law subjects of contract, torts, and property, which are controlled by judges, a few observers have identified a conservative turn in court decisions that are more favorable to businesses and less solicitous of injured individuals.[94] But it is still too early to evaluate the full impact of these efforts. President George W. Bush has several remaining

91 Echeverria, "Changing the Rules by Changing the Players," supra.
92 See Croley, "Majoritarian Difficulty," supra 740–1.
93 Stephen J. Ware, "Money, Politics and Judicial Decisions: A Case Study of Arbitration Law in Alabama," 15 *J. L. & Pol.* 645, 686 (1999).
94 See Jay M. Feinman, *Un-Making Law: The Conservative Campaign to Roll Back the Common Law* (Boston: Beacon Press 2004).

years of prospective appointments in his reshaping of the federal judiciary, and his appointments to the Supreme Court have only just been seated.

Given widespread perceptions that judges wield formidable power to affect society by their decisions, and that their ideological views shape their legal decisions, it seems inevitable that political battles to control who becomes federal and state judges will remain a dominant feature of the U.S. legal culture. The combatants are collectively caught in a trap that propels the conflict onward. Conservatives, in their own minds, are merely redressing the earlier liberal capture of the courts; liberals see it as a conservative takeover. Both sides charge their opponents with inappropriately politicizing the judiciary by using ideological litmus tests to select judges, while both on their own end engage in precisely that. After eight years of President Bush stocking the judiciary with conservatives, if a liberal is elected President, liberal groups will clamor for a full slate of liberal judges to offset the damage, which conservatives will mightily resist (filibustering if need be) to preserve their gains. Even if one side or the other would prefer to abstain from efforts to pack the judiciary – out of concern to preserve judicial integrity – the dynamics of the situation almost compel a continuing battle over judicial appointments, if only to keep judgeships out of the clutches of less-restrained ideological opponents who lack similar qualms. No side can trust others to stand down, so all sides must engage in this effort.

11

Instrumentalism in legislation and administration

Today there is an incalculably mammoth amount of state and federal legislation, covering virtually every conceivable subject, and an immense volume of administrative law, with more than seventy-five thousand pages of administrative rules, regulations, and proceedings published each year in the *Federal Register*. Administrative agencies gather knowledge and apply scientific expertise to establish regulatory schemes that effectuate legislative policies, and to monitor the achievement of legislatively established goals. Administrative law is thus a purely instrumental creature, created to carry out legislatively determined ends. Legislation, as Part 1 conveys, as been understood in consummately instrumental terms as well, for more than two centuries.

Battles over and through legislation and administrative regulations are no novelty. James Madison warned in *Federalist* 10 of the dangers of competing "factions," which had already made their presence felt in the state legislatures of the day. These battles were especially heated at the outset of the twentieth century. Louis Jaffe wrote in the 1937 *Harvard Law Review*:

> Indeed, our entire economy is honeycombed with violent and bitter intra and inter group conflict.... The power of special interests pervades our entire legal and governmental structure.... [I]t must be understood that these interests will, in one way or another, be effective, be it in the legislative or in the administrative process.[1]

Hence, the group conflict happening today in the legislation and administrative regulatory arenas is old stuff. This is not to say, however, that what is happening today is not different in any significant respects from the past. One crucial difference is that the entire surrounding legal milieu, as laid out in preceding chapters, has become more instrumental in orientation. Well-armed and organized combatants now take the battle to every legal arena in a way calculated to turn the weight of the entire legal apparatus in support of their agenda.

---

1 Louis L. Jaffe, "Law Making by Private Groups," 51 *Harvard L. Rev.* 201, 252 (1937).

Views on "public interest" in government – public choice theory

Another critical difference has to do with shifts in views about the "public interest:" what it means, how or whether it can be identified, and whether it is being pursued by public officials.

Several versions of this ideal have circulated in the U.S. legal culture. Theorists in the "civic republican" tradition assert that through dialogue and deliberation among competing factions, a policy can emerge that represents the common public interest.[2] Contemporary revivalists of civic republicanism urge that government officials, legislators, and members of the administrative bureaucracy must seek input from all sides with an open mind, and aim toward formulating a position and producing a course of action that serves all.[3] Another version of the public interest is the idea, typical among New Dealers, that administrative officials are neutral, apolitical decision-makers who apply expertise to render independent substantive judgments that advance the general public interest.[4]

Civic republicanism and faith in the scientific or technical expertise of agencies share the underlying faith that a common public interest exists apart from the interests of any particular group or groups. In this sense, they are variations of the same idea, merely arriving at the public interest in distinct ways, the former through open dialogue and the latter through expertise. They can work together, the former to operate when determining the legislative goals, and the latter when administratively carrying out those goals.

A fundamentally different understanding of the "public interest" accepts the endemic presence of an irreducible pluralism of interests in society. This view was influential among political scientists under the label "interest group pluralism" in the 1950s,[5] though its roots date to the turn of the century. Legislative and administrative processes in some way aggregate or balance the interests of the contesting groups within society, each seeking to advance its own interests, arriving at an equilibrium that represents the "public interest." For this process to operate properly and fairly, it is essential that all contesting groups have access to decision-makers to insure that their positions are appropriately considered, weighed, and reflected in the final decision. In the administrative context, this means that parties affected by agency actions should be given notice and opportunities to participate. Administrative expertise in this understanding involves an apolitical fine tuning that arrives at just the right balance.

---

2 See Cass Sunstein, "Interest Groups in American Public Law," 38 *Stanford L. Rev.* 29 (1985).
3 See Mark Seidenfeld, "A Civic Republican Justification for the Bureaucratic State," 105 *Harvard L. Rev.* 1511 (1991).
4 See Thomas W. Merrill, "Capture Theory and the Courts: 1967–1983," 72 *Chicago-Kent L. Rev.* 1039, 1048–50 (1997).
5 See Robert Dahl, *A Preface to Democratic Theory* (Chicago: Chicago Univ. Press 1956); Truman, *The Government Process*, supra.

Theorists have tended to emphasize the qualitative differences between these understandings, as Cass Sunstein does (comparing republican with pluralist):

> Under the pluralist view, politics mediates the struggle among self-interested groups for scarce social resources. Only nominally deliberative, politics is a process of conflict and compromise among various social interests. Under the pluralist conception, people come to the political process with preselected interests that they seek to promote through political conflict and compromise....
>
> The pluralist conception treats the republican notion of a separate common good as incoherent, potentially totalitarian, or both. The common good [in the pluralist conception] consists of uninhibited bargaining among the various participants, so that numbers and intensities of preferences can be reflected in political outcomes. The common good amounts to an aggregation of individual preferences.[6]

To summarize, one understanding of the "public interest" – coming in two variations, civic republican or expertise – involves a common good that is shared by all within the community, whereas the second involves an accommodation or balance of different interests that remain distinct. The second version is less ambitious than the first. Compared with a set of views to be discussed next, however, they share an important quality: Both were optimistic that the public interest (differently understood) could be identified and achieved legislatively and administratively.

As with so much covered earlier, the 1960s and 1970s was a crucial period, when the consensus assumptions that reigned in the 1950s gave way to cynicism and skepticism about government. The attractiveness as well as the accuracy of the assumption that administrative agencies operate through apolitical technocratic or scientific expertise were widely doubted. The belief that agencies are "captured" by the industries they regulate became popular.[7] It was pointed out that business interests participate actively in the administrative process, and that employees in administrative agencies anticipate future employment in these businesses. "[T]o the extent that belief in an objective 'public interest' remains," wrote Richard Stewart in his influential 1975 overview of administrative regulation, "the agencies are accused of subverting it in favor of the private interests of regulated and client firms."[8]

A seminal article was published in 1971 by George Stigler, who argued that "regulation is acquired by the industry and is designed and operated primarily for its benefit."[9] Stigler characterized the government's coercive power as a *product* that is *bought* by those willing to pay the most. Regulated industries benefit in various ways: Licensing requirements set up barriers to entry for new competitors; the establishment of standards based on existing products inhibit potential alternatives; price-setting prevents costly competition; subsidies boost profitability. The railroads

---

6 Cass R. Sunstein, "Interest Groups in American Public Law," 38 *Stanford L. Rev.* 29, 32–3 (1985).
7 See Merrill, "Capture Theory and the Courts," supra 1050–3.
8 Richard Stewart, "The Reformation of American Administrative Law," 88 *Harvard L. Rev.* 1669, 1682–3 (1975).
9 George J. Stigler, "The Theory of Economic Regulation," 2 *Bell J. Econ. & Manag.* 3 (1971).

and airlines benefited in several of these ways from the Interstate Commerce Commission and the Civil Aeronautics Board. In effect, Stigler argued, industries utilize the regulatory power of government to help them maintain cartels. Administrative agencies operate as industry enforcers.[10]

Building upon the work of Stigler and others, a school of thought called "public choice" theory swept through political science and law in the 1980s and 1990s, to become the leading framework for analyzing legislative and administrative activities. The dominance of this theory was so complete that it was confidently said in 1984 that public choice theory "long ago put public interest theories of politics to rest."[11]

Public choice theory, which is linked to the economic analysis of law described in Chapter 7, has a startlingly cynical cast. It begins with the assumption that all people – including legislators and administrative officials – are rational maximizers of their self-interest.[12] The primary objective of politicians is to ensure their own reelection. Voters typically do not monitor legislators on the multitude of individual bills they consider. What they know of the candidates, and what they base their election decisions on, are the positive and negative images projected by campaigns. So legislators find it rational to maximize their total amount of campaign contributions. Interest groups and individuals, as rational maximizers of their objectives, channel or withhold funds to politicians in a way most likely to obtain the legislation they desire.

This economic perspective on the political process was summarized by William Landes and Richard Posner:

> In the economists' version of the interest group theory of government, legislation is supplied to groups or coalitions that outbid rival seekers of favorable legislation. The price that the winning group bids is determined both by the value of legislative protection to the group's members. . . . Payments take the form of campaign contributions, votes, implicit promises of future favors, and sometimes outright bribes. In short, legislation is "sold" by the legislature and "bought" by the beneficiaries of the legislation.[13]

Needless to say, this is a purely instrumental view of law.

A great deal of legislation, in this view, involves legally imposed and sanctioned transfers of wealth secured by well-financed and organized interest groups at the expense of hapless groups or the unorganized in society.[14] Legislators are paid by beneficiaries of the legislation they produce through campaign contributions,

---

10 See Richard A. Posner, "Theories of Economic Regulation," 5 *Bell J. Econ. & Manag.* 335 (1974).
11 Joseph P. Kalt and Mark A. Zupan, "Capture and Ideology in the Economic Theory of Politics," 75 *Am. Econ. Rev.* 279, 279 (1984), quoted in Jonathan R. Macey, "Public Choice and the Legal Academy," 86 *Georgetown L.J.* 1975, 1977 (1998).
12 An excellent introduction to public *choice* theory is Daniel A. Farber and Philip P. Frickey, *Law and Public Choice: A Critical Introduction* (Chicago: Univ. of Chicago Press 1991). See also Symposium on the Theory of Public Choice, 74 *Virginia L. Rev.* 167 (1988); J. Mashaw, "The Economics of Politics and the Understanding of Public Law," 65 *Chicago-Kent L. Rev.* 123 (1989).
13 William Landes and Richard A. Posner, "The Independent Judicial in an Interest-Group Perspective," 18 *J. L. & Economics* 875, 877 (1975).
14 Posner, *Problems of Jurisprudence,* supra 354–5.

through services and perks provided to them by lobbyists, and with the expectation of one day securing high-paid positions in corporations or as lobbyists upon leaving public service. Administrative agency employees, in this view, are also rational maximizers of their self-interest, working to enhance their prospects for promotion and raises, and for increasing their chances of landing lucrative employment in industries upon leaving government.

It's not quite correct to conclude that public choice theory insists that there is no such thing as the "public interest," a topic about which it has little to say. What it insists is that government officials are not seeking the public interest. Legislative and administrative officials are using their positions of legal authority to maximize their own self-interest.

Because small groups with a lot to gain tend to organize effectively and be vigilant in pursuit of their shared aims, they are more successful in extracting benefits from the legislative and administrative arenas. These private benefits are often socially inefficient in that they cost more overall than the private gains they generate. Milk producers, for example, band together to secure legislatively or administratively imposed price supports at the expense of consumers of milk, each of whom must pay more. Large groups with members who suffer small individual harms or who stand to gain minor benefits, like the general public, are difficult to organize and must combat a strong incentive among members of the group to sit back and free ride on the efforts of others (obtaining the gains without any expenditure). As these examples imply, the basic prescription that comes out of public choice theory, consistent with its economic roots, is that the government should stay out of economic regulation, which amounts to legal coercion for private benefit.

Public choice theory, while highly influential among contemporary theorists, has many critics.[15] Opponents point out that it has difficulty explaining the deregulation that has taken place in the airline, telecommunications, and banking industries. Its assertions are belied by the existence of public interest groups, such as consumer groups, environmental groups, women's groups, and religious groups, which are supported by people who stand to gain less as individuals than what they contribute financially. It also paints an overly cynical, one-dimensional view of what motivates legislators and administrative employees.[16] Studies of voting behavior suggest that legislators at least some of the time are motivated by a desire to advance the public good.[17] Legislators are not constantly driven by concerns about reelection, especially given that incumbents have a formidably high reelection rate. Critics have also worried that public choice theory, by its very formulation, will encourage legislators and administrators to behave in a self-seeking manner, constituting a self-fulfilling

---

15 A comprehensive summary of these criticisms, as well as of administrative theory more generally, can be found in Steven B. Croley, "Theories of Regulation: Incorporating the Administrative Process," 98 *Columbia L. Rev.* 1 (1998).

16 See Edward L. Rubin, "Public Choice in Practice and Theory," 81 *California L. Rev.* 1657 (1991).

17 Id. 43. See also Daniel A. Farber and Philip P. Frickey, "The Jurisprudence of Public Choice," 65 *Texas L. Rev.* 873 (1987).

theory that undermines the orientation of public officials to pursue the public good.[18]

Even critics concede, however, that it has explanatory power. The charge of cynicism often leveled against public choice theory is unfair if the theory presents a realistic view of cynical – or rather, self-seeking – government officials. The theory is not to blame for the actions of the people it purports to explain. Public choice theory also reflects the prevailing mood about the conduct and motivations of government officials. Recent surveys show that a majority of the public see legislation as the product of interest groups activities,[19] and 58% of Americans believe there is "widespread corruption in Washington."[20]

Now for a closer look at the reality of legislative and administrative activities. The main focus that follows is on the federal level, though the same activities take place in the states as well.

The effort to influence legislators and administrators

A sophisticated and hugely expensive effort is made by private interests to influence the legislative and administrative apparatuses of the government for their own benefit. Money, in vast amounts, is the lifeblood of this system. So entrenched and pervasive is this activity that it constitutes an integrated structural aspect of the governing system on both the state and federal levels, although not officially acknowledged as such.

The major players seeking to influence or control the law can be roughly divided into financial interests and ideological interests, with significant overlaps, fuzzy cases, and strategic mutual support. Financial interests take three basic forms: individual corporations, associations (corporate trade groups as well as labor unions), and institutes. Ideological interests – women's rights groups, consumer groups, religious groups, libertarian groups, etc. – mainly take the form of advocacy groups. These entities combine in multilayered ways. Corporations participate in and fund trade associations which act to further the collective interests of their industry. Corporations (and their officers) and trade associations also create or fund political action committees (PACs), institutes, or "527 groups" – often with innocuous public-service–sounding names like "Citizens for the Right to Know" or "Traditional Values Coalition" – which lobby for their interests or place ads in the media to propogate their views. Owing to the central role that money plays in this system, financial interests dominate and will take up the bulk of emphasis in the following discussion, although ideological interests exert a significant influence in selected matters.

18 See Jerry Mashaw, "The Economics of Politics and the Understanding of Public Law," 65 *Chicago-Kent L. Rev.* 123 (1989).
19 See Farber and Frickey, "Law and Public Choice," supra 12; see also *Money, Politics, and Campaign Finance Reform Law in the States* edited by David Schultz (Durham, N.C.: Carolina Academic Press 2002).
20 Richard Morin and Claudia Deane, "In Abramoff Case, Most See Evidence of Wider Problem: Poll Shows Strong Support for Reform of Lobbying," *Washington Post*, January 10, 2006, A7.

Serving as intermediaries between these entities and government officials are a legion of professional lobbyists. Corporations, trade associations, institutes, and advocacy groups have lobbyists on staff as well as retain outside lobbyists to obtain access to and maintain contact with government officials for the purposes of influencing law-making and the regulatory process. Many lobbyists are located in small consulting firms or major law firms with lobbying practices. Money spent on lobbying has reached astronomical heights in the past few years, as will be detailed shortly.

The targets of these efforts are legislators, their staff members, well-placed members of state and federal administrations, and administrative agency officials at all levels (upper level political appointees and career bureaucrats). The greater authority a public official has, the more attention he or she receives. Leaving aside outright criminal bribery, this attention takes on several forms: making direct campaign contributions, sponsoring campaign fund-raising events, providing contributions to third-party supporters (political parties, political action committees, mutually favored institutes or organizations), supplying supportive work (drafting desired legislation, administrative regulations, and briefing papers), funding or securing funding for lavish trips at home and abroad for "informational" purposes (golf resorts being a favorite destination), subsidizing travel on private jets, supplying free social dinners and entertainment (including high-profile sporting events), employing close relatives as lobbyists or consultants, and offering the prospect of well-compensated future employment to legislators and their staff, and to administrative officials, upon departure from government service.[21] Less pleasant forms of attention include threats to withhold the aforementioned benefits, going to higher ups to assert pressure, and orchestrating "grassroots" pressure (prompting constituents to contact legislators).

Government officials are by no means the passive recipients of entreaties by lobbyists. Legislators, especially, aggressively seek out and utilize the resources offered by lobbyists to advance their own agenda; so intertwined are the connections that sometimes their respective agendas and identities are joined. This effort was refined in the "K-Street Project" (named after the main location of lobbying firms), undertaken by Congressman Tom DeLay following the Republican takeover of the House of Representatives in the 1994 elections. DeLay, who would rise to the position of House Majority Leader until forced to resign in the aftermath of the Abramoff lobbying scandal, informed trade associations and lobbying firms that they must fire Democrats and hire Republicans if they wished to have access to influential lawmakers.[22] "We're just following the old adage," he explained unrepentantly, "of punish your enemies and reward your friends." DeLay's goal was to secure a

---

21 "Summary Report: Influence Inc., Lobbyists Spending in Washington" (2000 Edition), at www.opensecrets.org/pubs/lobby. See Glen Justice, "With Attention on Delay, A Flurry of Filings (Better Late than Never, Some Say)," *New York Times*, June 13, 2005, A 13
22 Thomas B. Edsall, "Lobbyists Emergence Reflects Shift in Capital Culture," *Washington Post*, Jan. 12, 2006, A1.

permanent Republican majority in the House, as well as to enhance his own grip on power, which could best be accomplished by controlling the money spigot. In the early 1990s, money from lobbyists was about evenly distributed between Democrats and Republicans; by the mid-2000s, this money went two to one in favor of Republicans.[23]

The degree of intimate mixing between politicians and lobbyists – including spouses and other relatives of legislators and their staffs who work as lobbyists or consultants – is shocking to outsiders. Lobbyists have served as treasurers for the campaign committees of seventy-nine legislators and for eight hundred political action committees since 1998, raising campaign funds for Democrats as well as Republicans.[24] In the run up to an election, many lobbyists temporarily set aside lobbying to become campaign consultants for incumbents; after an election they return to lobby the very legislators they helped to victory.[25] Lobbyists, moreover, held all of the top positions at the 2004 Republican National Convention.

The front-page Abramoff affair,[26] reportedly ensnaring a dozen members of Congress and their staffs and executive branch officials in a corruption investigation, is the product of a culture in which money and favors flow from lobbyists and their clients to public officials with the expectation (or at least hope), implicit or explicit, of obtaining favorable legal action in return. In an unrelated case that broke at the same time, Congressman Randy Cunningham pleaded guilty to receiving bribes of $2.4 million.[27] Although money is an ever-present medium in politics, not since the Gilded Age has the mix of money and politics been this pervasive or this blatant.

There are numerous signs that the culture has changed for the worse in recent years. Twenty years ago, an uproar ensued when it became public that Senator Lloyd Bensten held a breakfast meeting for lobbyists who contributed funds to his campaign; but today lobbyists sponsor fundraisers for various senators and representatives every day that Congress is in session.[28] Representative Roy Blunt became acting majority leader upon DeLay's resignation; Blunt's wife is a lobbyist for Philip Morris, which contributes substantial sums to his campaign, and he has built a network of connections with lobbyists. Representative John Boehner, who prevailed in the contest with Blunt to permanently replace DeLay as majority leader, for years

---

23 Todd S. Purdom, "Go Ahead, Try to Stop K Street," *New York Times*, January 8, 2006, Week in Review 1.

24 See Elizabeth Brown and Shaylyn Cochran, "PAC-Men Lobbyists," Report by the Center for Public Integrity, available at http://www.publicintegrity.org/lobby/report.aspx?aid=750. See also Jonathan Weisman and Charles R. Babcock, "K Street's New Ways Spawn More Pork: As Barriers with Lawmakers Fall, 'Earmarks' Grow," *Washington Post*, January 27, 2006, A1.

25 Edsell, "Lobbyists Emergence Reflects Shifts in Capital Culture," supra 1.

26 Sheryl Gay Stolberg, "Lobbyist Accepts Plea Deal and Becomes Star Witness in a Wider Corruption Case: Tremors Across the Capital," *New York Times*, Jan. 4, 2006, A1; Anne E. Kornblut, "Abramoff Accord: Bribery Investigation is Expected to Reach into Congress," *New York Times*, Jan. 4, 2006, A1.

27 See Tony Perry, "Rep. Cunningham Pleads Guilty to Bribery, Resigns," *Los Angeles Times*, Nov. 29, 2005, A1.

28 Edsell, "Lobbyists Emergence Reflects Shift in Capital Culture," supra.

ran a weekly meeting with a dozen top business lobbyists (called his "K-Street Cabinet").[29] Fourteen former Boehner staffers work as lobbyists, and Boehner says he "regrets" an incident in 1996 when he handed out "checks from tobacco interests to members of Congress on the House floor."[30] "Yes, I am cozy with lobbyists," Boehner admitted, "but I have never done anything unethical."[31] It is almost a prerequisite for the majority leader position to have developed extensive networks of lobbyists, given that fellow members tend to back the person who promises to provide them with future campaign support.[32] The public is not oblivious to the situation: A poll found that 77% of respondents believe that reports of lobbyists bribing members of Congress are not isolated incidents but are "the way things work in Congress."[33] Two respected decades-long observers of Washington politics, Norman Ornstein (of the conservative American Enterprise Institute) and Thomas Mann (of the liberal The Brookings Institution), wrote in a joint essay that "We have never seen the culture so sick or the legislative process so dysfunctional."[34]

How much money and how it is distributed

Money flows in this system in four basic ways: direct contributions to electoral candidates ("hard" money); "soft money" contributions to political parties which can be spent on campaign office and staff expenses, support activities, and issue advocacy; expenditures on issue advocacy by independent "527 groups" (named after an Internal Revenue Service provision that specifies their tax status); and lobbying activities (covered in the next Part). The money frequently goes to or through organized PACs. Caps and other restrictions are imposed on hard money and soft money (following reform legislation in 2003) contributions but, as yet, 527 groups and lobbyists have few restrictions, encouraging the flow of increasing sums of money in these latter categories. The 527 groups – MoveOn.org and Swift Boat Veterans for Truth, for example – have proliferated in recent years.[35] Such groups are prohibited from coordinating with campaigns or making direct contributions to federal candidates (though they can give to state candidates). Ads paid for by 527 groups cannot say "vote for" or "vote against," or "elect" or "defeat," with

29 Mike Allen and Perry Bacon, Jr., "Can This Elephant be Cleaned Up?," *Time*, January 23, 2006, 27.
30 Sheryl Gay Stolberg, "Push to Control Lobbying Produces Unexpected Shifts and Alliances," *New York Times*, January 18, 2006, A17.
31 Quoted in Jim VandeHei and Shailagh Murray, "Post-Abramoff Mood Shaped Vote for DeLay's Successor," *Washington Post* February 3, 2006, A1.
32 See Carl Hulse, "In Election, a Fight to Lead the G.O.P. in a Crucial Year," *New York Times*, January 30, 2006, A16.
33 "Public Perception of Congress," New York Times/CBS News Poll, *New York Times*, January 27, 2006, A21.
34 Norman Ornstein and Thomas E. Mann, "If You Give a Congressman a Cookie," *New York Times*, January 19, 2006, A23.
35 See David Schultz, Introduction, "Money, Politics, and Campaign Financing in the States," supra 12.

respect to any particular candidate, but they have skirted this restriction – typically by showing the image of the candidate and making an unmistakable favorable or unfavorable "informational" reference.[36]

For federal elections alone, in the 2004 election cycle, a total of $2.5 billion dollars in hard and soft money was donated to candidates, parties, and PACs.[37] Of this amount, business interests gave a total of $1.5 billion dollars (55% to Republicans), dwarfing all other contributors; the next highest category, ideological groups, gave $72.7 million (51% to Republicans); labor groups gave $61.6 million (87% to Democrats).[38] For the same election cycle, 527 groups reported expenditures of $479.8 million.[39] The amount of money raised and spent by 527 groups in the 2004 election cycle was *double* the 2002 cycle, and five-times the 2000 election cycle.[40]

Three-quarters of the money given to candidates by corporations and interest groups goes to incumbents. This is a sensible allocation of funds for contributors who hope to curry favor with law makers given that incumbents in Senate and House races prevail 80% to 90% of the time. Incumbent candidates who also raise the most money in a race, a frequent conjunction, prevail more than 90% of the time.[41] Politicians in leadership positions, particularly chairs of committees with oversight over corporate interests and members of important committees, attract a relatively larger share of contributions from the interests affected by the committees. The pharmaceutical industry reportedly supplied $387,824 in the 2000 election to Orrin Hatch, then the Chairman of the Senate Judiciary Committee, and $124,372 in the 2002 election to Max Baucus, then Senate Finance Committee Chairman.[42] In the 2004 election cycle, Chair of the House Education Committee, John Boehner, received $172,000 from financial groups that handled student loans.[43]

The giving pattern of corporations is suggestive. Traditionally, corporations allocate their money about evenly overall between Republican and Democratic candidates (which is consistent with supporting incumbents because electoral offices are almost evenly divided between these two parties); but corporations give Republican

36 See Anna Nibley Baker and David B. Magleby, "Interest Groups in the 2000 Congressional Elections," in *The Other Campaign: Soft Money and Issue Advocacy in the 2000 Congressional Election* (Oxford: Rowman & Littlefield Pub. 2003) 53.
37 "2004 Cycle," PoliticalMoneyLine, at http://www.feinfo.com.
38 "2004 Election Overview," opensecrets.org, at http://www.opensecrets.org/overview. A portion of this went from one category to another, and thus is counted twice in the overall figure.
39 "Total 527 Receipts and Expenditures, 2003–2004," opensecrets.org, at http://opensecrets.org/527s/527new.asp?cycle=2004.
40 See "527s in 2004 Shatter Previous Records for Political Fundraising," December 16, 2004, Center for Public Integrity, at http://www.publicintegrity.org/527. The figures compiled by these different organizations vary, without explanation. The organizations tracking these expenditures take their numbers from public filings, but these are updated on a constant basis and filing requirements are complied with.
41 Mark Dixon, "Almost Unbeatable: Money and Incumbency, 2002," January 26, 2005, The Institute for Money in State Politics, at www.followthemoney.org.
42 Tom Hamburger, "U.S. Flip on Patents Shows Drug Makers' Growing Clout," *Wall Street Journal*, February 6, 2003, p. A4.
43 Anya Kamenetz, "Robbing Joe College to Pay Sallie Mae," *New York Times*, December 12, 2005, A25.

Party organizations twice the amount they give to Democratic Party groups.[44] The most recent statistics show a developing disparity, with an increasing share of corporate donations going to Republican candidates. For example, in 2005 (a non-election year), United Parcel Service gave $550,125 to Republicans and $226,173 to Democrats; AT&T gave $435,300 and $199,000, respectively; General Electric gave $346,650 and $193,350.[45] In the past, these same donors favored Republicans by only a small margin. The overall contribution pattern suggests that corporations want to remain in the good graces of the winner regardless of party, but they also perceive the Republican Party to be friendlier to their interests.

Many major corporations spread their campaign contributions over more than half the states for state level offices, allocating more money to states in which they have immediate financial interests at stake. Energy companies (oil, gas, electric utilities) gave $49.4 million in contributions for state level candidates in the 2004 election cycle, with the most money going to candidates in Texas, California, Illinois, Florida, and Alaska.[46] Pharmaceutical companies and their trade association, Pharmaceutical Research and Manufacturers of America (PhRMA), channeled the bulk of their funds to candidates in state legislatures that were considering various types of legislation aimed at reducing the cost of purchasing drugs.[47]

Substantial contributions also flow from nonbusiness groups, especially labor unions. Labor unions ranked first and second highest among individual donors to candidates from the 1990s through the early 2000s cumulatively, with more than 90% of their money directed to Democrats. The American Federation of State, City, and Municipal Employees gave $30.6 million, and the National Education Association gave $21.1 million. The Association of Trial Lawyers of America gave $19.9 million, 88% to Democrats.[48] In the 2004 election cycle, the Service Employee's International Union reported the fourth highest expenditure by a 527 group, $47.7 million, presumably supporting Democrats. Additional major contributors to elections include the National Rifle Association, Planned Parenthood, AFL-CIO, and the Sierra Club, among other advocacy groups. Notwithstanding the significant amounts spent by nonbusiness interests, however, businesses and their trade associations are the dominant direct and indirect financial contributors to campaigns by a large margin.

In view of this enormous flow of money, public skepticism about the loyalty and independent judgment of government officials is understandably high. According to a nationwide poll conducted in November 2005 (before the Abramoff scandal

---

44 Edwin Bender, "Energy Companies Build Power Base in State Houses," October 6, 2004, The Institute for Money in State Politics, at www.followthemoney.org; Sue O'Connell, "Big Tobacco in the States: A Strategy of Targeted Campaign Giving," May 5, 2005, The Institute for Money in State Politics, at www.followthemoney.org.
45 "2004 Cycle," PoliticalMoneyLine, supra.
46 See Bender, "Energy Companies Build Power Base in State Houses," supra 2–3.
47 See Paul Richards, "Drug Firms Prescribe Cash for Political Ills: Pharmaceutical Money in State Politics," October 27, 2003, The Institute for Money in State Politics, at www.followthemoney.org.
48 "The Top 100 Donors," opensecrets.org, at http://opensecrets.org/pubs/toporgs/topdonors.asp.

metastasized), 90% of respondents thought big companies had too much influence on government (up from 83% the year before); 85% felt likewise about political action committees, and 74% about lobbyists.[49]

The explosion and penetration of lobbying

Until recently, most of the concern about money co-opting law-makers has been directed at campaign contributions. In the past decade, huge sums of money have begun to flow into lobbying activities. Lobbying covers a broad category of activities that involves attempts to influence law-makers and public officials with legal responsibilities, ranging from a breakfast meeting with a member of Congress to commenting before an administrative rule-making proceeding. There is a close synergy between lobbying and campaign contributions: Lobbyists donate contributions, direct additional donations from clients, and throw campaign fundraising events that cost tens of thousands of dollars (and sometimes more) to raise substantial sums for the campaign coffers of legislators. In contrast to the strict legal limits and relatively close monitoring of campaign contributions, disclosure requirements for lobbying activities were enacted only in 1995, with few significant limits on amounts and negligible efforts at enforcement. Public records indicate that almost $2 billion was spent on federal lobbying in 2003; $2.1 billion in 2004; and in excess of $2.3 billion in 2005.[50]

About 14,000 lobbyists (out of a total of about 30,000 registered lobbyists) reported engaging in lobbying efforts in 2004 to influence members of Congress, White House officials, and officials in administrative agencies.[51] Again, business interests dominate. Ranked as the most profligate spender by far, the United States Chamber of Commerce spent $198 million on lobbying between 1998 and 2004. During this same time span, individual corporations also reported spending large amounts on lobbying, with these top spenders: Altria Goup, Inc. ($125 million); Verizon Communications, Inc. ($105 million); General Electric Co. ($105 million). Ranked by industry, pharmaceuticals and health products ($758 million) was first, followed by insurance companies ($644 million) and electric utilities ($588 million).

The huge infusion of money into lobbying in the past decade coincided with an increase in the number of former members of Congress entering the lobbying business upon leaving government service, in some cases commanding million-dollar salaries to make contact with former colleagues on behalf of clients.[52] This career

49 Claudia H. Deutsch, "Take Your Best Shot, New Surveys Show that Big Business Has a P.R. Problem," *New York Times*, December 9, 2005, C14.
50 "Lobby Databases," Political Money Line, supra. Alex Knott, "Special Report: Industry of Influence Nets Almost $13 Billion, April 7, 2005, at www.publicintegrity.org/lobby. The 2005 total is a projected one based upon the first six months of the year.
51 These statistics are taken from the "Special Report," supra compiled by the Center for Public Integrity from disclosure records.
52 See Jeffrey H. Birnbaum, "Lawmaker-Turned-Lobbyist: A Growing Trend on the Hill," *Washington Post*, June 20, 2004, A1.

path was relatively uncommon two decades ago, but is now so routine as to be almost expected. Effective lobbying depends upon access to officials. Congressional alumnae retain privileges that grant them free access to the congressional floor and gym, enabling them to mingle with legislators. Congressional staff members also routinely move into lobbying firms, as do heads and high-ranking members of administrative agencies. In 2004, almost 250 former members of Congress and former heads of administrative agencies worked as lobbyists. More than two thousand federal employees and White House aides have registered as lobbyists since 1998. Lobbyists who advocate for the airline industry, to offer just one example, include ten former members of Congress, two former Secretaries of the U.S. Department of Transportation, and three high-ranking officials in the Federal Aviation Administration.[53]

Movement goes in both directions. The current Bush Administration has appointed a large number of former lobbyists to high-ranking positions in the agencies or departments they previously lobbied. A brief sampling will convey the breadth of this initiative:

Anne-Marie Lynch, Deputy Assistant Secretary, Department of Health and Human Services, former lobbyist for PhRMA;

Thomas Scully, head of federal Center for Medicare and Medical Services, former for-profit hospital lobbyist;

Daniel E. Troy, Chief Counsel, Food and Drug Administration (FDA), former lobbyist for pharmaceutical companies (who had previously initiated suits against the FDA);

Thomas Sansonetti, Chief Counsel, Natural Resources Division, Justice Department, former lobbyist for National Mining Association and for coal producers;

Steven Giles, Assistant Secretary, Interior Department, former lobbyist for oil industry;

Gale Norton, Secretary of Interior Department, former lobbyist for oil, gas, mining, and logging companies;

Bennett Raley, Assistant Secretary for Water and Science, Interior Department, former lobbyist for industry against Clean Air Act;

James Peltier, Deputy Secretary for Water and Science, Interior Department, former (and subsequent) lobbyist for farmers on water supply issues;

Rebecca Watson, Assistant Secretary for Land and Minerals Management, Interior Department, former lobbyist for gas, timber, and petroleum companies;

William Myers, Chief Counsel, Interior Department, former lobbyist for mining and beef industry;

Lisa Jaeger, Deputy General Counsel and Acting General Counsel, Environmental Protection Agency (EPA), former lobbyist for electric, oil, and chemical companies;

Jeffrey Holmstead, Assistant Administrator, Air and Radiation, EPA, former lawyer and lobbyist for farm, chemical, and utility companies;

Adam J. Sharp, Associate Assistant Administrator, Office of Prevention, Pesticides and Toxics, EPA, former staff lobbyist for American Farm Bureau Federation;

53 See Executive Summary, "Delay, Dilute and Discard: How the Airline Industry and the FAA Have Stymied Aviation Security Recommendations," Report, Public Citizen, at www.citizen.org.

David Safavian, Chief Procurement Officer, former lobbyist for companies that seek government contracts;

Mark Rey, Undersecretary for National Resources and Environment, Agriculture Department, former lobbyist for forest-related industries.

Several of these individuals went from working as lobbyists, to stints as agency officials, then returned to positions as lobbyists. Officials are subject to a one-year moratorium from lobbying upon departure from office, but during this period they can work as consultants and lawyers.

Have private interests seized control of the government?

Demonstrating a causal link between official legal actions and the flow of money from private interests to public officials is notoriously elusive. It is not enough to surmise that the parties collectively expending billions of dollars in this endeavor must be getting something for their largess. It is not enough to wonder skeptically whether administrative officials would act contrary to the desires of their once and future employers in industry. It is not enough to raise the obvious question: How likely is it that politicians would vote against the desires of a group or interest that supplies them with tens of thousands of dollars in direct campaign contributions, that sponsors fundraising events that generate tens of thousands of dollars more, that independently airs supportive campaign ads, that showers them with fancy dinners and trips, that employs their wife or husband or son or daughter as a lobbyist or consultant, and that might employ them at remuneration many times their current pay upon leaving office? Under such circumstances, truly virtuous public officials would not be influenced, and such officials exist, but the cumulative inducement to favor supportive interests is mighty.

Compelling as such innuendo might be, it is still innuendo. Legislators, of course, will *never* (except when indicted with ample evidence compiled against them) admit that their vote was influenced by campaign contributions or perks from lobbyists – they vote their convictions regardless of contributions. Sometimes this denial can be pierced. A statistical study of congressional voting patterns in bankruptcy reform legislation in 2001 that controlled for the policy preferences of the legislator found a "significant correlation" between campaign contributions and votes. About fifteen legislators who would be expected to oppose the legislation based upon their policy positions instead voted for it after receiving contributions (with the dangling prospect of future contributions) from a credit card coalition that fought for the legislation.[54] The Bankruptcy Abuse Prevention and Consumer Protection Act of 2005, which sharply restricted consumer bankruptcies, confirmed the power of the credit card lobby. It is open knowledge within the bankruptcy bar that this Act was the product of a heavy lobbying effort by the credit industry (which literally drafted

---

54 See Stephen Nunez and Howard Rosenthal, "Bankruptcy 'Reform' in Congress: Creditors, Committees, Ideology, and Floor Voting in the Legislative Process," 20 *J. Law, Econ. & Org.* 527 (2004).

parts of the bill).[55] Incensed by the unfairness of the Act, a bankruptcy judge was moved to observe in a ruling that it contains an "inane" filing prerequisite that appears designed mainly to disqualify people from eligibility regardless of whether they are otherwise appropriate candidates for a bankruptcy. "Apparently," the Judge wrote, "it is not the individual consumers of this country that make the donations to the members of Congress that allow them to be elected and re-elected and re-elected and re-elected."[56]

A number of studies have identified official actions in different areas that appear to benefit industry to the detriment of the public. Agency actions have increased the risk to the flying public,[57] have increased pollution and allowed private exploitation of public resources,[58] and have loosened meat regulation while raising the risk of bacterial contamination,[59] among other instances of questionable actions.[60] In each situation, officials offer a colorable explanation for why their actions further the public interest.

Another way to get at this issue is through examples of dubious government actions by officials who were past (and future) lobbyists. According to reports, President George W. Bush appointed former lobbyists, lawyers, or spokespersons for industries to more than one hundred high-level administrative positions with oversight authority over industries they formerly represented.[61] At the direction of these appointees, a disquieting number of policy initiatives, rule changes, agreements, and enforcement actions (or their cancellation or settlement) were implemented by government agencies with results that were unquestionably advantageous to industry. An industry-supported Labor Department alteration in the meaning of "management" resulted in several million employees falling outside labor requirements that mandate overtime pay. Food and Drug Administration (FDA) lawyers made unprecedented appearances in private law suits, arguing in defense of

---

55 See Jean Braucher, "Rash and Ride-Through Redux: The Terms for Holding on to Cars, Homes and Other Collateral Under the 2005 Act," 13 *Am. Bankr. Inst. L. Rev.* 457 (2005).

56 In Re: Guillermo Alfonso Sosa, Melba Nelly Sosa, Debtors, Case No. 05-20097-FM, United States Bankruptcy Court, Western District of Texas, Order to Dismiss, December 22, 2005, 5.

57 Marc C. Niles, "On the Hijacking of Agencies (and Airplanes): The Federal Aviation Administration, 'Agency Capture,' and Airline Security," 10 *Am. U.J. Gender Soc. Pol'y & L.* 381 (2002).

58 Patrick Parenteau, "Anything Industry Wants: Environmental Policy Under Bush," 6 *Vermont J. Environmental L.* 2 (2004–05).

59 Dion Casey, "Agency Capture: The USDA's Struggle to Pass Food Safety Regulations," 7 *Kan. J.L. & Pub. Pol'y* 142 (1998).

60 See John Shepard Wiley, "A Capture Theory of Antitrust Federalism," 99 *Harvard L. Rev.* 713 (1986); Mark Seidenfeld, "Bending the Rules: Flexible Regulation and Constraints on Agency Discretion," 51 *Admin. L. Rev.* 429 (1999).

61 Investigative reports that detail these efforts are Dan Fagin, "Erasing the Rules: Committed to Making the EPA More Business-Friendly, the Bush Administration has Staffed Key Positions with Industry Lawyers and Lobbyists," *Newsday*, October 12, 2004; Kenneth T. Walsh, "Back to Business," *U.S. News & World Report*, January 21, 2002; Anne C. Mulkern, "Watchdog or Lapdogs? When Advocates Become Regulators: Bush Has Installed More Than 100 Top Officials Who Were Once Lobbyists, Attorneys, or Spokespeople for the Industries They Oversee," *Denver Post*, May 23, 2004.

pharmaceutical companies being sued for harm caused by inadequate warnings. Interior Department attorneys entered an extremely favorable settlement for ranchers who had numerous grazing violations on federal land. The Environmental Protection Agency (EPA) issued a rule change (later overturned by a federal appellate court) easing the application of Congressional mandates that coal-burning power plants and oil refineries upgrade their facilities to reduce pollution, saving industry hundreds of millions of dollars. Within days of the change, two key agency employees resigned, one to work for a utility company and the other to work as a lobbyist.[62] The EPA also proposed to relax reporting requirements on the release of toxic chemicals.[63] The Consumer Product Safety Commission, the FDA, The National Highway Traffic Safety Administration, and the Office of Thrift Supervision have all issued new regulations that restrict state tort law, state pollution and safety standards, and state regulation of business practices.[64] There are more examples.[65] In several instances, administrators implemented as official agency policy precisely the same proposals they previously had promoted as industry lobbyists when appearing before the agency.

Yet another class of questionable conduct involved attempts to slant scientific studies in favor of ideologically preferred outcomes. A primary justification of the administrative system is the need for scientific expertise to help inform and accomplish legislative policy objectives. Several respected scientific journals have expressed alarm about the politicization of science by Bush agency appointees so extensive and systematic that it compromises the scientific integrity of certain agencies.[66] Advisory boards were stacked with people with strong industry ties; research scientists with years of independent study were replaced by scientists who worked for industry; and research findings unfavorable to industry interests were omitted or deemphasized in reports.[67] The scientific issues affected range from determining the danger level of lead for children, to identifying the environmental consequences of oil drilling in Alaska, to confirming (or, in this instance, disputing) the existence of global warming.[68] Conservative religious views resulted in agency actions that

62 Fagin, "Erasing the Rules," supra.
63 Jim Jeffords and Julie Fox, "A Dark Cloud Over Disclosure," *New York Times*, March 10, 2006, A31.
64 Stephen Labaton, "Silent Tort Reform Is Overriding States' Power," *New York Times*, March 10, 2006, C5.
65 The disaster caused by Hurricane Katrina, and the failure of FEMA to adequately respond in its aftermath, exposed the extent to which the Bush Administration stacked upper level agency positions with less-than-qualified people, often with ties to industry that raised questions about their independence. See Karn Tumulty, Mark Thompson, and Mike Allen, "How Many More Mike Browns Are Out There?" *Time*, October 3, 2005, 49.
66 Donald Kennedy, "An Epidemic of Politics," *Science*, January 31 2003, 625; "Faith-Based Reasoning," *Scientific American*, June 2001, 8; "Problems With the President,"I, March 29, 2001, 499.
67 This is a select summary taken from a detailed report, "Politics and Science in the Bush Administration," United States House of Representatives Committee on Government Reform – Minority Staff Special Investigations Division, August 2003.
68 See "Report by E.P.A. Leaves out Data on Climate Change," *New York Times*, June 19, 2003.

downplayed the benefits of condom use as a means to prevent sexually transmitted diseases, distorted the connection between abortion and breast cancer, and shaped health policies related to human immunodificiency virus prevention programs for gays. A report by the independent Government Accountability Office found that senior officials at the FDA, under the influence of religious conservatives, decided that the "morning-after pill" would not be approved for sale without a prescription months before the completion of the scientific review of the issue.[69] A high-level career FDA official resigned in protest of this politicization of the scientific process.

A particularly alarming concern is the apparent politicization of the U.S. Department of Justice. The Department of Justice is the nations' main law enforcement body, with the obligation to carry out the law. Though not ordinarily thought of as an administrative agency, it has certain rule-making and regulatory functions. Most of the attorneys in the Department are career lawyers who hold their positions without respect to who is president, but the top administrators are political appointees. The mission of the Department can be compromised if political considerations influence legal determinations. Two examples of this came out of the Voting Rights Division. Tom DeLay orchestrated a redistricting effort in the Texas state legislature that broke up districts with strong blocks of Democratic voters and split them among Republican districts, which successfully increased the number of Republican members of the House. The plan required prior approval by the Justice Department. The staff lawyers and two voting rights analysts unanimously concluded in a seventy-three page report that the plan violated the Voting Rights Act because it improperly diluted minority voting power; in a highly unusual action, this determination was overruled by the head of the division.[70] The plan was upheld by a three-judge panel, and is now on appeal to the Supreme Court. Similarly, a Republican-pushed plan in Georgia imposed a requirement that voters either have a driver's license or a special identification card (at a cost of $20, and not widely available). Staff lawyers opposed the plan on the grounds that it would disenfranchise tens of thousands of poor black voters; again, political appointees decided otherwise.[71] A federal district court invalidated the plan, likening it to a poll tax from the Jim Crow era. Both plans were designed by proponents to enhance the electoral successes of the Republican Party. Politically appointed officials in both instances overruled the legal analysis of staff lawyers, albeit denying that their decisions were influenced by political considerations.

69 See Government Accountability Office Report to Congressional Requesters: "FDA Decision Process to Deny Initial Application for Over-the-Counter Marketing of the Emergency Contraceptive Drug Plan B Was Unusual," GAO-06–109, November 2005. Mark Kaufman, "Review of 'Plan B' Pill is Faulted: Report Calls FDA Actions 'Unusual,'" *Washington Post*, November 15, 2005, A1.
70 Dan Eggen, "Justice Staff Saw Texas Districting As Illegal: Voting Rights Finding on Map Produced by DeLay Was Overruled," *Washington Post*, December 2, 2005, A1.
71 Dan Eggen, "Politics Alleged in Voting Cases: Justice Officials Are Accused of Influence," *Washington Post*, January 23, 2006, A1.

Piercing the "public interest" shield – the PhRMA example

Industry defenders insist that it is misleading to overemphasize the cozy relationships legislators and agency officials have with business interests and their lobbyists. Non-business interest groups (especially unions) spend lots of money as well, and pro-union laws and regulations have been enacted. Moreover, there are ample environmental laws and regulations costly to business, environmental groups have long worked closely with the EPA, and EPA employees have left government to work in environmental groups. Although groups opposed to business interests appear in far fewer administrative proceedings owing to more limited resources,[72] this does not mean business interests have greater influence. The opinions of groups that oppose the business lobby are sometimes accorded more weight by agency decision-makers.[73] Participation by business interests is essential to the intelligent shaping of legal regulation, defenders assert, because they possess key information about the economic costs and consequences of proposed regulation.[74] Finally, it is also often said that what's good for business is good for the economy and good for employees, and thus in the public interest.

These are legitimate points. The task is to discern what is truly in the public interest as opposed to self-interested actions that invoke this claim as cover. A closer examination of the efforts of the multi-billion dollar pharmaceutical industry will demonstrate that cautious skepticism about the motivations of industry and legislators and administrative officials is warranted.[75] In recent years, the pharmaceutical industry has consistently ranked first in lobbying expenditures and among the top fifteen in campaign contributions. The industry allocates its money at both the federal and state levels, concentrated where their interests are most at stake. More than twenty former members of Congress, evenly split between Democrats and Republicans, have registered as lobbyists for the drug industry.

A rare inside look at the industry and its strategies was provided when a confidential 2003 budget and planning memorandum prepared by PhRMA, the industry's trade association, was made public.[76] PhRMA proposed to spend $150 million (by itself) in the following fiscal year, a 23% increase from the year before, of which $72.7 million was directed at Congress, $4.9 million at the FDA, and $48.7 million at the state level. This large amount was attributable to the pending federal Medicare

---

72 See Croley, "Theories of Regulation," supra.
73 See Cornelius M. Kerwin, *Rulemaking: How Government Agencies Write Law and Make Policy,* 3rd ed. (Washington, D.C.: CQ Press 2003).
74 See Jody Freeman, "The Private Role in Governance," 75 *NYU L. Rev.* 543 (2000).
75 Where not otherwise indicated, the following information is taken primarily from Paul Richards, "Drug Firms Prescribe Cash for Political Ills: Pharmaceutical Money in State Politics," October 27, 2003, The Institute for Money in State Politics, at www.followthemoney.org; and Bob Young and Michael Surrusco, "The Other Drug War: Big Pharma's 625 Washington Lobbyists," July 2001, Public Citizen: Congress Watch, at www.citizen.org.
76 See Robert Pear, "Drug Companies Increase Spending Efforts to Lobby Congress and Governments," *New York Times,* June 1, 2003, p. 33.

drug coverage bill, and to pending bills in various states aimed at reducing the costs to residents of purchasing drugs. One million dollars was allocated to a network of economists who would be paid to place op-ed pieces in newspapers against price control regulations, and another $2 million was earmarked to fund think tanks that would produce favorable research and policy papers. PhRMA's lobbying agenda, laid out in the internal memo, included: resisting attempts by consumers to purchase cheaper drugs from abroad (Canada or via the internet), and fighting state initiatives to provide drug discounts for the public. The detriment to the public of this agenda is as plain as the financial benefits to pharmaceutical companies.

One of PhRMA's tactics is to create and fund "independent" groups to advocate positions that favor the drug industry. It created "Citizens for Better Medicare," which spent $65 million in issue advocacy ads about prescription drugs across the nation in the 2000 campaign, running almost one third of all the ads broadcast in the country by non-party groups.[77] PhRMA also provided funding and expertise for "Citizens for the Right to Know," a group that advocated more prescription drug benefits in managed care plans.[78] PhRMA was also closely linked to the "Traditional Values Coalition," which lobbied against legislation that would allow the importation of drugs from Canada and Europe.[79] Each of these organizations operated under the guise of grassroots campaigns.

In the late nineties, Congress was interested in promoting drug testing for children, which drug companies were reluctant to undertake owing to low expected revenues. The industry agreed to engage in the testing on the condition that Congress grant a six-month extension for patent protection on expiring drugs. The tests would cost about $4 million per drug, whereas the patent extensions were worth more than $1 billion in sales, inflicting higher costs on consumers.[80] Senators who opposed this exorbitant boon to pharmaceutical companies at public expense advocated that the government instead arrange and pay directly for the research to be done. The "Coalition for Children's Health," which received funding from PhRMA and was headed by a former pharmaceutical lobbyist, lobbied Congress on behalf of the deal, which went through. PhRMA has also lobbied effectively on the state level. Of the eighteen states considering bills in 2003 to provide for the sale of discounted drugs, only one bill passed.

The crowning success for the pharmaceutical lobby was the 2003 enactment of a drug prescription benefit in Medicare coverage. Among other benefits to the industry, which lobbied mightily for the bill, a provision in the legislation prohibits the federal government from negotiating for reduced prices from drug companies based upon bulk purchases, a practice that is common among other national governments (one reason why drugs are more expensive in the United States than elsewhere). The 204 Republicans who voted for the bill in the House had received an

77 Young and Surrusco, "The Other Drug War," supra 8.
78 "Summary: Influence Inc.: Lobbyists Spending in Washington (2000), 4, at www.opensecrets.org.
79 Richards, "Drug Firms Prescribe Cash for Political Ills," supra 10.
80 See "Executive Summary: The Other Drug War II" (2003), 4–5, Public Citizen; Congress Watch, at www.citizen.org.

average of $28,504 in campaign contributions from the drug industry, compared with $8,122 received by the twenty-five Republicans who opposed it; the sixteen Democrats who supported the bill had received an average of $16,296, compared with $11,791 received by Democrats who voted against.[81] Senator Richard Durbin of Illinois was quoted as saying, *before* the bill passed, that "PhRMA, this lobby, has a death grip on Congress."[82]

Soon after the bill passed, the head of Medicare, Thomas Scully (formerly a lobbyist for the hospital industry), resigned and became a lobbyist for drug companies.[83] A few months after the legislation was enacted, a controversy erupted when it was disclosed that influential Representative Billy Tauzin – a twenty-four-year congressional veteran, chairman of a committee with oversight over pharmaceuticals, and a member of the committee that drafted the Medicare drug legislation – had engaged in negotiations to become the President of PhRMA at a reported annual salary of $2 million. Tauzin denied that he had talks with PhRMA while working on the legislation. A year later, Tauzin became President of PhRMA.[84]

Battles over and through law – the U.S. Chamber of Commerce

To appreciate the full scope of the effort to seize and wield the law instrumentally, consider the U.S. Chamber of Commerce.[85] Armed by revenues from industry contributors that totaled $135 million in 2003, the Chamber of Commerce pursues a strategic course of action in every legal arena. The Chamber works at the national level and across the states. It leads all other single entities in lobbying expenditures, spending almost $40 million in 2003 and $53 million in 2004 to advocate business-friendly positions.

The Chamber is also very active in elections. According to Chamber President Tom Donohue, in the 2004 election, "the Chamber put 215 people on the ground in 31 states; sent 3.7 million pieces of mail and more than 30 million e-mails; made 5.6 million phone calls."[86] After the election, Donohue crowed about the Chamber's successful efforts and its anticipated fruits: "The expanded numbers of

---

81 "Money and Medicare," November 24, 2003, Center for Responsive Politics, www.capitaleye.org.
82 Quoted in Pear, "Drug Companies Increase Spending on Efforts to Lobby Congress and Governments," supra.
83 Paul Krugman, "The K Street Prescription," *New York Times*, January 20, 2006, A17.
84 See Gerard Shields, "Tauzin Takes Pharmacy Industry Post," *The Advocate* (Baton Rouge, La.), December 16, 2004, B1–2; Editorial, "The Drug Lobby Scores Again," *New York Times*, December 17, 2004, A34.
85 For background on the Chamber of Commerce, which provides the main basis for this account, see Taylor Lincoln, et al., "Tom Donohue: U.S. Chamber of Commerce President Oversees Renegade Corporations While Pushing Limits to Corporate Accountability" (February 2005) Public Citizen: Congress Watch, at www.citizen.org.; John Gibeaut, "Back in Business," 91 *ABA Journal* 40 (2005); Jeffrey H. Birnbaum, "A Quiet Revolution in Business Lobbying: Chamber of Commerce Helps Bush Agenda," *Washington Post*, February 5, 2005, A1; Gretchen Morgenson and Glen Justice, "Taking Care of Business, His Way," *New York Times*, February 20, 2005, Sunday Business, 1; Dan Zagert, "The Right Wing's Drive for Tort Reform," 279 *Nation*, October 25, 2004.
86 Tom Donohue, "President's Update – November 2004," December 6, 2004, Memo to U.S. Chamber of Commerce Board of Directors (on file with author) 1.

pro-business votes in the Senate and the House – along with a team of reasonable regulators and appointees in the executive branch – will mean a more favorable hearing for some of our key priorities, including legal reform, comprehensive energy legislation, permanent tax relief, market-based healthcare, and pension reform, and balanced workplace, environmental and corporate governance rules."[87] Rewarding Donohue's optimism, in 2005, Congress enacted legislation designating federal courts as having primary jurisdiction over large class action suits (to which federal judges are perceived as less hospitable than state courts), which has long been coveted by major corporations.

The Chamber also engaged in a self-described "targeted campaign" in sixteen state Supreme Court and state Attorney General electoral contests in 2004,[88] to secure the election of pro-business candidates. Stanton D. Anderson, the Chamber's Chief Legal Officer, claimed that the Chamber "won every race in which we were involved."[89] Anderson touts this successful effort to seat friendly judges as "an example of what the business community can do." The Chamber has put an estimated $50 million into state judicial elections since 1998, an investment warranted by the potentially billions of dollars of judgments faced by corporations in civil lawsuits at the state level.[90] The Chamber uses aggressive tactics: A federal court and a state court in Missouri, and an elections commission in Ohio, ruled that the Chamber aired improper advocacy ads in the 2000 judicial elections.

The Chamber also has its own in-house litigation firm, the National Chamber Litigation Group, which actively brings suits and intervenes in ongoing litigation to defend business interests. Among other cases, the Chamber recently sued the Securities and Exchange Commission (SEC) seeking to invalidate a new rule issued by the SEC designed to secure better oversight over fund managers which requires that three fourths of the board of directors of mutual funds be independent.[91]

The Chamber of Commerce has thus implemented a well-funded and well-executed effort to get the laws and regulations it desires enacted, to have like-minded executive branch and administrative agency officials carry out these laws, to litigate cases that advance its agenda, and to insure that receptive judges preside over these cases. It is a formidable, carefully orchestrated effort to seize the law in the legislative, executive, administrative, and judicial arenas that has scored notable successes.

This is just one player. Multiply its efforts many-fold across all of these arenas by all of the groups and entities mentioned in this and earlier chapters and the full scope of these activities can come dimly into view.

---

87 Id. 3.
88 Id.
89 Quoted in Emily Heller, "Business and the Bench: U.S. Chamber of Commerce Scores Big in Backing Judicial Elections Nationwide," 51 *Palm Beach Daily Business Review*, November 9, 2004.
90 See Mike France, et. al., "The Battle Over the Courts: How Politics, Ideology, and Special Interests are Compromising the U.S. Justice System," 3901 *Business Week*, September 27, 2004.
91 *U.S. Chamber of Commerce v. Securities & Exchange Com'n.*, 412 F.3d 1(2005).

"Lawyers, lawyers everywhere"

About 40% of the members of the House of Representatives over the years have been lawyers by occupation, with a higher percentage for Senators.[92] No other single occupational group is close. Their office staff and the staffs of congressional committees are dominated by lawyers. Executive branch departments and administrative agencies are filled with lawyers. Many lobbyists are lawyers. Washington is a lawyers' town. Lawyers are also prevalent in parallel positions in state governments. All of these lawyers were trained in law school to see the law as an empty vessel to be utilized to achieve ends. This perspective on law was reinforced in legal practice. This is the view of law they bring when entering government office.

92 "Lawyers, Lawyers Everywhere" is the title of a chapter in Mark C. Miller, *The High Priests of American Politics: The Role of Lawyers in American Political Institutions* (Knoxville: Univ. of Tenn. Press 1995). See also Miller's Chapter Four.

Part 3

Corroding the rule of law

12

Collapse of higher law, deterioration of common good

In the past two-hundred-plus years, the period traced out in this book, the U.S. legal culture has been deprived of two sets of ideals that provided the foundation for law for more than a millennium. Both of these sets of ideals, in different ways, were central to the rule of law.

The defining characteristic of the first set of ideals was that law consists of fundamental principles that even the sovereign law-maker is bound to obey. This was the classical understanding of the rule of law – the notion that there are legal limits on law itself. The non-instrumental views of law described in the first chapter – divine law, natural principle, reason, customs descended from time immemorial – were the source of these controlling legal principles.[1] Owing to these qualities, it was thought, the law had a built-in integrity, a core of good and right. These non-instrumental views of law grounded, provided content for, and set limits on the law itself. The shift to an instrumental understanding of law had the effect, therefore, of removing a foundational source of grounding, content, and limits on the law, leaving law an empty vessel without built-in restraints.

The defining characteristic of the second set of ideals was that law represents the common good or public welfare. This quality made the law *of and for* the community, deserving of obedience by citizens. This too is an essential element and companion of the rule of law because, in conjunction with the first set of ideals, it supplies the justification for *why* law is entitled to rule. Although the instrumental view of law was meant to supplant the first set of ideals, this second set was supposed to carry on. The common good ideal supplied a key component of the instrumental view of law: Law is an instrument *to serve the public good*. As earlier chapters show, however, the forces and developments that undermined the non-instrumental view of law also tended to undermine the notion of the common good.

This chapter poses the question: What are the prospects for the rule of law if the law lacks any core integrity and is not tied to the service of the public good? This discussion will convey the central role and function formerly played by these classical ideas and the critical vacuum left by their demise. Integral parts are missing from what once was an organic whole of interconnected ideas about law.

---

1 See Tamanaha, *On the Rule of Law*, supra.

Collapse of higher limits on law

As indicated in Chapter 1, natural law and principle, reason, and customs from time immemorial were thought to be the source of, to be binding upon, and to be superior to the positive law of the state. Thomas Aquinas famously asserted "A law that is unjust seems not be a law."[2] "Hence every human positive law has the nature of law to the extent that it is derived from the Natural law. If, however, in some point it conflicts with the law of nature it will no longer be law but rather a perversion of law."[3] Echoing this position, Blackstone wrote that "This law of nature . . . is of course superior in obligation to any other. . . . [N]o human laws are of any validity, if contrary to this; and as such of them as are valid derive all their force, and all their authority, mediately or immediately, from this original."[4] The central idea, again, is that the non-instrumental views of law established *legal limits on the law itself* – that legal officials are legally bound to higher law. This was at the core of early English understandings of the ancient constitution and the common law. "In an age when people's minds were becoming deeply, if dimly, imbued with the fear of some sort of sovereignty or absolutism, it must have satisfied many men's minds to be able to argue that the laws of the land were so ancient as to be the product of no one's will, and to appeal to the almost universally respected doctrine that law should be above will . . ."[5]

This view of the primacy of unwritten law over legislation was standard at the establishment of the colonies. The 1677 Charter of Fundamental Laws of West New Jersey "began with the provision that the 'common law or fundamental rights' of the colony should be 'the foundation of government, which is not to be altered by the Legislative authority.'"[6] A similar provision was in the first Charter of the Massachusetts Bay Colony (1629). Historian Daniel Boorstin found in the colonial period a "widely accepted assumption that there were definite limits which the legislators were not free to transgress,"[7] limits composed of what were understood to be ancient common law prescriptions as well as certain passages of scripture. The prevailing belief was that "the primary and normal way of development of civil institutions was by custom and tradition rather than by legislative or administrative fiat."[8] Leading up to and following the Revolution, a number of state courts invalidated legislation thought to be contrary to natural law or fundamental common law rights.[9]

---

2 Thomas Aquinas, *Summa Theologiae*, trans. R. J. Henle (South Bend, Ind.: University of Notre Dame Press 1993) 96.4 sec.4.
3 Id. 95.2.
4 Quoted in Boorstein, *Mysterious Science of the Law*, supra 49.
5 Pocock, *Ancient Constitution and the Feudal Law*, supra 51–2.
6 Quoted in Leonard W. Levy, *Origin of the Bill of Rights* (New Haven: Yale Univ. Press 1999) 7.
7 Boorstein, *The Americans*, supra 20.
8 Id.
9 Charles G. Haines, "Political Theories of the Supreme Court From 1789–1835," 2 *Am. Pol. Sci. Rev.* 221, 222–223 (1908).

Belief in natural law and in the primacy of the common law continued to influence jurists throughout the nineteenth century, as indicated in earlier chapters. A 1905 study of the jurisprudence of the preceding century found that "Several American courts have asserted the doctrine that the judiciary can disregard a statute which plainly violates the fundamental principles, although it may not contravene any particular constitutional provision."[10] A highly effective mechanism judges utilized to control legislation was to render narrow or defeating constructions. "Indeed, one of the rules of statutory construction, 'statutes in derogation of the common law are to be construed strictly,' constituted for many years a check on legislative innovation far more subtle but scarcely less stringent than written constitutional limitations."[11] Roscoe Pound remarked as late as 1910 that "Judges and jurists do not hesitate to assert that there are extra-constitutional limits to legislative power which put fundamental common-law dogmas beyond the reach of statutes."[12]

In the course of the first half of the twentieth century, when the non-instrumental understanding of the common law gave way to the instrumental view, also swept away was the notion that the common law and natural principles constitute limits on legislation. Their demise, it must be repeated, cannot be attributed to advocacy of instrumental views of law alone. The implications of the Enlightenment, the secularization of society, doubts about the existence of objective moral principles, a culturally heterogeneous and class-differentiated populace, pitched battles within society among groups with conflicting economic interests in the late nineteenth century, an increasingly specialized economy with complex regulatory regimes far beyond the ken of common law concepts, the disenchantment of the world in the twentieth century – all these contributed to undermining old notions of natural principles and inviolate common law. After this denouement, the only substantive restrictions on legislation were those found in the words of the Constitution.

Constitutional enforcement of substantive limits on law-making, while similar in function to classical rule of law limits such as natural law, is different in two key respects. Classical rule of law limits were thought to exist entirely apart from the will of law-makers. The Declaration of Independence reflected this understanding: "We hold these truths to be self-evident, that all men are created equal, that they are endowed by their Creator with certain unalienable Rights . . . " The 9th Amendment of the Constitution announced the same sentiment: "The enumeration in the Constitution, of certain rights, shall not be construed to deny or disparage others retained by the people." A widely shared understanding at the time was that "Common law and written constitutions expressed and elaborated these notions [of fundamental rights and limits on government], but did not create them."[13] Up through the early twentieth century, as Roscoe Pound observed, it was still thought by many judges that the Bill of Rights was "merely declaratory of fundamental

10 Simeon Baldwin, *The American Judiciary* (New York: Century Co. 1920[1905]).
11 Jacobs, *Law Writers and the Courts*, supra 10.
12 Pound, "Law in Books and Law in Action," supra 27.
13 Tribe, *American Constitutional Law*, supra 561.

natural rights;" and "legislation is to be judged by those rights and not by the constitutional texts in which they are declared."[14]

This view did not survive the twentieth century. As belief in natural law waned, the Supreme Court came to characterize rights and restraints on legislative powers in positivist terms tied to the language of the Constitution. The only limits on legislation were those limits specified in the Constitution (though not always restricted to the explicit text). Identical to ordinary legislation, such limits were the product of will-based law-making. "[I]n the American *written Constitution*," wrote eminent constitutional scholar Edward Corwin, "higher law at last attained a form which made possible the attribution to it of an entirely new sort of validity, the validity of a *statute emanating from the sovereign people*."[15] The supremacy of the Constitution came to be understood as grounded on "its rootage in popular will."[16] Every provision of the Constitution can be altered by amendment (albeit with higher hurdles to scale). Hence constitutional limits on legislation represent contingent acts of will by law-makers that exist only as long as they remain in the document. This understanding is radically unlike former limits imposed by natural principles and common law principles, which were not the product of human will but were immanent principles of right.

The second difference is that traditional natural law conceptions constituted absolute prohibitions: Offending positive laws were invalid, as Aquinas and Blackstone pronounced. Modern constitutional analysis, however, frequently takes a balancing approach to rights. A willingness to balance the different interests at stake is a product of viewing law and rights in instrumental terms, seen as supporting particular interests or ends rather than constituting ends in themselves.

The consequences of the collapse

Constitutional restrictions provide a new form of limitation that accomplishes some of the work done by the older understandings, but it does so in a reduced sense. It is law limiting itself, raised up on a pedestal, but still a contingent body of law that can be changed through amendment (or re-interpretation) if so desired. Lost in this transformation was the time-honored understanding that there are certain things the government and legal officials absolutely cannot do with and through law – that the law possesses integrity unto itself and must comport with standards of good and right. The elimination of this former standard is highlighted in legal theorist Joseph Raz's description of what, under modern understandings, can be entirely consistent with the rule of law: "A non-democratic legal system, based on the denial of human rights, on extensive poverty, on racial segregation, sexual inequalities, and racial persecution, may, in principle, conform to the requirements of the rule

---

14 Pound, "Law in Books and Law in Action," supra 28.
15 Corwin, "'Higher Law' Background of American Constitutional Law," supra 89 (emphasis in original).
16 Id. 4.

of law..."[17] To satisfy the rule of law, the government must abide by and apply stable, certain, and general rules set out publicly in advance. Beyond these minimal formal characteristics, the law can consist of any content whatsoever and serve any end whatsoever.

The traditional and the modern understandings of law are fundamentally antithetical in this respect: The traditional view insists that law consists of and is limited by principles consistent with reason, or community norms representing the good and right, whereas the instrumental understanding is that law is an empty vessel that can be applied to achieve any end.

When law was thought to have an inviolable, built-in principled integrity, invocations of that core provided a source within law to resist malign uses of the law. Instrumentalism, in contrast, entails only means–ends reasoning. Once an end has been decided upon, law can be used in any way possible to advance the designated end, without limit. Instrumental questions may be raised about the efficiency of law in achieving the ends designated, but as long as the formal or procedural requirements of law are met, there can be no *legal* objections against using law in an abhorrent or evil fashion. Moral opposition may be raised to such repulsive uses of law, but it will lack legal standing – a difference that matters mightily in the realm of symbolism and political discourse.

The "torture memo" offers a supreme example. In pursuit of the end of combating terrorism, law was used to justify torture, which should be unacceptable to a principled law. If law was understood to have its own internal integrity, a principled core of right, any attempt to justify torture in legal terms would have been beyond plausibility, dismissed out of hand rather than contemplated as an arguable matter. The torture might still have taken place, of course, but with the understanding of the government officials involved that they were embarking upon a patently illegal course of action for reasons they considered absolutely compelling. This action would represent a challenge to the power of law (at least until legal institutions mounted their response), but it would have confirmed that law is principled in nature.

When the law has been deprived of its own integrity, there is little to separate law from any other tool or weapon. The legitimacy of law then rides on the rightness of the ends the law is utilized to advance. That is the next subject.

Historical primacy of the "common good" ideal

A constant refrain in the history of the rule of law ideal is that the law is, and should be, for the common good. Plato asserted that the laws should be "for the sake of what is common to the whole city."[18] Aristotle wrote that a "true government"

---

17 Joseph Raz, "The Rule of Law and its Virtue," in *The Authority of Law*, supra 211.
18 Plato, *Laws*, translated by T. Pangle (New York: Basic Books 1980) 715b.

must have just laws, and just laws are oriented toward the "common interest."[19] Aquinas defined law as "an ordinance of reason for the common good."[20] Germanic customary law in the Medieval period tied the primacy of the law to the traditional order of the whole community.[21] Locke insisted that, as a matter of natural law, the legislative power "in the utmost bounds of it, is limited to the public good of society."[22] "It is an ancient principle ... that governmental powers should be exercised for public purposes only[.]"[23]

This idea has been central the the U.S. legal tradition from its inception. The Mayflower Compact – *the* founding political document of the colonies – written two generations before Locke's famous *Second Treatise*, was a covenant to form a "civill body politick for our better ordering and preservation . . . to enacte, constitute, and frame such just and equall lawes, ordinances, acts, constitutions, and offices, from time to time, as shall be thought most meete and convenient for the general good of the Colonie, unto which we promise all due submission and obedience."[24] The very first charge against King George in the Declaration of Independence was his refusal to assent to laws "the most wholesome and necessary for the public good."

The negative corollary of the assertion that legal power is legitimate only when used to further the common good is that it is inappropriate for law to benefit particular groups within society at the expense of the common good. This too has been a constant theme in the U.S. political–legal culture from the founding. Article VII of the Massachusetts Constitution shows the tight connection between the common good ideal and its negative corollary: "Government is instituted for the common good; for the protection, safety, prosperity and happiness of the people; and not for the profit, honor, or private interest of any one man, family, or class of men." Historian of the Revolution Bernard Bailyn observed that the founder's goal was that "the system would lead to the selection as representatives those who would be likely to stand above special interests and pursue the true interests of all their constituents, as well as the common good of society."[25]

To recount the historical primacy of this ideal is not to say it has always been believed or honored. Innumerable political writers have noted that law regularly serves particular interests, often those of the elite or most powerful. According to Plato, Thrasymachus declared that "justice is the interest of the stronger."[26] Karl Marx famously said much the same. But this point is not exclusive to radical critics

---

19 Aristotle, *The Politics*, translated by E. Barker (Cambridge: Cambridge Univ. Press 1988) 68–9.
20 Aquinas, *Summa Theologica*, supra 90.4.c.2.
21 See Fritz Kern, *Kingship and Law in the Middle Ages* (New York: Harper Torchbooks 1956).
22 Locke, *Second Treatise of Government*, supra Chap. XI, Section 135.
23 Jacobs, *Law Writers and the Courts*, supra 100.
24 Mayflower Compact, quoted in Corwin, "Higher Law Background of American Constitutional Law," supra 65.
25 Bernard Bailyn, *To Begin the World Anew: the Genius and Ambiguities of the American Founders* (New York: Vintage Books 2003) 117.
26 Plato, *The Republic* (New York: Random House 1991) Book I, 344.

of the legal order. Liberal icon Adam Smith observed that "Laws and government may be considered in this and indeed in every case as a combination of rich to oppress the poor, and preserve to themselves the inequality of goods which would otherwise be soon destroyed by the attacks of the poor . . . "[27]

Clear-eyed about law even as a young man, in 1873, Oliver Wendell Holmes wrote that "This tacit assumption of the solidarity of interests of society is very common, but seems to us to be false . . . in the last resort a man rightly prefers his own interest to that of his neighbors. And this is as true in legislation as in any other form of corporate action."[28] "[W]hatever body may possess the supreme power for the moment is certain to have interests inconsistent with others which have competed unsuccessfully. The more powerful interests must be more or less reflected in legislation; which, like every other device of man or beast, must tend in the long run to aid the survival of the fittest."[29] Legislation, he said, "is necessarily made a means by which a body, having the power, puts burdens which are disagreeable to them on the shoulders of everyone else."[30] The only prospect for tempering this tendency that Holmes could envision was the spread of an educated sympathy among the dominant groups to "reduce the sacrifice" required of minorities. Accordingly, he said, "it is no sufficient condemnation of legislation that it favors one class at the expense of another; for much or all legislation does that, and none the less when the *bona fide* object is the greatest good of the greatest number."[31]

Awareness that reality often disappoints the ideal does not, in itself, discredit the ideal. Even Holmes thought law could and should promote sound social policy. The underlying point of these accounts, including from skeptics, is that what entitles the law to obedience, at least in the eyes of the citizenry, is the claim that it furthers the public good. Unless one is in a favored position, why abide by the rule of law if the law mainly secures the advantage of some in society at the expense others?

Judicial tainting of the notion of the common good

Two main sources have contributed to the deterioration of the notion of the common good within the U.S. political–legal culture, one particular to law and the second related to general social attitudes. The legal contribution was the malodorous stain left by courts that invoked the general welfare or public purpose notion when striking legislation in the late nineteenth century. As described earlier, judges in this period scrutinized the legislatively designated public purpose behind a statute to determine whether, by their own lights, it was real and weighty enough to overcome the liberty

27 Adam Smith, *Lectures on Jurisprudence*, edited by R. L. Meek, D. D. Raphael, and P. G. Stein (Oxford: Clarendon Press 1978) 208.
28 Oliver Wendell Holmes, "The Gas Stoker's Strike," 7 *American L. Rev.* 582, 583 (1873).
29 Id.
30 Id.
31 Id. 584.

interest at stake.[32] The Missouri Supreme Court, in 1897, invalidated legislation that prohibited mining and manufacturing companies from the abusive practice of paying employees their wages in scrip exclusively redeemable at company stores: "If [the statute] can stand, it is difficult to see an end to such legislation, and the government becomes one of special privileges, instead of a compact 'to promote the general welfare of the people.'"[33] Time and again courts utilized this reasoning to void legislation that extended protection to employees and unions, as well as other types of legislation. In the name of prohibiting laws that favored special interests, the courts appeared to be protecting the special interests of employers and capital.

Judges could no longer be trusted to decide questions about legitimate public purposes. In the mid-1903s, under pressure from critics, courts abdicated a monitoring role in economic legislation. The question of whether legislation furthers the common good was left to the legislature without any oversight. This development eliminated a key structural feature of the system. The founding generation invested faith in the judiciary to stand above and serve as an effective check on special interests. "[T]he independence of the judges may be an essential safeguard," wrote Alexander Hamilton in the *Federalist Papers*, ".... [which] not only serves to moderate the immediate mischiefs of those [laws] which may have been passed, but it operates as a check upon the legislative body in passing them[.]"[34]

Modern pluralism and skepticism and the common good

Even without the damage done to the common good ideal by the aforementioned court decisions, problems would have arisen for this notion owing to the increasing heterogeneity of views within society and to doubts about law and morality that have spread in the course of the past century. Early in the twentieth century, when it first became evident that uncertainty and disagreement might pose formidable challenges to the idea of the public good, the Realists, like others of their time, placed an inordinate faith in the capacity of social science to help point the way. The difficulties in resolving these questions were glossed over in the spirit of consensus that prevailed in the Second World War and its aftermath. The clashes of the 1960s and 1970s changed all that. Disputes now exist over what social justice requires, over the proper trade-offs between liberty and equality or between formal and substantive equality, over the enforcement of moral and religious norms in public and private spheres, over the rights of women, minorities, and gays and lesbians, over the appropriate distribution of resources and opportunities, over the conditions of employment, over the balance between economic development and the environment, and so on. The old faith that science will supply answers to these questions now smacks of naïvete – the natural and social sciences are themselves

32 An excellent exploration of these decisions can be found in Jacobs, *Law Writers and the Courts*, supra.
33 *State v. Loomis*, 115 Mo. 307, 316 (1893).
34 Hamilton, Federalist 78, in *Federalist Papers*, supra 477.

caught up in the battles among groups, with contrary studies enlisted to serve all sides.

Some people reject the very ideal of the public good as a fiction; they deny that a single common good exists that spans the differences among contesting groups within society. Many of those who do not reject the ideal outright nonetheless have no confidence that the public good can be identified with certainty, or agreed upon. Modern epistemological doubt leads many to believe that these disputes are impossible to resolve in principle. Reflected in the academic phrase "incommensurable paradigms," it is thought that people on opposing sides begin from fundamentally incompatible starting premises, which precludes coming to agreement. Characteristic of this view is the final riposte in an argument – "I guess we just see the world differently" – after which the disputing parties walk away convinced in the soundness of their position, seeing no need to further contemplate the opposition. These attitudes fuel the militant "groupism" that is a standout feature of contemporary social-political-legal discourse.

Using every available legal channel, today, a multitude of groups aggressively pursue their agendas: women's groups, immigrant groups, gay rights groups, fundamentalist Christian groups, racial or ethnic groups, environmental groups, labor unions, libertarians, consumer groups, trade associations, merchants associations, professional associations, and more. All of these groups, many in direct opposition to one another in various legal arenas – in cause litigation, in battles over judicial appointments, in legislative and administrative lobbying – routinely claim to be acting in the name of the common good or public welfare.

Under such circumstances, it perhaps makes sense to strive to find the most acceptable balance among the competing interests. Pound proposed this as the appropriate goal of legal instrumentalism. A balance among competing interests, it should be recalled, is not the same as the classical ideal of a shared common good. "The goal of representation," Alexander Hamilton wrote, was "not to mirror the infinity of private interests in the way a pure democracy would do, but to meld the contesting forces into the permanent and collective interests of the nation."[35] The idea was to find a position that "in the end would benefit all."[36]

Current attitudes toward law, however, often do not even strive for the less ambitious goal of balancing. Combatants are not seeking to find a compromise or balance among competing interests: individuals and groups vigorously seek to secure the legal enforcement of their particular agenda to the exclusion of or conquest over others. Dialogue with opponents is dismissed as pointless: Groups have their own truths, so it is better to prevail over the other side than to risk being prevailed upon. This set of attitudes – admittedly a construct, but one evident in public discourse – comprises an aggressive posture that strives for nothing less than victory within and through the law.

35 Bailyn, *Begin the World Anew*, supra 118.
36 Id. 119.

Those who promoted the instrumental view of law in the early twentieth century, like Karl Llewellyn, insisted that the proper use of this instrument is to advance the social good. A realistic idealist knows that the struggle to achieve the common good is arduous and unceasing. In Llewellyn's words:

> One matter does need mention here, however: the eternal dilemma of the law, indeed of society; and of the law because the law purports peculiarly among our instruments to 'represent' the whole. There is, amid the welter of self-serving groups, clamoring and struggling over this machine that will give power over others, the recurrent emergence of some wholeness, some sense of responsibility which outruns enlightened self-interest, and results in action apparently headed (often purposefully) for the common good.[37]

The trajectory traced out in this book reflects the gradual adoption of the idea that law is an instrument, coinciding with the gradual loss of faith in the idea of a common good. Llewellyn and Pound, and other proponents of the instrumental view of law, aware of the presence of competing factions and the pull of self-interest, knew that it would be difficult to achieve the common good in law. What they failed to anticipate was the extent to which the very notion of the common good would itself become so problematic.

Battles to seize the law and their consequences

The combatants over and through law, it is critical to recognize, do not necessarily envision themselves as pursuing their particular group interests *at the expense of* the common good. Building upon a cluster of familiar ideas that have persisted in the U.S. political–legal culture for more than two centuries, it is possible to pursue one's own particular agenda through law with the conviction that one is thereby promoting the public good. These ideas, which have coursed through earlier chapters, are: the liberal idea that the public good is advanced as if by an invisible hand when individuals pursue their own good; the Social Darwinist idea that society involves a competitive struggle in which the fittest survive, which helps society progress;[38] the marketplace of ideas image, in which ideas are tested under fire, with truth and merit emerging victorious, or as Holmes put it, "the best test of truth is the power of the thought to get itself accepted in the competition of the market";[39] the democratic ethos that whatever prevails in a political contest has earned the stamp of community consent; and the adversarial legal system in which parties are wrung through a litigation procedure that produces deserving winners and losers.

Common to these ideas is that they encourage participants to exclusively pursue their individual or group agenda, they involve a process of competitive combat,

---

37 Karl Llewellyn, "A Realistic Jurisprudence – the Next Step," supra 461.
38 See Hofstadter, *Social Darwinism in American Thought*, supra.
39 *Abrams v. United States*, 250 U.S. 616, 630 (1919) (Holmes, J., dissenting).

they invest faith in the capacity of the process to select or produce the correct outcome, they draw upon metaphors to discredit interference with the "natural" workings of the process as improper meddling that causes distortions, and they suggest that winning is verification of right or entitlement. The victors or survivors or products of these processes, by having gone through and prevailed, are anointed with representing the common good, almost by definition.

The losers don't see it that way. They complain that the process unfairly rewards those with greater resources, that the system has a built-in tilt against them, that the decision-makers are biased or corrupt, that on the merits they should prevail, that competition or combat is not a proper way to decide what is right, that winners are the most rapacious or unscrupulous rather than deserving. But these complaints have little traction. If there is no way to agree upon a shared common good, if positions cannot somehow be combined or superseded at a higher level, there appears to be no alternative to leaving it to the ordeal of combat to pick winners.

The idea that the law represents the common good is hard pressed to hold up under these circumstances. The law is little more than the spoils that go to winners in contests among private interests, who, by their victory, secure the prize of enlisting the coercive power of the legal apparatus to enforce their agenda. What keeps the losing combatants in line, what convinces them to abide by the rule of law, is not the normative obligation generated by the fact that the law represents the common good. Losers comply owing to the threat that the legal apparatus will apply force to secure compliance over the unwilling, and out of the hope that they might prevail in future contests to take their turn to wield the law.

This is a barren vision indeed – a war of all against all within and through law. It is rule of some groups over others *by* and through the law, more so than a community united under a rule of law that furthers the common good.

From the very outset, the constitutional system anticipated that a clash of interests would dominate the political–governmental scene, but the matters covered in this book are not merely a contemporary reprise of this old story. Bailyn identified a critical element required of the participants in the system:

> Tension, balance, adversarial clashes leading to conciliating moderation lay at the core of the *Federalist* writers' thought – but they knew that a mechanically tense, self-balancing system did not activate or maintain itself. Its success would depend in the end on the character of the people who managed it and would allow themselves to be ruled by it – their reasonableness, their common sense, their capacity to rise above partisan passions to act for the common good and remain faithful to constitutional limits.[40]

That people were motivated by self-interest, that human nature had its dark corners, the founders understood well. But they also believed that government officials can, and must, have virtue and be motivated to further the common good.

---

40 Bailyn, *Begin the World Anew*, supra 123.

The *Federalist* authors also posited faith in lawyers, "who truly form no distinct interest in society," to rise above the clash of special interests and work for the general welfare.[41] Today, as earlier chapters suggest, public officials increasingly act as servants of particular (and their own) interests, and lawyers manipulate legal rules and processes in the service of their clients, their own financial interests, and their causes. The orientation to the common good ideal that the founders counted on now has a distinctly old fashioned, almost obsolete feel.

41 Hamilton, Federalist 35, *Federalist Papers,* supra 200.

13

The threat to legality

The U.S. legal system, to put it dramatically, is in danger of becoming less of a system of law. Concentrating on judging, this assertion will be demonstrated through two themes that have shown up at various points throughout this book. The first theme is that the rule-bound character of the legal system is reduced when achieving purposes or focusing on ends becomes the paramount goal of judges in their decisions. The second theme is that a legal system requires that judges render decisions according to the applicable rules, not according to their own political views or preferences. It is antithetical to the very notion of "the rule of law" for legal decisions to be determined by the personal views of the individual judge. Both of these themes raise vexing issues about the separation of law and politics in the decision-making of judges. The legal quality of the system – the reality of the rule of law – hinges upon how these issues are dealt with in contemporary law.

Antithesis between rule-bound and purpose orientation

Friedrich Hayek offered a highly influential definition of the rule of law: "Stripped of all technicalities, this means that government in all its actions is bound by rules fixed and announced before-hand – rules which make it possible to foresee with fair certainty how the authority will use its coercive powers in given circumstances and to plan one's individual affairs on the basis of this knowledge."[1] In legal theory circles, this is labeled the "formal" understanding of the rule of law, as elaborated in Chapter 7, because it focuses only on the formal characteristics of law rather than on its content. The core idea is that the government must abide by legal rules declared publicly in advance.

The formal rule of law is complementary to an instrumental view of law when considered in connection with legislative declarations of law. Both the formal rule of law and an instrumental approach hold that law is an empty vessel that can consist of any content whatsoever to serve any end desired. Lon Fuller, as indicated earlier, remarked that the formal rule of law is "indifferent toward the substantive aims of

---

1 F. A. Hayek, *The Road to Serfdom* (Chicago: Univ. of Chicago Press 1994) 80.

the law and is ready to serve a variety of such aims with equal efficiency."[2] That is precisely how the instrumental approach portrays law: open with respect to content and ends.

When moving from legislation to judging, however, the proposition that *judges should strive to achieve purposes and ends when deciding cases*, which has also been promoted as an aspect of the instrumental view of law, raises a direct conflict with the formal rule of law. Proponents of an instrumental approach to law, from Pound, to the Realists, to the legal process school, to contemporary legal pragmatists, have urged that judges pay attention to social consequences and strive to achieve legislative purposes and social policies when deciding cases. Sensible as this might sound, this approach has detrimental consequences for the rule-bound nature of the system.

Hayek argued that an attempt by a judge to achieve particular results in particular cases is inconsistent with the rule of law. "[W]hen we obey laws, in the sense of general abstract rules laid down irrespective of their application to us, we are not subject to another man's will and are therefore free. It is because the lawgiver does not know the particular cases to which his rules will apply, and it is because the judge who applies them has no choice in drawing the conclusions that follow from the existing body of rules and the particular facts of the case, that it can be said that laws and not men rule."[3] Alexander Hamilton similarly wrote, "To avoid an arbitrary discretion in courts, it is indispensable that they should be bound down by strict rules and precedents, which serve to define and point out their duty in every particular case that comes before them . . ."[4]

The fundamental tension between following rules and striving for purposes or ends cannot be eradicated because it strikes at the very meaning of a legal rule. "At the heart of the word 'formalism,'" wrote legal philosopher Fredrick Schauer, "lies the concept of decisionmaking according to *rule*."[5] What makes a rule a "rule" is that it specifies in general terms in advance a mandate that decision-makers must follow to the exclusion of – screening out – any other considerations. The rule provides a sufficient and obligatory reason for the decision. This is so without regard to the purpose behind the rule or the consequences of the applying the rule:

> In summary, it is exactly a rule's rigidity, even in the face of applications that would ill serve its purpose, that renders it a rule. This rigidity derives from the language of the rule's formulation, which prevents the contemplation of every fact and principle relevant to a particular application of a rule. . . . Formalism in this sense is therefore indistinguishable from "rulism," for what makes a regulative rule a rule, and what

---

2 Lon Fuller, *The Morality of Law*, 2nd revised ed. (New Haven: Yale Univ. Press 1969) 153.
3 Friedrich Hayek, *The Constitution of Liberty* (Chicago: Univ. of Chicago Press 1960) 153.
4 Hamilton, Madison, and Jay, Federalist 78, *Federalist Papers*, supra 478.
5 Fredrick Schauer, "Formalism," 97 *Yale L.J.* 509, 510 (1988) (emphasis in original). Also informative on this subject is Schauer's *Playing by the Rules: A Philosophical Examination of Rule Based Decision Making in Law and Life* (Oxford: Clarendon Press 1991).

distinguishes it from a reason, is precisely the unwillingness to pierce the generalization even in cases in which the generalization appears to the decisionmaker to be inapposite.[6]

If achieving a purpose or end is allowed to prevail over a rule, the rule is relegated to "a mere rule of thumb, defeasible when the purposes behind the rule would not be served."[7] A rule of thumb is not a binding rule.

Legal philosopher David Lyons made the same basic point: A legal system in principle cannot combine being rule-bound and trying to achieve ends (what he calls "optimizing outcomes"). It is not just that these are contrasting orientations, but that achieving ends swallows up being rule-bound. "To insist on maximum promotion of satisfactions and on deference to past authoritative decisions only when that deference could reasonably be expected to have such optimific consequences is to deny that courts are bound in the slightest degree by statutes or precedent."[8] Lyons' point is that if a judge is free to decide whether applicable legal rules ought to be followed, the judge is not bound by the rules.

In addition to the fact that striving to achieve purposes or ends diminishes the binding quality of legal rules, these are starkly dissimilar tasks. Striving to achieve a purpose or end in law, legal theorist Duncan Kennedy observed, "involves the expression, interaction and measurement of values in conflict, and the assessment of the implications for those conflicting values of infinitely complex factual situations."[9] "Rule application, in sharp contrast, involves the objective or 'cognitive' operation of identifying particular factual aspects of situations followed by the execution of unambiguous prescriptions for official action."[10] Although rule application is more involved than this description implies, there is no doubt that the task of achieving purposes or ends – which requires a judge to grapple with hard issues of value and social policy, and to determine likely future consequences – is more complicated, far more uncertain, and far less ascertainable than strictly applying legal rules to an existing situation.[11]

There are multiple reasons why attention to purposes and ends raises complex non-legal questions and can lead to decisions that are contrary to a legal rule. Some legal rules on the books are obsolete and inconsistent with current policies, so vindicating the latter will vitiate the former. Some statutes are poorly drafted or embody purposes and policies that are internally at odds (the product of political compromise). The main problem, however, is inherent to the nature of legal rules and will arise in the best conceived legal regimes. Legal rules are set forth in general terms in advance and cannot anticipate or account for every eventuality that might arise.

6 Schauer, "Formalism," supra 535.
7 Id.
8 David Lyons, "Legal Formalism and Instrumentalism – A Pathological Study," 66 *Cornell L. Rev.* 949, 967 (1981).
9 Duncan Kennedy, "Legal Formality," 2 *J. Legal Studies* 351, 364 (1973).
10 Id.
11 See also Unger, *Knowledge and Politics*, supra 89; Unger, *Law in Modern Society*, supra 192–200.

Contemplate the situation in which a poorly educated and slow-witted but not incompetent person signs a legally binding contract with punitive terms; the harsh terms of the contract are explained to the party, who willingly signs without realizing that a much better contract could be obtained across the street. A judge committed to the formal rule of law will duly enforce the contract according to its terms regardless of the outcome. A judge focused on ends will find a way to ameliorate or avoid the onerous contractual terms, even though the conditions for a valid contract have clearly been met. Either way there is an unpalatable consequence: The judge who enforces the contract will impose a harsh result; the judge who avoids the contract will ignore binding legal rules and tread on the legal rights and expectations of a contracting party.

The situation is further complicated because alternative views of the purposes of contract law circulate within the legal culture. The judge in this scenario is moved by consideration of fairness, but other possible considerations are enhancing economic efficiency, preserving the sanctity of promise or agreements, encouraging desirable business practices, protecting vulnerable segments of the populace, achieving certainty in contractual relations, and more. There is no preestablished hierarchy among alternative values and purposes, and no set method for resolving clashes among these alternatives. In tort cases, similarly, judges routinely weigh such considerations as the deterrence effect, compensation for victims, moral responsibility for actions that cause harm, availability of products for consumers at affordable prices, consequences for the economy, costs of injuries to society, implications for insurance, problems caused by excessive litigation, taxing the resources of the court, and so forth. The analysis relies on contestable political, scientific, moral, and economic issues, and on highly speculative predictions of future consequences, all matters about which judges have no particular expertise or reliable information. A judge who considers these purposes and ends when applying legal rules is at sea in an embarrassingly rich set of unconstrained options.

Yet a further level of complication exists because most purposive approaches, following the legal process school, invoke not just the purpose of a legislative or common law provision – hard enough to discern – but also the purpose of an entire area of law and of the legal system as a whole. At each higher level of generality there is more room for disagreement and more contestable choices must be made. Conflicts may also arise between specific purposes and general purposes. Moreover, explicitly stated purposes will not necessarily be consistent with real underlying purposes. Take the South Dakota abortion ban: The facial purpose is to ban abortions, but the immediate, driving purpose (as stated by its proponents) is to provoke litigation that leads to the overtuning of *Roe*. When law is primarily treated as a means to an end in a context of sharp disagreement, it is not evident that specific legal regimes or the legal system as a whole will have overarching or internally consistent purposes.

Finally, it should be recognized that the very notion of searching for a purpose behind legislation or common law doctrines trades on an abstraction. Since legislators often have different motives, intentions, and purposes in mind, and the common law is the product of innumerable judicial decisions partaking of different streams within the law, identifying *the* purpose is invariably a judicial construction[12] – a fiction. The legal process school admitted as much when it proposed that, when searching for the purpose, the judge should presume that legislation was the product of "reasonable persons pursuing reasonable purposes reasonably."

Judges who advocate focusing on purposes and ends concede that this orientation is in tension with being bound to legal rules. Judge Richard Posner, a tireless campaigner for pragmatism in judging, acknowledges that "Pragmatic reasons do not sound very lawlike . . . "[13] Supreme Court Justice Stephen Breyer, also known as a pragmatist judge, advocates that a constitutional or legislative text should be interpreted "in light of its purpose" with attention to "consequences," including "contemporary conditions, social, industrial, and political, of the community to be affected."[14] Breyer contrasts this purposive approach with "textualist" or "literalist" approaches, most identified with Justice Scalia;[15] textualists decide cases based upon the (public) meaning of the words of the constitutional or legislative provision at the time of enactment without particular attention to purpose or consequences. Breyer concedes that his approach under certain circumstances "would leave the Court without a clear rule" and that "a court focused on consequences may decide a case in a way that radically changes the law."[16]

Advocates of a "purposive" approach and advocates of a "pragmatic" approach to judging do not agree on all points (and there are difference within these approaches), it should be noted, though they tend to substantially overlap, and will be treated here together. They have the similar effect of orienting judicial decision-making toward ends, pointing outside legal rules and drawing in non-legal considerations, requiring judges to make complex decisions about values and policies and about the likely future social and economic consequences of decisions. In these respects, both lessen the rule-bound orientation of the judge.

Unstable combination of rule-bound and purpose-oriented

Although legal theorists have put forward compelling arguments that rule-bound judging and a focus on purposes and ends *cannot in principle* be combined, this combination has, in fact, taken place in the U.S. legal culture as a result of the developments laid out in Parts 1 and 2 of this book. Phillipe Nonet and Philip Selznick wrote in 1978 that judicial decision-making was in the process of evolving

---

12 See William N. Eskridge, *Dynamic Statutory Interpretation* (Cambridge, Mass.: Harvard Univ. Press 1994) 25–34.

13 Posner, "Forward: A Political Court," supra 98.

14 Stephen Breyer, *Active Liberty: Interpreting Our Democratic Constitution* (New York: Knopf 2005) 18. For a more elaborate account of striving for purposes, see Aharon Barak, *Purposive Interpretation in Law* (Princeton: Princeton Univ. Press 2005).

15 Antonin Scalia, *A Matter of Interpretation: Federal Courts and the Law* (Princeton: Princeton Univ. Press 1996).

16 Breyer, *Active Liberty*, supra 129, 119.

away from an emphasis on formal legality toward utilizing instrumental rationality to achieve policies and purposes. In the same year, legal theorist Patrick Atiyah commented on the notable shift in judicial decision-making toward "pragmatism," involving greater judicial attention to achieving ends.[17] Roberto Unger wrote in 1975 that "the courts... are caught between two roles with conflicting demands: the role of the traditional formalist judge, who asks what the correct interpretation of rules of law is, and the role of the calculator of efficiencies, who seeks to determine what course of action will most effectively serve a given goal..."[18] A study that interviewed judges on four state Supreme Courts conducted in the late 1960s found that judges fell into three categories in their perception of their judicial role. About half considered themselves to be strict law appliers, a fourth considered themselves to be law-makers, and another fourth considered themselves to be pragmatists who partook of both roles while aiming at just results and sound policy.[19] Although more recent studies are lacking, it is a fair to surmise, given the discussion in earlier chapters, that a greater proportion of contemporary judges are judicial pragmatists, though no doubt the other two orientations are also well represented. Judicial decisions today regularly cite policy considerations, consider the purposes behind the law, and pay attention to law's social consequences.

This apparent shift in judging orientation toward greater consideration of purposes and ends has not been wholesale, as the aforementioned study indicates. Moreover, movement has not taken place in only in one direction; theorists have noted a "new formalism" in contract law, for example, which partakes of aspects of both rule formalism and pragmatism.[20] Some judges remain strictly rule-oriented while others have become more pragmatic; the same judge might be rule-oriented in certain cases but pragmatic in others.

Despite this multifarious reality, the official line of the legal culture is still that judges are rule-bound in their decisions. In his opening statement in the Senate hearings for his appointment to the Supreme Court, Judge Alito declared that "The judge's only obligation, and it's a solemn obligation, is to the rule of law. And what that means is that in every single case the judge has to do what the law requires."[21] Justice Alito, who, like Justice Scalia, has avowed his fidelity to the text, joins the bench with Justice Breyer, who advocates a more purposive and consequentialist approach. This mix of judicial philosophies among judges exists at all levels of the judiciary. Individual judges sometimes shift from one philosophy to another. Scalia will respect longstanding precedent even if wrongly decided (as adjudged by original

---

17 See Atiyah, *From Principle to Pragmatism*, supra.

18 Unger, *Knowledge and Politics*, supra 99.

19 K. N. Vines, "The Judicial Role in the American States," in *Frontiers of Judicial Research*, edited by J. B. Grossman and J. Tanenhaus (New York: J. Wiley 1969); see also J. T. Wold, "Political Orientations, Social Backgrounds, and Role Perceptions of State Supreme Court Judges," 27 *Western Pol. Quarterly* 239 (1974).

20 See Mark L. Movsesian, "Rediscovering Williston," 62 *Wash. & Lee L. Rev.* 207 (2005).

21 Transcript of Alito Opening Statement before Senate Judiciary Committee, *New York Times*, Jan. 10, 2006, A18.

meaning), out of an unwillingness to disrupt settled legal understandings. Scalia concedes that this is a "pragmatic exception" to his textualist approach,[22] so even an extremist of the rule-bound ilk may invoke pragmatic considerations.

The result of this mish-mash of contrasting orientations is a system of judging suspended in uncertain and shifting space, with some judges freed of the shackles of being rigidly rule-bound, yet not entirely comfortable with this freedom, and other judges insisting on being rule-bound (though not every time). There is no common rule of decision judges follow to determine when they should stick with the rules or depart from the rules to achieve ends – nor is it clear that such a rule can be formulated. Not only are the legal rules less binding because of more purposive and pragmatic reasoning, but also the legal system as a whole manifests a greater degree of unpredictability because judges have different orientations among themselves.

Legal theorists who have considered the situation concur that it is detrimental to the rule of law.[23] What this analysis does not resolve is whether these changes have been for the better. Nonet and Selznick construed this development positively, though their assessment assumed the ability to obtain a consensus about the social good. It is conceivable that judges individually and collectively are able to moderate the tensions identified earlier, considering puposes yet still following rules in a manner that maintains a robust rule of law system, still largely certain, equal in application, and predictable. Not enough information about judicial reasoning and its consequences is presently available to know for sure.

The problem explored here, it should be recognized, is a perennial one that every system of law must manage. In earlier periods of the common law, it showed up in the contrast between judges strictly applying the law versus doing equity in the individual case. But two critical factors must be borne in mind, factors which render the current situation different from prior moments in the Anglo-American legal tradition. First, when there is a high degree of homogeneity or consensus in society, which the judges reflect, judicial decisions that focus on ends will still be relatively certain and predictable because most people will share in and correctly anticipate the outcomes of these decision. Society today, however, is marked by dissensus Second, large consequences can following from a seemingly slight shift in orientation. Judges formerly were explicitly oriented toward strictly following the law, but they were never completely blind to ends. With the rise of instrumentalism, judges are encouraged to strive to achieve purposes and ends, while paying attention to the legal rules. Both orientations consider rules and ends. The former approach makes it clear, however, that the rules control, unless the outcome is absolutely absurd or impossibly outrageous (a high threshold rarely met). The latter approach makes consideration of ends a routine matter, and thus always a threat to affect the application of the legal rules. The difference between these two orientations, in practice, can be vast.

---

22 Scalia, *A Matter of Interpretation,* supra 140.
23 See Tamanaha, *On the Rule of Law,* supra Chapters 5 and 6.

If judges individually and collectively have indeed found an ideal combination of being rule-bound while considering purposes and ends, surely it is a precarious balance to maintain. Pressure is put on this balance by the growing view that it is naïve or false to believe that judges can rule in an objective or unbiased fashion. Skepticism about judicial objectivity is the greatest looming contemporary threat to legality.

Modern skepticism about judicial objectivity

All of the classic phrases used to capture the rule of law ideal – "the rule of law, not man"; a "government of laws, not men"; law is reason, not passion; law is objective, not subjective – identify the law with the image of the objective judge.[24] Judges are mere "mouthpieces of the law." Their fidelity is to the law alone. They are unbiased, neutral, evenhanded, devoid of non-legal influences. Chief Justice John Marshall insisted that "Courts are mere instruments of law, and can will nothing."[25]

A major theme of earlier chapters was the spread of skepticism about this portrayal of judicial decision-making, challenged by the Legal Realists, lent support by the 1937 "switch in time" and the apparently political decisions of the Warren Court and its successors, exacerbated in the contemporary legal culture by the penetration of postmodern views that background and subjectivity inevitably color perception. A recent book by Lee Epstein and Jeffrey A. Segal, political scientists who have conducted leading studies of judicial decision-making, approvingly quotes a pioneer in the field, C. Herman Pritchett, "that judges 'are influenced by their own biases and philosophies, which to a large degree predetermine the position they will take on a given question. Private attitudes, in other words, become public law."[26] Judge Posner wrote a review of the Rehnquist Court's final term that he entitled "A Political Court," asserting that "The evidence of the influence of policy judgments, and hence of politics, on constitutional adjudication on the Supreme Court is everywhere at hand."[27] Although Posner's statement is directed at judging on the Supreme Court, he clearly believes that judges generally are influenced by their personal ideology and other non-legal factors when deciding cases.[28] In a comprehensive study of federal appellate judging, prominent legal scholar Cass Sunstein (and co-authors) flatly stated that "No reasonable person seriously doubts that ideology, understood as normative commitments of various sorts, helps to explain judicial votes."[29]

24 Id. 122–6.
25 *Osborn v. Bank of United States*, 22 US (9 Wheaton) 736, 866 (1824).
26 Lee Epstein and Jeffrey A. Segal, *Advice and Consent: The Politics of Judicial Appointments* (New York: Oxford Univ. Press 2005) 3.
27 Richard A. Posner, "Foreword: A Political Court: The Supreme Court 2004 Term," 119 *Harvard L. Rev.* 32, 46 (2005).
28 See Scherer, *Scoring Points*, supra.
29 Cass R. Sunstein, David Schkade, and Lisa Michelle Ellman, "Ideological Voting on Federal Courts of Appeals: A Preliminary Investigation," 90 *Virginia L. Rev.* 301, 352 (2004).

This perception has also penetrated the public, fueled by the rampant politiciza-tion of the judicial appointments process in recent years. "When asked if 'in many cases judges are really basing their decisions on their own personal beliefs' 56% [of the public] agree and only 36% disagree."[30] Yet, confirming the continuing hold of the objective judge ideal, a poll taken during the Alito hearings found that 69% of the public believe that the personal views of a Justice should not have a role in their decisions.[31]

For the sake of reducing the degree of complexity, the discussion in the preceding Part assumed that judges objectively resolve questions about the interpretation of the law and about the appropriate purpose, or social policy, or the right outcome in a given case. But questions about subjectivity cannot be kept apart from the debate over whether judges should be strictly rule-oriented or should also focus on purposes and ends. Text-oriented critics of purposive or pragmatist approaches object that the latter involve expansive inquiries (as just indicated) beyond the interpretation and application of legal rules, inquiries that invite judges to draw upon their subjective views.

Similar criticisms about the necessity for personal judicial choices have been lodged against the other main theory of interpretation, the principles approach, promoted by Ronald Dworkin and others,[32] who urge that judges consider in their decisions background moral or political principles. Textualists (Scalia) and pragma-tists (Posner) argue that "principles" approaches are plagued by controversial ques-tions of value. Although proponents of the principles approach think these questions are resolvable on some objective basis, critics insist that under this approach value choices are merely couched in the terminology of broader principles.[33]

Questions about judicial objectivity also apply to textualist or literalist app-roaches that claim to strictly apply legal rules. The historical evidence of meaning is often lacking or ambiguous, alternative readings of legal provisions are regularly available, their application to novel or unanticipated circumstances involves choices (especially for phrases that were written more than a century ago), and open-ended standards and principles require judgments to be made.[34] Moreover, even self-proclaimed text-bound judges will make exceptions, as Scalia does, which suggests that they are able to maneuver when they so desire. As mentioned earlier, studies have found correlations between the personal attitudes and legal decisions of avowed textualists.

So whether one is a textualist or a purposivist, or an advocate of legal principles, the same fundamental question must be confronted: To what extent do judges'

---

30 Judges and the American Public's View of Them," Results of Maxwell Poll, conducted in October 2005, available at www.maxwell.syr.edu.
31 "Poll: Americans Undecided on Alito," CBS News, Jan. 9, 2006, available at http://www. CBSNews.com.
32 See Dworkin, *Law's Empire*, supra.
33 See Posner, "A Political Court," supra 85; Scalia, *A Matter of Interpretation*, supra.
34 Both sides of these arguments are developed in Breyer, *Active Liberty*, supra and Scalia, *A Matter of Interpretation*, supra.

subjective views infect their purportedly objective legal decisions on the correct application of legal rules (and, when permitted, the correct identification of purposes and ends)?

Many observers, to repeat the challenge, take Legal Realism and postmodernism to have taught that the aforesaid distinction between an objective perspective and a subjective perspective is, at a deep level, illusory. A judge's personal preferences inevitably color that judge's conclusion about the correct interpretation of the legal rules and about the correct ends in a case. The judge's subjectively desired ends shape how the judge selects, interprets, and utilizes the applicable legal rules. Judges who attempt in good faith to render decisions in an objective fashion, striving to screen out the influence of subjective views, will nevertheless fail, according to this view, because the process operates subconsciously, beneath their awareness.

The threat posed to the rule of law by this set of ideas cannot be overstated. If judges substantially base their legal decisions – whether involving rule application alone, or some combination of rules and ends – upon their personal views, then the rule of law ideal would be a fraud. Judges are still constrained in that they must work within acceptable legal conventions, but these conventions and the available body of rules and exceptions are capacious enough to provide judges the leeway to reach desired outcomes much of the time. "The 'law' ... becomes mere instruments or barriers that judges must utilize strategically to advance their *a priori* political objectives."[35] The private will of the particular judge, not the law, is determinative.

Furthermore, when the total body of judges is made up of individuals who hold divergent personal views, the formal rule of law in the sense of stability, certainty, predictability, and equality of application, cannot be sustained, because the outcomes of cases will vary in accordance with the divergent personal views of judges. Ex ante, every legal dispute is a crapshoot, the outcome of which can be predicted only after the case is assigned, when the personal predilections of the individual judge are known. Supreme Court watchers already have this mindset, routinely engaging in vote counting along political lines.[36]

So described – a legal system shot through with subjectively influenced, willful judging – the threat to the rule of law seems dire. A more careful examination, however, reveals that things are not quite as bad as this scenario suggests. Not yet anyway. The threat to the rule of law posed by this complex of ideas is not that judges are incapable of rendering decisions in an objective fashion. Rather, the threat is that judges come to *believe* that it cannot be done or that most fellow judges are not doing it. This skepticism, if it becomes pervasive among lawyers, judges, and the public, will precipitate a self-fulfilling collapse in the rule of law.

---

35 Cornell W. Clayton, "The Supply and Demand Sides of Judicial Policy-Making (Or, Why Be So Positive About the Judicialization of Politics?)" 65 *Law & Contemp. Probs.* 69 (2002).

36 See Molly McDonough, "Pitching to a New Lineup: Supreme Court Practitioners Will Aim Their Arguments At Different Justices," *ABA Journal Report,* February 3, 2006, at http://www.abanet. org/journal/report/f3sct.html.

This skepticism is based upon a widely shared misunderstanding of Legal Realism and postmodernism, neither of which deny that there is a real and meaningful difference between instructing judges to render decisions objectively, dictated by the law, versus instructing judges to make whatever decisions they think right.

Realists and the possibility of judicial objectivity

The Realist critique of rule formalism came in two versions. Radical rule skeptics, like Jerome Frank in his most extreme moments (before he became a judge), denied that legal rules determined judicial decisions. Judges arrive at decisions they subjectively prefer, then work backward, manipulating legal rules to support these predetermined ends. The more moderate Realist critique, in contrast, was not entirely skeptical of legal rules, only of certain unrealistic claims about the rules. They put forth a negative argument that denied that rule application is a purely mechanical process, and they denied formalist claims that there are no gaps or conflicts in the applicable legal rules. Judges regularly have leeway within the applicable body of legal rules and exceptions, and they are regularly required or able to make choices. Unlike the arguments of radical rule skeptics, the more moderate critique does not deny that judges decide cases in accordance with rules, and does not claim that decisions are always determined by what judges personally prefer.

Karl Llewellyn and Felix Cohen asserted that there is a shared craft to legal interpretation and legal argument that make it a relatively stable and predictable exercise that is not entirely the product of the personal views of judges. Cohen criticized the "hunch" theory of judging (of Frank and Hutcheson) for improperly denying "the relevance of significant, predictable, social determinants that govern the course of the judicial decision."[37] He added that "actual experience does reveal a significant body of predictable uniformity in the behavior of courts."[38] Cohen insisted that judicial decisions must be understood as "more than an expression of individual personality";[39] they are the product of an institutional legal context that insures consistency. He speculated – calling it "guesswork" – that a judge's decisions may be affected by the attitudes of his class, but Cohen also insisted that "judges are craftsmen, with aesthetic ideals, concerned with the aesthetic judgments that the bar and the law schools will pass upon their awkward or skillful, harmonious or unharmonious, anomalous or satisfying, actions and theories."[40] The shared understandings and practices of legal argument provide constraints on judges. After opining that the ambiguity of legal material allows judges "to throw

37 Cohen, "Transcendental Nonsense and the Functional Approach," supra 843.
38 Id.
39 Id.
40 Id. 845.

the decision this way or that," Llewellyn tempered this by recognizing that "while it is possible to build a number of different logical ladders up out of the same cases and down again to the same dispute, there are not so many that can be built defensibly."[41]

John Chipman Gray, whom the Realists admired, recognized that judges "decide cases otherwise than they would have decided them had the precedents not existed, and follow the precedents, although they may think that they ought not to have been made."[42] Realist hero Holmes once said, "It has given me the great pleasure to sustain the Constitutionality of laws that I believe to be as bad as possible, because I thereby helped to mark the difference between what I would forbid and what the Constitution permits."[43] It was his view that, notwithstanding the presence of discretion, judicial decisions can and should conform to the law.[44] Holmes' critique of the majority in the *Lochner* case was precisely that the personal (and class) laissez faire views of the judges were an *improper* basis for a constitutional decision. "I strongly believe," Holmes wrote, "that my agreement or disagreement has nothing to do with the right of a majority to embody their opinions in law."[45] When called upon to make decisions that turn on policy, Holmes felt that the duty of judges was to find the correct social policy, not simply enact their own preference.[46]

According to Justice Benjamin N. Cardozo, another favorite of the Realists:

> In countless litigations, the law is so clear that judges have no discretion. They have the right to legislate within gaps, but often there are no gaps. We shall have a false view of the landscape if we look at the waste spaces only, and refuse to see the acres already sown and fruitful.... Judges have, of course, the power, though not the right, to ignore the mandate of a statute and render judgment in spite of it. They have the power, though not the right, to travel beyond the walls of the intersticies, the bounds set to judicial innovation by precedent and custom. None the less, by that abuse of power they violate the law...[47]

Cardozo acknowledged that the personal views of judges have an impact, but not to a degree that is completely outcome determinative: "So sweeping a statement exaggerates the element of free volition. It ignores the factors of determinism which cabin and confine within narrow bounds the range of unfettered choice."[48] "The judge, even when he is free, is still not wholly free."[49]

---

41 Llewellyn, The Bramble Bush, supra 73.
42 John Chipman Gray, *The Nature and Sources of the Law* (New York: Columbia Univ. Press 1909) 34.
43 Quoted in Menand, *Metaphysical Club*, supra 67.
44 See M. Cohen, *Law and the Social Order*, supra 213.
45 *Lochner v. New York*, 198 U.S. 90 (Holmes, J. dissenting).
46 See White, *Social Thought in American*, supra 208–9.
47 Benjamin N. Cardozo, *The Nature of the Judicial Process* (New Haven: Yale Univ. Press 1921) 129.
48 Id. 170.
49 Id. 141.

Most Realists took a middle position that avoided either extreme of mechanical reasoning or rule skepticism, articulated here by philosopher Morris Cohen:

> [T]he judge's *feelings* as to right and wrong must be logically and scientifically trained. This trained mind sees in a flash of intuition that which the untrained mind can succeed in seeing only after painfully treading many steps. They who scorn the idea of the judges as a logical automaton are apt to fall into the opposite effort of exaggerating as irresistible the force of bias or prejudice. But the judge who realizes before listening to a case that all men are biased is more likely to make a conscientious effort at impartiality than one who believes that elevation to the bench makes him at once an organ of infallible logical truth.[50]

The Realist reminder that judges are subject to subconscious influences was meant to help them be vigilant toward and overcome these influences, not a call to surrender to their inevitability.

Chemerinsky's earlier quoted declaration that the Realists "exploded the myth" that judges could decide "cases apart from their views and ideology" fails to appreciate this more nuanced view. The Realists believed and advocated that judicial decisions should not be entirely the products of judges' personal views and ideology, and they did not consider this a hopeless demand.

Postmodernism and judicial objectivity

The Realists do not have final say on the matter, of course, and they lived before late-twentieth-century postmodernism drove deep doubts about the possibility of objectivity into society and the legal culture. Postmodernism suggests that "The human subject is an embodied agent, acting and judging in a context that can never be wholly objectified, with orientations and motivations that can never be fully grasped or controlled."[51] Judges, under this view, subconsciously see the law through an ideologically colored lens, no matter how sincerely motivated they might be to decide objectively.

This is not the place to put forth a detailed response to postmodernism,[52] but a quick answer can be given that accepts the basic proposition while resisting its skeptical implications. Judges indeed approach the law from the standpoint of their personal views. More immediately, however, they see the law from within the lens of the legal tradition into which they have been indoctrinated, and from within the conventions of legal practice and judging in which they participate. The totality of the legal tradition – the legal language, the corpus of legal rules, concepts, principles, and ideas, legal processes and practices, hierarchical legal institutions, the craft of lawyering – has the effect of stabilizing legal meaning and providing restraints on the influence of the subjective views. Law is a socially produced and shared activity

---

50 M. Cohen, *Law and the Social Order*, supra 182–3.
51 Tarnas, *The Passion of the Western Mind*, supra 396.
52 See generally Tamanaha, *Realistic Socio-Legal Theory*, supra.

that participants are not free to do in any way they desire. Unacceptable moves and interpretations that do not comport with shared understandings of legal rules within the legal tradition simply "will not write." Judges who stretch legal rules beyond recognition risk disapproval from colleagues on a shared panel or rebuke upon appellate review. These are social and institutional mechanisms of perpetuating and enforcing conformity in the interpretation of legal rules.

This account incorporates the postmodern insight about the influence of background views on how people see the world, merely adding the reminder that the legal tradition itself is such a body of background views, which becomes an integrated aspect of the judge's own perspective.[53] The Realists said as much in their emphasis on the craft of lawyering. Subconscious personal influences are not completely suppressed under this account, but must pass through a filtering perspective. This still leaves ample flexibility, and willful judges can always manipulate legal rules to achieve the ends they desire (though at the risk of reversal). But most judges most of the time appear to consciously strive to render decisions in an objective fashion, and there is sufficient stability and constraint within the legal tradition to make this process meaningful.

Excluding the Supreme Court, this assertion is borne out by the high percentage of unanimous decisions rendered by panels of judges with contrasting ideological views.[54] The bulk of empirical studies of judicial decision-making suggests that "ideological values play a less prominent role in the lower federal courts."[55] Studies of appellate course decisions have found that, although political considerations show up in decisions, legal doctrine appears to have an overarching influence.[56] Judges routinely follow binding precedent.[57] Judge Posner sweepingly claims that "There is almost no legal outcome that a really skillful legal analyst cannot cover with a professional varnish."[58] But he is well versed on studies of judicial decision-making, and carefully conditions (italicized here) the reach of his skepticism: "It is no longer open to debate that ideology ... plays a significant role in the decisions even of lower court judges *when the law is uncertain and emotions aroused.*"[59] In many cases, the law is relatively clear and the judge is not emotionally involved in the outcome. A comprehensive study by Sunstein, Schkade, and Ellman demonstrated

53 See Id. Chaps. 7 and 8.
54 See Harry T. Edwards, "Collegiality and decision-making on the D.C. Circuit," 84 *Virginia L. Rev.* 1335 (1998); Patricia M. Wald, "A Response to Tiller and Cross," 99 *Columbia L. Rev.* 235 (1999).
55 D. Songer and S. Haire, "Integrating Alternative Approaches to the Study of Judicial Voting: Obscenity Cases in the US Court of Appeals," 36 *Am. J. Pol. Sci.* 963, 964 (1992). For a review of political science studies on judicial decision-making up through the mid-1990s, see Tamanaha, *Realistic Socio-Legal Theory,* supra Chap. 7.
56 See Frank B. Cross, "Decisionmaking in the U.S. Circuit Courts of Appeals," 91 *California L. Rev.* 1457 (2003); Frank B. Cross and Emerson H. Tiller, "Judicial Partisanship and Obedience to Legal Doctrine: Whistleblowing on the Federal Courts of Appeals," 107 *Yale L.J.* 2155 (1998).
57 Gregory C. Sisk, Michael Heise, Andrew P. Morriss, "Charting the Influence on the Judicial Mind: An Empirical Study of Judicial Reasoning," 73 *NYU L. Rev.* 1377 (1998).
58 Posner, "A Political Court," supra 52.
59 Id. 48.

ideology-correlated differences (though not in all categories of cases) in the voting patterns of Democratic and Republican appointed federal appellate judges, but still found that there was a great deal of agreement in their legal decisions: "It would be possible to see our data as suggesting that most of the time, the law is what matters, not ideology."[60]

None of this denies that with respect to the Supreme Court there is compelling evidence to believe that the personal views of the judges have a substantial impact on their decisions.[61] This is a unique court, however, the conduct of which cannot be extrapolated to others. The danger is that the Supreme Court example, and the politicization that now surrounds all judicial appointments, may have begun to infect others. Studies suggest that as lower level federal judicial appointments have become more ideologically charged in the past few decades, the voting behavior of lower court judges has shown an uptick in partisanship.[62]

The significance of a consciously rule-bound orientation

Although postmodernism suggests that subjective influences on perception are pervasive and not entirely repressible, nothing within postmodernism doubts that the conscious orientation of actors has real consequences for individual and social action. Conscious orientation is a fundamental causal factor in behavior. The theory that our shared and acted upon ideas and beliefs substantially construct social reality is built upon the causal efficacy of intentional orientations. We each see confirmation of this, usually without reflecting upon it, every day in our own purposeful behavior. So even accepting the irreducible presence of subconscious influences on perspective and judgments, objectivity in legal decisions is real and achievable in the conscious attitudes and motivations of judges. Therein lies the reality and prospects for the rule of law.

Imagine two judges, both with politically conservative personal views: One decides cases with a conscious orientation that strives to abide by the binding dictates of applicable legal rules to come up with the most correct legal interpretation in each case (the Consciously Bound judge, CB); a second judge decides cases with a conscious orientation that strives to achieve ideologically preferred ends in each case and interprets and manipulates the legal rules to the extent necessary to achieve the ends desired (the Consciously Ends-Oriented judge, CEO).

Add four realistic conditions to this scenario. First, notwithstanding this conscious orientation, CB is subconsciously influenced by and sees the law through background personal views; the legal interpretations of CB are thus not completely free of political influences in this subconscious sense. Second, CEO is not able to achieve ends with total disregard for conventional legal understandings because the

60 Sunstein, Schkade, Ellman, "Ideological Voting on Federal Courts of Appeals," supra 336.
61 See Spaeth and Seagal, "Attitudinal Model and the Supreme Court Revisited," supra.
62 See Scherer, *Scoring Points*, supra.

decisions must be legally plausible and maintain the external appearance of being rule-bound; the legal interpretations of CEO are thus not completely devoid of legal constraints. Third, in a large (but not total) subset of cases, the legal rules allow for more than one legally plausible outcome, though usually one outcome can be ranked as more legally compelling or defensible than the others. Finally, in a subset of cases, the legal rules are open or invite the judge to render a judgment based upon non-legal factors. Note that these conditions accept all of the major points made by the Legal Realists as well as postmodernism.

Now, imagine that, in a given case, both judges arrive at precisely the same outcome, supported by identical written decisions; had they been sitting together on a panel, they would have joined opinions. They are led to the same result and use the same reasoning because both judges adopt the same theory of constitutional interpretation. The difference is that CB settles upon the theory as the correct way to interpret the Constitution following a sincere and exhaustive study of constitutional law, whereas CEO settles upon the theory because it tends to support the outcomes the judge personally prefers, and CEO is willing to depart from or "adjust" the theory when necessary to achieve the desired end in particular cases.

Would we evaluate the judges' respective decisions as equivalent? They are literally identical in *external* form and in consequence. A strong argument can be made, however, that these externally identical decisions are not equivalent: CB's decision is faithfully law-abiding while CEO's decision is an abusive exercise of power in the guise of law.

This scenario is meant to tease out the essential difference between subconscious influences on judging and willful judging. The sophisticated modern recognition that judges' background views subconsciously influence their interpretation of the law at some deep level is correct. It is also correct that sometimes the law runs out or calls upon the making of judgments by judges. Too often, however, a leap is made from these points to the conclusion that, therefore, judges are deluded, naïve, or lying when they claim that their decisions are determined by the law. To the extent that a judge is consciously rule-bound when engaging in judging, the judge is correct in claiming to be rule-bound *in the only sense that this phrase can be humanly achieved.* Since judging is a human practice, it is absurd to evaluate the decision-making of judges by reference to a standard that is impossible to achieve, inevitably finding them wanting. There are other aspects to proper judging, such as not favoring one side or the other, but being consciously rule-bound is the essence of a system of the rule of law. CB's decisions are determined by the law in this sense, whereas CEO's decisions are not.

To be sure, owing to subconscious influences on how the law is seen, the legal decisions of CB's with conservative views would differ somewhat from those of CB's with liberal views, but their legal decisions would also substantially overlap (as Sunstein's study showed). In contrast, the decisions of conservative CEOs and liberal CEOs would diverge markedly, with only minimal overlap (when the applicable law and legal conventions allow little wiggle room). As this contrast shows, a system composed entirely of CBs would be rule-bound and largely predictable based upon the strength of legal considerations. This analysis leads to the perhaps odd – but consistent – assertion that the decisions of all CB judges are *objectively* determined by the law, even when their decsions diverge.

Now imagine an entire system filled with CEOs. That would be a system that is "legal" in external form only, markedly different in operation from a CB-filled system. The judges in this scenario in each case willfully strive to achieve ends, manipulating the legal rules as required (even if for well-meaning reasons), restrained by the law only in the weak sense that unavoidable legal conventions will sometimes preclude certain outcomes. Skeptics like Judge Posner and political scientists who dismiss the significance of the conscious orientation of judges toward being rule-bound, miss this larger picture of the substantial contrast between a CB-populated system and a CEO-populated one.

Statistical correlations that political scientists have documented between the decisions of judges and their personal ideologies are, to some degree, a reflection of irrepressible subconscious influences, and to some degree a reflection of the openness of the law – open either because the legal answer is unclear or the law calls upon the judge to make a non-legal determination (factors that are more prevalent at higher level courts). These statistically demonstrated correlations, however, are never total and are higher for certain judges than for others.[63] With respect to those judges who manifest relatively higher correlations between their personal attitudes and their legal decisions when compared with judges in the same circumstances (Rehnquist and Douglas, in certain classes of cases, had correlations above 90%),[64] it is fair to surmise that their conscious orientation is less rule-bound in comparison with their colleagues. From the standpoint of the rule of law, they can be condemned for this reason.

A pragmatic judge who focuses on outcomes is more like a CEO judge (though not necessarily with the same unrestrained manipulative orientation towards legal rules) than a CB judge. "The way I approach a case as a judge," Posner stated, "is first to ask myself what would be a reasonable, sensible result, as a lay person would understand it, and then, having answered that question, to ask whether that result is blocked by clear constitutional or statutory text, governing precedent, or any other conventional limitation on judicial discretion."[65] This is not "decision-making *according to* rule," but decision-making according to the judge's sense of what is right, all things considered, unless prohibited by the law. An outcome that is not disallowed by the law, and thus acceptable for a judge who reasons like Posner, might not be the strongest legal outcome. A consciously rule-bound judge, in contrast, would feel obliged to search out and apply the strongest legal decision.

---

63 For a collection of such studies for lower federal courts, see Scherer, *Scoring Points*, supra.
64 See Tamanaha, *Realistic Socio-Legal Theory*, supra Chap. 7.
65 Richard A. Posner, "Tap Dancing," *The New Republic Online*, at http://www.tnr.com/doc.mhtml?i=w060130&S=heymanposner013106.

This is not an abstract point of no consequence. Posner offered his description of judging in a debate over the legality of the Bush Administration's warrantless surveillance program to combat terrorism. Security experts and the public are sharply divided over the program in terms of value, necessity, and the consequences to privacy and liberty interests. A pragmatic judge searching for a "reasonable" result "as a lay person would understand it" could easily come down on either side of the issue, and throw up plausible legal arguments to justify either outcome. But this does not mean that a decision *according to* the law would lead equally to both outcomes. Aiming toward an end, a judge reasoning pragmatically might pass over the stronger argument in favor of the weaker, because the weaker argument cannot be categorically ruled out. In that instance, the individual who happens to be the judge will dictate the outcome, not the law. This example illustrates the legitimate concern of opponents of the pragmatic approach that it invites judges to render contestable value decisions, that it would diminish equality of application, and that it would generate uncertainty in the law.

The *sine qua non* of the rule of law is striving to decide cases according to the law. Over time, the decisions of Posner's pragmatist judge, who resembles a CEO judge in approaching legal rules with a controlling end in mind, would diverge from the decisions of a judge who is oriented toward doing what the law requires (rather than doing what the law does not disallow).

The present threat to the rule of law, to return to the key point, is not that it is impossible for judges to be consciously rule-bound when rendering their decisions, striving to set aside subjective preferences and abide by the legal rules. Rather the threat comes from the *belief* that it cannot be done or the *choice* not to do it. In the present atmosphere, with prevailing misunderstandings about the Realist position and about the implications of postmodernism, judges may become convinced that to decide in a rule-bound fashion is a chimerical or naïve aspiration. They may think other judges are instrumentally manipulating legal rules to reach ends they personally desire – even when the judges insist otherwise – cloaking their personal preferences in legal logic. The temptation to do so is magnified when judges recognize that their ideological views were a major consideration in securing their appointment, and that everyone involved expects that these views will influence their legal decisions.

Nothing can be done about the subconscious springs of human intellect. What is not inevitable is that a judge would cross over from abiding by the binding quality of law, sincerely striving to figure out what the law requires (however uncertain), to instrumentally manipulating the legal rules to reach a particular end, much as a lawyer does in service of the client. A judge will be bound by the law only to the extent that the judge believes it is possible to be bound by the law and sees it as his or her solemn obligation to render legally bound and determined decisions. Living up to this obligation is the particular virtue of judging.

What cannot be known is the cumulative effect of the spread and permeation of legal instrumentalism documented in earlier chapters in this book: of several generations of legal education that inculcates in law students a purely instrumental attitude toward legal rules, reinforced by the instrumental orientation that pervades the daily practice of law, encouraged by the example of a political Supreme Court and by the spread of theories like legal pragmatism, which urge judges to consider ends when deciding cases, worsened by the openly instrumental views taken toward the selection and appointment of judges. All of these factors egg judges on to downplay the binding aspect of legal rules and give themselves over to a more instrumental approach, allowing greater reign to their personal views. If judges succumb to this invitation, the decisions they render will be driven by personal preferences more so than the law, furthering the aims of the groups that helped seat them as judges. Judges will then become another set of combatants in the pitched battle to use the law as a weapon.

Epilogue

To forestall a fundamental misunderstanding of this book – one easy to fall into given its emphasis on the untoward consequences of moving from a non-instrumental to an instrumental view of law – let me first make clear what I am not arguing. I am not advocating a return to former non-instrumental understandings of law, which appears impossible. Nor am I a legal romanticist inclined toward a utopian view of the reality that accompanied former non-instrumental understandings of law. I do not vouch for the veracity of claims that law embodied principle, reason, and the customs and order of the community. Indeed, I explicitly noted that the common law claim to represent customs from time immemorial was largely a fiction, and I observed that what were identified as natural law principles often merely reflected and bolstered the status quo. Non-instrumental versions of law were guilty of their own sins. Two centuries ago and before, law inured to the benefit of the powerful and was often draconian and intolerant of dissent. To the extent that, under non-instrumental views of law, there was less overt conflict over law and greater apparent consensus within society, this was to some degree the result of an enforced homogeneity in the socio-legal order which suppressed or eliminated contrary groups, granting them little or no recognition within the law.

As suggested by the radical skeptic in the Introduction (and again in Chapter 2), self-described non-instrumental law was instrumental in its own way. In a detailed historical study of eighteenth-century English property law, which marked the high point of purportedly non-instrumental common law, Marxist historian E.P. Thompson confirmed the underlying instrumentalism:

> [W]e can stand no longer on that traditional ground of liberal academicism, which offers the eighteenth century as a society of consensus, ruled within the parameters of paternalism and deference, and governed by a "rule of law" which attained (however imperfectly) toward impartiality. That is not the society which we have been examining; we have not observed a society of consensus; and we have seen the law being devised and employed, directly and *instrumentally*, in the imposition of class power.[1]

---

1 E. P. Thompson, "The Rule of Law" (from *Whigs and Hunters: The Origin of the Black Act*), in *The Essential E. P. Thompson* (N.Y.: The New Press 2001) 435 (emphasis added).

The common law of this period was shaped by judges loyal to the landed gentry, protecting their property interests against arbitrary regal power while draping the law in claims about customs of the people and reason and principle. "Thus the law . . . may be seen instrumentally as mediating and reinforcing existent class relations and, ideologically, as offering to these a legitimation."[2]

Acknowledging that non-instrumental law had instrumental aspects might appear to vitiate the central theme of this book. It would seem to suggest that the shift from non-instrumental to instrumental understandings of law was merely superficial. But there is more to consider. "If the law is evidently partial and unjust, then it will mask nothing, legitimize nothing, contribute nothing to any class's hegemony," wrote Thompson. "The essential precondition for the effectiveness of law, in its function as ideology, is that it shall display an independence from gross manipulation and shall seem to be just. It cannot seem to be so without upholding its own logic and criteria of equity; indeed, on occasion, by actually *being* just."[3] Thompson's point is that the often-repeated non-instrumental claims about law, honored initially by the elite for the sake of securing credibility, carried their own implications and imposed their own demands. They conferred benefits upon others unintended by the elite, and regularly hamstrung those in power who wished to wield the law instrumentally for their own advantage. "The law, in its forms and traditions, entailed principles of equity and universality which, perforce, had to be extended to all sorts and degrees of men."[4]

For this reason, even recognizing that the law did not live up to its idealized characterizations, it is a grave error to dismiss traditional non-instrumental views of law as mere rhetoric. "The rhetoric and the rules of a society are something a great deal more than sham. In the same moment they may modify, in profound ways, the behavior of the powerful, and mystify the powerless. They may disguise the true realities of power, but, at the same time, they may curb that power and check its intrusions."[5] Thompson's conclusion carries additional weight because he felt compelled by the evidence to draw it, despite its inconsistency with doctrinaire Marxist assumptions that law is an unadulterated instrument of class domination, inciting the ire of disappointed fellow Marxists. Anyone who doubts Thompson's conclusion about the benefits offered by the rule of law must merely examine the situation in those countries around the world where it is lacking – at blighted societies in which power has its way with scant restraint, and the powerless have little protection.

Thompson's findings bear directly on the focus this book. The preceding pages trace out the implications of a centuries-long shift in prevailing characterizations of law, a shift that discarded glorified rhetoric about law, rhetoric that was, however, more than just a sham. Some might think that stripping away the non-instrumental

2 Id. 436.
3 Id. 436.
4 Id. 437.
5 Id. 438.

veneer is good because then everyone can see law for what it is, allowing an open contest to control the law. This exploration poses the question of whether an unanticipated price may be paid for stripping the law of it non-instrumental claims, dissolving former restraints on the instrumental uses of law, turning law into a pure instrument of coercive power.

The answer is equivocal, for two stories can be read in these pages.

The main story is the arc of the increasing spread and penetration in the past two centuries of the idea that law is purely a means to an end. Concomitantly there has been a heightening of group-based disagreement, exacerbated by deep skepticism about whether an overarching common public good exists, or whether it can be agreed upon. The consequence of this combination of ideas and events, I have argued, is that in every legal arena battles are taking place between groups seeking to seize control of and wield the law as a weapon in their struggle against other groups. Groups strive to influence (by financial inducement) legislators to write laws that further their agendas, to influence administrative officials to issue and enforce regulatory regimes they desire, to stock the benches with judges who personally favor their positions, and to actively bring cases before these judges to obtain rulings that advance their objectives. Through this multi-pronged strategy, they endeavor to mold the law to their liking, and to use the law to change society, the economy, and the political system to their liking. The public coercive power of law in many of these instances is enlisted for partisan or private purposes. In all of these arenas, groups with opposing agendas face off against one another. Those groups that are well organized or amply funded possess a formidable advantage in these contests over law. The resultant fractious battles and the consummately instrumental view of law that feeds them threaten to corrode the rule of law, I have argued, by encouraging legal actors and the citizenry to see legal rules and processes as tools to be manipulated or weapons to be wielded to achieve preferred ends, rather than as obligatory public commands that further the common good, worthy of compliance and respect.

But these pages tell another story as well. Group conflict over and through law has been a constant of the U.S. legal culture, ebbing and flowing over time, heightening at the turn of the last century, rising to another peak today. This story suggests that groups and legal officials in the United States have long perceived and utilized law – especially legislation – instrumentally to achieve their objectives. So there is nothing new or especially alarming in the developments and events canvassed in this book. The battles are troublesome, to be sure, but they are a normal feature of law in situations of social conflict, and are not inevitably destabilizing. The developments chronicled in this book merely retell an old story in updated vernacular. Notwithstanding such battles, this second story suggests, there remains a core baseline of consensus over fundamentals within U.S. society and the legal culture. The legal system still delivers the goods, sufficiently satisfying the demands placed upon it by the populace to remain efficacious and generally respected. Moreover, legal institutions and ideas are an integrated, constitutive aspect of society, a background infrastructure for social and economic intercourse, a massive inertial presence, so deeply a part of the culture and society that catastrophic events would be required to bring it down. The rule of law tradition in the U.S. legal culture has sturdy roots. The aforesaid battles, although real, involve highly publicized controversies that do not penetrate the bulk of everyday law.

The situation has not played out sufficiently to discern which of these two interpretations (or some other one) turns out to be correct. Those inclined toward the more consoling second interpretation must consider that earlier episodes in the U.S. legal culture did not take place in an environment steeped in an instrumental view of law and skepticism about the public good. Whatever tempering effects former non-instrumental views might have had, either in setting limits on law or in softening pursuit of individual or group interests, has disintegrated, at least to some extent. This is a real change that must have consequences. For this reason, it is perhaps unduly optimistic to think that this is just another recurrence of a relatively common social-legal phenomenon.

The most portentous development chronicled in these pages is the progressive deterioration of ideals fundamental to the system of law and government: that the law is a principled preserver of justice, that the law serves the public good, that legal rules are binding on government officials (not only the public), and that judges must render decisions in an objective fashion based upon the law. The notion that law is a means to an end would be a positive component if integrated within a broader system with strong commitments to these four ideals. If law is seen as an instrument without the nourishing, enriching, containing soil of these ideals, however, there is nothing to keep law from devolving to a matter of pure expediency. The ideal that law has a principled core has suffered the most of the four ideals, undermined by modern relativism. The public good ideal has also undergone deterioration, for the same reason and, furthermore, owing to widespread cynicism about and among government officials. The third and fourth ideals have not yet succumbed, it would appear, but they are under heavy pressure, especially from the politicization of the judiciary. All four of these ideals are further undermined by the fact that legal education, and the practice of law, teach and reinforce the message that law is an empty vessel and legal rules are tools to be manipulated to achieve ends. Lawyers have thoroughly internalized this view of law – and lawyers occupy leading roles in society, business, politics, government, and law.

The judiciary is in a pivotal position with respect to restraining the excesses of legal instrumentalism. In the past, judges served as a check against the instrumental uses of legislation and government power for private interests, but this role was discredited in the early twentieth century and will not be easy to revive. Nonetheless, by institutional design, the judiciary remains the final check to ensure that other governmental bodies act in accordance with the law, and it is the institution of final resort in disputes among citizens, entities, and groups. It is true that American jurisprudence obsesses inordinately about the position of the judge (in an era when less than 2% of federal civil cases actually go to trial, and disputes are increasingly resolved through arbitration), but there is a legitimate reason for this. Symbolically, judges epitomize the law. When judges become embroiled in political disputes or render nakedly political decisions, they become targets for forces who seek to utilize the law to advance their ends. If an instrumental attitude toward the application of law comes to pervade judicial decision-making – with judges routinely manipulating legal rules to justify outcomes, rather than abiding by the binding dictates of the law – the last redoubt of the law as a system of binding rules will be lost. The imminent politicization of the judiciary, therefore, has outsized consequences for the entire legal system.

These final observations are styled an "Epilogue" because which of these two stories turns out to be correct has yet to be determined. It depends upon whether we are collectively able to manage these battles and temper the rampant instrumental manipulation of the law for particular ends so that it does not undermine the intangible but essential collective commitment to legality.

Looking forward, three simple and perhaps obvious points can be made. First, legislators must be genuinely oriented toward enacting laws that are in the *common* good or *public* interest. The fact that these involve hotly contested issues with no oracle to consult to divine what is ultimately correct makes it all the more essential that legislators never lose sight of the primacy of this overarching orientation. Second, government officials must see it as their solemn duty to abide by the law in good faith; this duty is not satisfied by the manipulation of law and legal processes to achieve objectives. Third, judges, when rendering their decisions, must be committed to searching for the strongest, most correct *legal* answer; they must resist the temptation to succumb to the power they have to exploit the inherent indeterminacy of law to produce results they desire. These three points do not offer answers to any of the hard issues legislators, government officials, and judges must confront daily when carrying out their obligations. Rather, they are the minimal conditions necessary for a properly functioning instrumental system of law. Moreover, they are the most that can be achieved in a system of law created through human efforts – and that is good enough.

Alas, to offer these three points sounds fatuous in the face of the magnitude of the problems identified in the preceding pages. This book attempts to uncover and bring attention to the underlying dynamics that have led to and that structure and constrain our current situation. Our trajectory points directly toward turbulent waters with threatening shoals. We must pay heed to the signs now.

Index